AF364253

Textbook of
Digital Image Processing

Textbook of
Digital Image Processing

M. Anji Reddy

Director, Institute of Science & Technology
Jawaharlal Nehru Technological University
Hyderabad, A. P., India.

Y. Hari Shankar

Guest Faculty, Centre for Environment
Jawaharlal Nehru Technological University
Hyderabad, A. P., India.

BSP BS Publications

A unit of **BSP Books Pvt., Ltd.**

4-4-309, Giriraj Lane, Sultan Bazar,
Hyderabad - 500 095 - A.P.
Phone : 040 - 23445605, 23445688

© 2014, *by Publisher*

Published by :

BS Publications

A unit of **BSP Books Pvt., Ltd.**

4-4-309/316, Giriraj Lane, Sultan Bazar,
Hyderabad - 500 095
Phone : 040 - 23445605, 23445688
e-mail : info@bspbooks.net

ISBN : 978-93-85433-36-8 (HB)

Jawaharlal Nehru Technological University

Prof. K. Rajagopal
Vice-Chancellor

Hyderabad - 500 072 A.P. (India)
Phone : 040 - 23156109 (O)
    040 - 23156116 (R)
Fax : 040 - 23156112
E-mail : *jntuadm@hd2vsnl.net.in*
www. jntu.ac.in

Foreword

Imaging technology used to be a single unified field in early years. Today it has expanded and diversified into several branches based on imaging technology as well as applications. However there is a need for beginners as well as practicing engineers to have a textbook covering the basic syllabi of Digital Image Processing, which would give an overall exposure to the subject.

This book, by Dr. M. Anji Reddy and Y. Hari Shankar, which is unique in its comprehensive integration of the theory and application of digital image processing fulfils this need. A good coverage of introduction of imaging technology and basic digital image processing has been provided in the initial chapters. These chapters will be very useful for students and other beginners who want to pursue this field for its specific applications. All the basic elements of imaging technology beginning from segmentation, edge detection, image compression, object recognition have been discussed in great detail. Topics specific to remote sensing, digital image processing such as transformations, multi-image operations, etc., have also been covered in good length. All imaging technologies have been covered in great detail and all concepts have been discussed.

Dr. Reddy, with his experience, has been able to sift and sort the topics to make this book a valuable and important tool at a very fundamental level, and an asset for undergraduate students and researchers alike to provide the necessary impetus for engaging in effective applications of this wide field of imaging technology. I am very happy that such an important and timely publication is brought out by one of our faculty to meet the present needs of this book on an advanced topic. I wish that all concerned will not only use it as a book of knowledge and information but also take the benefit for teaching and research purpose.

K. Rajagopal
Vice-Chancellor

Preface

Digital Image Processing is a rapidly evolving field with growing applications in science and engineering. Image processing holds the possibility of developing the ultimate machine that could perform the visual functions of all living beings. Many theoretical as well as technological breakthroughs are required before we could build such a machine. In the meantime, there is an abundance of image processing applications, which can serve mankind with the available and anticipated technology in the near future. Over the years of teaching and R & D experience, we have had the feeling that there is a definite need for a systematic textbook covering the whole subject, including both its basic foundations and its applications. It is our objective that this book should, at least in part, help to fulfill this requirement.

This book addresses the fundamentals of the major topics of Digital image processing representation, processing techniques and communication. Attention has been focused on mature topics with the hope that the level of discussion provided would enable an engineer or a scientist to decide on a image processing system and conduct research on advanced and newly emerging areas. Image representation includes tasks ranging from acquisition, digitalization, and display to mathematical characterization of images for subsequent processing. Often, a proper representation is a pre-requisite to an efficient processing technique such as enhancement, filtering and restoration, analysis, reconstruction from projections, image compression, and image processing problems and techniques.

Thus this book has been oriented towards students, engineers and technicians, who are basically external to the field of Digital Image Processing and who would like to understand at least part of this field, by using it from time to time, without the help of professionals of Digital Image Processing. The aim here is to get the speciality much closer to the end user, and to help him to be autonomous in more circumstances. All those, who are involved in the developmental activities, even in the field of Agriculture, will benefit greatly from this up-to-date work.

We are deeply indebted to the many people who have contributed in making the completion of this book possible. Our sincere thanks to Prof. K. Rajagopal, Hon'ble Vice-Chancellor, JNT University, Hyderabad, for giving foreword to this book.

We acknowledge the help extended to us by Dr. T. Vijayalakshmi, Dr. A. Sivasankar, lecturers, JNT University; Ms. V. Padmaja, Mr. K. Kiran, Mr. Y. Ram Mohan - research scholars, for their help in preparing the book. We have a word of appreciation for the services extended to me by Mr. Naresh, and management of BS Publications for their support in publishing this textbook.

It is our duty and responsibility to show gratitude and love to our parents, who have been perennial source of inspiration. Indeed with great pleasure, we express special regards and affection to our families who took care of other duties, while preparing the manuscript. Finally we express; love and affection to Chandu and Rajiv for making the work enjoyable.

- Authors

Contents

Chapter 1
Introduction to Imaging Technology

Chapter 2

Basic Digital Image Processing

Chapter 3

Segmentation and Edge Detection

Chapter 4

Morphological and Other Area Operations

Chapter 5

Image Compression (Image Coding)

Chapter 6
Pattern Recognition (Object Recognition)

Chapter 7
Digital Image Processing – SOFTWARES

Overview

Chapter 1. Introduction to Imaging Technology

This chapter considers how the image is held and manipulated inside the memory of a computer. Memory models are important because the speed and quality of image-processing software is dependent on the right use of memory. Most image transformations can be made less difficult to perform if the original mapping is carefully chosen. Aquisition of image from different sources is dealt in detail.

Chapter 2. Basic Digital Image Processing

Basic Digital Image Processing deals with low-level image processing operations. The techniques (algorithms) in this chapter are independent of the position of the pixels. The levels processing to be applied on an image in a typical processing sequence are low first, then medium, then high.

Low level processing is concerned with work at the binary image level, typically creating a second "better" image from the first by changing the representation of the image by removing unwanted data, and enhancing wanted data.

Medium-level processing is about the identification of significant shapes, regions or points from the binary images. Little or no prior knowledge is built to this process so while the work may not be wholly at binary level, the algorithms are still not usually application specific.

High level preprocessing interfaces the image to some knowledge base. This associates shapes discovered during previous level of processing with known shapes of real objects. The results from the algorithms at this level are passed on to non image procedures, which make decisions about actions following from the analysis of the image.

This chapter combines other techniques and operations on single images that deal with pixels and their neighbors (spatial operations). The techniques include spatial filters (normally removing noise by reference to the neighboring pixel values), weighted averaging of pixel areas (convolutions), and comparing areas on an image with known pixel area shapes so as to find shapes in images (correlation). There are also discussions on edge detection and on detection of "interest point". The operations discussed are as follows.

- Spatially dependent transformations
- Templates and Convolution
- Other window operations
- Two-dimensional geometric transformations
- Enhancement and Filtering
- Restoration

Chapter 3. Segmentation and Edge Detection

Segmentation is concerned with splitting an image up into segments (also called regions or areas) that each holds some property distinct from their neighbor. This is an essential part of scene analysis – in answering the questions like where and how large is the object, where is the background, how many objects are there, how many surfaces are there... Segmentation is a basic requirement for the identification and classification of objects in scene.

Segmentation can be approached from two points of view by identifying the edges (or lines) that run through an image or by identifying regions (or areas) within an image. Region operations can be seen as the dual of edge operations in that the completion of an edge is equivalent to breaking one region onto two. Ideally edge and region operations should give the same segmentation result: however, in practice the two rarely correspond. Some typical operations are:

- Region operations
- Basic edge detection
- Second-order edge detection
- Pyramid edge detection
- Crack edge detection
- Edge following.

Chapter 4. Morphological and Other Area Operations

Morphology is the science of form and structure. In computer vision it is about regions or shapes – how they can be changed and counted, and how their areas can be evaluated. The operations used are as follows.

- Basic morphological operations
- Opening and closing operations
- Area operations.

Chapter 5. Image Compression

Compression of images is concerned with storing them in a form that does not take up so much space as the original. Compression systems need to get the following benefits: fast operation (both compression and unpacking), significant reduction in required memory, no significant loss of quality in the image, format of output suitable for transfer or storage. Each of this depends on the user and the application. The topics discussed are as follows.

- Introduction to image compression
- Run Length Encoding
- Huffman Coding
- Modified Huffman Coding
- Modified READ
- Arithmetic Coding
- LZW
- JPEG
- Fractal compression
- Wavelet compression
- Image compression standards

Chapter 6. Pattern (Object) Recognition

A pattern recognition system finds patterns in the real world from an image of the world, using object models that are known a priori. This chapter will discussed different steps in pattern recognition and introduce some techniques that have been used for pattern recognition in many applications. The architecture and main components of pattern recognition are presented and their role in pattern recognition systems of varying complexity is discussed. The chapter covers the following topics:

- System component
- Complexity of pattern recognition
- Pattern representation
- Feature detection
- Recognition strategy
- Verification

Chapter 7. Digital Image Processing-Softwares

Software for Image Processing is available from many vendors but for a beginner in this field we have introduced three software each of which support customisation. This chapter gives a synopsis of the capabilities of the following software:

- MATLAB
- EASI/PACE
- ERDAS IMAGINE

The various modules and capabilities of these software are presented briefly.

CHAPTER 1

Introduction to Imaging Technology

1.1 Introduction

Digital Image Processing (DIP) is a technology that allows people to manipulate and analyze data in the form of digital images, is quickly becoming a basic tool for survival in the information age. Image processing helps people take a new look at the familiar world around them. Too often we "look at" phenomena and don't really observe them. Once phenom ena are digitized into images, however, what was previously invisible, or unrecognizable to the human eye, can become apparent. Digital image processing is a tool to visualize and explore connections between things in a new way.

A digital image is a picture which is divided into a grid of "pixels" (picture elements) in which each pixel is defined by three numbers and displayed on a computer screen [54]. The first two numbers give the x and y coordinates of the pixel, and the third number, or z coordinate, gives the intensity value, relative to all the other pixels in the image. The x and y coordinates of each pixel relate it to the actual location on the CCD (sensor) of the photoelement that collected the light which is displayed in that pixel. The z coordinate is a measure of the amount of light collected by that photoelement.

The image shown in Fig. 1.1 has been divided into M = 16 rows and N = 16 columns.

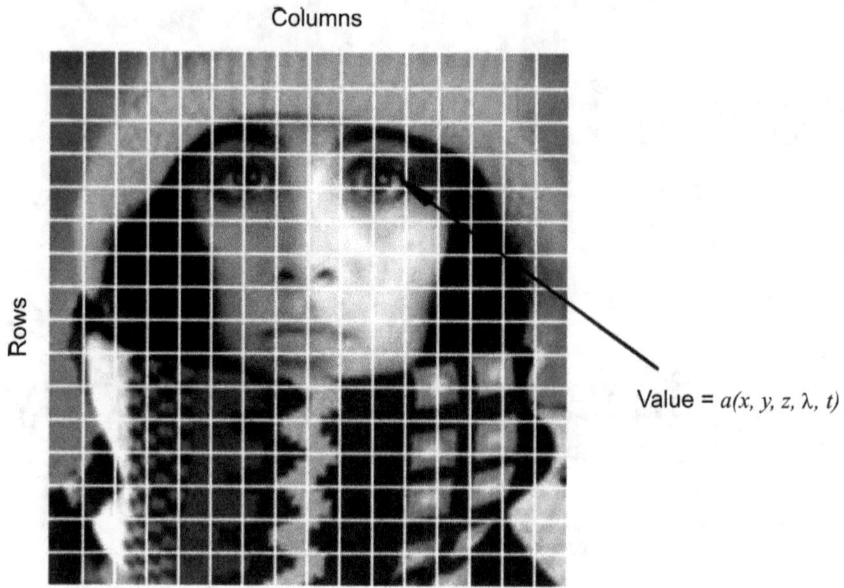

Fig. 1.1 Digitization of a continuous image. The pixel at coordinates [m = 3, n = 10] has the integer brightness value 110.

Definition :

A digital image a [m, n] described in a 2-Dimensional (2D) discrete space is derived from an analog image a (x, y) in a 2D continuous space through a *sampling* process called digitization.

The 2D continuous image a (x, y) is divided into M *rows* and N *columns*. The intersection of a row and a column is termed a *pixel*. The value assigned to the integer coordinates [m, n] with {m = 0, 1, 2, $M - 1$} and {n = 0, 1, 2,..., $N - 1$} is a [m, n]. In fact, in most cases a (x, y)—which we might consider to be the physical signal that impinges on the face of a 2D sensor is actually a function of many variables including depth (z), colour (γ), and time (t). A digital image is a matrix of digital numbers.

1.2   Digital Image Representation

Images are stored in computers as a 2-dimensional array of numbers. The numbers can correspond to different information such as colour or gray scale intensity, luminance, chrominance, and so on.

Before we can process an image on the computer, we need the image in digital form. To transform a continuous tone picture into digital form requires a digitizer. The most commonly used digitizers are scanners and digital cameras. The two functions of a digitizer are sampling and quantizing. Sampling captures evenly spaced data points to represent an image. Since these data points are to be stored in a computer, they must be converted to a binary form. Quantization assigns each value a binary number.

Figure 1.2 shows the effects of reducing the spatial resolution of an image. Each grid is represented by the average brightness of its square area (sample).

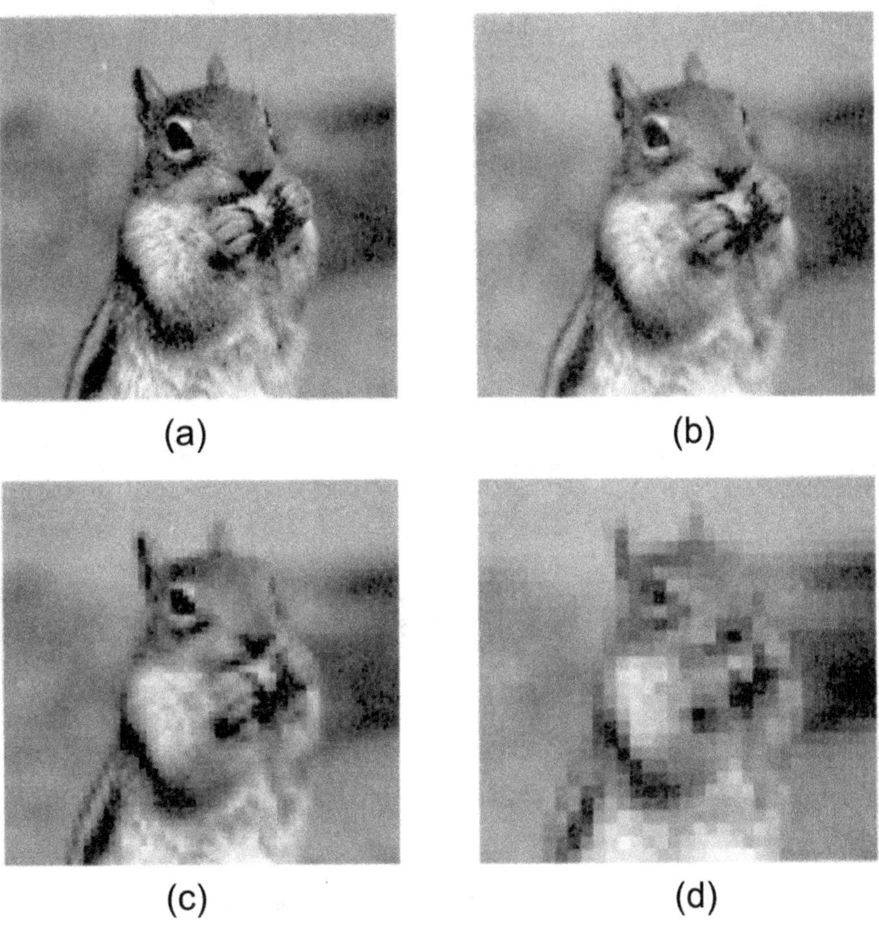

(a)   (b)

(c)   (d)

Fig. 1.2 Example of sampling size: (a) 512 x 512, (b) 128 x 128, (c) 64 x 64, (d) 32 x 32.

Figure 1.3 shows the effects of reducing the number of bits used in quantizing an image. The banding effect prominent in images sampled at 4 bits/pixel and lower is known as false contouring or posterization.

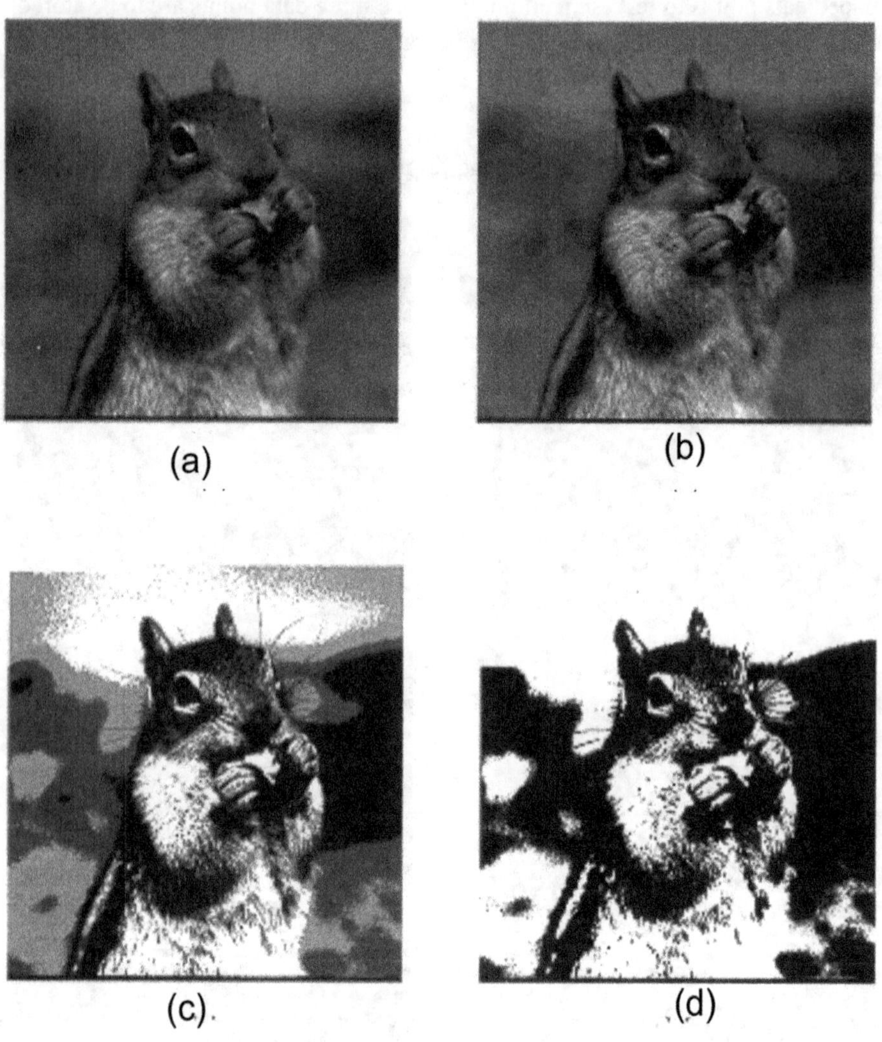

Fig. 1.3 Various quantizing level: (a) 6 bits; (b) 4 bits; (c) 2 bits; (d) 1 bit.

A picture is presented to the digitizer as a continuous image. As the picture is sampled, the digitizer converts light to a signal that represents brightness.

A transducer makes this conversion. An analog-to-digital (AID) converter quantizes this signal to produce data that can be stored digitally. This data represents intensity. Therefore, black is typically represented as 0 and white as the maximum value possible.

1.3 The Electromagnetic Radiation

Radiation is energy that travels as energy and spreads out as it goes. Electromagnetic radiation is a propagating wave in space with electric and magnetic components.

These components oscillate at right angles to each other. The electromagnetic waves are made up of two parts. The first part is an electric field the second part is a magnetic field hence they are called electromagnetic waves. The two fields are at right angles to each other. Electromagnetic energy passes through space at the speed of light in the form of sinusoidal waves. The wavelength is the distance from wavecrest to wavecrest (see Fig. 1.4).

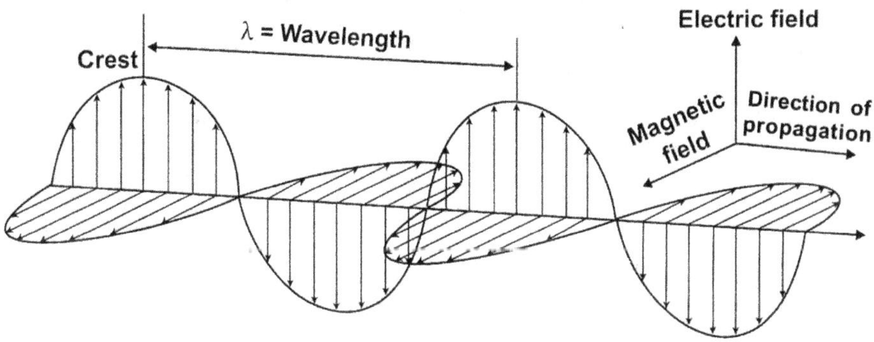

Fig. 1.4 Propagation of Electromagnetic wave.

The Electromagnetic Spectrum

The Electromagnetic spectrum is a Sequential arrangement of all electromagnetic waves arranged according to frequency and wavelength [19].

The Electromagnetic (EM) spectrum actually is a concept that scientists created to a bunch of types of radiation when they want to talk about them as a group. When white light is passed through a prism it is separated out into all the colours of the rainbow; this is called the visible spectrum. So white light is a mixture of all colours.

The electromagnetic spectrum encompasses all possible wavelengths of electromagnetic radiation. Light is a particular type of electromagnetic radiation that can be seen and sensed by the human eye, but this energy exists at a wide range of wavelengths. The micron is the basic unit for measuring the wavelength of electromagnetic waves. The sun, earth, and other bodies radiate electromagnetic energy of varying wavelengths. The spectrum of waves is divided into sections based on wavelength. The shortest waves are gamma rays, which have wavelengths of 10^6 microns or less. The longest waves are radio waves, which have wavelengths of many kilometers. The range of visible light consists of the narrow portion of the spectrum, from 0.4 microns (blue) to 0.7 microns (red). The visible spectrum is just one small part of the electromagnetic spectrum as shown in Fig. 1.5.

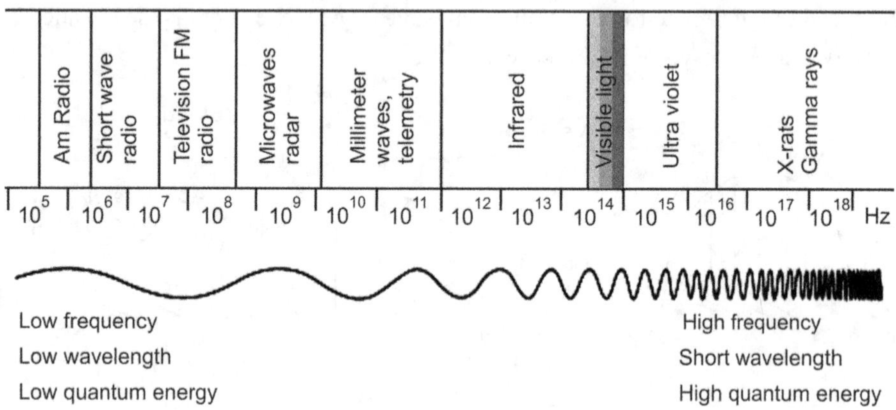

Fig. 1.5 The electromagnetic spectrum.

Electromagnetic energy at a particular wavelength λ (in vacuum) has an associated frequency (η) and photon energy E. These quantities are related according to the equations :

$$\lambda = c/v \ \& \ E = hv$$

Where c is the speed of light (3×10^8 m/s)

h = 6.626×10^{-34} J·sec is Planck's constant, or, in alternative units, h = 4.136 μeV/GHz.

The Table 1.1 below shows the important regions in the electromagnetic region from the Image processing perspective and their important measures.

Table 1.1 Frequency ranges.

Type of Radiation	Frequency Range (Hz)	Wavelength Range	Type of Transition	Description
Radio Waves	$10^5 - 10^{10}$	3000m-3cm	Nuclear spin flips under magnetization	Signals in AM/FM Radio
Microwaves	$10^{10} - 10^{12}$	3cm-0.3mm	Molecular rotations and electron spin flips	Used in radar and in home appliances
Infrared	$10^{12} - 10^{14}$	0.3mm-2.5mm	Molecular vibrations	Emission of heat
Near-infrared	$1 - 4 \times 10^{14}$	2.5 mm-750nm	Outer electron and molecular vibrations	Emission of heat
Visible light	$4 - 7.5 \times 10^{14}$	750nm-400nm	Outer electron	Light detected by human eye
Ultraviolet	$10^{15} - 10^{17}$	400nm-1nm	Outer electron	Produces Sunburn
X-rays	$10^{17} - 10^{20}$	1nm-1pm	Inner electron	Gets picture of bones
Gamma rays	$10^{20} - 10^{24}$	<1pm	Nuclear	Nuclear emission rays

Radio waves

Radio waves have a much longer wavelength than light waves. The longest waves are several kilometers in length. The shortest ones are only millimeters long. Radio waves make the electrons in a piece of copper wire move; this means that they generate electric currents in the wire. In fact it works both ways: alternating currents in a copper wire generate electromagnetic waves, and electromagnetic waves generate alternating currents. Radio and television transmitters and receivers use the electric currents at "radio frequencies" (RF). They are used for radio broadcasts, amateur radio, television, and mobile phones. Different parts of the radio spectrum have been allocated to the various services.

Microwave region

Microwaves have wavelengths that can be measured in centimeters. The longer microwaves, those closer to a foot in length, are the waves which heat our food in a microwave oven. Microwaves are good for transmitting information from one place to another because microwave energy can penetrate haze, light rain and snow, clouds, and smoke. Shorter microwaves are used in remote sensing. These microwaves are used for radar like the doppler radar used in weather forecasts. Microwaves, used for radar, are just a few inches long.

Infrared region

The term "infrared" refers to a broad range of frequencies, beginning at the top end of those frequencies used for communication and extending up the the low frequency (red) end of the visible spectrum. The wavelength range is from about 1 millimeter down to 750 nm. The range adjacent to the visible spectrum is called the "near infrared" and the longer wavelength part is called "far infrared".

In interactions with matter, infrared primarily acts to set molecules into vibration. Infrared spectrometers are widely used to study the vibrational spectra of molecules. These radio/light waves have a very short wavelength; their wavelength is longer than visible light. Infra-red can be detected by special infra-red film. Infra-red has a longer wavelength (less energy) than Red light.

The visible region

The narrow visible part of the electromagnetic spectrum corresponds to the wavelengths near the maximum of the Sun's radiation curve. In interactions with matter, visible light primarily acts to set elevate electrons to higher energy levels. White light may be separated into its spectral colours by dispersion in a prism as shown in Fig. 1.6 and Plate No. 1.

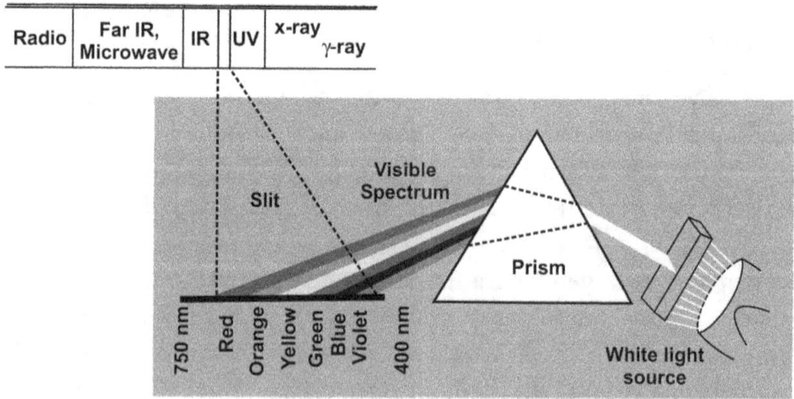

Fig. 1.6 White light split into spectral colours of visible region.

An easy way of remembering the order of colours in the visible region is 'Richard Of York Gave Battle In Vain. = Red, Orange, Yellow, Green, Blue, Indigo, and Violet'.

Ultraviolet region

The region just below the visible region in wavelength is called the near ultraviolet region. It is absorbed very strongly by most solid substances, and even absorbed appreciably by air. The shorter wavelengths reach the ionization energy for many molecules, so the far ultraviolet has some of the dangers attendent to other ionizing radiation. The tissue effects of ultraviolet include sunburn, but can have some therapeutic effects as well. The sun is a strong source of ultraviolet radiation, but atmospheric absorption eliminates most of the shorter wavelengths. The eyes are quite susceptible to damage from ultraviolet radiation.

These waves have very high energy and very short wave lengths; shorter than visible light. Some animals like honey bees can see ultra-violet light. It is the Ultraviolet which is thought to cause skin cancer. UV light has a shorter wavelength (more energy) than visible light.

X-Ray region

X-ray was the name given to the highly penetrating rays which emanated when high energy electrons struck a metal target. Within a short time of their discovery, they were being used in medical facilities to image broken bones. We now know that they are high frequency electromagnetic rays that are produced when the electrons are suddenly decelerated - these rays are called bremsstrahlung radiation, or "braking radiation". X-rays are also produced when electrons make transitions between lower atomic energy levels in heavy elements. X-rays produced in this way have definite energies just like other line spectra from atomic electrons. They are called characteristic X-rays since they have energies determined by the atomic energy levels.

In interactions with matter, X-rays are ionizing radiation and produce physiological effects which are not observed with any exposure of non-ionizing radiation, such as the risk of mutations or cancer in tissue.

Gamma ray region

Gamma-rays have the smallest wavelengths and the most energy than any other wave in the electromagnetic spectrum. These waves are generated by radioactive atoms and in nuclear explosions. Gamma-rays can kill living cells, a fact which medicine uses to its advantage, using gamma-rays to kill cancerous cells.

Gamma-rays are the most energetic form of light and are produced by the hottest regions of the universe. They are also produced by such violent events as supernova explosions or the destruction of atoms, and by less dramatic events, such as the decay of radioactive material in space. Things like supernova explosions (the way massive stars die), neutron stars and pulsars, and black holes are all sources of celestial gamma-rays.

They have very high energy and pass even through metals. So they can be used for finding tiny cracks in metals. Some radioactive materials produce gamma rays. Gamma rays and X-Rays can cause cancer, but gamma rays can also be used to destroy cancer cells which is called radiotherapy.

1.3.1 Nature of Electromagnetic Radiation

As a result development of understanding the nature of electromagnetic energy, it is presently possible to furnish a consistent and unambiguous theoretical explanation for all optical phenomena using a combination of Maxwell's electromagnetic wave theory and modern quantum theory. Maxwell's theory deals primarily with the propagation and macroscopic optical effects of electromagnetic energy, while quantum theory is concerned with the atomic molecular absorption and emission aspects of radiation.

The four differential equations that form the basis of electromagnetic theory are quite generally referred to as "Maxwell's equations," and they express in mathematical terms all the facts determined prior to 1860 by such workers as Coulomb, Oersted, Ampere, Biot, Savart, Henry, Faraday, and Gauss. They predict that electric and magnetic fields may exist in regions where no electric charges are present, and that when the fields at one point in space vary with time, then some point in space at some other time, and consequently, changes in the fields propagate throughout space. The propagation of such a disturbance is called an electromagnetic wave.

Because of the paramount importance of Maxwell's equations, they will be briefly introduced at this point.

1.3.2 Wave Nature : Maxwell's Equations

The electromagnetic state at a point in a vacuum can be specified by two vectors: E, the electric field (in volts per meter) and H, the magnetic field (in ampere turns per meter). These vector quantities are completely independent of each other in the static case, and are determined by the distribution of all charges and currents in space. In the dynamic case, however, the fields are not independent, but rather their space and time derivatives are interrelated as expressed by the curl (∇) equations

$$\nabla \times E = -\mu_o \frac{\partial H}{\partial t} \qquad \qquad .....(1.1)$$

$$\nabla \times H = \varepsilon_o \frac{\partial E}{\partial t} \qquad \qquad .....(1.2)$$

Where $\mu_o \equiv$ permeability of the vacuum $= 4\pi \times 10^{-7}$ h/m and $\varepsilon_o \equiv$ permittivity of the vacuum $= 8.85 \times 10^{-12}$ farads/m.

The divergence conditions :

$$\nabla . E = 0 \qquad \qquad .....(1.3)$$

$$\nabla . H = 0 \qquad \qquad ....(1.4)$$

indicate that there is no charge at the point in question, and this is true in both the static and dynamic case. The four equations above are "Maxwell's equations" for a vacuum.

It can be seen that both fields satisfy the same formal partial differential equation

$$\nabla^2 (X) = \frac{1}{c^2} \frac{\partial^2 (X)}{\partial t^2} \qquad \qquad .....(1.5)$$

where $X = E$ or H, and $c = \dfrac{1}{\mu_o \varepsilon_o}$, and this is called the wave different kinds of physical phenomena. The major implication of the equation is that changes in the fields E or H propagate through space with a speed equal to the constant value c, which is known as the speed of light, and has a measured value of 2.9979×10^8 m/s.

The Maxwell curl equations are precisely the same for isotropic nonconducting media as they are vacuum, except that the vacuum constants μ_o and ε_o are replaced by corresponding constants for the medium, denoted μ and ε.

It can be shown, for the case where the spatial variation occurs in the z direction, that the function

$$E_z t = Eo \cos (K_z - \omega t)$$

is a solution to the wave equation, provided $V = \dfrac{\omega}{K_z}$.

This is the fundamental solution to the wave equation, and represents a plane harmonic wave, and the solution is of the same form for the magnetic field. It can be shown that the magnetic and electric components are perpendicular to each other and that these plane waves are both perpendicular to the direction of propagation (see Fig. 1.1).

Poynting's theorem states that the time rate of flow of electromagnetic energy per unit area is given by a vector, called the poynting vector, which is defined as the cross product of the electric and magnetic field vectors, and energy flux of the wave.

In summary, it can be seen that all electromagnetic radiation is energy in transit and can be regarded as a wave motion, and magnetic fields that are always mutually perpendicular to each other and to the direction of propagation, and this rate of propagation is constant in a vacuum.

1.3.3 Particulate Nature : Quantum Viewpoint

As far as electromagnetic radiation is concerned, the basic idea of quantum theory is that radiant energy is transmitted in indivisible packets whose energy is given in integral parts, of size hv, (where h is Planck's constant = 6.6252×10^{-34} j-s, and v is the frequency of the radiation), and these are called quanta or photons. In this basic way quantum theory differs from Maxwell's theory, which implies that energy is supplied continuously in wave.

The dilemma of the simultaneous wave and particulate views of electromagnetic energy may be conceptually resolved by considering that energy is not supplied continuously throughout a wave, but rather that it is carried by photons, and that the classical wave theory does not give the intensity of energy at a point at that point, thus the classical concept of a wave yields to the idea that a wave simply describes the probability path for the motion of the individual photons.

The particular importance of the quantum approach for remote sensing is that it provides the concept of *discrete* energy levels in materials, and the values and arrangement of these levels is different for each different material. Information about a given material is thus available in electromagnetic radiation as a consequence of transitions between these energy levels, a transition to a higher energy level being caused by the absorption of energy, or from a higher to a lower energy. The amounts of energy either absorbed or emitted correspond precisely to the energy difference between the two levels involved in the transition. Because the energy levels are different for each material, the amounts of energy a particular substance can absorb or emit are different for each material, the amounts of energy a particular substance can absorb or emit are different from those of any other materials. Consequently, the positions and intensities of the bands in the spectrum of a given material are characteristic of that material.

1.4 Elements of Visual Perception :
The Human Visual System (HVS)

The human visual system is made of 3 key parts: the eye, the conducting nerves, and the brain. Each of these parts are similar in function to man made imaging systems [23]. The image that one perceives is processed by the human visual system in many subtle ways. One must always keeps these concepts in mind when designing any digital imaging system, as the final recipient of most imaging systems is the human visual system.

The human eye is a remarkable organ, whose sensitivity and performance characteristics approach the absolute limits set by quantum physics [19]. The eye is able to detect as little as a single photon as input, and is capable of adjusting to ranges in light that span many orders of magnitude. No camera has been built that even partially matches this performance.

Sight, or vision, is a rapidly occurring process that involves continuous interaction between the eye, the nervous system, and the brain [29]. When someone looks at an object, what he really sees is the light reflected from the object. This reflected light passes through the lens and falls on the retina of the eye. Here the light induces nerve impulses that travel through the optic nerve to the brain, which in turn sends appropriate signals over through other nerves to muscles and glands.

1.4.1 Structure of the Human Eye

The eye is shaped like a ball, with a slight bulge at the front. It is this bulge that a person sees when looking at the eyes of someone else. When the eyelids are closed, the bulge is covered. The rest of the eye is protected by the bones of the skull. Each part of the human eye has a special function.

Cornea and sclera

The eye is made of three coats, or tunics. The outermost coat consists of the cornea and the sclera; the middle coat contains the main blood supply to the eye and consists of the choroid, the ciliary (Fig. 1.7) body, and the iris. The innermost layer is the retina. The sclera, or the white of the eye, is composed of tough fibrous tissue. On the exposed area of the eye the scleral surface is covered with a mucous membrane called the conjunctiva. This protects the eye from becoming dry. The cornea, a part of the sclera, is the transparent window of the eye through which light passes. The focusing of light begins in the cornea [19].

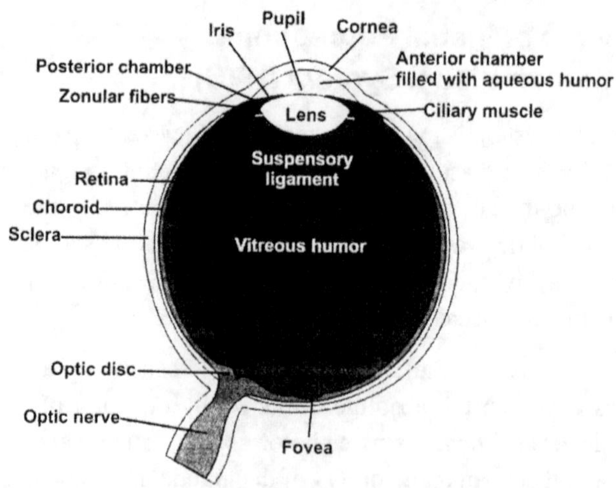

Fig. 1.7 Sketch of a cross-section of the eye.

Behind the cornea is a watery fluid called the aqueous humor. This fluid fills a curved, crescent-shaped space, thick in the center and thinner toward the edges. The cornea and the aqueous humor together make an outer lens that refracts, or bends, light and directs it toward the center of the eye.

Iris

Behind the aqueous humor is a coloured ring called the iris (Fig. 1.8). The colour of the iris is inherited and does not affect vision. The iris is like a muscular curtain that opens and closes. It controls the amount of light entering the eye through the pupil, an opening in the iris. The pupil looks like a black spot. Light from everything a person sees must go through the pupil. When more or less light is needed to see better, the pupil becomes larger or smaller through the movement of the muscle in the iris. The aqueous humor flows through the pupil into a small space between the iris and the lens.

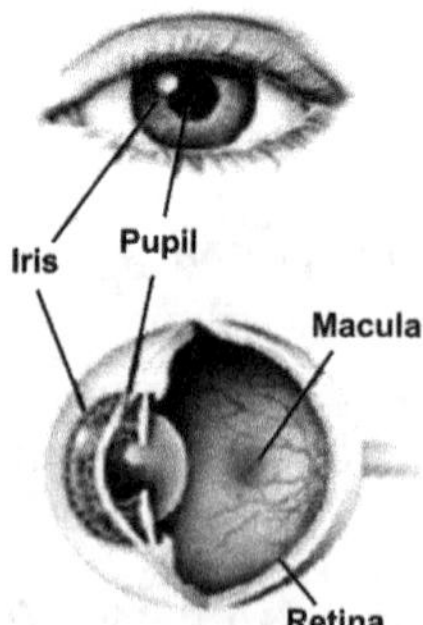

Fig. 1.8 The Iris in frontal (top) and cross sectional (bottom) view of the eye.

The choroid is a layer of blood vessels and connective tissue squeezed between the sclera and the retina. It supplies nutrients to the eye. The ciliary body is a muscular structure that changes the shape of the lens.

Lens

Behind the pupil and iris are the crystalline lens and the ciliary muscle. The muscle holds the lens in place and changes its shape. The lens is a colourless, nearly transparent double convex structure, similar to an ordinary magnifying glass. Its only function is to focus light rays onto the retina. The lens is made of elongated cells that have no blood supply. These cells obtain nutrients from the surrounding fluids i.e., the aqueous humor in front and the vitreous body, a clear jelly, behind. The shape of the lens is essentially that of a flattened globe and it can be changed by the movement of the ciliary muscles surrounding it. Hence, the eye can focus clearly on objects at widely varying distances. The ability of the lens to adjust from a distant to a near focus is called *accommodation* [29].

By contracting, the ciliary muscle pushes the lens to make it thicker in the middle. By relaxing, the muscle pulls the lens and flattens it. To see objects clearly when they are close to the eyes the lens is squeezed together and thickened. To see distant objects clearly it is flattened. For people with normal vision, the relaxed ciliary muscle flattens the lens enough to bring objects into sharp focus if they are 20 feet (6 meters) or more from the eye. To see closer objects clearly, the ciliary muscle must contract in order to thicken the lens. Young children can see objects clearly at distances as close as 2½ inches (6.4 centimeters). After about age 45 most people must have objects farther and farther away in order to see them clearly. The lens becomes less elastic as a person grows older.

Retina

The retina is a soft, transparent layer of nervous tissue made up of millions of light receptors. The retina is connected to the brain by the optic nerve [29]. All of the structures needed to focus light onto the retina and to nourish it are housed in the eye, which is primarily a supporting shell for the retina. When light enters the eye it passes through the lens and focuses an image onto the retina.

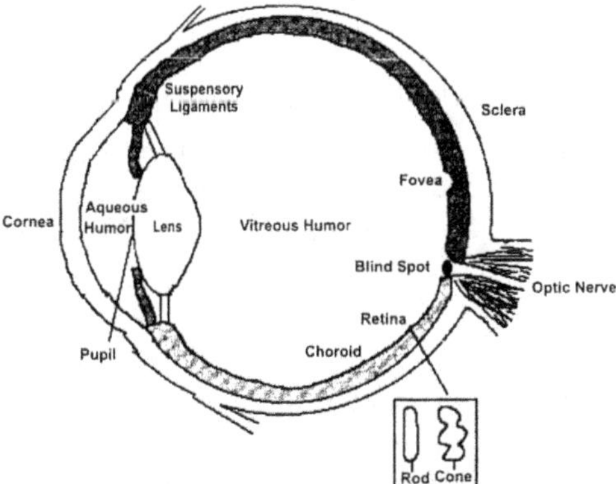

Fig. 1.9 Cross-section of eye showing the Retina, Rods & Cones.

The retina has several layers, one of which contains special cells named for their shapes—*rods* and *cones*. Light-sensitive chemicals in the rods and cones react to specific wavelengths of light and trigger nerve impulses. These impulses are carried through the optic nerve to the visual center in the brain. Here they are interpreted, and sight occurs. Light must pass through the covering layers of the retina to reach the layer of rods and cones. There are about 75 to 150 million rods and about 7 million cones in the human retina. Rods do not detect lines, points, or colour. They perceive only light and dark tones in an image. The sensitive rods can distinguish outlines of objects in almost complete darkness.

The rods make it possible for people to see in darkness or at night. Cones are the keenest of the retina's receptor cells. They detect the fine lines and points of an image. The cones, for example, make it possible to read these words. There are three types of cones that receive colour sensations. One type absorbs light best in wavelengths of blue-violet and another in wavelengths of green; a third is sensitive to wavelengths of yellow and red.

Macula

The macula or macula lutea is an oval yellow spot near the center of the retina of the human eye (Fig. 1.10). It has a diameter of about 1.5 mm. Near its center is the fovea, a small pit that contains the largest concentration of cone cells in the eye and is responsible for central vision.

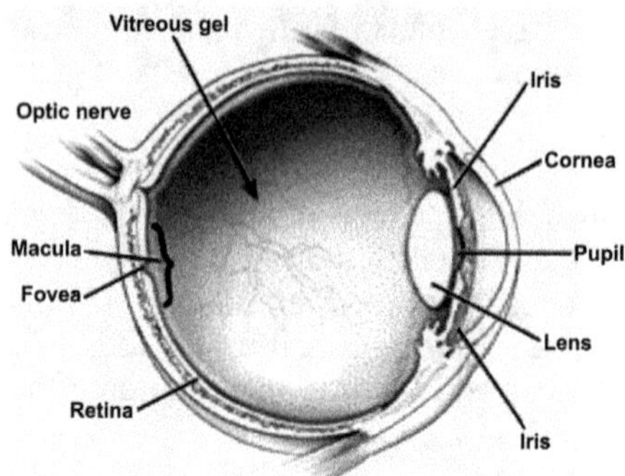

Fig. 1.10 Cross-section of eye showing the Macula.

Whereas loss of peripheral vision may go unnoticed for some time, damage to the macula will result in loss of central vision, which is usually immediately obvious. The progressive destruction of the macula is a severe disease known as macular degeneration.

Fovea

The fovea is a spot located in the center of the macula (Fig. 1.11). The fovea is responsible for our sharp central vision, which is necessary in humans for reading, watching television or movies, driving, and any activity where visual detail is of primary importance [29].

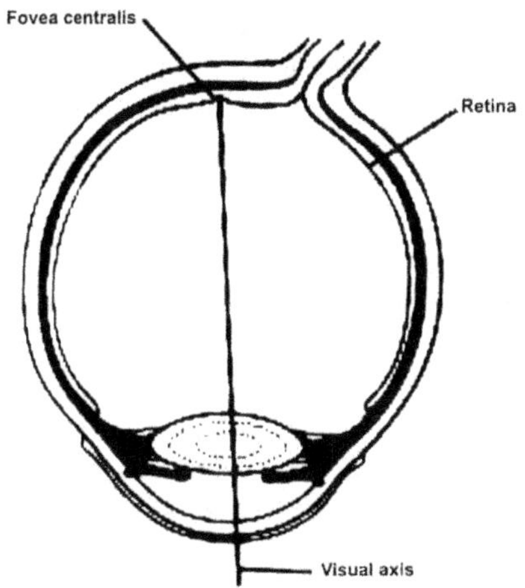

Fig. 1.11 Diagram showing the fovea and visual axis.

At the center of the fovea there is a pit with a diameter of about 0.2 mm. It has a high concentration of cone cells and virtually no rods. Compared to the rest of the retina, the cones in the foveal pit are smaller and more densely packed (in a hexagonal pattern), and they are not obscured by a layer of nerve cells and blood vessels; all of this together accounts for the sharp vision associated with them. The fovea is largely responsible for the colour vision in humans which is superior to most other mammals.

The foveal pit is located exactly on the optical axis: when we focus on an object, then the object, the center of the pupil and the fovea will form a straight line. Surrounding the foveal pit is the foveal rim, where the neurons displaced from the pit are located. This is the thickest part of the retina.

The foveal rim is a circular indentation in the retina of about 1.5 mm in diameter, considering the fovea as a 1.5 mm × 1.5 mm square sensor array, the density of cones is ~150,000 elements per square mm the number of cones in the region of highest acuity in the eye (fovea) is about 337,000 (150,000 × 1.5 × 1.5) elements whereas a CCD (Charge Coupled Device) imaging chip of medium resolution can have this number of elements in a receptor array no larger than 5 mm × 5 mm but much poorer than the ability of the eye to resolve detail.

Visual purple

Rods detect images in the dark because the cells contain a rose-red pigment called visual purple, or rhodopsin. When exposed to bright light, visual purple undergoes a chemical change in which it loses its colour. This causes the rods to lose their sensitivity to light, thus enabling the eye to endure glaring light. Before the eye can see in the dark, visual purple must be re-formed in the retina. As more visual purple is produced, the eye's sensitivity to light increases. Thus when a person enters a darkened motion-picture theater his eyes do not contain much visual purple. As the visual purple is re-formed, the person can see better. In a short time his eyes' sensitivity to light is multiplied about 2,000 times. Visual purple can be produced only if the body has a sufficient quantity of vitamin A. Lack of vitamin A in the diet may lead to night blindness.

1.4.2 Image Formation in the Eye

Human vision is the process of using light reflected from the surrounding world as a way of modifying activity. Generally, with humans, we say that the surrounding environment is *interpreted* by visual input. This usually implies some form of conscious understanding of the 3D world from the 2D projection that is formed on the retina of the eye.

In this section we will briefly overview the human visual system and try to understand the ways in which this system uses *computation* as a means of interpreting its input. Although not strictly correct, this analogy between machine vision and biological vision is currently the best model available. Moreover, the models interact in an ever increasing fashion: we use the human visual system as an existing proof that visual interpretation is even possible in the first place and its response to optical illusions as a way to guide our development of algorithms that replicate the human system; and we use our understanding of machine vision and our ability to generate ever more complex computer images as a way of modifying, or evolving, our visual system in its efforts to interpret the visual world.

Functioning of the eye

Any understanding of the function of the human eye serves as an insight into how machine vision might be solved. Indeed it was some of the early work by Hubel and Wiesel on the receptive fields in the retina that has led to the fundamental operation of spatial filtering that nowadays dominates so much of early image processing.

The eye is considered by most neuroscientists as actually part of the brain. Light enters the eye through the transparent *cornea*, passes through the *aqueous humor*, the *lens*, and the *vitreous humor*, where it finally forms an image on the *retina*. It is the muscular adjustment of the lens, known as *accommodation* that focuses the image directly on the retina. If this adjustment is not correctly accomplished, the viewer suffers from either nearsightedness (Myopia) or farsightedness (Hypermetropia). Both conditions are easily corrected with optical lenses [19].

The retina itself is a complex tiling of photoreceptors called rods and cones which are at the *back* of the retina, when stimulated by light produce electrical signals that are transmitted to the brain via the *optic nerve*. The location of the optic nerve on the retina obviously prohibits the existence of photoreceptors at this point. This point is known as the *blind spot* and the viewer does not perceive any light that falls upon it.

The rods and cones do not have a continuous physical link to the optic nerve fibres. Rather, they communicate through three distinct layers of cells, via junctions known as *synapses*. These layers of cells connect the rods and cones to the *ganglion cells*, which respond to the photostimulus according to a certain *receptive field*. Thus the light passes through the various cell layers to these receptive fields, and is then transmitted via various synaptic junctions back towards the optic nerve fibre.

Very little is known about what happens to the optic signal once it begins its voyage down the optic nerve. The optic nerve has inputs arriving from both the left and right sides of both eyes, and these inputs split and merge at the *optic chiasma*. Moreover, what is seen by one eye is slightly different from what is seen by the other, and this difference is used to deduce *depth* in stereo vision. From the optic chiasma, the nerve fibres proceed in two groups to the *striate cortex*, the seat of visual processing in the brain. A large proportion of the striate cortex is devoted to processing information from the fovea.

Vision

The optic nerve delivers its impulses to a special area of the brain called the visual center. This is where people "see" objects in the sense of recognizing and reacting to what their eyes look at. In other words, seeing always involves the brain's visual center. Here sensation turns into perception. The brain must learn by experience to analyze correctly the impulses it receives from the eyes. For instance, the lens system of the eye, like that of a camera, transmits its light pattern upside down. The brain has to learn that the impulses received from the upper part of the retina represent the lower part of the object sighted and vice versa.

In the brain also are located the centers that control all the eye's muscular movements, such as the opening and closing of the iris, the focusing of the main lens, and the movement of the eyeball. The eyeball's movement is voluntary. Other eye adjustments are reflexes [29].

Binocular and stereoscopic vision

Most individuals use both eyes to see an object. This type of sensory perception is known as binocular vision. Thus two images of the object are formed—one on the retina of each eye. Impulses from both images are sent to the brain (Fig. 1.12). Through experience these impulses are interpreted as two views of the same object. Because the eyes are about 2½ inches (6.4 centimeters) apart from pupil to pupil and therefore are looking at the object from different angles, the two views are not exactly alike. This is known as the stereoscopic effect. If the object is far away, the difference between the images is slight. If it is a few inches away, the difference is very great.

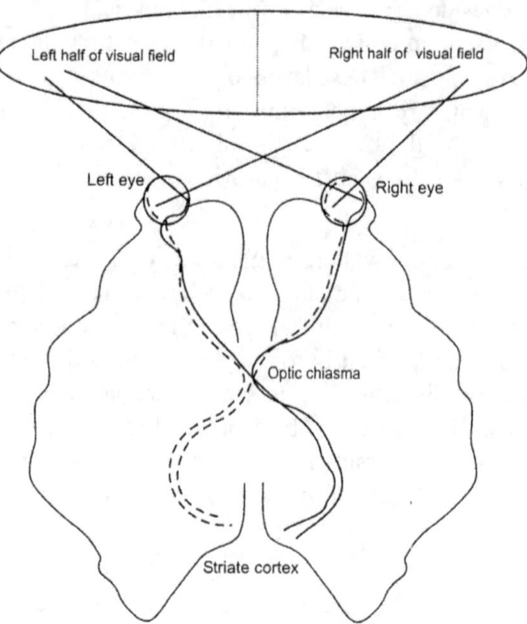

Fig. 1.12 Overview of the visual pathways from
eyes to striate cortex in the Brain

The brain makes good use of this phenomenon. It learns to judge the distance of an object way the brain perceives what is called perspective. It estimates differences in distance between two different objects or between two parts of the same object by the degree of difference between the images it receives from the two eyes.

The eyes are turned up, down, and sideways by long muscles. At one end these muscles are attached to the top, bottom, and sides of the eyeball. At the other end, these muscles are attached to the bony walls of the eye socket. They are regulated with the most delicate precision so that normally they turn both eyes toward the same object at exactly the same time.

Persistence of Vision and Motion Pictures

While the eyes are in motion they cannot see an object clearly. The image on the retina must come to rest, if only for a fraction of a second. That is why, when the eyes scan a line of type, they move across it in a series of quick jerks.

On the other hand, when the image has registered on the retinas, the vision of it persists from 1/50 to 1/25 part of a second. That is how the eyes receive the impression of video pictures. A movie consists of a rapid series of still pictures that are flashed on a screen, with about 1/60 of a second of complete darkness after each image. But persistence of vision fills in the dark moment. It blends each picture perfectly with the one that went before to create the same impression that true motion produces.

1.4.3 Brightness Adaptation and Discrimination

Rods are sensitive to very low levels of illumination and are responsible for our ability to see in dim light (scotopic vision). They contain a pigment with a maximum sensitivity at about 510 nm, in the green part of the spectrum. The rod pigment is often called visual purple since when it is extracted by chemists in sufficient quantities the pigment has a purple appearance. Scotopic vision is completely lacking in colour; a single spectral sensitivity function is colour-blind and thus scotopic vision is monochromatic [30].

Colour vision is provided by the cones, of which there are three distinct classes each containing a different photosensitive pigment. The three pigments have maximum absorptions at about 430, 530, and 560 nm and the cones are often called blue, green, and red. The mono chromatic lights at 430, 530, and 560 nm are not blue, green, and red respectively but violet, blue-green, and yellow-green. The use of short, medium, and long-wavelength cones is a more logical nomenclature.

The existence of three spectral sensitivity functions provides a basis for colour vision since light of each wavelength will give rise to a unique ratio of short, medium, and long-wavelength cone responses. The cones therefore provide us with colour vision (photopic vision) that can distinguish remarkably fine wavelength changes.

Digital images are displayed as a discrete set of intensities; the eye's ability to discriminate between different intensity levels is an important consideration in presenting image-processing results. The range of light intensity levels to which the human visual system can adapt is enormous—on the order of 10^{10}—from the scotopic threshold to the glare limit [19].

The essential point in interpreting the impressive dynamic range is that the visual system cannot operate over such a range *simultaneously*. Rather, it accomplishes this large variation by changes in its overall sensitivity, a phenomenon known as *brightness adaptation*. The total range of distinct intensity levels it can discriminate simultaneously is rather small when compared with the total adaptation range. For any given set of conditions, the current sensitivity level of the visual system is called the *brightness adaptation level* [30].

If the background illumination is held constant and the intensity of the other source, instead of flashing, is allowed to vary incrementally from never being perceived to always being perceived, the typical observer can discern a total of one to two dozen different intensity changes. Roughly, this result is related to the number of different intensities a person can see at any one point in a monochrome image. This result does not mean that an image can be represented by such a small number of intensity values because, as the eye roams about the image, the average background changes, thus allowing a *different* set of incremental changes to be detected at each new adaptation level. The net consequence is that the eye is capable of a much broader range of *overall* intensity discrimination. In fact, the eye is capable of detecting objectionable contouring effects in monochrome images whose overall intensity is represented by fewer than approximately two dozen levels.

Brightness perception

Digital images are often presented as a collection of discrete intensities. Therefore, it is important to understand how the human eye perceives brightness. The way that the human eye achieves this feat is to adapt the sensitivity of the eye to a small range at each moment. Therefore, although it is possible for the eye to see in a large range of intensities, it can only view a small range at any given time. Subjective intensity is therefore dependent upon the general light intensity that the eye is receiving. From experimental evidence, two different adaptation modes are observed. They are the scotopic and photopic vision. A diagram of this adaptation is shown on Fig. 1.13.

In the Fig. 1.13 B_a corresponds to Brightness for any given set of conditions and B_b corresponds to level below which all stimuli are perceived as black.

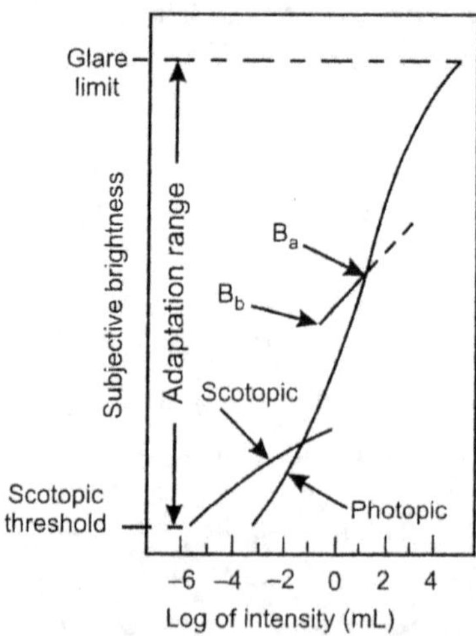

Fig. 1.13 Diagram showing photopic and scotopic vision [30].

Fig. 1.13 shows a plot of the log of the true intensity verses the subjective brightness that one perceives. The line labeled "B" on the diagram shows the actual range that the eye can perceive at any given adaptation level. In normal and bright light conditions, this line will move along the photopic vision line as indicted on Fig. 1.13. However, in dark conditions, this line will move along the scotopic vision curve. This vision curve represents the eye's ability to adapt to low light intensity conditions.

Brightness discrimination is also an important topic in the study of the human visual system. Brightness discrimination can be thought of as the ability to detect changes in intensity at any given adaptation level. This ability of the eye can be quantified by using an experimental setup where a subject is to look at a field of uniform brightness, with a small part of it of a different intensity. A diagram of this setup is given on Fig. 1.14.

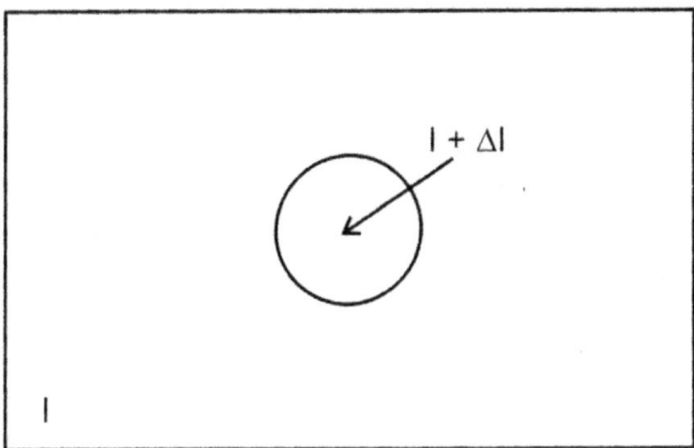

Fig. 1.14 Diagram showing an experimental setup to quantify brightness discrimination

In the above Fig. 1.14, "I" is the intensity of the background, while "ΔI" is the change in intensity. With this setup, a subject can be asked to tell when the change in intensity is detectable. Using this test, a quantity known as the Weber ratio can be established. The Weber ratio can be defined as $\Delta I_c/I$, where ΔI_c is the change in intensity where 50% of the test subjects report as detectable for a certain I. Therefore, a small value for the Weber ratio indicts the ability to distinguish between slight changes in intensity, while a large Weber ratio means poor brightness discrimination .

In addition to the processes described above, other high order, non-linear processing also occurs during brightness perception. One example of such event is the Mach band effect. An example of this effect is shown in the Fig. 1.15.

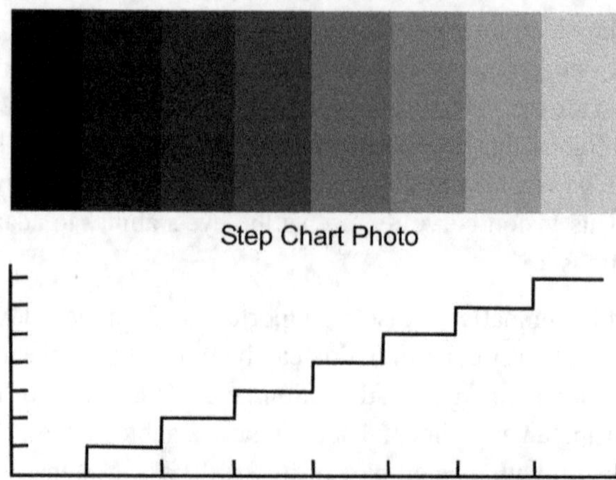

Fig. 1.15 Diagram showing the Mach band effect (30).

The top panel on figure shows a series of bands in which the light intensity over each band is uniform. The bottom panel shows a plot of the intensity of the top panel. As can be seen, the intensity is in a step-wise pattern. However, the observer will perceive that the right side of each band is darker and the left side is lighter. This effect came to be because the eye has lower sensitivity to high and low spatial frequencies when compared to mid frequencies. Due to this effect, one can keep in mind that when designing an imaging system, perfect reproduction of edges is often not necessary as the human eye is not able to detect such perfection. Another important phenomenon that occurs in brightness perception is known as simultaneous contrast. This is when a diagram showing the Mach band effect.

Object of certain intensity appears to be of a different intensity when viewed in a different background . An example of this is shown on Fig. 1.16 below.

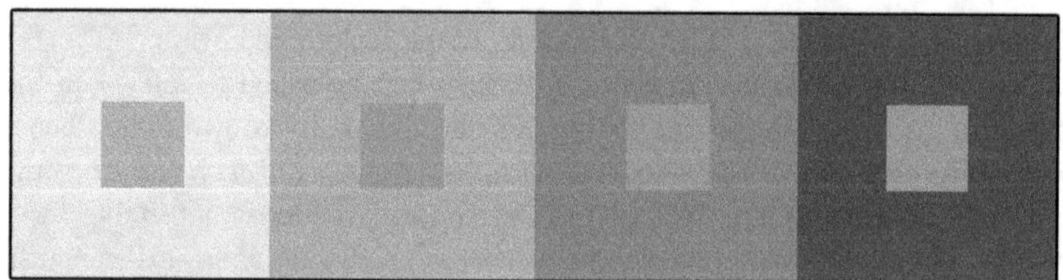

Fig. 1.16 Diagram showing simultaneous contrast.

The small square in each of the four large squares on Fig. 1.16 is of the same intensity. However, the small square that is located in lighter large squares appears darker than the small square in the dark large square. This goes to show that the background that an object is in will influence that perceived intensity of the object.

Colour perception

As was mentioned earlier, the colour is detected by three different cone cells in
the retina. Each of these cone cells are sensitive to certain wavelengths of light.
The three wavelengths of light that the cones are sensitive to are known as the
three primary colours (blue, green, red). Other colours in the spectrum are
perceived by the brain as a combination of these three colours. The Fig. 1.17
shows a diagram of this concept [29].

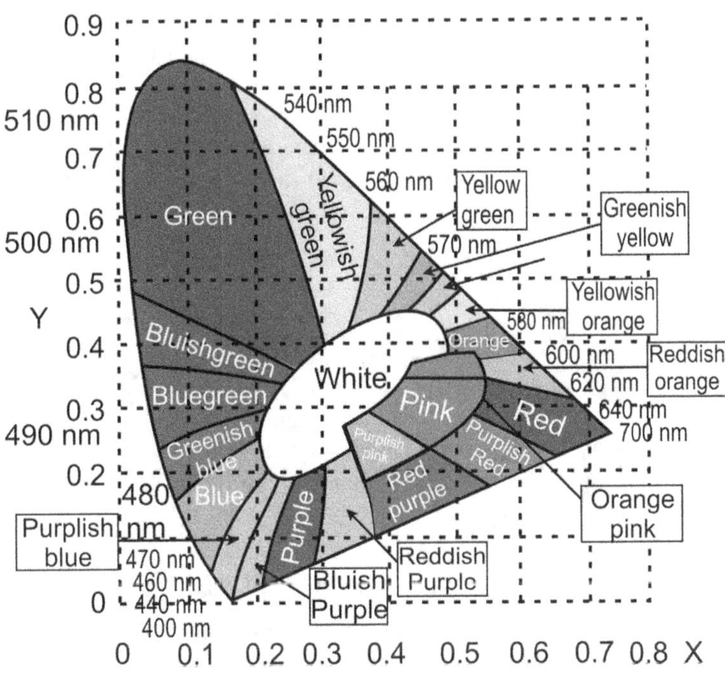

Fig. 1.17 Diagram showing colours obtained using
the mixture of the three primary colours.

The three corners in Fig. 1.17 represent the three primary colours. In the
center, where there is roughly an even mixture of the three colours, is white. Any
other colour can be seen as the mixture of the three primary colours.

Higher order processing

As was mentioned earlier, higher order processing exists in the human visual
system so that the image that is viewed is often different from the original image
[34]. A category of this processing is called optical illusions. In this, the brain
processes the image and fills in non-existent information about the image. An
example of this is shown on Fig. 1.18.

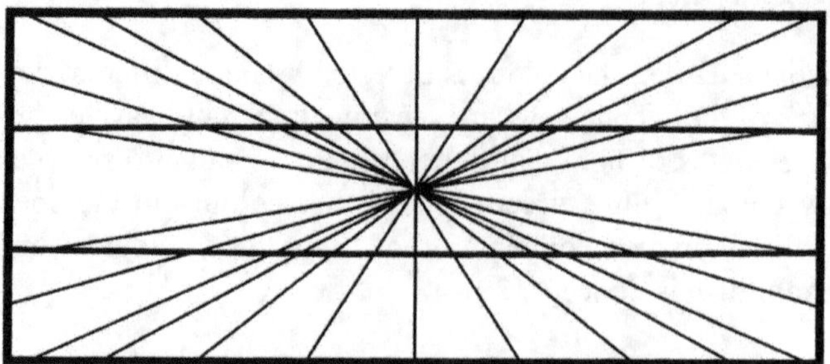

Fig. 1.18 Example of an optical illusion [30].

In this optical illusion, the two horizontal lines appear to be bending near the middle. However, they are in fact straight lines. Another example of an optical illusion is shown on Fig. 1.19. In this illusion there appears to be spirals in the figure. However, the spirals are in fact just circles.

Fig. 1.19 Example of an optical illusion [30].

1.5 The Image Model

Images can be denoted by two-dimensional functions of the order $f(x, y)$. The value or amplitude of f at spatial coordinates (x, y) is a positive scalar quantity whose physical meaning is determined by the source of the image [51]. In most of the monochromatic image values are said to span the gray scale. When an image is generated from a physical process, its values are proportional to energy radiated by a physical source (e.g., electromagnetic waves).

As a consequence, $f(x, y)$ must be nonzero and finite; that is, $0 < f(x, y) < \infty$

The function $f(x, y)$ may be characterized by two components:

(i) the amount of source illumination incident on the scene being viewed, and

(ii) the amount of illumination reflected by the objects in the scene.

Appropriately, these are called the illumination and reflectance components and are denoted by $i(x, y)$ and $r(x, y)$, respectively. The two functions combine as a product to form $f(x, y)$:

$$f(x, y) = i(x, y)\, r(x, y) \qquad \qquad .....(1.6)$$

Where

$$0 < i(x, y) < \infty \qquad \qquad .....(1.7)$$

and

$$0 < r(x, y) < 1. \qquad \qquad .....(1.8)$$

Eq. (1.8) indicates that reflectance is bounded by 0 (total absorption) and 1 (total reflectance). The nature of $i(x, y)$ is determined by the characteristics of the imaged objects. It is noted that these expressions also are applicable to images formed via transmission of the illumination through a medium, such as a chest X-ray. In this case, we would deal with a transmissivity instead of a reflectivity function, but the limits would be the same as in eq. (1.8), and the image function formed would be modeled as the product in eq. (1.6).

The values given in eq. (1.7) and (1.8) are theoretical bounds. The following average numerical figures illustrate some typical ranges of $i(x, y)$ for visible light. On a clear day, the sun may produce in excess of 90,000 lm/m^2 of illumination on the surface of the Earth. This figure decreases to less than 10,000 lm/m^2 on a cloudy day. On a clear evening, a full moon yields about 0.1 lm/m^2 of illumination. The typical illumination level in a commercial office is about 1000 lm/m^2. Similarly, the following are some typical values of $r(x, y)$: 0.01 for black velvet, 0.65 for stainless steel, 0.80 for flat –white wall paint, 0.90 for silver-plated metal, and 0.93 for snow.

We call the intensity of a monochrome image at any coordinates (x_0, y_0) the gray level (L) of the image at that point. That is,

$$L = f(x_0, y_0) \qquad \qquad .....(1.9)$$

From eq. (1.8 & 1.9), it is evident that l lies in the range

$$L_{min} \le l \le L_{max} \qquad \qquad .....(1.10)$$

In theory, the only requirement on L_{min} is that it be positive, and on L_{max} that it be finite, In practice, $L_{min} = i_{min}\, r_{min}$ and $L_{max} = i_{max}\, r_{max}$. Using the preceding average office illumination and range of reflectance values as guidelines, we may expect $L_{min} \approx 10$ and $L_{max} \approx 1000$ to be typical limits for indoor values in the absence of additional illumination. The interval $[L_{min}, L_{max}]$ is called the gray scale. Common practice is to shift this interval numerically to the interval white on the gray scale. All intermediate values are shades of gray varying from black to white.

1.5.1 Image Types

Each pixel of an image is typically associated to a specific 'position' in some 2D region, and has a value consisting of one or more quantities (samples) related to that position [54]. Digital images can be classified according to the number and nature of those samples:

(i)   Binary (bilevel) images
(ii) Grayscale images
(iii) Colour images
(iv) False-colour images or Pseudo-colour images
(v)   Multi-spectral images
(vi) Thematic images
(vii) Video images

The term digital image is also applied to data associated to points scattered over a three-dimensional region, such as those produced by tomographic equipment. In that case, each datum is called a voxel [51].

Binary Images

A binary image is a digital image that has only two possible values for each pixel. Binary images are also called bi-level or two-level. The names black-and-white, B&W, monochrome or monochromatic are often used for this concept, but may also designate any images that have only one sample per pixel, such as grayscale images. Binary images often arise in digital image processing as masks or as the result of certain operations such as segmentation, thresholding, and dithering. Some input/output devices, such as laser printers, fax machines, and bilevel computer displays, can only handle bilevel images [21].

A binary image is usually stored in memory as a bitmap, a packed array of bits. Binary images can be interpreted as subsets of the two-dimensional integer lattice Z2; the field of morphological image processing was largely inspired by this view. For example, a binary image of 5×5 digital image can be seen as below :

$$
\begin{matrix}
0 & 1 & 0 & 1 & 1 \\
1 & 0 & 0 & 1 & 1 \\
0 & 0 & 1 & 1 & 1 \\
1 & 1 & 0 & 1 & 1 \\
1 & 1 & 1 & 0 & 0
\end{matrix}
$$

Grayscale Image

Grayscale digital image is an image in which the value of each pixel is a single sample. Displayed images of this sort are typically composed of shades of gray, varying from black at the weakest intensity to white at the strongest, though in principle the samples could be displayed as shades of any colour, or even coded with various colours for different intensities. Grayscale images are distinct from black-and-white images, which in the context of computer imaging are images with only two colours, black and white; grayscale images have many shades of gray in between. In most contexts other than digital imaging, however, the term "black and white" is used in place of "grayscale"; for example, photography in shades of gray is typically called "black-and-white photography". The term monochromatic in some digital imaging contexts is synonymous with grayscale, and in some contexts synonymous with black-and-white. Grayscale images are often the result of measuring the intensity of light at each pixel in a single band of the electromagnetic spectrum (for example visible light).

Grayscale images intended for visual display are typically stored with 8 bits per sample, which allows 256 intensities (i.e., shades of gray) to be recorded, typically on a non-linear scale. The accuracy provided by this format is barely sufficient to avoid visible banding artifacts, but very convenient for programming. Technical uses (e.g. in medical imaging or remote sensing applications) often require more levels, to make full use of the sensor accuracy (typically 10 or 12 bits per sample) and to guard against roundoff errors in computations. Sixteen bits per sample (65536 levels) appears to be a popular choice for such uses. The following satellite image in single band is a classical example of grayscale image (Fig. 1.19a).

Fig. 1.19 (a) A Gray scale image.

Colour Images

A digital colour image is a digital image that includes colour information for each pixel [21]. For visually acceptable results, it is necessary and almost sufficient to provide three samples (colour channels) for each pixel, which are interpreted as coordinates in some colour space. The RGB colour space is commonly used in computer displays, but other spaces such as YUV, HSI, CMY and are often used in other requirements. Plate 2 shows the colour image of remotely sensing data obtained by Indian remote sensing satellite sensing systems. This colour image is the result of the combination of three band (three samples) digital data.

False-colour Images

A false-colour or pseudo-colour image is a colour image derived from a grayscale one by mapping each pixel value to a colour according to a table or function. A familiar example is the encoding of altitude in physical relief maps, where negative values (below sea level) are usually represented by shades of blue and positive values by greens and browns. Although false colouring does not increase the information contents of the original image, it can make some details more visible, by increasing the distance in colour space between successive gray levels.

More importantly, false colouring allows the visual comparison of pixel values between non-adjacent regions of the image. This is not possible when the image is displayed in shades of gray, because our eye perceives intensity changes rather than intensity values — so that the same gray level will appear darker or lighter depending on its surround. For this reason, the altitude scale in a relief map would be mostly useless if it was displayed in shades of gray. Hues, in contrast, are perceived in a more "absolute" fashion. So, in a false-colour relief map, there is little danger of confusing negative altitudes with positive ones; and the relative altitude of two mountains is clearly perceived, even if they lie at opposite ends of the map [35].

Multi-spectral Images

Multi-spectral images are images of the same object (Earth or planetary surface), taken in different bands of visible or infrared region of electromagnetic spectrum [52]. This is the main type of images acquired by Remote sensing (RS) radiometers. Usually satellites have 3 to 7 or more radiometers, IRS has 4, France's SPOT has 3, Landsat has 7. Each one acquires one digital image, in RS called scene, in a small band of visible spectra, ranging 0.7 μm to 0.4 μm, called red-green-blue (RGB) region, and going to infra-red wavelengths of 0.7 μm to 10 or more μm, classified as NIR-Near InfraRed, MIR-Midle InfraRed and FIR-Far InfraRed or Thermal. In the Landsat case we have 7 scenes comprising a 7 band multi spectral image. Plate 3 shows the satellite multispectral image aquired by IRS 1D LISS III sensor. Plate 4 shows the images taken in different spectral bands along with the composites.

Thematic Images

Thematic images are image products of classification processing of multispectral images of any terrain. The classification process differentiates various types of earth surface features such as land, water, forest, lake, structure etc. In principle, the multispectral image depicts all the features without any discrimination. In digital image processing, image classification is a very popular methodology to classify all the pixels into number of groups. The classification is mainly based on the known values called as training datasets. Each group of pixels form a class and each class will be represented by a colour and all the colours are displayed. As a result, a classified output is displayed (plate 5). Here each class or group of pixels / gray values form one type of feature on the ground. Such images are called as thematic images [60].

Video Images

Video images can be regarded as a three-dimensional generalization of still images, where the third dimension is time [43]. Each *frame* of a video sequence can be compressed by any image compression algorithm. A method where the images are separately coded by JPEG is sometimes referred as *Motion JPEG* (*M-JPEG*). A more sophisticated approach is to take advantage of the *temporal* correlations; i.e. the fact that subsequent images resemble each other very much. This is the case in the latest video compression standard MPEG (*Moving Pictures Expert Group*).

1.5.2 Image Quality

Image quality for digital capture from originals is a measure of the completeness and the accuracy of the capture of the visual information. Image quality depends on the project's planning and implementation methods. Project designers need to consider what standard practices they will follow for input resolution and bit depth, layout and cropping, image capture metric (including colour management), and the particular features of the capture device and its software. Benchmarking quality for any given type of source material can help one select appropriate image quality parameters that capture just the amount of information needed from the source material for eventual use and display. By maximizing the image quality of the digital master files, managers can ensure the on-going value of their efforts, and ease the process of derivative file production.

The clarity of a digital image depends on the number of "bits" the computer uses to represent each pixel. The most common type of representation in popular usage today is the "8-bit image", in which the computer uses 8 bits, or 1 byte, to represent each pixel. This yields 2^8 or 256 brightness levels - possible colours or shades of gray available within a given image. Other more expensive programs and computers can utilize 12 bits or 16 bits per pixel, yielding 2^{12} (4,096) and 2^{16} (65,536) brightness levels to represent the shading in an image.

Quality is necessarily limited by the size of the digital image file, which places an upper limit on the amount of information that is saved [52]. The size of a digital image file depends on the size of the original and the resolution of capture (number of pixels per inch in both height and width that are sampled from the original to create the digital image), the number of channels (typically 3 : Red, Green, and Blue: "RGB"), and the bit depth, that is the number of data bits used to store the image data for one pixel.

Measuring the accuracy of visual information in digital form implies the existence of a capture metric i.e., the rules that give meaning to the numerical data in the digital image file. For example, the visual meaning of the pixel data Red = 246, Green = 238, Blue = 80 will be a shade of yellow, which can be defined in terms of visual measurements. Most devices in RGB using software are based on the video standards defined in international agreements.

Bit depth is an indication of an image's tonal qualities. Bit depth is the number of bits of colour data which are stored for each pixel; the greater the bit depth, the greater the number of gray scale or colour tones that can be represented and the larger the file size [50]. The most common bit depths are :

- Bitonal or binary, 1 bit per pixel; a pixel is either black or white
- 8 bit gray scale, 8 bits per pixel; a pixel can be one of 256 shades of gray
- 8 bit colour, 8 bits per pixel ("indexed colour"); a pixel is one of 256 colours
- 24 bit colour (RGB), 24 bits per pixel; each 8-bit colour channel can have 256 levels, for a total of 16 million different colour combinations

While it is desirable to be able to capture images at bit depths greater than 24 (which only allows 256 levels for each colour channel), standard formats for storing and exchanging higher bit-depth files have not yet evolved, so that we expect that (at least for the next few years) the majority of digital master files will be 24-bit.

1.6 Colour models

A colour model or colour space is a way of representing colours and their relationship to each other. Different image processing systems use different colour models for different reasons. The colour picture publishing industry uses the CMY colour model. Colour CRT monitors and most computer graphics systems use the RGB colour model. Systems that must manipulate hue, saturation, and intensity separately use the HSI colour model. Human perception of colour is a function of the response of three types of cones. Because of that, colour systems are based on three numbers. These numbers are called tristimulus values. In this section, we will explore the RGB, CMY, HSI, and YC_bC_r colour models [21].

There are numerous colour spaces based on the tristimulus values. The YIQ colour space is used in broadcast television. The XYZ space does not correspond to physical primaries but is used as a colour standard. It is fairly easy to convert from XYZ to other colour spaces with a simple matrix multiplication. Other colour models include Lab, YUV, and UVW.

All colour space discussions will assume that all colours are normalized and the brightness values lie between 0 and 1.0. This is easily accomplished by dividing the colour by its maximum value. For example, an 8-bit colour is normalized by dividing by 255.

1.6.1 The RGB Model

The RGB colour space consists of the three additive primaries: red, green, and blue. Spectral components of these colours combine additively to produce a resultant colour.

The RGB model is represented by a 3-dimensional cube with red green and blue at the corners on each axis (Fig. 1.20) and Plate 6. Black is at the origin. White is at the opposite end of the cube. The gray scale follows the line from black to white. In a 24-bit colour graphics system with 8 bits per colour channel, red is (255,0,0). On the colour cube, it is (1,0,0).

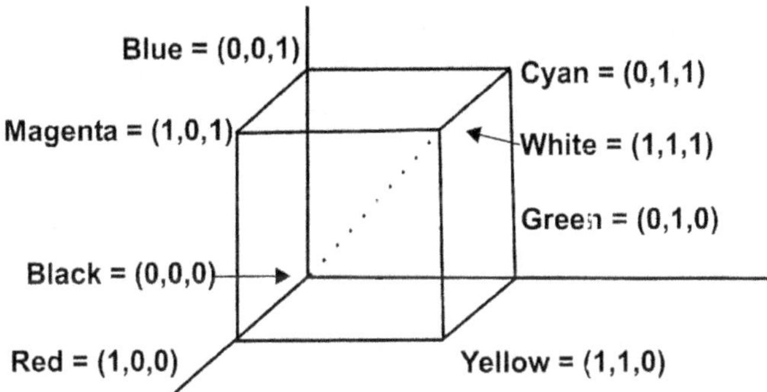

Fig. 1.20 RGB colour cube [21].

The RGB model simplifies the design of computer graphics systems but is not ideal for all applications. The red, green, and blue colour components are highly correlated. This makes it difficult to execute some image processing algorithms. Many processing techniques, such as histogram equalization, work on the intensity component of an image only. These processes are easier implemented using the HSI colour model.

Many times it becomes necessary to convert an RGB image into a gray scale image, perhaps for hardcopy on a black and white printer.

To convert an image from RGB colour to gray scale, use the following equation:

Gray scale intensity = 0.299R + 0.587G + 0.114B

This equation comes from the NTSC standard for luminance.

Another common conversion from RGB colour to gray scale is a simple average :

Gray scale intensity = 0.333R + 0.333G + 0.333B

This is used in many applications. It is also used in the RGB to HSI colour space conversion.

Because green is such a large component of gray scale, many people use the green component alone as gray scale data. To further reduce the colour to black and white, we can set normalized values less than 0.5 to black and all others to white. This is simple but doesn't produce the best quality [40].

1.6.2 The CMY/CMYK Image Model

The CMY colour space consists of cyan, magenta, and yellow. It is the complement of the RGB colour space since cyan, magenta, and yellow are the complements of red, green, and blue respectively [21]. Cyan, magenta, and yellow are known as the subtractive primaries. These primaries are subtracted from white light to produce the desired colour. Cyan absorbs red, magenta absorbs green, and yellow absorbs blue. You could then increase the green in an image by increasing the yellow and cyan or by decreasing the magenta (green's complement). Hence, this model is suited for applications like printers and copiers. This is because, it needs to display colours *reflected* from the surface of the paper.Since black is extensively used in printing, an additional colour, black is also added. If just the CMY model were to be used, then to print black colour, equal proportions of CMY would be required, and in the highest proportion. This causes considerable wastage of coloured ink. Hence, a separate black ink is used.

The values of C, M, and Y are found internally using the following formula :

$$\begin{bmatrix} C \\ M \\ Y \end{bmatrix} = \begin{bmatrix} 1 \\ 1 \\ 1 \end{bmatrix} - \begin{bmatrix} R \\ G \\ B \end{bmatrix}$$

Because RGB and CMY are complements, it is easy to convert between the two colour spaces. To go from RGB to CMY, subtract the complement from white :

$$C = 1.0 - R$$

$$M = 1.0 - G$$

$$Y = 1.0 - B$$

and to go from CMY to RGB :

$$R = 1.0 - C$$

$$G = 1.0 - M$$

$$B = 1.0 - Y$$

Most people are familiar with additive primary mixing used in the RGB colour space. Children are taught that mixing red and green yield brown. In the RGB colour space, red plus green produces yellow. Those who are artistically inclined are quite proficient at creating a desired colour from the combination of subtractive primaries [21]. The CMY colour space provides a model for subtractive colours Fig. 1.21 (a & b) and Plates 7 and 8.

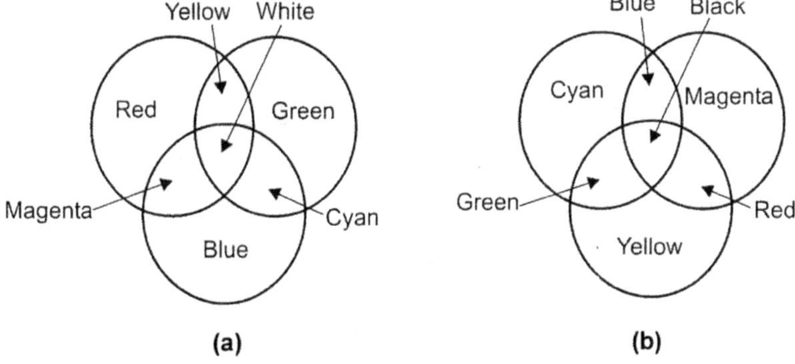

Fig. 1.21 (a) Additive colours and **(b)** substractive colours

Remember that these equations and colour spaces are normalized. All values are between 0.0 and 1.0 inclusive. In a 24-bit colour system, cyan would equal 255 - red (Fig. 1.21 a, b). In the printing industry, a fourth colour is added to this model. The three colours - cyan, magenta, and yellow - plus black are known as the process colours. Another colour model is called CMYK. Black (K) is added in the printing process because it is a more pure black than the combination of the other three colours. Pure black provides greater contrast. There is also the added impetus that black ink is cheaper than coloured ink.

To make the conversion from CMY to CMYK:

$$K = \min(C, M, Y)$$

$$C = C - K$$

$$M = M - K$$

$$Y = Y - K$$

To convert from CMYK to CMY, just add the black component to the C, M, and Y components.

1.6.3 The HSI Image Model

Since hue, saturation, and intensity are three properties used to describe colour, it seems logical that there be a corresponding colour model, HSI [36]. When using the HSI colour space, you don't need to know what percentage of blue or green is to produce a colour. You simply adjust the hue to get the colour you wish. To change a deep red to pink, adjust the saturation. To make it darker or lighter, alter the intensity.

Many applications use the HSI colour model. Machine vision uses HSI colour space in identifying the colour of different objects. Image processing applications - such as histogram operations, intensity transformations, and convolutions - operate on only an image's intensity. These operations are performed much easier on an image in the HSI colour space. For the HSI is modeled with cylindrical coordinates, see Fig. 1.22. The hue (H) is represented as the angle 0, varying from $0°$ to $360°$. Saturation (S) corresponds to the radius, varying from 0 to 1. Intensity (I) varies along the z axis with 0 being black and 1 being white.

When $S = 0$, the colour is a gray of intensity 1. When $S = 1$, the colour is on the boundary of top cone base. The greater the saturation, the farther the colour is from white/gray/black (depending on the intensity). Adjusting the hue will vary the colour from red at $0°$, through green at $120°$, blue at $240°$, and back to red at $360°$. When $I = 0$, the colour is black and therefore H is undefined. When $S = 0$, the colour is grayscale. H is also undefined in this case. By adjusting 1, a colour can be made darker or lighter. By maintaining $S = 1$ and adjusting I, shades of that colour are created.

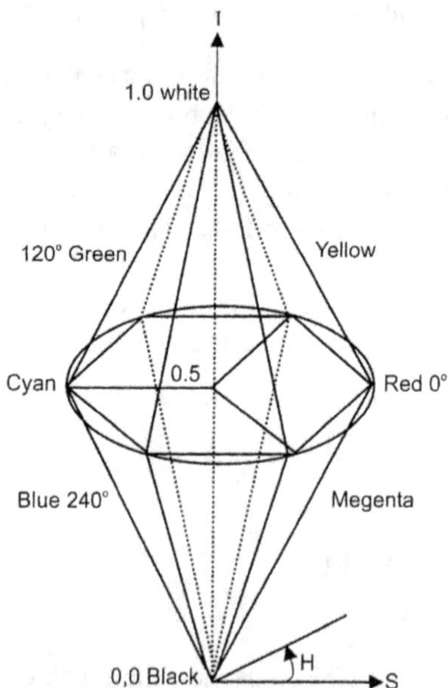

Fig. 1.22 Double cone model of HSI colour space.

The following formulas show how to convert from RGB space to HSI :

$$I = \frac{1}{3}\,(R + G + B)$$

$$S = I - \frac{3}{R+G+B}\,[min\ (R,\ G,\ B)]$$

$$H = cos^{-1}\left[\frac{\frac{1}{2}\left[(R-G)+(R-B)\right]}{\sqrt{(R-G)^2+(R-B)(G-B)}}\right]$$

If *B* is greater than *G*, then $H = 360^0 - H$.

To convert from HSI to RGB, the process depends on which colour sector H lies in. For the RG sector ($0° \le H \le 120°$):

$$b = \frac{1}{3}\,(I{-}S)$$

$$r = \frac{1}{3}\left[1+\frac{Scos(H)}{cos(60°-H)}\right]$$

$$g = 1 - (\,r + b\,)$$

For the *GB* sector ($120° \le H \le 240°$):

$$H = H{-}120°$$

$$g = \frac{1}{3}\left[1+\frac{Scos(H)}{cos(60°-H)}\right]$$

$$r = \frac{1}{3}\,(1 - S)$$

$$b = 1{-}(r + b)$$

For the *BR* sector ($240° \le H \le 360°$):

$$H = H - 240°$$

$$g = \frac{1}{3}\left[1+\frac{Scos(H)}{cos(60°-H)}\right]$$

$$r = \frac{1}{3}\,(1 - S)$$

$$b = 1 - (r + b)$$

The values r, g, and b are normalized values of R, G, and B. *To* convert them to R, G, and B values use:

$$R = 3Ir,\ G = 3Ig,\ 100B = 3Ib.$$

Remember that these equations expect all angles to be in degrees. To use the trigonometric functions in C, angles must be converted to radians.

1.6.4 The YC_bC_r Image Model

YC_bC_r is another colour space that separates the luminance from the colour information. The luminance is encoded in the Y and the blueness and redness encoded in C_bC_r. It is very easy to convert from RGB to YC_bC_r

$$Y = 0.29900R + 0.58700G + 0.11400B$$

$$C_b = -0.16874R - 0.33126G + 0.50000B$$

$$C_r = 0.50000R - 0.41869G - 0.08131B$$

and to convert back to RGB

$$R = 1.00000Y + 1.40200C_r$$

$$G = 1.00000Y - 0.34414C_b - 0.71414C_r,$$

$$B = 1.00000Y + 1.77200C_b$$

There are several ways to convert to/from YC_bC_r. This is the CCIR (International Radi Consultive Committee) recommendation 601-1 and is the typical method used in JPEG compression [40].

1.7   Image Acquisition

Imaging is the short term for image acquisition, the process of sensing our surroundings and then representing the measurements that are made in the form of an image. The sensing phase distinguishes image acquisition from image creation and acquisition can be accomplished using an existing set of data, and does not require a sensor.

1.7.1 Passive and Active Image Acquisition

We can classify imaging as either passive or active. Passive imaging employs energy sources that are already present in the scene, whereas active imaging involves the use of artificial energy sources to probe our surroundings. Passive imaging is subject to the limitations of existing energy sources; the sun for example, is a convenient source of illumination, but only during daylight hours. Active imaging is not restricted in this way, but it is invariably a more complicated and expensive procedure, since we must supply and control a source of radiation in addition to an imaging instrument.

In simple words, if the photograph of any object is taken using an ordinary camera without flash, it is said to be passive image acquisition where as the photograph taken with flash is said to be active image acquisition.

Active imaging predominates in the medical field, where precise control over radiation sources is essential in order to facilitate an accurate diagnosis and safeguard the patient's health. Active imaging is also becoming an important tool in remote sensing. Earth - orbiting satellites that carry sensors tuned to the visible region of the EM spectrum are unable to acquire useful images for areas of the surface that are in darkness, or that suffer from excessive cloud cover. Satellites equipped with synthetic aperture radar, on the other hand can acquire data continuously, regardless of the time of day or the weather conditions.

1.7.2 Energy Source

All regions of the Electromagnetic spectrum are suited to imaging. Nevertheless, there are good reasons to prefer light for imaging, which are as follows:

- Light is familiar, and is inherently safe.
- Light can be generated reliably and cheaply.
- Light is easy to control and process with optical hardware.
- Light can be detected easily.

The last point is important. Sensors for the visible and near-IR regions of the spectrum can be manufactured cheaply from silicon- that exhibits a useful response to radiation at these wavelengths. Also, the use of silicon allows a sensor to be integrated with its associated signal processing electronics, further reducing manufacturing costs.

For the reasons given above, we shall concentrate on imaging equipment that uses light. We shall examine in detail how images are acquired by an electronic camera and compare its performance with that of our own imaging ' hardware': our eyes.

Illumination and reflection

An image is defined as a two dimensional function, $f(x,y)$ where the x and y variables are the plane coordinates. The intensity or gray level at any coordinates (x,y) is defined by the value or amplitude of f. The function $f(x,y)$ relies on the two very important components. The first component is the amount of illumination (energy) source on the object of interest [21]. The second component is the amount of illumination reflected by the object of interest. The function $f(x,y)$ can be rewritten as follows:

$$f(x, y) = i(x, y) \, r(x, y)$$

Everything that can be seen is seen only when light from that object travels to our eyes. Whether it be a luminous object meaning it generates light of its own or an illuminated object meaning it reflects the light which is incident upon it, you can only view the object when light from that object travels to your eye. Visible light represents only a small spectrum of the electromagnetic spectrum. Visible light has wavelength that ranges from 400nm to 700nm as shown in Fig. 1.23. Intensity of light is proportional to the number of photons of each wavelength.

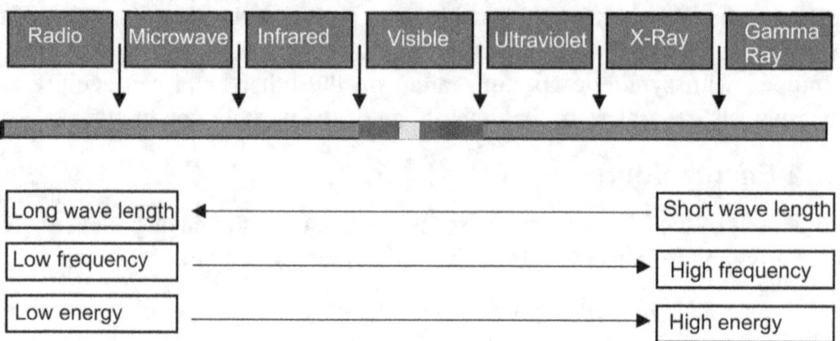

Fig. 1.23 Visible region of EM spectrum and its transformations.

Light is known to be moving in a predictable way or pattern. If a beam of light approaches a flat mirror and reflects off the flat mirror, then the behavior of such an event is predicted by the law of reflection. Fig. 1.24 illustrates the law of reflection [21]. The incident ray is denoted by I in the diagram and the reflected ray is denoted by R in the diagram. The N in the diagram is known as the normal line which cuts the incident ray and reflected ray into two equal angles.

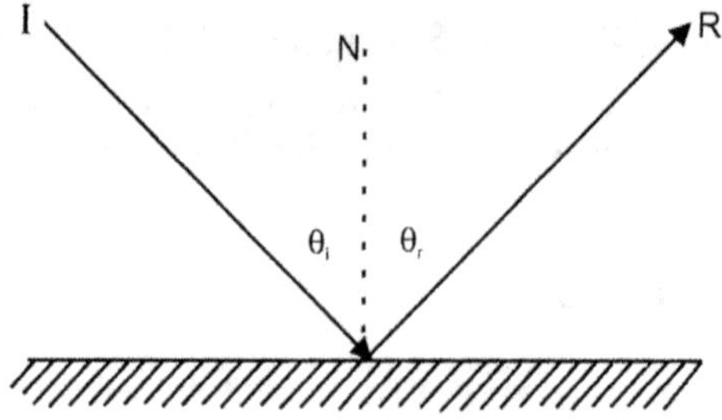

Fig. 1.24 Law of reflection.

None of us are light generating objects. We are illuminated objects like the moon, and the sun can be considered as an illuminating source. We make our presence visibly known by reflecting light to the eyes of those who observe our way. It is only by reflection that we can be seen as well as other objects in the world. It is surprising to see how we take for granted illumination and reflection in our everyday life.

1.7.3 Camera Optics

A camera uses a lens to focus part of the visual environment onto a sensor. The most important characteristics of lens are its magnifying power and its light gathering capacity [19]. The former can be specified by a magnification factor.

$$m = \text{image size / object size}$$

by similar triangles, we can also say that

$$(v / u) = (\text{image size / object size})$$

Where u is the distance from an object to the lens and v is the distance from the lens to the image plane. Hence

$$m = v / u \qquad\qquad .....(1.11)$$

It is usual to express the magnifying power of a lens in terms of its focal length, f, the distance from the lens to the point at which parallel incident rays converge (Fig. 1.24). Focal length is given by the lens equation,

$$1/ f = 1/ u + 1/v \qquad\qquad .....(1.12)$$

The units for f are usually millimeters.

We can combine Eqs. (1.11) and (1.12) and rearrange to give an expression for f in terms of u and m :

$$f = (um) / (m + 1)$$

This is useful, since it allows us to select an appropriate lens for any desired magnification and object distance. Consider, for example, a scenario in which we need to form an image of a 10-cm-wide object, 50 cm away, on a sensor measuring 10mm across. The magnification factor we require is

$$m = (\text{image size/object size}) = (10 / 100) = 0.1$$

Hence the focal length should be

$$f = (um) / (m + 1) = [(500 \times 0.1) / 1.1] = 45.5$$

i.e., we need a lens with a focal length of approximately 45 mm.

The light gathering capacity of a camera lens is determined by its aperture. This can be no larger than the diameter of the lens itself, and it is usually made smaller than this by means of a diaphragm – a circular hole of size, incorporated into the lens. It is normal to express the aperture of a lens as an 'f number' – a dimensionless value obtained when focal length is divided by aperture diameter. Most lenses offer a sequence of fixed apertures (e.g., f 2.8, f 4, f 5.6, f 8, f 11) that progressively halve the total amount of light reaching the sensor.

All lenses suffer from defects or aberrations, which can affect image quality. Spherical aberration arises when central and off- center rays are brought to a focus at different distances from the lens, resulting in blurred images. Coma occurs for obliquely – incident light when the off-centre rays come to a focus to one side of the central ray position, producing comet-shaped images of point objects. The surface of best focus for a lens is domed rather than planer; with the result that focus varies across an image acquired using a flat sensor. Field curvature measures the severity of this effect. Geometric distortion may also be a problem, particularly for lenses with small focal lengths. The tendency for straight lines to be bowed inwards, towards the centre of image, is termed pincushion distortion; the tendency for straight lines to be bowed outwards is termed barrel distortion.

The lens of a camera typically consists of several separate lens elements, designed so that, I combination, they partially compensate for the aforementioned aberrations. The effects of aberrations can also be reduced by making the lens aperture as small as possible. This confers additional benefits: depth of field (the range of distances at which an object will be in focus) is increased; also, small apertures restrict the passage of light to the central part of the lens, which has the highest resolving power. However, small apertures also cut down the amount of light falling on the sensor, thereby reducing the sensitivity of the instrument and, consequently, the quality of the image.

1.7.3.1 Image formation in a pin-hole camera

In order to better understand how to model vision and replicate it such as on a computer, we need to go another step in understanding the image acquisition project. The role a camera plays in machine vision is similar to how the eye performs in human vision [40]. The pinhole camera is considered the simplest and the most ideal model of a camera function. This model has a very small hole through which light enters. The Fig. 1.25 below illustrates perspective projection where we map three dimensions onto two.

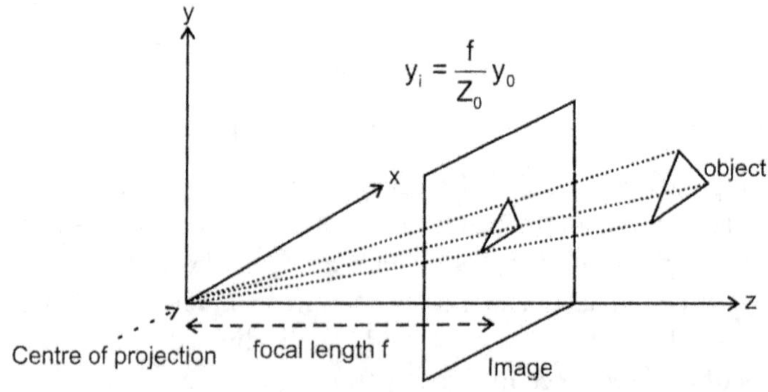

Fig. 1.25 Image formation in pin hole camera.

Perspective projection relations :

A perspective projection is defined as the projection of a three-dimensional object onto a two-dimensional surface through the use of straight lines which goes through a single point. Through geometry, it shows that if the define f as the distance between the image plane and the center of projection, then we image coordinates (x_i, y_i) have relations to the source object coordinates (x_o, y_o, z_o) by the following equation.

$$x_i = \frac{f}{z_o} x_o$$

1.7.3.2 Image Formation in a Convex Lens Camera

A converging lens is a lens that converges rays of light traveling parallel to its principal axis. Converging lens are known to have an oval shape and are thicker across their center while being thinner at the upper and lower edges as shown in Fig. 1.26. Image models give us the geometric and photometric information of a scene and the image itself. Pin-hole, thin lens, and Gaussian thick lens model use three dimensional image models. In a pin-hole model, a small hole is placed between the scene and the image sensor. The thin lens model is an improved version of the pin-hole model where a thin lens is placed at the finite aperture. The addition of the thin lens helps it to capture photometric effects that include the sharpness of the image. It also captures the accumulation of light from a finite distance.

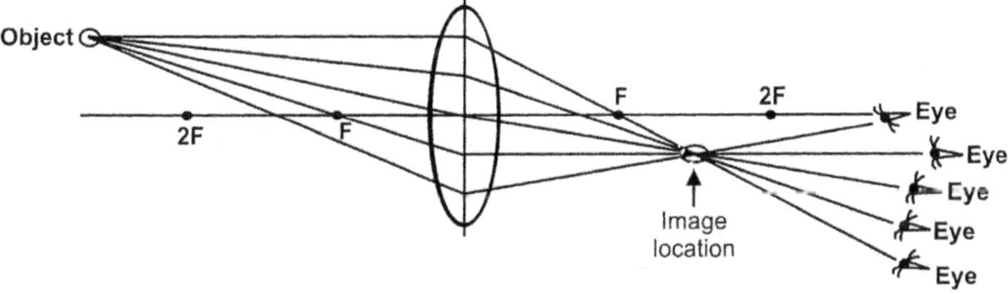

Fig. 1.26 Radiance, irradiance, and luminance [19].

Radiance and irradiance are defined as the power emerging from the object and is measured in unit of watt (W). Luminance is defined as the total amount of energy the observer receives from an illuminated source and has units in lumens (lm).

1.7.4 CCD and CMOS

Both CMOS and CCD imagers are constructed from silicon. This gives them fundamentally similar properties of sensitivity over the visible and near-IR spectrum. Thus, both technologies convert incident light (photons) into electronic charge (electrons) by the same photo conversion process. Both technologies can support two flavors of photo element - the photo gate and the photodiode. Generally, photodiode sensors are more sensitive, especially to blue light, and this can be important in making colour cameras. Colour sensors can be made in the same way with both technologies; normally by coating each individual pixel with a filter colour (e.g. red, green, blue).

1.7.4.1 Basic operation of CCD

A charge-coupled device (CCD) gets its name from the way the charges on its pixels are read after an exposure. After the exposure the charges on the first row are transferred to a place on the sensor called the read out register. From there, the signals are fed to an amplifier and then on to an analog-to-digital converter. Once the row has been read, its charges on the readout register row are deleted, the next row enters, and all of the rows above march down one row. The charges on each row are "coupled" to those on the row above so when one moves down, the next moves down to fill its old space. In this way, each row can be read-one row at a time.

CCDs capture light on the small photo sites on their surface and get their name from the way that charge is read after an exposure. To begin, the charges on the first row are transferred to a read out register.

After the exposure is complete, the charge is transferred row by row into a read-out register and from there to an output amplifier, analog/digital converters and on for processing. This row-by-row processing of the CCD's light "data" is where the sensor gets the term "Charge-Coupled" in its name. One row of information is transferred to the read-out register, and the rows behind it are each shifted one row closer to the register. After being "read out," the charge is released and the register is empty again for the next charge. Repeat the process a number of times, and eventually you read out the entire contents of the CCD sensor. The structure of a CCD sensor and its basic functioning in a camera is shown in Fig. 1.27 [28].

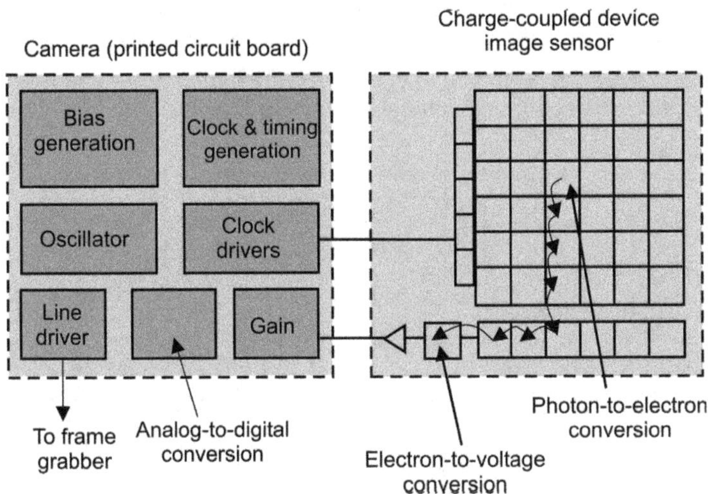

Fig. 1.27 The structure of CCD.

1.7.4.2 Basic principle of CMOS

Recent advances in CMOS sensors bring them closer to their CCD counterparts in terms of image quality, but CMOS sensors remain unsuitable for cameras where the highest possible image quality is required. CMOS sensors provide a lower total cost for the cameras since they contain all the logics needed to build cameras around them. They make it possible to produce smaller-sized cameras. Large-sized sensors are available, providing mega pixel resolution to a variety of network cameras. A current limitation with CMOS sensors is their lower light sensitivity. While this drawback is not an issue in bright environments, in low light conditions it becomes apparent. The result is either a very dark or a very noisy image.

Image sensors are manufactured in wafer foundries. Here the tiny circuits and devices are etched onto silicon chips. The biggest problem with CCDs is that there isn't enough economy of scale. They are created in foundries using specialized and expensive processes that can only be used to make CCDs. Meanwhile, more and larger foundries across the street are using a different process called Complementary Metal Oxide Semiconductor (CMOS) to make millions of chips for computer processors and memory. This is by far the most common and highest yielding process in the world. The latest CMOS processors, such as the Pentium III, contain almost 10 million active elements. Using this same process and the same equipment to manufacturer, CMOS image sensors cut costs dramatically because the fixed costs of the plant are spread over a much larger number of devices. (CMOS refers to how a sensor is manufactured, and not to a specific sensor technology.) As a result of this economy of scale, the cost of fabricating a CMOS wafer is lower than the cost of fabricating a similar wafer using the more specialized CCD process. The structure of a CMOS sensor along with its basic functioning in a camera is given in Fig. 1.28.

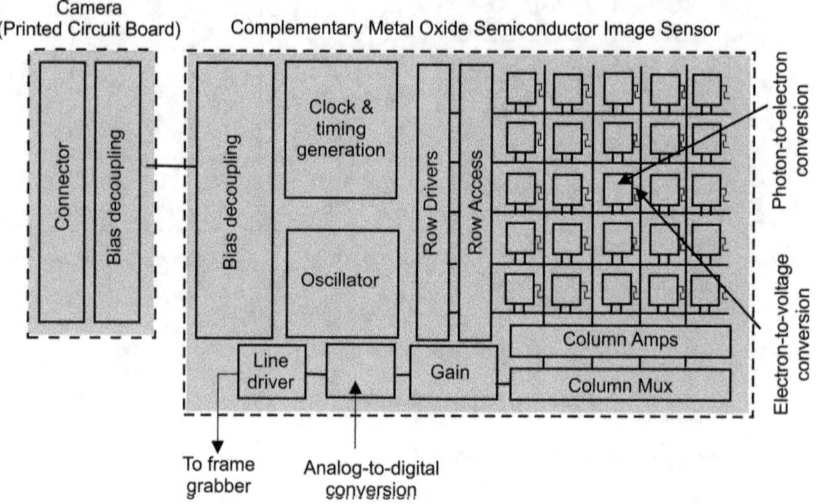

Fig. 1.28 The structure of CMOS.

Table 1.2 shows the feature comparision of CCD and CMOS sensors. The basic differences can be found out from this table, whereas Tabe 1.3 shows the feature comparision, clearly showing that CCD is superior to CMOS.

Table 1.2 Feature Comparison of CCD and CMOS.

Feature	CCD	CMOS
Signal out of pixel	Electron packet	Voltage
Signal out of chip	Voltage (analog)	Bits (digital)
Signal out of camera	Bits (digital)	Bits (digital)
Fill factor	High	Moderate
Amplifier mismatch	N/A	Moderate
System Noise	Low	Moderate to High
System Complexity	High	Low
Sensor Complexity	Low	High
Camera components	PCB + multiple chips + lens	Chip + lens
Relative R & D cost	Depends on Application	Depends on Application
Relative system cost	Depends on Application	Depends on Application

Table 1.3 Performance Comparison of CCD and CMOS.

Performance	CCD	CMOS
Responsivity	Moderate	Slightly better
Dynamic Range	High	Moderate
Uniformity	High	Low to Moderate
Uniform Shuttering	Fast, common	Poor
Speed	Moderate to High	Higher
Windowing	Limited	Extensive
Anti-blooming	High to none	High
Biasing and Clocking	Multiple, higher voltage	Single, low-voltage

1.7.4.3 Scanners

In recent years scanners have become an integrated part of our daily lives. Scanner technology is used everywhere and in various forms. There are four popularly used scanners which are flat bed scanners, sheet fed scanners, handheld scanners and drum scanners. These are briefly described as :

- **Flat bed scanners**, also called desktop scanners, (Fig. 1.29) are the most versatile and commonly used scanners.

Fig. 1.29 A Flat bed scanner.

- **Sheet-fed scanners** are similar to flatbed scanners except the document is moved and the scan head is immobile. A sheet-fed scanner looks a lot like a small portable printer.

- **Handheld scanners** use the same basic technology as a flatbed scanner, but rely on the user to move them instead of a motorized belt. Poor Image quality but faster and quicker response to capturing text.

- **Drum scanners** are used by the publishing industry to capture incredibly detailed images. They use a technology called a photo multiplier tube (PMT). In PMT, the document to be scanned is mounted on a glass cylinder. At the center of the cylinder is a sensor that splits light bounced from the document into three beams. Each beam is sent through a colour filter into a photo multiplier tube where the light is changed into an electrical signal.

Principle of operation

The basic principle of a scanner is to analyze an image and process it in some way. Image and text capture (optical character recognition or OCR) allows us to save information to a file on your computer. One can then alter or enhance the image, print it out or use it on the web page.

Core Components of the Scanner : The core component of the scanner is the CCD array. The CCD is the most common technology for image capture in scanners. CCD is a collection of tiny light-sensitive diodes, which convert photons (light) into electrons (electrical charge). These diodes are called **photo sites**. In a nutshell, each photo site is sensitive to light — the brighter the light that hits a single photo site, the greater the electrical charge that will accumulate at that site.

Scanning Process: There are a series of steps the scanner goes through before it stores the scanned document in any image format. The document is placed on the glass and the cover is closed. The cover provides a uniform background that the scanner uses to determine a reference point for determining the size of the object. The internal lamp illuminates the object. The scan head comprised of mirrors, filter and CCD array is moved over the document till a complete pass is performed over the entire document. The data which is scanned can be kept as an image in the buffer of the scanner and after the user approves of a draft of the document within the scanner the image is converted into any of the file formats for storage purposes i.e. JPEG, BMP etc.

The document is placed on the **glass plate** and the **cover** is closed. The inside of the cover in most scanners is flat white, although a few are black. The cover provides a uniform background that the scanner software can use as a reference point for determining the size of the document being scanned. Most flatbed scanners allow the cover to be removed for scanning a bulky object, such as a page in a thick book.

1.7.5 Image Acquisition Using a Single Sensor

The most familiar sensor of this type is the photodiode, which is constructed of silicon materials and whose output voltage waveform is proportional to light. The use of a filter in front of a sensor improves selectivity (Fig. 1.30). For example, a green (pass) filter in front of a light sensor favors light in the green band of the colour spectrum. As a consequence, the sensor output will be stronger for green light than for other components in the visible spectrum.

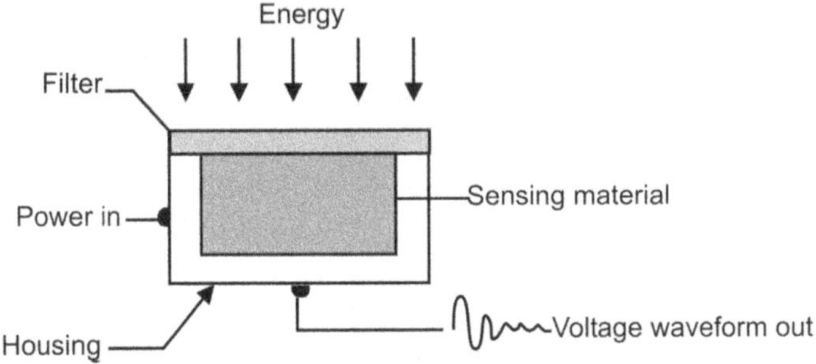

Fig. 1.30 The components of a single imaging sensor [30].

In order to generate a 2-D image using a single sensor, there has to be relative displacements in both the x- and y-directions between the sensor and the area to be imaged. Fig. 1.31 shows an arrangement used in high-precision scanning, where a film negative is mounted onto a drum whose mechanical rotation provides displacement in one dimension. The single sensor is mounted on a lead screw that provides motion in the perpendicular direction. Since mechanical motion can be controlled with high precision, this method is an inexpensive (but slow) way to obtain high-resolution images. Other similar mechanical arrangements use a flat bed, with the sensor moving in two linear directions. These types of mechanical digitizers sometimes are referred to as *microdensitometers*.

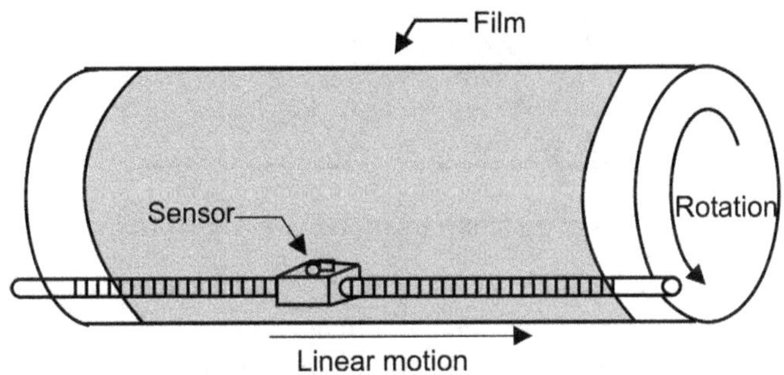

Fig. 1.31 A single sensor with motion used to generate a 2-D image [30].

Another example of imaging with a single sensor places a laser source coincident with the sensor. Moving mirrors are used to control the outgoing beam in a scanning pattern and to direct the reflected laser signal onto the sensor. This arrangement also can be used to acquire images using strip and array sensors, which are discussed in the following two sections.

1.7.6 Image Acquisition using Sensor Strips

A geometry that is used much more frequently than single sensors consists of an in-line arrangement of sensors in the form of a sensor strip, as Fig. 1.32 shows.

The strip provides imaging elements in one direction. Motion perpendicular to the strip provides imaging in the other direction, as shown in Fig. 1.32.This is the type of arrangement used in most flat bed scanners. Sensing devices with 4000 or more in-line sensors are possible. In-line sensors are used routinely in airborne imaging applications, in which the imaging system is mounted on an aircraft that flies at a constant altitude and speed over the geographical area to be imaged. One-dimensional imaging sensor strips that respond to various bands of the electromagnetic spectrum are mounted perpendicular to the direction of flight. The imaging strip gives one line of an image at a time, and the motion of the strip completes the other dimension of a two-dimensional image. Lenses or other focusing schemes are used to project the area to be scanned onto the sensors.

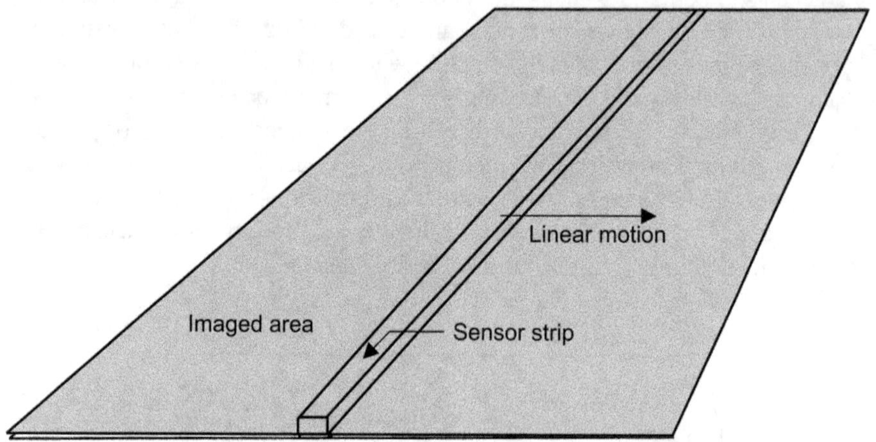

Fig. 1.32 Image acquisition using a linear sensor strip [30].

Sensor strips mounted in a ring configuration are used in medical and industrial imaging to obtain cross-sectional ("slice") images of 3-D objects, as Fig. 1.33 shows. A rotating X-ray source provides illumination and the portion of the sensors opposite the source collect the X-ray energy that pass through the object (the sensors obviously have to be sensitive to X-ray energy). This is the basis for medical and industrial computerized axial tomography (CAT) imaging. It is important to note that the output of the sensors must be processed by reconstruction algorithms whose objective is to transform the sensed data into meaningful cross-sectional images.In other words, images are not obtained directly from the sensors by motion alone; they require extensive processing. A 3-D digital volume consisting of stacked images is generated as the object is moved in a direction perpendicular to the sensor ring. Other modalities of imaging based on the CAT principle include magnetic resonance imaging (MRI) and positron emission tomography (PET) [30].The illumination sources, sensors, and types of images are different, but conceptually they are very similar to the basic imaging approach shown in Fig. 1.33.

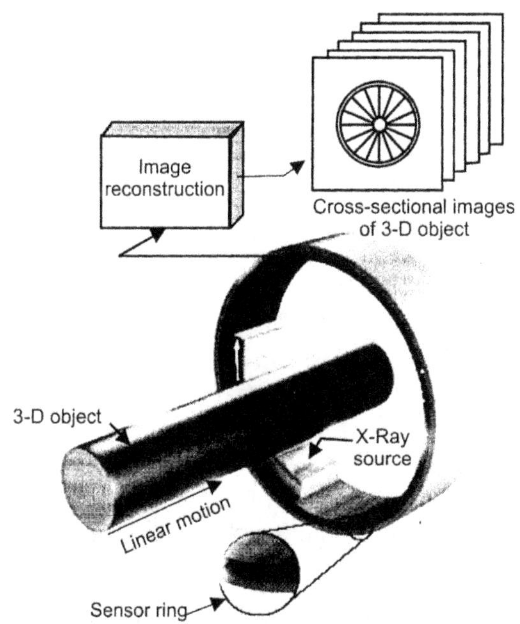

Fig. 1.33 Image acquisition using a circular sensor strip [30].

1.7.7 Image Acquisition Using Sensor Arrays

Numerous electromagnetic and some ultrasonic sensing devices frequently are arranged in an array format. This is also the predominant arrangement found in digital cameras. A typical sensor for these cameras is a CCD array, which can be manufactured with a broad range of sensing properties and can be packaged in rugged arrays of elements or more. CCD sensors are used widely in digital cameras and other light sensing instruments. The response of each sensor is proportional to the integral of the light energy projected onto the surface of the sensor, a property that is used in astronomical and other applications requiring low noise images. Noise reduction is achieved by letting the sensor integrate the input light signal over minutes or even hours. Since the sensor array shown in Fig. 1.34(c) is two dimensional, its key advantage is that a complete image can be obtained by focusing the energy pattern onto the surface of the array. Motion obviously is not necessary, as is the case with the sensor arrangements discussed in the preceding two sections. The principal manner in which array sensors are used is shown in Fig. 1.34.

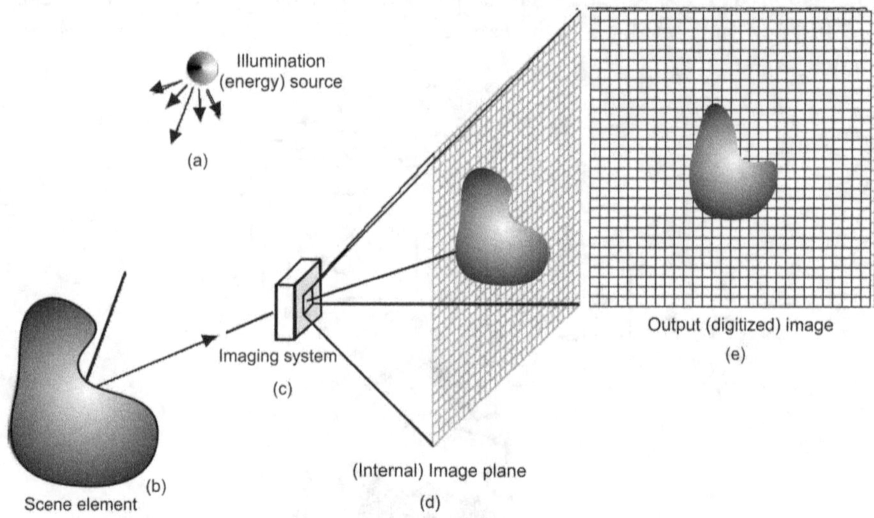

Fig. 1.34 An example of the digital image acquisition process. (a) Energy ("illumination") source. (b) An element of a scene. (c) Imaging system. (d) Projection of the scene onto the image plane. (e) Digitized image [30].-

The Fig. 1.34 shows the energy from an illumination source being reflected from a scene element, but, as mentioned at the beginning of this section, the energy also could be transmitted through the scene elements. The first function performed by the imaging system shown in Fig. 1.34 (c) is to collect the incoming energy and focus it onto an image plane. If the illumination is light, the front end of the imaging system is a lens, which projects the viewed scene onto the lens focal plane, as Fig. 1.34 (d) shows. The sensor array, which is coincident with the focal plane, produces outputs proportional to the integral of the light received at each sensor. Digital and analog circuitry sweep these outputs and convert them to a video signal, which is then digitized by another section of the imaging system. The output is a digital image, as shown diagrammatically in Fig. 1.35 (e).

1.7.8 Three-dimensional imaging

A camera creates images that are projections of some limited part of our three-dimensional world onto a two-dimensional plane. If we can somehow invert this projective transformation, we can recover information about the three-dimensional world from images. Unfortunately, a single image does not contain sufficient information to invert the projection. There is ambiguity because a given feature in the image could correspond to a large distant object or a small nearby object. This ambiguity can be resolved using multiple view of the scene.

1.7.9 Stereoscopy

Our two eyes give us binocular vision. A point in the scene that we are viewing projects onto one point on the retina of the left eye and a different point on the retina of the right eye. The points are different because our eyes are separated by a few centimeters. The separation of the points is termed the disparity. There is an inverse relationship between disparity and depth in the scene; disparity will be relatively large for points in the scene that are near to us and relatively small for points that are far away.

Following this principle, stereoscopic imaging uses a pair of images of the same scene obtained from cameras located at slightly different positions. Standard formulae exist to calculate depth from disparity, given adequate knowledge of imaging geometry (i.e. camera separation and focal length). However, a major problem is the detection of corresponding points in the left and right images, a process known as stereo matching.

1.7.10 Computerized Axial Tomography (CAT)

CAT scans take the idea of conventional X ray imaging to a new level. Instead of finding an outline of the bones and the organs, the CAT scan machine forms a full three dimensional model of the insides of the patient. The doctors can then examine at a time one narrow slice to pinpoint area of interest.

The CAT machine produces X rays, a very powerful form of electromagnetic energy. X ray are the same thing as visible light photons but they have more energy.

This energy allows X rays to become almost invisible and pass through the soft insides and bones and cartilages inside the human body.

X ray image is basically a shadow when you shine a bright source of light on one side of the body and a piece of film registers the silhouette of the bones. But the shadows of object cannot give a complete picture of the objects shape. In order to show a complete picture the body has to be rotated 360 degrees in the longitudinal axis for all the parts of the body to be visible. In the conventional CAT scan X ray machine image the same thing happens. If a larger bone is between the X ray machine and smaller bone, the larger bone covers the smaller bone on the film. For the smaller bone to be visible you have to turn the body or rotate the X ray machine.

Scanning Procedure

To a layman the CAT machine is more or less a huge donut tipped on one of its side. The patient sleeps on a platform which slowly moves inside the core of the machine. The X ray tube is mounted on the core of the movable ring around the edges of the hole of the machine. The ring also supports an array of X ray detectors directly opposite the X ray tube. A motor move the X ray tube such that the X ray tube and the X ray detectors revolve round the body. Each full revolution scans a slice of the horizontal portion of the body mounted on the platform (Fig. 1.35). Also some movement of the platform pushes it further into the machine core so that the tube and detectors can scan another slice of the body.

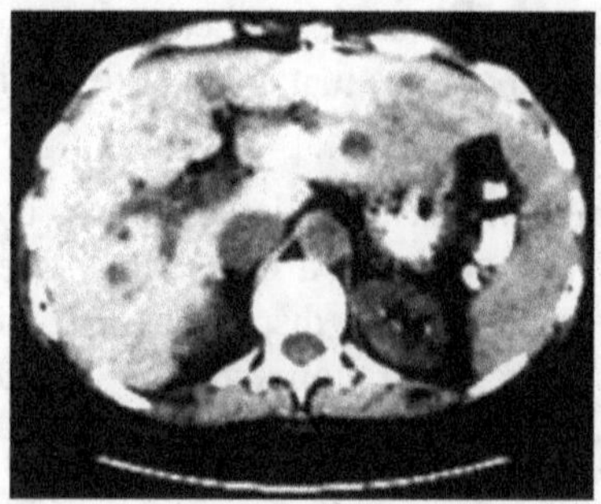

Fig. 1.35 A CAT scanned Liver slice

Since the scans cover the human body slice by slice in the complete 360 degrees revolution, the scans are more comprehensive than conventional X-ray scans. In today's medical world doctors use these CAT scans to treat an array of ailments from Head trauma to cancer.

1.8   Image Sampling and Quantization

The first step involved in digitizing an image is called sampling. The density of the image is apportioned at fixed increments. The increment size should be determined by the ultimate purpose of the final image. Quantization is the conversion of the sampled image into numeric values [5]. For example, white is read as "1" and black is read as "0".

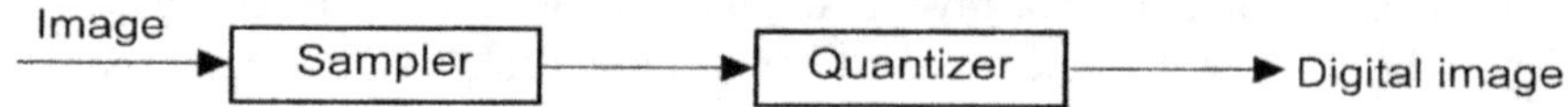

Fig. 1.36 Image sampling procedure.

Spatial resolution is the smallest discernible detail in an image. Spatial resolution is determined by the sampling frequency. The terms spatial frequency and spatial resolution are interchangeable. Gray-level resolution is the smallest discernible grey-level changing. The number of gray-levels is usually a power of 2 such as 8 bits, 16 bits, or 32 bits. Sampling is the process of measuring the value of the image function f (x, y) at discrete image, known as a pixel. A digital image is a two-dimensional array of these pixel. Pixel are indexed by x and y coordinates, with x and y taking integer values. The Fig. 1.36 shows the various stages from capturing a raw image to get a dgital image.

A CCD sensor consists of a discrete array of photosites, so it has, in effect, already sampled the radiation pattern that falls on it. However, in conventional video cameras these samples are converted into an analogue video signal for compatibility with the majority of video equipment in use today.

A single frame from a standard video signal is already discrete in the y dimension, consisting of either 525 or 625 lines of data. Sampling the signal that correspond to each line. This makes the image discrete spatially in the x dimension.

Video standards enforce a particular sampling rate for a video signal. An RS-170 video signal, for instance, has 485 active lines and each frame must have aspect ratio of 4:3, so there must be $485 \times (4/3) = 646$ samples per lines. In practice, a few lines and samples are trimmed from the signal to give an array of pixels with dimensions 640×480. To produce such an image, a temporal sampling rate of around 12 MHz is required.

With a digital 'still picture' camera, things are somewhat simpler, as there is no need to convert samples from the CCD into an analogue form and then resample, neither is there a requirement to conform to broadcast video standards. Such cameras typically produce images with dimensions of 1024×768, 1280×1024, etc. These dimensions are chosen to suit display standards originating from the computer industry (e.g., SVGA). Much higher resolutions than those of broadcast video are possible, and a 4:3 aspect ratio is not enforced (although this is often preferred).

Other types of imaging equipment operate under different constraints. In medicine, for example, radioisotope imaging devices produce images that are, of necessity, sampled very coarsely [36]. This is because images are formed from gamma ray photons emitted radioactive material inside the patient. For safety reasons, the quantity of this material is small, hence there are relatively few photons emitted. It is therefore necessary to integrate photon counts over a relatively large area in order to obtain statistically meaningful results. An area the size of the chest, for example, might be represented by a 64×64-pixel array.

In deciding whether a digital image has been sampled appropriately, we must consider the rapidity with which the value of $f(x, y)$ changes as we move across the image. This rate of change is measured by spatial frequency. Gradual changes in $f(x, y)$ are characterized by low spatial frequencies and can be represented adequately in a coarsely-sampled image; rapid changes are characterized by high spatial frequencies and can be represented accurately only in a densely-sampled image [40]. Wherever possible, the sampling that we choose for an image should satisfy the Nyquist criterion. Essentially, this states that the sampling frequency should be at least double the highest spatial frequency found in the image. If we sample an image coarsely, such that the Nyquist criterion is not met, then the image may suffer from the effects of aliasing.

1.8.1 Sampling Pattern

When sampling an image, we need to consider not only the sampling rate, but also the physical arrangement of the samples. A rectangular pattern, in which pixels are aligned horizontally and vertically into rows and columns, is by far the most common. Unfortunately, a rectangular sampling pattern leads to ambiguities in pixel connectivity. Fig. 1.37 (a) suggests that the chain of shaded pixels labeled A - D separates two regions of unshaded pixels, but this is not so; if we allow B and C to be connected diagonally, then it follows that E and F are also connected – in which case, the chain is not continuous and the two groups of unshaded pixels form a single region.

A second problem with rectangular pattern is an inconsistency in distance measurement. Suppose that each pixel in Fig. 1.36 (a) represent of these scene that is 1mm wide and 1mm high. The distance between pixels C and D is thus 1 mm; however, the distance between pixel B and C is not 1mm but 2 mm, by simple trigonometry. Hence, the actual distance traveled when by a fixed number of pixels in the image depends on the direction in which we move.

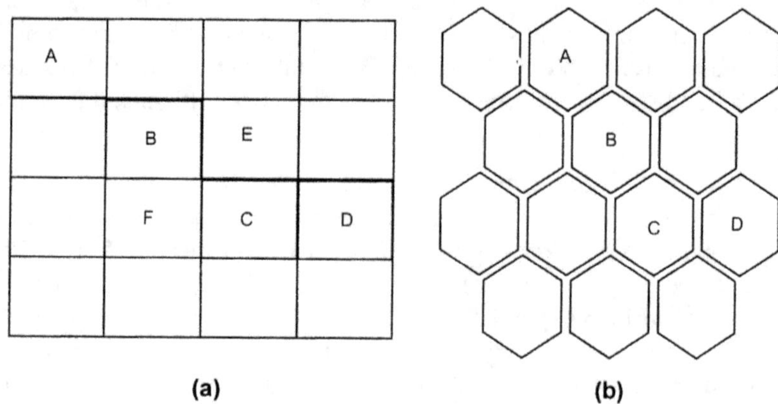

Fig. 1.37 Connectivity of different sampling patterns (a) Rectangular pattern (b) Hexagonal pattern.

These problems would be solved by a hexagonal sampling pattern (Fig. 1.37 (b)). Here, diagonal neighbors are properly connected, and the distance traveled in an image does not depend on direction. Despite these advantages, a hexagonal pattern seldom used, it cannot portray accurately the large number of horizontal and vertical features found in many images, and, in any case, sensors and display hardware generally do not support hexagonal sampling [51].

The rectangular and hexagonal patterns described above are uniform, with the result that one part of an image is as important as any other part. This is useful in images intended for eventual human interpretation, for which predication of where viewers will direct their attention is impossible. In other situations, where attention can be predicted or controlled, a non-uniform sampling scheme may be profitable. In particular, a log-polar sampling pattern has some interesting and useful properties. Fig. 1.38 shows an array of pixels that conforms to this pattern. The pixels of this array sectors with a fixed angular size and a radial size that increases logarithmically with increasing distance from the centre. This gives high resolution near the centre of the array and low resolution and wide field of view in the periphery. However, a camera using a sensor with this sampling pattern must always point towards the most interesting or important part of the scene, to ensure that it lies in the centre of the array and is therefore imaged at the highest possible resolution. This is known as an attentive vision strategy.

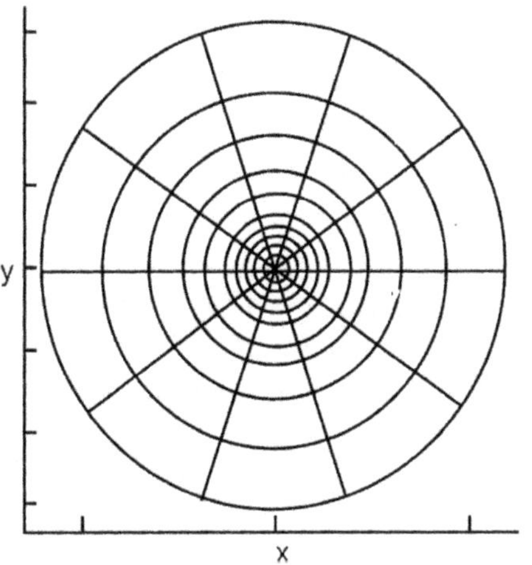

Fig. 1.38 A log-polar array of pixels.

Note that the photoreceptor distribution in the human retina broadly resemble that of a log-polar array. The part of the image that forms on the fovea is densely sampled by the tightly packed, well connected cones in that part of the retina; the remainder of the image is coarsely sampled by a more sparse population of rods. The human visual system supports attentive vision by means of eye, head and even body movements, thereby ensuring that the features of interest are always imaged using the fovea.

A pixel coordinate in a log-polar array is specified by a radial index, r, and a sector index, θ. If we plot these indices in Cartesian space, it becomes clear that changes in scale cause translations along the r axis, whereas rotation causes a cyclic shift along the θ axis. This greatly simplifies scale- and rotation-invariant object recognition and matching tasks.

1.8.2 Quantization

It is usual to digitize the values of the image function, f (x. y), in addition to its spatial coordinates. This process of quantization involves replacing a continuously varying f (x, y) with a discrete set of quantisation levels that we use; the more levels we use, the better the approximation.

Conventionally, a set of n quantization levels comprises the integers 0,1,2…n –1,0 and n-1 are usually displayed or printed as black and white, respectively, with intermediate levels rendered in various shades of grey. Quantization levels are therefore commonly referred to as grey levels. The collective term for all the grey levels, ranging from black to white, is a greyscale [17].

For convenient and efficient processing by a computer, the number grey levels, n, is usually an integral power of two, we may write.

$$n = 2^b$$

Where b is the number of bits used for quantization. b is typically 8, giving us images with 256 possible grey levels ranging from 0 (black) to 255 (white). Some ADCs (Analog to digital converters) are not capable of quantising to 8 bits, producing 6-bit or 7-bit images instead (although these may subsequently be represented in memory using 8 bits per pixel). The specialized equipment used in medicine and astronomy may produce images quantized using 10 or even 12 bits.

(a)   (b)   (c)

Fig. 1.39 Effect of quantization on image interpretation. (a) 4 levels, (b) 16 levels, (c) 256 levels.

Fig. 1.39 shows how the number of quantization levels affects image quality. The differences between 8-bit and 6-bit images are almost imperceptible. Coarser quantization creates a 'false contouring' effect in an image, although this will not necessarily hamper interpretation.

1.9 Pixel Relationships

1.9.1 Pixel Neighbors

Consider a pixel p with coordinates (x,y).

4-neighbors of p: all the horizontal and vertical neighbors

$$N_4(p): (x+1,y),\ (x-1,y),\ (x,y+1),\ (x,y-1)$$

	$(x, y-1)$	
$(x-1, y)$	(x, y)	$(x+1, y)$
	$(x, y+1)$	

Diagonal neighbors of p:

$$N_D(p): (x+1,y+1),\ (x+1,y-1),\ (x-1,y+1),\ (x-1,y-1)$$

$(x-1, y-1)$		$(x+1, y-1)$
	(x, y)	
$(x-1, y+1)$		$(x+1, y+1)$

8-neighbors of p:

$N_8(p)$: *All the 4- and diagonal neighbors*

$(x-1, y-1)$	$(x, y-1)$	$(x+1, y-1)$
$(x-1, y)$	(x, y)	$(x+1, y)$
$(x-1, y+1)$	$(x, y+1)$	$(x+1, y+1)$

1.9.2 Adjacency

Consider V as a set of gray-level values, and p and q as two pixels.

4-adjacency: two pixels p and q from V are 4-adjacent if q is in $N_4(p)$.

8-adjacency: two pixels p and q from V are 8-adjacent if q is in $N_8(p)$.

m-adjacency: two pixels p and q from V are m-adjacent if q is in $N_4(p)$, or in $N_D(p)$ and $N_4(p) \cap N_4(q)$ has no pixels whose values are from V.

Pixel Arrangement			8-Adjacent Pixels			m-Adjacent Pixels		
0	1	1	0	1	1	0	1	1
0	1	0	0	1	0	0	1	0
0	0	1	0	0	1	0	0	1

V{1}: The set V consists of pixels with value 1.

Two image subsets S_1, S_2 are adjacent if at least one pixel from S_1 and one pixel from S_2 are adjacent.

Digital Path

A sequence of adjacent pixels from pixel p with coordinates x,y to pixel q with coordinates (s,t) is called a digital path or curve [1]. The number of these pixels is called the length of the path. If p and q are the same pixel, then the path is called closed. There are 4- 8-, or m- paths depending on the adjacency under consideration.

Connectivity, Regions and Boundaries

If S is a subset of pixels in an image, then two pixels in S are called connected if there exists a path between them whose pixels are all in S. For a pixel in S, the set of pixels connected to it is called a connected component of S. If it only has one connected component then S is called a connected set [46].

If R is an image subset, it is called a region if R is a connected set. The boundary of a region is the set of pixels in R that have at least one neighbor which is not in R. If R is the entire image, then the boundary is defined by the extreme position image pixels.

Edges are formed from pixels whose derivatives exceed a specific value [1].

Distance measures

Definition of Distance Function or Metric : A function D of two pixels p,q: D(p,q) is a distance function, if :

(a) $D(p, q) \geq 0$ $(D(p, q) = 0,$ if $p = q)$.

(b) $D(p, q) = D(q, p)$.

(c) $D(p, q) \leq D(p, z) + D(z, q)$ (z is a third pixel).

Assume that the coordinated of pixels p and q are (x, y) and (s, t) respectively.

Euclidean Distance : $D_e(p, q) = \sqrt{(x-s)^2 - (y-t)^2}$

D_4 *Distance* : $D_4 (p, q) = |x - s| + |y - t|$

$$
\begin{array}{ccccc}
 & & 2 & & \\
 & 2 & 1 & 2 & \\
2 & 1 & 0 & 1 & 2 \\
 & 2 & 1 & 2 & \\
 & & 2 & & \\
\end{array}
$$

D_8 *Distance* : $D_8 (p, q) = \max (|x - s|, |y - t|)$

$$
\begin{array}{ccccc}
2 & 2 & 2 & 2 & 2 \\
2 & 1 & 1 & 1 & 2 \\
2 & 1 & 0 & 1 & 2 \\
2 & 1 & 1 & 1 & 2 \\
2 & 2 & 2 & 2 & 2 \\
\end{array}
$$

D_m Distance : Note that the previous distances are depending only on the pixel coordinates and not on the path between pixels. The D_m distance is defined as the shortest m-path between the points (considering m-adjacency).

1.9.3 Image Operations on a Pixel Basis

Numerous references are made in the following chapters to operations between images, such as dividing one image by another. Images are represented in the form of matrices. As we know, matrix division is not defined. However, when we refer to an operation like "dividing one image by another," we mean specifically that the division is carried out between corresponding pixels in the two images. Thus, for example, if f and g are images, the first element of the image formed by "dividing" f by g is simply the first pixel in f divided by the first pixel in g; the assumption is that none of the pixels in g have value 0. Other arithmetic and logic operations are similarly defined between corresponding pixels in the images involved [15].

1.10 Satellite Image Processing

Many types of remote sensing images are routinely recorded in digital form and then processed by computers to produce images for interpreters to study. The simplest form of digital image processing employs a microprocessor that converts the digital data tape into a film image with minimal corrections and calibrations. At the other extreme, large mainframe computers are employed for sophisticated interactive manipulation of the data to produce images in which specific information has been extracted and highlighted [35].

Digital processing did not originate with remote sensing and is not restricted to these data. Many image-processing techniques were developed in the medical field to process X-ray images and images from sophisticated body-scanning devices. For remote sensing, the initial impetus was the program of unmanned planetary satellites in the 1960s that telemetered, or transmitted, images to ground receiving stations [35]. The low quality of the images required the development of processing techniques to make the images useful. Another impetus was the Landsat program, which began in 1972 and provided repeated worldwide coverage in digital format. A third impetus is the continued development of faster and more powerful computers, peripheral equipment, and software that are suitable for image processing.

Satellite Image Processing – Overview

Image-processing methods may be grouped into three functional categories; these are defined below together with lists of typical processing routines.

(i)   Image restoration compensates for data errors, noise, and geometric distortions introduced during the scanning, recording, and playback operations.

- Restoring periodic line dropouts
- Restoring periodic line striping
- Filtering of random noise
- Correcting for atmospheric scattering
- Correcting geometric distortions

(ii)   Image enhancement alters the visual impact that the image has on the interpreter in a fashion that improves the information content.

- Contrast enhancement
- Intensity, hue, and saturation transformations
- Density slicing
- Edge enhancement
- Making digital mosaics
- Producing synthetic stereo images

(iii)   Information extraction utilizes the decision-making capability of the computer to recognize and classify pixels on the basis of their digital signatures.

- Producing principal-component images
- Producing ratio images
- Multispectral classification
- Producing change-detection images

(iv) *Image classification*

Image classification of remotely sensed digital data is a process of classifying all the pixels into number of classes or groups or clusters based on some known data. The known data is called training data set and each class represents one type of feature on the earth surface. This is a very sophisticated technique for information extraction based on the spectral signatures. There are broadly two types of classification methods (i) supervised classification and (ii) unsupervised classification. In supervised classification, the classification process is based on the training data set and digital signatures. Some of the supervised classifiers are minimum distance to mean methods, average method, maximum likelyhood classifier, baysian classifier and parallelopiped classifier. In unsupervised classification, all the pixels are classified based on the inherent property of the pixels by using predefined algorithms.

1.11 Questions

1. Explain in detail about different active acquisition methods to acquire range images.

2. (a) Explain the effect of Sampling and Quantization of digital image.

   (b) For the given image segment let $V = \{0, 2\}$. Compute the D_4, D_8 and D_m distances between p and f.

$$
\begin{array}{cccc}
3 & 1 & 2 & 1^f \\
2 & 2 & 0 & 2 \\
1 & 2 & 1 & 1 \\
1 & 0 & 1 & 2
\end{array}
$$

   image segment : (p)

3. Explain about RGB and CMY color models.

4. What is meant by digital image processing ? What are the various ways to define an image ? What are the applications of digital image processing.

5. Explain the connectivity relations between the pixels. With an example of each.

6. (a) What are the various input, output & storage devices required for an image processing? Give an example of each.

   (b) For the given image segment. Let $V = \{1,2\}$.Compute the D_4,D_8 and D_m distances between p and f.

$$
\begin{array}{cccc}
3 & 1 & 2 & 1^f \\
2 & 2 & 0 & 2 \\
1 & 2 & 1 & 1 \\
1 & 0 & 1 & 2
\end{array}
$$

   image segment : (p)

7. (a) Explain with a block diagram about each module of the entire image processing system.

   (b) Explain about various distance measures.

8. With a brief note on various elements of digital image processing system, explain image acquisition devices in detail.

9. Explain in detail about 2-D sampling theory with necessary derivations and graphical illustrations.

10. (a) Explain in detail about different colour co-ordinate systems.

   (b) Describe the chromaticity diagram.

11. (a) Explain how an image can be represented in digital form?

   (b) Explain how image is obtained in camera model.

12. (a) Explain the procedure of converting Analog image into Digital form.

   (b) Explain the following terms with respect to Image.

      (i) Adjacency   (ii) connectivity   (iii) Distance measure

13. (a) Compare electronic imaging with human vision in terms of resolution.

   (b) Explain the various elements of an image processing system.

14. (a) Explain the terms translation, scaling and rotation with respect to image.

$$(p) \begin{matrix} 3 & 1 & 2 & 1^{(q)} \\ 2 & 2 & 0 & 2 \\ 1 & 2 & 1 & 1 \\ 1 & 0 & 1 & 1 \end{matrix}$$

15. Derive expressions for image plane co-ordinates, assuming that camera and world co-ordinate systems are not coincident.

16. What are the elements required to acquire digital images? Explain in detail about various imaging systems.

17. (a) Write a short note on image model.

   (b) Explain in detail about different types of CCD sensors used for image acquisition.

18. With a brief note on satellite imagery technique, explain in detail about various methods of acquiring images from satellite.

19. (a) Explain how an image is formed? Discuss about various elements of an image processing system.

   (b) Listout the applications of image processing.

20. (a) Explain about

      (i) 4-connectivity

      (ii) 8-connectivity and

      (iii) m-connectivity with an example of each.

   (b) What are the applications of ALU operations in image processing?

CHAPTER 2

Basic Digital Image Processing

This Chapter covers the Statistical and Frequency domain Transformations in detail. Before that a brief discussion on the fundamental steps in Digital image processing is given.

2.1 Fundamental Steps in Digital Image Processing

The Operations that are routinely carried out in Digital Image Processing are briefly listed below. The intention is to convey an idea of all the methodologies that can be applied to images for different purposes and possibly with different objectives. The discussion in this section may be viewed as a brief overview.

Image acquisition is the process of sensing our surroundings and then representing the measurements that are made, in the form of an image [1]. The sensing phase distinguishes image acquisition from image creation; acquisition can be accomplished using an existing set of data, and does not require a sensor.

Image enhancement is the step in which the principal objective is to process an image so that the result is more suitable than the original image for a specific application [5]. The word "specific" is important, since the processing techniques for the image depend upon the application.

Image enhancement techniques can be divided into two broad categories namely, Spatial domain methods, which operate directly on pixels, and Frequency domain methods, which operate on the Fourier transform of an image.

Image restoration is an area that also deals with improving the appearance of an image. However, unlike enhancement, which is subjective, image restoration is objective, in the sense that restoration techniques tend to be based on mathematical or probabilistic models of image degradation [6]. Enhancement, on the other hand, is based on human subjective preferences regarding what constitutes a "good" enhancement result. Color image processing is an area that has been gaining importance because of the significant increase in the use of digital images over the Internet.

Morphological processing is very important step in digital image processing in evaluation of objects through images. Morphology is the science of form and structure. In computer vision it is about regions or shapes – how they can be changed and counted, and how their areas can be evaluated. The operations used in morphological processing are basic morphological operations, opening and closing operations and area operations.

Segmentation is concerned with splitting an image up into segments (also called regions or areas) that each holds some property distinct from their neighbor [7]. This is an essential part of scene analysis – in answering the questions like where and how large is the object, where is the background, how many objects are there, how many surfaces are there... Segmentation is a basic requirement for the identification and classification of objects in scene. Segmentation can be approached from two points of view by identifying the edges (or lines) that run through an image or by identifying regions (or areas) within an image [15]. Region operations can be seen as the dual of edge operations in that the completion of an edge is equivalent to breaking one region onto two. Ideally edge and region operations should give the same segmentation result: however, in practice the two rarely correspond. Some typical operations are, region operations, basic edge detection, second-order edge detection, pyramid edge detection, crack edge detection and edge following.

Representation and Analysis of Visual Images entails the fundamental concepts and tools of computational vision and digital image processing. It cover the following areas: imaging and optics, multi-scale and differential image decompositions, alignment and displacement estimation, range estimation, statistical image modeling and its use in compression, enhancement and synthesis.

Pattern recognition system finds objects in the real world from an image of the world, using object models which are known a priori.

Statistical techniques and operations deal with low-level image processing operations. The techniques (algorithms) are independent of the position of the pixels. The levels of processing to be applied on an image in a typical processing sequence are first, low then medium, then high. Low level processing is concerned with work at the binary image level, typically creating a second "better" image from the first by changing the representation of the image by removing unwanted data, and enhancing wanted data.

Compression of images is concerned with storing them in a form that does not take up so much space as the original. Compression systems need to get the following benefits: fast operation (both compression and unpacking), significant reduction in required memory, no significant loss of quality in the image and format of output suitable for transfer or storage. Each of this depends on the user and the application.

Medium-level processing is about the identification of significant shapes, regions or points from the binary images. Little or no prior knowledge is built to this process so while the work may not be wholly at binary level, the algorithms are still not usually application specific. High level preprocessing interfaces the image to some knowledge base. This associates shapes discovered during previous level of processing with known shapes of real objects. The results from the algorithms at this level are passed on to non image procedures, which make decisions about actions following from the analysis of the image.

2.2 Gray-level Transformation

As is discussed in previous chapter, a digital image is a matrix of digital numbers. That is there are a large number of digital numbers in any given image and these digital numbers or intensity values are filled in pixels. Statistically, all these numbers form ungrouped data set and such data set is difficult to understand spatially. Information extraction from such a ungrouped data set is also a difficult process and sometimes is not possible. Hence, it is necessary to convert or transform the ungrouped intensity values into grouped data using frequency distribution or Histogram method.

The image histogram is a valuable tool used to view the intensity profile of an image. The histogram provides information about the contrast and overall intensity distribution of an image. The image histogram is simply a bar graph of the pixel intensities [19]. The pixel intensities are plotted along the x-axis and the number of occurrences for each intensity represents the y-axis. Figure 2.1 shows a sample histogram for a simple image.

Dark images have histograms with pixel distributions towards the left-hand (dark) side. Bright images have pixels distributions towards the right hand side of the histogram. In an ideal image, there is a uniform distribution of pixels across the histogram. Plate 9 shows the example of sample dark image and its corresponding histogram.

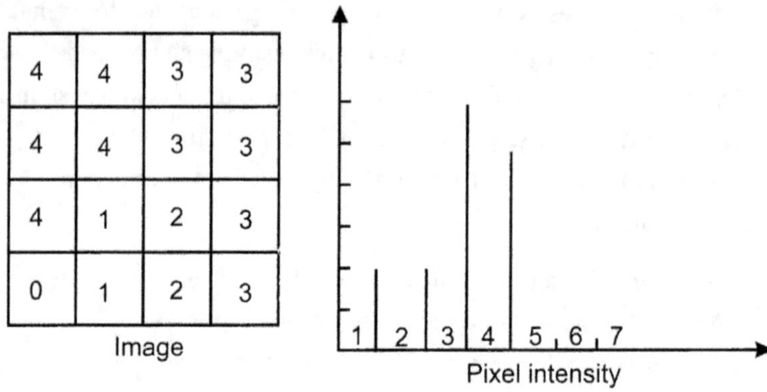

Fig. 2.1 Sample image with histogram.

2.2.1 Intensity Transformation

Intensity transformation is a point process that converts an old pixel into a new pixel based on some predefined function. These transformations are easily implemented with simple look-up tables [20]. The input-output relationship of these look-up tables can be shown graphically. The original pixel values are shown along the horizontal axis and the output pixel is the same value as the old pixel. Another simple transformation is the negative.

Look-up table techniques

Point processing algorithms are most efficiently executed with look-up tables (LUTs). LUTs are simply arrays that use the current pixel value as the array index (Fig. 2.2). The new value is the array element pointed by this index. The new image is built by repeating the process for each pixel. Using LUTs avoids needless repeated computations. When working with 8-bit images, for example, you only need to compute 256 values no matter how big the image is.

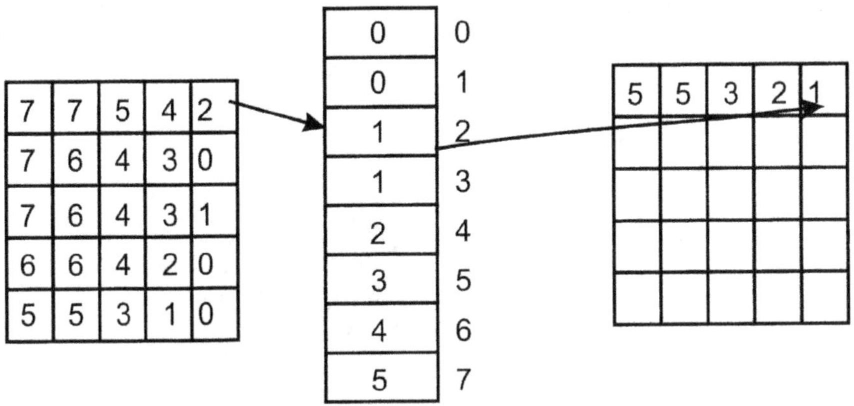

Fig. 2.2 Operation of a 3-bit look-up-table

Notice that there is bounds checking on the value returned from operation. Any value greater than 255 will be clamped to 255. Any value less than 0 will be clamped to 0. The input buffer in the code also serves as the output buffer. Each pixel in the buffer is used as an index into the LUT. It is then replaced in the buffer with the pixel returned from the LUT. Using the input buffer as the output buffer saves memory by eliminating the need to allocate memory for another image buffer.

One of the great advantages of using a look-up tables is the computational savings. If you were to add some value to every pixel in a 512×512 gray-scale image, that would require 262,144 operations. You would also need two times that number of comparisons to check for overflow and underflow. You will need only 256 additions with comparisons using a LUT. Since there are only 256 possible input values, there is no need to do more than 256 additions to cover all possible outputs.

Gamma correction function

The brightness of an image can be adjusted with a gamma correction transformation. This is a nonlinear transformation that maps closely to the brightness control on a CRT. Gamma correction functions are often used in image processing to compensate for nonlinear responses in imaging sensors, displays and films [22]. The general form for gamma correction is:

$$\text{output} = \text{input}^{1/g}$$

If g = 1.0, the result is null transform. If 0 < g < 1.0, then the g creates exponential curves that dim an image. If g > 1.0, then the result is logarithmic curves that brighten an image. RGB monitors have gamma values of 1.4 to 2.8. Figure 2.3 shows gamma correction transformations with gamma = 0.45 and 2.2.

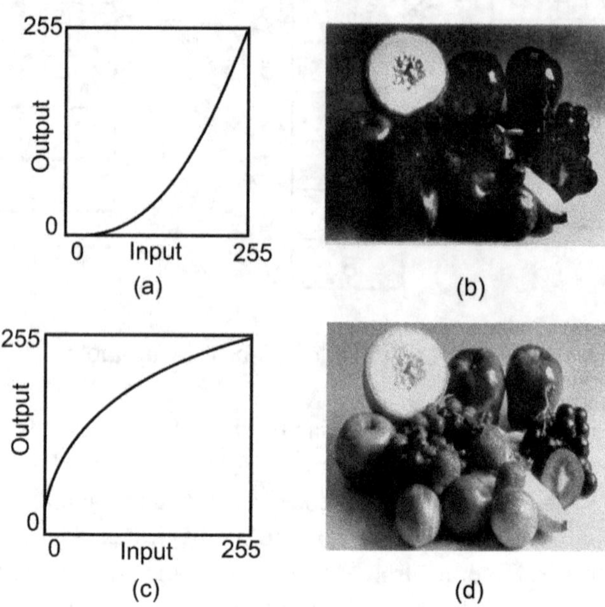

Fig. 2.3 (a) Gamma correction transformation with gamma = 0.45; (b) gamma corrected image; (c) gamma correction transformation with gamma = 2.2; (d) gamma corrected image.

Contrast stretching is an intensity transformation. Through intensity transformation, contrasts can be stretched, compressed, and modified for a better distribution. Fig. 2.4 shows the transformation for contrast stretch. Also shown is a transform to reduce the contrast of an image. As seen, this will darken the extreme light values and lighten the extreme dark value. This transformation better distributes the intensities of a high contrast image and yields a much more pleasing image.

Contrast stretching

The contrast of an image is its distribution of light and dark pixels. Gray-scale images of low contrast are mostly dark, mostly light, or mostly gray. In the histogram of a low contrast image, the pixels are concentrated on the right, left, or in the middle. Then bars of the histogram are tightly clustered together and use a small sample of all possible pixel values.

Fig. 2.4 (a) Contrast stretch transformation; (b) contrast stretched image; (c) contrast compression transformation; (d) contrast compressed image.

Images with high contrast have regions of both dark and light [32]. High contrast images utilize the full range available. The problem with high contrast images is that they have large regions of dark and large regions of white. A picture of someone standing in front of a window taken on a sunny day has high contrast. The person is typically dark and the window is bright. The histograms of high contrast images have two big peaks. One peak is centered in the lower region and the other in the high region [36]. See Figure 2.5.

Images with good contrast exhibit a wide range of pixel values. The histogram displays a relatively uniform distribution of pixel values. There are no major peaks or valleys in the histogram.

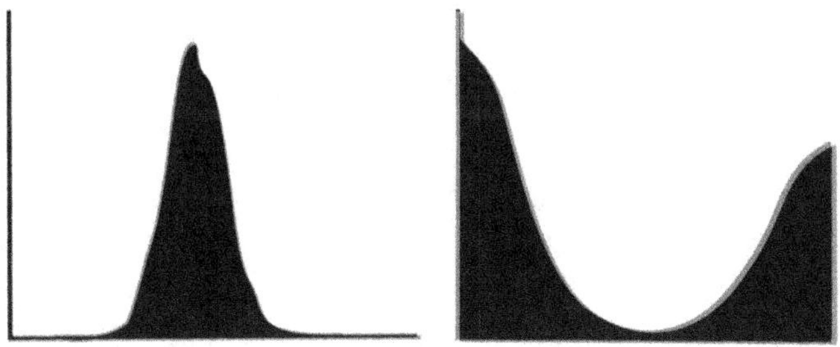

Fig. 2.5 Low and high contrast histograms.

Contrast stretching is applied to an image to stretch a histogram to fill the full dynamic range of the image. This is a useful technique to enhance images that have low contrast. It works best with images that have a Gaussian or near-Gaussian distribution.

The two most popular types of contrast stretching are basic contrast stretching and end-in-search.

Basic contrast stretching works best on images that have all pixels concentrated in one part of the histogram, the middle, for example. The contrast stretch will expand the image histogram to cover all ranges of pixels [41].

The highest and lowest value pixels are used in the transformation. The equation is :

$$\text{New pixel} = \frac{\text{old pixel - low}}{\text{high - low}} \times 255$$

Figure 2.6 shows how the equation affects an image. When the lowest value pixel is subtracted from the image it slides the histogram to the left. The lowest value pixel is now 0. Each pixel value is then scaled so that the image fills the entire dynamic range. The result is an image than spans the pixel values from 0 to 255.

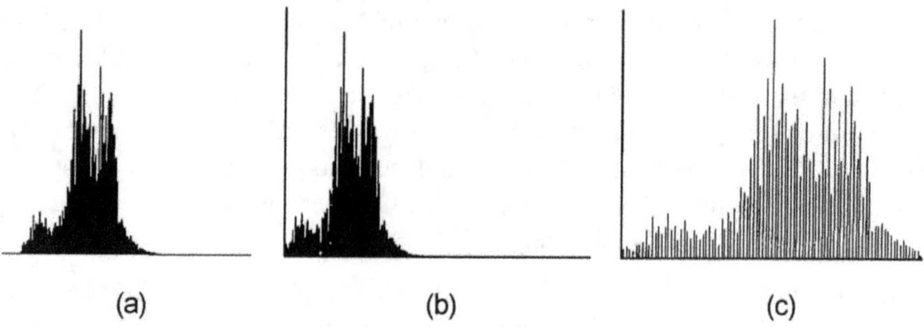

(a)   (b)   (c)

Fig. 2.6 (a) Original histogram; (b) histogram-low; (c) (high-low)*255/(high-low).

Posterizing reduces the number of gray levels in an image [43]. Thresholding results when the number of gray levels is reduced to 2. A bounded threshold reduces the thresholding to a limited range and treats the other input pixels as null transformations.

Bit-clipping sets a certain number of the most significant bits of a pixel to 0. This has the effect of breaking up an image that spans from black to white into several subregions with the same intensity cycles.

The last few transformations presented are used in esoteric fields of image processing such as radiometric analysis. The next two types of transformations are used by digital artists. The first called solarizing. It transforms an image according to the following formula:

$$output(x) = \begin{cases} x & for \quad x \leq threshold \\ 255 - x & for\ x > threshold \end{cases}$$

The last type of transformation is the parabola transformation. The two formulas are

$$output(x) = 255 - 255(x/128 - 1)^2$$

and

$$output(x) = 255(x/128 - 1)^2$$

End-in-search

The second method of contrast stretching is called ends-in-search. It works well for images that have pixels of all possible intensities but have a pixel concentration in one part of the histogram [46]. The image processor is more involved in this technique. It is necessary to specify a certain percentage of the pixels must be saturated to full white or full black. The algorithm then marches up through the histogram to find the lower threshold. The lower threshold, low, is the value of the histogram to where the lower percentage is reached. Marching down the histogram from the top, the upper threshold, high, is found. The LUT is then initialized as

$$output(x) = \begin{cases} 0 & for\ x \leq low \\ 255 \times (x - low)/(high - low) & for\ low \leq x \leq high \\ 255 & for\ x > high \end{cases}$$

The end-in-search can be automated by hard-coding the high and low values. These values can also be determined by different methods of histogram analysis. Most scanning software is capable of analyzing preview scan data and adjusting the contrast accordingly.

2.3 Histogram Equalization

Histogram equalization is one of the most important part of the software for any image processing. It improves contrast and the goal of histogram equalization is to obtain a uniform histogram. This technique can be used on a whole image or just on a part of an image.

Histogram equalization will not "flatten" a histogram. It redistributes intensity distributions. If the histogram of any image has many peaks and valleys, it will still have peaks and valley after equalization, but peaks and valley will be shifted. Because of this, "spreading" is a better term than "flattening" to describe histogram equalization. Plate 10 shows the histogram plots with their mean and standard deviation.

Because histogram equalization is a point process, new intensities will not be introduced into the image. Existing values will be mapped to new values but the actual number of intensities in the resulting image will be equal or less than the original number of intensities [50].

Operation

1. Compute histogram
2. Calculate normalized sum of histogram
3. Transform input image to output image.

The first step is accomplished by counting each distinct pixel value in the image. You can start with an array of zeros. For 8-bit pixels the size of the array is 256 (0-255). Parse the image and increment each array element corresponding to each pixel processed.

The second step requires another array to store the sum of all the histogram values. In this array, element 1 would contain the sum of histogram elements 1 and 0. Element 255 would contain the sum of histogram elements 255, 254, 253,... , 1 ,0. This array is then normalized by multiplying each element by (maximum-pixel-value/number of pixels). For an 8-bit 512 x 512 image that constant would be 255/262144.

The result of step 2 yields a LUT you can use to transform the input image.

Figure 2.7 shows steps 2 and 3 of our process and the resulting image. From the normalized sum in Figure 2.7 you can determine the look up values by rounding to the nearest integer [51]. Zero will map to zero; one will map to one; two will map to two; three will map to five and so on.

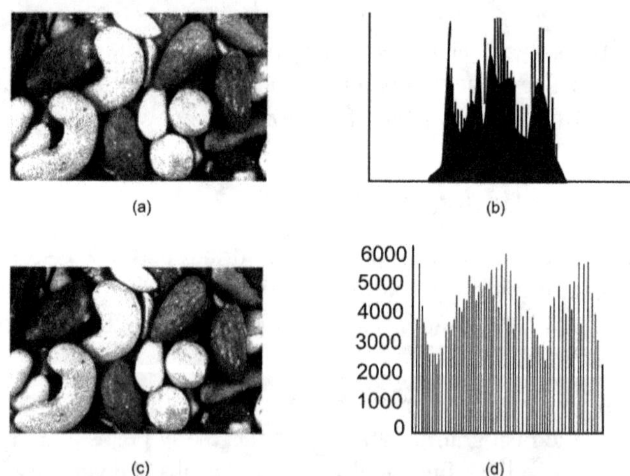

Fig. 2.7 (a) Original image; (b) Histogram of original image; (c) Equalized image; (d) Histogram of equalized image.

Histogram equalization works best on images with fine details in darker regions. Some people perform histogram equalization on all images before attempting other processing operations [53]. This is not a good practice since good quality images can be degraded by histogram equalization. With a good judgment, histogram equalization can be a powerful tool.

Histogram Specification

Histogram equalization approximates a uniform histogram. Some times, a uniform histogram is not what is desired. Perhaps you wish to lighten or darken an image or you need more contrast in an image. These modification are possible via histogram specification.

Histogram specification is a simple process that requires both a desired histogram and the image as input. It is performed in two easy steps.

The first is to histogram equalize the original image.

The second is to perform an inverse histogram equalization on the equalized image.

The inverse histogram equalization requires to generate the LUT corresponding to desired histogram, then compute the inverse transform of the LUT. The inverse transform is computed by analyzing the outputs of the LUT. The closest output for a particular input becomes that inverse value.

2.4 Multi-image Operations

Frame processes generate a pixel value based on an operation involving two or more different images [56]. The pixelwise operations in this section will generate an output image based on an operation of a pixel from two separate images. Each output pixel will be located at the same position in the input image (Fig. 2.8).

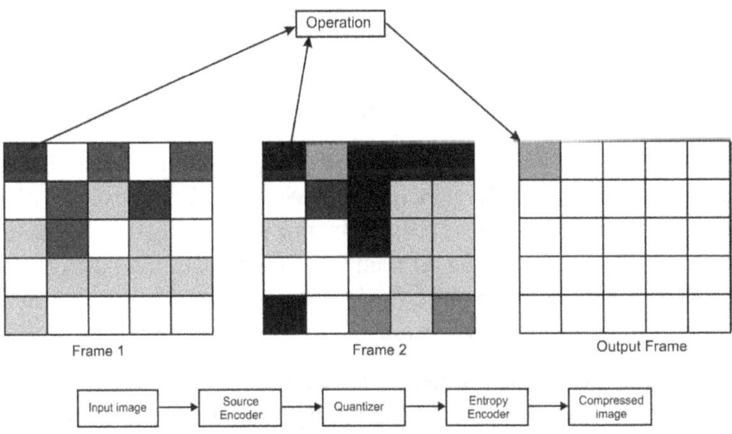

Fig. 2.8 Working of Frame process.

2.4.1 Addition

The first operation is the addition operation (Fig. 2.9). This can be used to composite a new image by adding together two old ones. Usually they are not just added together since that would cause overflow and wrap around with every sum that exceeded the maximum value. Some fraction, a, is specified and the summation is performed

$$New - Pixel = aPixel1 + (1 - a)Pixel2$$

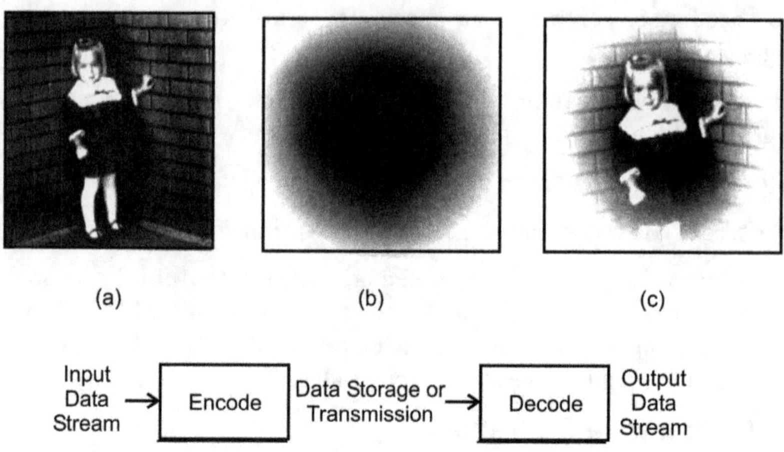

(a)   (b)   (c)

Fig. 2.9 (a) Image 1, (b) Image 2; (c) Image 1 + Image 2.

This prevents overflow and also allows you to specify 'a' so that one image can dominate the other by a certain amount. Some graphics systems have extra information stored with each pixel. This information is called the alpha channel and specifies how two images can be blended, switched, or combined in some way.

2.4.2 Subtraction

Background subtraction can be used to identify movement between two images and to remove background shading if it is present on both images [22]. The images should be captured as near as possible in time without any lighting conditions. If the object being removed is darker than the background, then the image with the objects is subtracted from the image without the object. If the object is lighter than the background, the opposite is done.

Subtraction practically means that the gray level in each pixel in one image is to subtract from gray level in the corresponding pixel in the other images.

$$result = x - y$$

where $x \geq y$, however , if $x < y$ the result is negative which, if values are held as unsigned characters (bytes), actually means a high positive value. For example:

$$-1 \text{ is held as } 255$$

$$-2 \text{ is held as } 254$$

A better operation for background subtraction is

$$result = |x - y|$$

i.e. x–y ignoring the sign of the result in which case it does not matter whether the object is dark or light compared to the background. This will give negative image of the object. In order to return the image to a positive, the resulting gray level has to be subtracted from the maximum gray-level, call it MAX. Combining this two gives

$$new\ image = MAX - |x - y|$$

2.4.3 Multi-image Averaging

A series of the same scene can be used to give a better quality image by using similar operations to the windowing. A simple average of all the gray levels in corresponding pixels will give a significantly enhanced picture over any one of the originals [20]. Alternatively, if the original images contain pixels with noise, these can be filtered out and replaced with correct values from another shot.

Multi-image modal filtering

Modal filtering of a sequence of images can remove noise most effectively. Here the most popular valued gray-level for each corresponding pixel in a sequence of images is plotted as the pixel value in the final image. The drawback is that the whole sequence of images needs to be stored before the mode for each pixel can be found.

Multi-image median filtering

Median filtering is similar except that for each pixel, the grey levels in corresponding pixels in the sequence of the image are stored, and the middle one is chosen. Again the whole sequence of the images needs to be stored, and a substantial sort operation is required [19].

Multi-image averaging filtering

Recursive filtering does not require each previous image to be stored. It uses a weighted averaging technique to produce one image from a sequence of the images.

OPERATION. It is assumed that newly collected images are available from a frame store with a fixed delay between each image.

1. Setting up - copy an image into a separated frame store, dividing all the gray levels by any chosen integer n. Add to that image n-1 subsequent images, the gray level of which are also divided by n. Now, the average of the first n image in the frame store.

2. Recursion - for every new image, multiply of the frame store by $(n-1)/n$ and the new image by $1/n$, add them together and put the result back to the frame store.

2.4.4 AND/OR

Image ANDing and ORing is the result of outputting the result of a boolean AND or OR operator [17]. The AND operator will output a 1 when both inputs are 1. Otherwise the Output is 0. The OR operator will output a 1 if either input is 1. Otherwise the output is 0. Each bit in corresponding pixels are ANDed or 0Red bit by bit.

The ANDing operation is often used to mask out part of an image. This is done with a logical AND of the pixel and the value 0. Then parts of another image can be added with a logical OR.

2.5   Spatially Dependent Transformation

Spatially dependent transformation is one that depends on its position in the image. Under such transformation, the histogram of gray levels does not retain its original shape: gray level frequency change depending on the spread of gray levels across the picture. Instead of $f(g)$, the spatial dependent transformation is $f(g, X, Y)$.

Simply thresholding an image that has different lighting levels is unlikely, to be as effective as processing away the gradations by implementing an algorithm to make the ambient lighting constant and then thresholding. Without this preprocessing the result after thresholding is even more difficult to process since a spatially invariant thresholding function used to threshold down to a constant, leaves a real mix of some pixels still spatially dependent and some not. There are a number of other techniques for removal of this kind of gradation [7].

Gradation removal by averaging

USE. To remove gradual shading across a single image.

OPERATION. Subdivide the picture into rectangles, evaluate the mean for each rectangle and also for the whole picture. Then to each value of pixels add or subtract a constant so as to give the rectangles across the picture the same mean [1].

This may not be the best approach if the image is a text image. More sophistication can be built in by equalizing the means and standard deviations or, if the picture is bimodal (as, for example, in the case of a text image) the bimodality of each rectangle can be standardized. Experience suggests, however that the more sophisticated the technique, the more marginal is the improvement.

Masking

USE. To remove or negate part of an image so that this part is no longer visible [15]. It may be part of a whole process that is aimed at changing an image by, for example putting an object into an image that was not there before. This can be done by masking out part of an old image, and then adding the image of the object to the area in the old image that has been masked out.

OPERATION. General transformations may be performed on part of a picture, for instance. ANDing an image with a binary mask amounts to thresholding to zero at the maximum gray level for part of the picture, without any thresholding on the rest.

2.6 Templates and Convolution

Template operations are very useful as elementary image filters. They can be used to enhance certain features, de-enhance others, smooth out noise or discover previously known shapes in an image [6].

Convolution

USE. Widely used in many operations. It is an essential part of the software kit for an image processor.

OPERATION. A sliding window, called the convolution window (template), centers on each pixel in an input image and generates new output pixels. The new pixel value is computed by multiplying each pixel value in the neighborhood with the corresponding weight in the convolution mask and summing these products.

This is placed step by step over the image, at each step creating a new window in the image the same size of template, and then associating with each element in the template a corresponding pixel in the image. Typically, the template element is multiply by corresponding image pixel gray level and the sum of these results, across the whole template, is recorded as a pixel gray level in a new image. This "shift, add, multiply" operation is termed the "convolution" of the template with the image.

If T(x, y) is the template ($n \times m$) and I(x, y) is the image ($M \times N$) then the convoluting of T with I is written as

$$T * I(X,Y) = \sum_{i=0}^{n-1} \sum_{j=0}^{m-1} T(i, j)I(X + i, Y + j)$$

In fact this term is the cross-correlation term rather than the convolution term, which should be accurately presented by

$$T * I(X,Y) = \sum_{i=0}^{n-1} \sum_{j=0}^{m-1} T(i, j)I(X - i, Y - j)$$

However, the term "convolution" loosely interpreted to mean cross-correlation, and in most image processing literature convolution will refer to the first formula rather than the second. In the frequency domain, convolution is "real" convolution rather than cross-correlation [20].

Often the template is not allowed to shift off the edge of the image, so the resulting image will normally be smaller than the first image. For example:

$$
\begin{array}{cc}
1 & 0 \\
0 & 1
\end{array}
\;*\;
\begin{array}{ccccc}
1 & 1 & 3 & 3 & 4 \\
1 & 1 & 4 & 4 & 3 \\
2 & 1 & 3 & 3 & 3 \\
1 & 1 & 1 & 4 & 4
\end{array}
\;=\;
\begin{array}{ccccc}
2 & 5 & 7 & 6 & * \\
2 & 4 & 7 & 7 & * \\
3 & 2 & 7 & 7 & * \\
* & * & * & * & *
\end{array}
$$

where * is no value.

Here the 2 x 2 template is opening on a 4 x 5 image, giving 3 x 4 result. The value 5 in the result is obtained from

$$(1 \times 1) + (0 \times 3) + (0 \times 1) + (1 \times 4)$$

Many convolution masks are separable. This means that the convolution can be per formed by executing two convolutions with 1-dimensional masks. A separable function satisfies the equation:

$$f(x,y) = g(x) \times h(y)$$

Separable functions reduce the number of computations required when using large masks This is possible due to the linear nature of the convolution. For example, a convolution using the following mask

$$
\begin{array}{rrr}
1 & 2 & 1 \\
0 & 0 & 0 \\
-1 & -2 & -1
\end{array}
$$

Can be performed faster by doing two convolutions using

$$
\begin{array}{c}
1 \\
0 \\
-1
\end{array}
\quad \text{and} \quad
\begin{array}{ccc}
1 & 2 & 1
\end{array}
$$

since the first matrix is the product of the second two vectors. The savings in this example aren't spectacular (6 multiply accumulates versus 9) but do increase as masks sizes grow.

Common Templates

Just as the moving average of a time series tends to smooth the points, so a moving average (moving up/down and left-right) smooth out any sudden changes in pixel values removing noise at the expense of introducing some blurring of the image [5]. The classical 3×3 template does this but with little sophistication. Essentially, each resulting pixel is the sum of a square of nine original pixel values. It does this without regard to the position of the pixels in the group of nine. Such filters are termed 'low-pass ' filters since they remove high frequencies in an image (i.e. sudden changes in pixel values while retaining or passing through) the low frequencies. i.e. the gradual changes in pixel values.

$$\begin{pmatrix} 1 & 1 & 1 \\ 1 & 1 & 1 \\ 1 & 1 & 1 \end{pmatrix}$$

An Alternative Smoothing Template Might Be

$$\begin{pmatrix} 1 & 3 & 1 \\ 3 & 16 & 3 \\ 1 & 3 & 1 \end{pmatrix}$$

This introduces weights such that half of the result is got from the centre pixel, 3/8ths from the above, below, left and right pixels, and 1/8th from the corner pixels-those that are most distant from the centre pixel [22].

A high-pass filter aims to remove gradual changes and enhance the sudden changes. Such a template might be (the Laplacian)

$$\begin{pmatrix} 1 & -1 & 1 \\ -1 & 4 & -1 \\ 1 & -1 & 1 \end{pmatrix}$$

Here the template sums to zero so if it is placed over a window containing a constant set of values, the result will be zero. However, if the centre pixel differs markedly from its surroundings, then the result will be even more marked.

The next table shows the operation or the following high-pass and low-pass filters on an image:

High-pass filter $\qquad \begin{pmatrix} 1 & -1 & 1 \\ -1 & 4 & -1 \\ 1 & -1 & 1 \end{pmatrix}$

$$
\text{Low-pass fitter} \begin{pmatrix} 1 & 1 & 1 \\ 1 & 1 & 1 \\ 1 & 1 & 1 \end{pmatrix}
$$

Original image

$$
\begin{matrix}
0 & 0 & 0 & 0 & 0 \\
0 & 1 & 1 & 1 & 0 \\
0 & 1 & 1 & 1 & 0 \\
0 & 1 & 1 & 1 & 0 \\
0 & 1 & 1 & 1 & 0 \\
0 & 1 & 6 & 1 & 0 \\
0 & 1 & 1 & 1 & 0 \\
0 & 0 & 0 & 1 & 0
\end{matrix}
$$

After high pass

$$
\begin{matrix}
2 & 1 & 2 \\
1 & 0 & 1 \\
1 & 0 & 1 \\
1 & -5 & 1 \\
-4 & 20 & -4 \\
2 & -4 & 2
\end{matrix}
$$

After low pass

$$
\begin{matrix}
4 & 6 & 4 \\
6 & 9 & 6 \\
6 & 9 & 6 \\
11 & 14 & 11 \\
11 & 14 & 11 \\
9 & 11 & 9
\end{matrix}
$$

Here, after the high pass, half of the image has its edges noted, leaving in the middle a zero, while the bottom half of the image jumps from -4 and -5 to 20, corresponding to the original noise value of 6.

After the low pass, there is a steady increase to the centre and the noise point has been shared across a number or values, so that its original existence is almost lost. Both high-pass and low-pass filters have their uses.

Edge detection

Templates such as A and B highlight edges in an area as shown in the next example

$$\begin{matrix} -1 & -1 \\ 1 & 1 \end{matrix} \quad \text{and} \quad \begin{matrix} -1 & 1 \\ -1 & 1 \end{matrix}$$

$$A \qquad\qquad B$$

Clearly template B has identified the vertical edge and A the horizontal edge. Combining the two, say by adding the result A + B above, gives both horizontal and vertical edges [19].

Original image

$$\begin{matrix} 0 & 0 & 0 & 0 & 0 & 0 \\ 0 & 0 & 0 & 0 & 0 & 0 \\ 0 & 0 & 0 & 0 & 0 & 0 \\ 0 & 0 & 3 & 3 & 3 & 3 \\ 0 & 0 & 3 & 3 & 3 & 3 \\ 0 & 0 & 3 & 3 & 3 & 3 \\ 0 & 0 & 3 & 3 & 3 & 3 \end{matrix}$$

After A

$$\begin{matrix} 0 & 0 & 0 & 0 & 0 \\ 0 & 0 & 0 & 0 & 0 \\ 0 & 6 & 6 & 6 & 6 \\ 0 & 6 & 0 & 0 & 0 \\ 0 & 6 & 0 & 0 & 0 \\ 0 & 6 & 0 & 0 & 0 \end{matrix}$$

After B

$$\begin{matrix} 0 & 0 & 0 & 0 & 0 \\ 0 & 0 & 0 & 0 & 0 \\ 0 & 3 & 0 & 0 & 0 \\ 0 & 6 & 0 & 0 & 0 \\ 0 & 6 & 0 & 0 & 0 \\ 0 & 6 & 0 & 0 & 0 \end{matrix}$$

$$\text{After A + B} \quad \begin{array}{ccccc} 0 & 0 & 0 & 0 & 0 \\ 0 & 0 & 0 & 0 & 0 \\ 0 & 3 & 6 & 6 & 6 \\ 0 & 0 & 0 & 0 & 0 \\ 0 & 0 & 0 & 0 & 0 \\ 0 & 0 & 0 & 0 & 0 \end{array}$$

See next chapter for a fuller discussion of edge detectors.

Storing the Convolution Results

Results from templating normally need examination and transformation before storage. In most application packages, images are held as one array of bytes (or three arrays of bytes for color). Each entry in the array corresponds to a pixel on the image [56]. The byte unsigned integer range (0-255) means that the results of an operation must be transformed to within that range if data is to be passed in the same form to further software. If the template includes fractions it may mean that the result has to be rounded. Worse, if the template contains anything other than positive fractions less than $1/(n \times m)$ (which is quite likely) it is possible for the result, at some point to go outside of the 0-255 range.

Scaling can be done as the results are produced. This requires either a prior estimation of the result range or a backwards rescaling when an out-of-rank result requires that the scaling factor be changed [32]. Alternatively, scaling can be done at the end of production with all the results initially placed into a floating-point array. The latter option assumed that there is sufficient main memory available to hold a floating-point array. It may be that such an array will need to be written to disk, which can be very time-consuming. Floating point is preferable because even if significantly large storage is allocated to the image with each pixel represented as a 4 byte integer, for example, it only needs a few peculiar valued templates to operate on the image for the resulting pixel values to be very small or very large.

Fourier transform was applied to an image. The imaginary array contained zeros and the real array values ranged between 0 and 255 [50]. After the Fourier transformation, values in the resulting imaginary and real floating-point arrays were mostly between 0 and 1 but with some values greater than 1000. The following transformation was applied to the real and imaginary output arrays:

$$F(g) = \{\log_2\text{-}[abs(g)] + 15\} \times 5 \text{ for all } abs(g) > 2^{-15}$$

$$F(g) = 0 \quad \textit{otherwise}$$

where abs(g) is the positive value of 'g' ignoring the sign. This brings the values into a range that enabled them to be placed back into the byte array.

Other Window Operations

Templating uses the concept of a window to the image whose size corresponds to the template. Other non-template operations on image windows can be useful.

Median Filtering

USE. Noise removal while preserving edges in an image.

OPERATION. This is a popular low-pass filter, attempting to remove noisy pixels while keeping the edge intact [46]. The values of the pixel in the window are stored and the median – the middle value in the sorted list (or average of the middle two if the list has an even number of elements)-is the one plotted into the output image.

Example. *The 6 value (quite possibly noise) in input image is totally eliminated using 3x3 median filter*

```
              0  0  0  0  0
              0  1  1  1  0
              0  1  1  1  0
              0  1  1  1  0
Input Image   0  1  1  1  0
              0  1  6  1  0
              0  1  1  1  0
              0  0  0  1  0
```

```
               1  1  1
               1  1  1
               1  1  1
Output image   1  1  1
               1  1  1
               1  1  1
```

Modal filtering is an alternative to median filtering, where the most popular from the set of nine is plotted in the centre.

k-Closet Averaging

USE: To reserve, to some extent, the actual values of the pixels without letting the noise get through the final image [52].

OPERATION: All the pixels in the window are stored and the 'k' pixels values closest in value to the target pixel – usually the centre of the window – are averaged. The average may or may not include the target pixel, if not included the effect is similar to a low-pass filter. The value 'k' is a selected constant value less than the area of the window.

An extension of this is to average of the 'k' value nearest in value to the target, but not including the 'q' values closest to and including the target. This avoids pairs of triples of noisy pixels that are obtained by setting q to 2 or 3.

In both median and k-closest averaging, sorting creates a heavy load on the system. However, with a little sophistication in the programming, it is possible to sort the first window from the image and then delete a column of pixels values from the sorted list and introduce a new column by slotting them into the list thus avoiding a complete re-sort for each window. The k-closet averaging requires differences to be calculated as well as ordering and is, therefore, slower than the median filter.

Interest Point

There is no standard definition of what constitutes an interest point in image processing. Generally, interest points are identified by algorithms that can be applied first to images containing a known object, and then to images where recognition of the object is required.

Recognition is achieved by comparing the positions of discovered interest points with the known pattern positions. A number of different methods using a variety of different measurements are available to determine whether a point is interesting or not. Some depend on the changes in texture of an image, some on the changes in curvature of an edge, some on the number of edges arriving coincidentally at the same pixel and a lower level interest operator is the Moravec operator.

Moravec Operator

USE. To identify a set of points on an image by which the image may be classified or compared.

OPERATION. With a square window, evaluate the sums of the squares of the differences in intensity of the centre pixel from the centre top, centre left, centre bottom and centre right pixels in the window. Let us call this the variance for the centre pixel. Calculate the variance for all the internal pixels in the image as

where

$$S = \{(0, a), (0, -a), (a, 0), (-a, 0)\}$$

Now pass a 3 × 3 window across the variances and save the minimum from the nine variances in the centre pixel. Finally, pass a 3 × 3 window across the result and set to zero the centre pixel when its value is not the biggest in the window.

Correlation

Correlation can be used to determine the existence of a known shape in an image [5]. There is a number of drawbacks with this approach to searching through an image. Rarely is the object orientation or its exact size in the image known. Further, if these are known for one object that is unlikely to be consistent for all objects.

A biscuit manufacturer using a fixed position camera could count the number of well-formed, round biscuits on a tray presented to it by template matching. However, if the task is to search for a sunken ship on a sonar image, correlation is not the best method to use.

Classical correlation takes into account the mean of the template and image area under the template as well as the spread of values in both template and image area [20]. With a constant image, i.e., with lighting broadly constant across the image and the spread of pixel values broadly constant then the correlation can be simplified to convolution as shown in the following technique.

USE. To find where a template matches a window in an image.

THEORY. If $N \times M$ image is addressed by $I(X,Y)$ and $n \times m$ template is addressed by $t(i,j)$ then

$$\text{corr} (X, Y) = \sum_{i=0}^{n-1} \sum_{j=0}^{m-1} \left[t(i,j) - I(X+i, Y+j) \right]^2$$

$$= \sum_{i=0}^{n-1} \sum_{j=0}^{m-1} \left[t(i,j)^2 - 2t(i,j) I(X+i, Y+j) + I(X+i, Y+j)^2 \right]$$

$$= \underbrace{\sum_{i=0}^{n-1} \sum_{j=0}^{m-1} \left[t(i,j) \right]^2}_{A} - \underbrace{2 \sum_{i=0}^{n-1} \sum_{j=0}^{m-1} t(i,j) I(X+i, Y+j) + \sum_{i=0}^{n-1} \sum_{j=0}^{m-1} \left[I(X+i, Y+j) \right]^2}_{B}$$

Where A is constant across the image, so can be ignored, B is t convolved with I, C is constant only if average light from image is constant across image (often approximately true).

OPERATION. This reduces correlation (subtraction, squaring, and addition), to multiplication and addition convolution. Thus normally if the overall light intensity across the whole image is fairly constant, it is worth to use convolution instead of correlation.

2.7 Transformations

Introduction

Most signal processing is done in a mathematical space known as the frequency domain [1]. In order to represent data in the frequency domain, some transforms are necessary. The signal frequency of an image refers to the rate at which the pixel intensities change. The high frequencies are concentrated around the axes dividing the image into quadrants. High frequencies are noted by concentrations of large amplitude swing in the small checkerboard pattern. The corners have lower frequencies. Low spatial frequencies are noted by large areas of nearly constant values. The section covers the following topics.

- Discrete Fourier Transform
- Fast Fourier Transform
- Discrete Cosine Transform
- Hadamard Transform
- Haar Transform
- Hotelling Transform
- Walsh transform

Much signal processing is done in a mathematical space known as the frequency domain. In order to represent data in the frequency domain, some transform is necessary. The most studied one is the Fourier transform.

In 1807, Jean Baptiste Joseph Fourier presented the results of his study of heat propagation and diffusion to the Institut de France [7]. In his presentation, he claimed that any periodic signal could be represented by a series of sinusoids. Though this concept was initially met with resistance, it has since been used in numerous developments in mathematics, science, and engineering. This concept is the basis for what we know today as the Fourier series. Fig. 2.10 shows how a square wave can be created by a composition of sinusoids [19]. These sinusoids vary in frequency and amplitude.

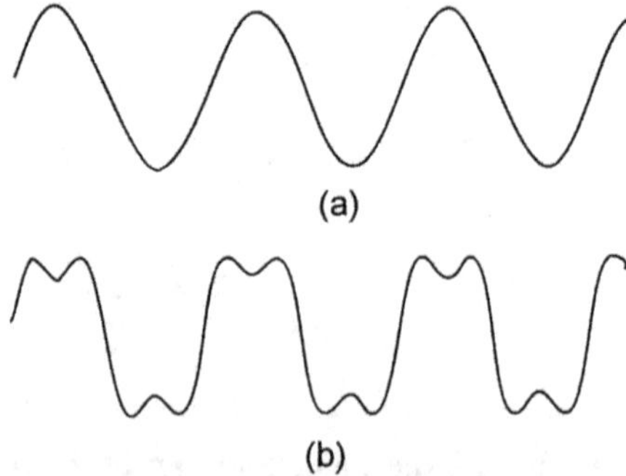

Fig. 2.10 (a) Fundamental frequency: sine(x); **(b)** Fundamental plus 16 harmonics: sine(x) + sine(3x)/3 + sine(5x)/5...

What this means to us is that any signal is composed of different frequencies. This applies to 1-dimensional signals such as an audio signal going to a speaker or a 2-dimensional signal such as an image.

A prism is a commonly used device to demonstrate how a signal is a composition of signals of varying frequencies. As white light passes through a prism, the prism breaks the light into its component frequencies revealing a full color spectrum.

The spatial frequency of an image refers to the rate at which the pixel intensities change. Fig. 2.11 shows an image consisting of different frequencies [6]. The high frequencies are concentrated around the axes dividing the image into quadrants. High frequencies are noted by concentrations of large amplitude swings in the small checkerboard pattern. The corners have lower frequencies. Low spatial frequencies are noted by large areas of nearly constant values.

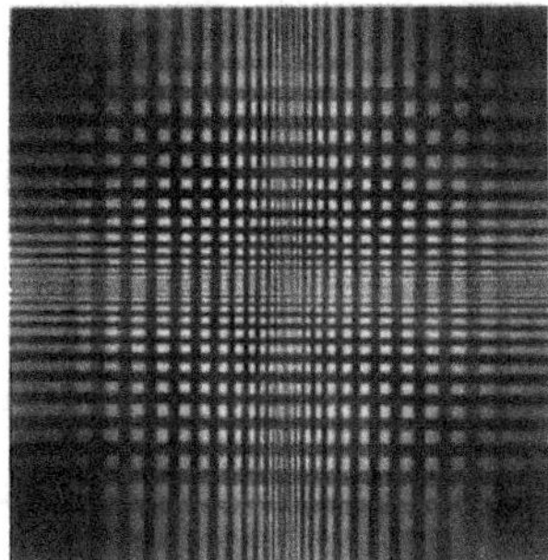

Fig. 2.11 Image of varying frequencies [53].

The easiest way to determine the frequency composition of signals is to inspect that signal in the frequency domain [53]. The frequency domain shows the magnitude of different frequency components. A simple example of a Fourier transform is a cosine wave. Fig. 2.12 shows a simple 1-dimensional cosine wave and its Fourier transform. Since there is only one sinusoidal component in the cosine wave, one component is displayed in the frequency domain. You will notice that the frequency domain represents data as both positive and negative frequencies.

Many different transforms are used in image processing (far too many begin with the letter H: Hilbert, Hartley, Hough, Hotelling, Hadamard, and Haar) [32]. Due to its wide range of applications in image processing, the Fourier transform is one of the most popular (Fig. 2.13). It operates on a continuous function of infinite length. The Fourier transform of a 2-dimensional function is shown mathematically as

$$H(u,v) = \int\limits_{-\infty}^{\infty}\int\limits_{-\infty}^{\infty} h(x,y)e^{-j2\pi(ux+vy)}\,dx\,dy$$

where

$$j = \sqrt{-1} \quad \text{and} \quad e^{\pm jx} = \cos(x) \pm j\sin(x)$$

It is also possible to transform image data from the frequency domain back to the spatial domain. This is done with an inverse Fourier transform

$$h(x,y) = \int_{-\infty}^{\infty} \int_{-\infty}^{\infty} H(u,v)e^{-j2\pi(ux+vy)}\,du\,dv$$

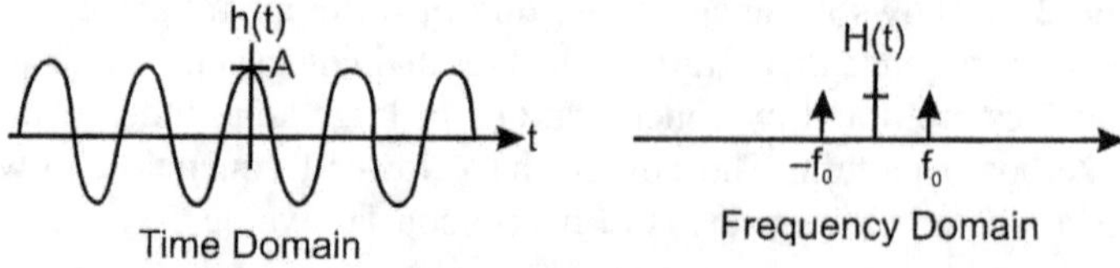

Fig. 2.12 Cosine wave and its Fourier transform.

It quickly becomes evident that the two operations are very similar with a minus sign in the exponent being the only difference [56]. Of course, the functions being operated on are different, one being a spatial function, the other being a function of frequency [40]. There is also a corresponding change in variables.

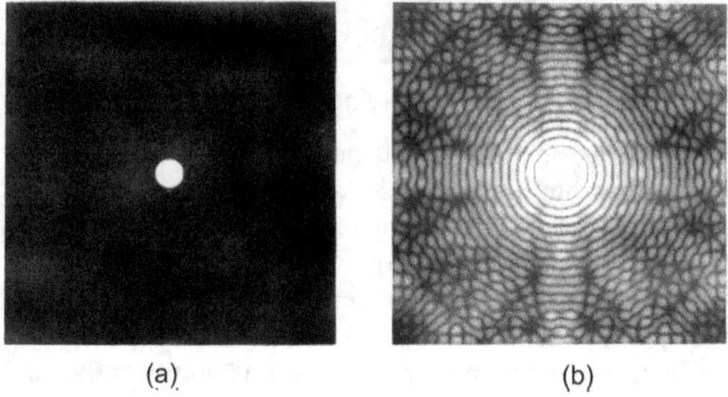

(a)   (b)

Fig. 2.13 Fourier Transform of a spot : (a) original image; (b) Fourier Transform.

In the frequency domain, u represents the spatial frequency along the original image's x axis and v represents the spatial frequency along the y axis. In the center of the image u and v have their origin.

The Fourier transform deals with complex numbers (Fig. 2.14). It is not immediately obvious what the real and imaginary parts represent. Another way to represent the data is with its sign and magnitude. The magnitude is expressed as

$$|H(u,v)| = \sqrt{R^2(u,v) + I^2(u,v)}$$

and phase as

$$\theta(u,v) = \tan^{-1}\left[\frac{I(u,v)}{R(u,v)}\right]$$

where R(u, v) is the real part and I(u, v) is the imaginary. The magnitude is the amplitude of sine and cosine waves in the Fourier transform formula. As expected, 0 is the phase of the sine and cosine waves. This information along with the frequency, allows us to fully specify the sine and cosine components of an image. Remember that the frequency is dependent on the pixel location in the transform. The further from the origin it is, the higher the spatial frequency it represents.

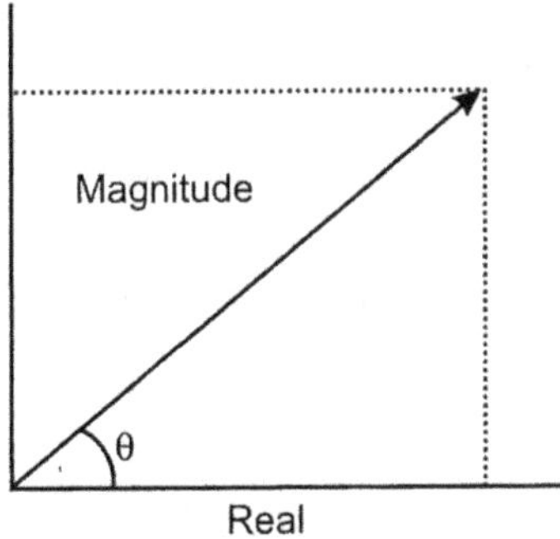

Fig. 2.14 Relationship between imaginary number and phase and magnitude.

2.7.1 Discrete Fourier Transform

When working with digital images, we are never given a continuous function, we must work with a finite number of discrete samples [43]. These samples are the pixels that compose an image. Computer analysis of images requires the discrete Fourier transform.

The Discrete Fourier transform (DFT) is a special case of the continuous Fourier transform [52]. Fig. 2.15 shows how data for the Fourier transform and the discrete Fourier transform differ. In Fig. 2.15 (a), the continuous function can serve as valid input into the Fourier transform [52]. In Fig. 2.15 (b), the data is sampled. There is still an infinite number of data points. In Fig. 2.15 (c), the data is truncated to capture a finite number of samples on which to operate. Both the sampling and truncating process cause problems in the transformation if not treated properly.

The formula to compute the discrete Fourier transform on an M × N size image is

$$H(u,v) = \frac{1}{MN}\sum_{x=0}^{M-1}\sum_{y=0}^{N-1} h(x,y)e^{-j2\pi(ux/M+vy/N)}$$

The formula to return to the spatial domain is

$$h(x, y) = \sum_{x=0}^{M-1} \sum_{y=0}^{N-1} H(u, v)e^{j2\pi(ux/M+vy/N)}$$

Again it can be seen that the operations for the DFT and inverse DFT are very similar. In fact, the code to perform these operations can be the same taking note of the direction of the transform and setting the sign of the exponent accordingly.

There are problems associated with data sampling and truncation. Truncating a data set to a finite number of samples creates a ringing known as Gibb's phenomenon [20]. This ringing distorts the spectral information in the frequency domain. The width of the ringing can be reduced by increasing the number of data samples. This will not reduce the amplitude of the ringing. This ringing can be seen in either domain. Truncating data in the spatial domain causes ringing in the frequency domain. Truncating data in the frequency domain causes ringing in the spatial domain.

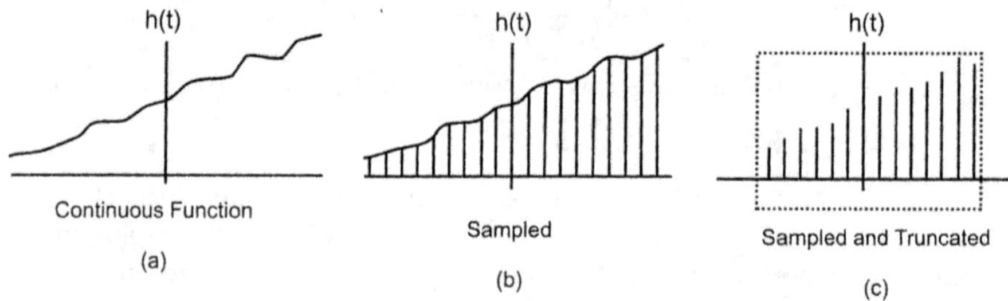

Fig. 2.15 (a) Continuous function; (b) sampled; (c) sampled and truncated

The Discrete Fourier transform expects the input data to be periodic, and the first sample is expected to follow the last sample. The amplitude of the ringing is a function of the difference between the amplitude of the first and last samples. To reduce this discontinuity, we can multiply the data by a windowing function (sometimes called window weighting functions) before the Fourier transform is performed.

There are a number of window functions, each with its set of advantages and disadvantages [53]. Fig. 2.16 shows some popular window functions. N is the number of samples in the data set. The Bartlett window is the simplest to compute requiring no sine or cosine computations. Ideally the data in the middle of the sample set is attenuated very little by the window function.

The equation for the Bartlett window is

$$w(n) = \begin{cases} \dfrac{2n}{N-1} & 0 \le n < \dfrac{N-1}{2} \\[2ex] 2 - \dfrac{2n}{N-1} & \dfrac{N-1}{2} \le n \le N-1 \end{cases}$$

The equation for the Hamming window is

$$w(n) = \frac{1}{2}\left[1 - \cos\left(\frac{2\pi n}{N-1}\right)\right]$$

The equation for the Hamming window is

$$w(n) = 0.54 - 0.46\cos\left(\frac{2\pi n}{N-1}\right)$$

The equation for a Blackman window is

$$w(n) = 0.42 - 0.5\cos\left(\frac{2\pi n}{N-1}\right) + 0.08\cos\left(\frac{4\pi n}{N-1}\right)$$

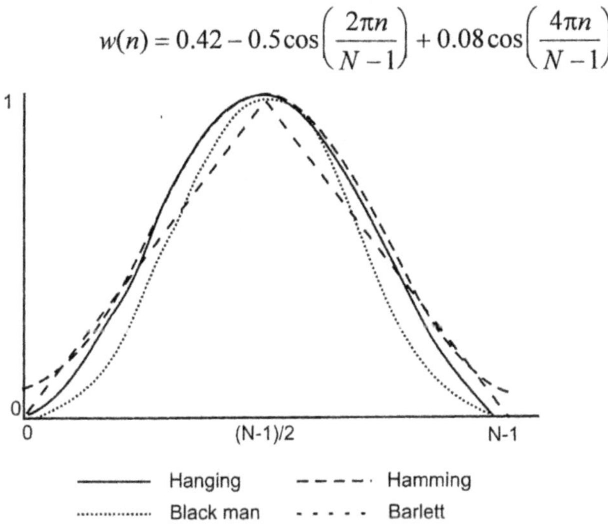

Fig. 2.16 1-dimensional window function

Just like many other functions, 1-dimensional windows can be converted into 2-dimensional windows by the following equation so that the original data is periodic [5].

$$f(x, y) = w\left(\sqrt{x^2 + y^2}\right)$$

There are some great discontinuities at the truncation edges. Window functions attenuate all values at the truncation edges. These great discontinuities are hence removed. Fig. 2.17 also shows the truncated function after windowing.

Window functions attenuate the original image data [19]. Window selection requires a compromise between how much you can afford to attenuate image data and how much spectral degradation you can tolerate.

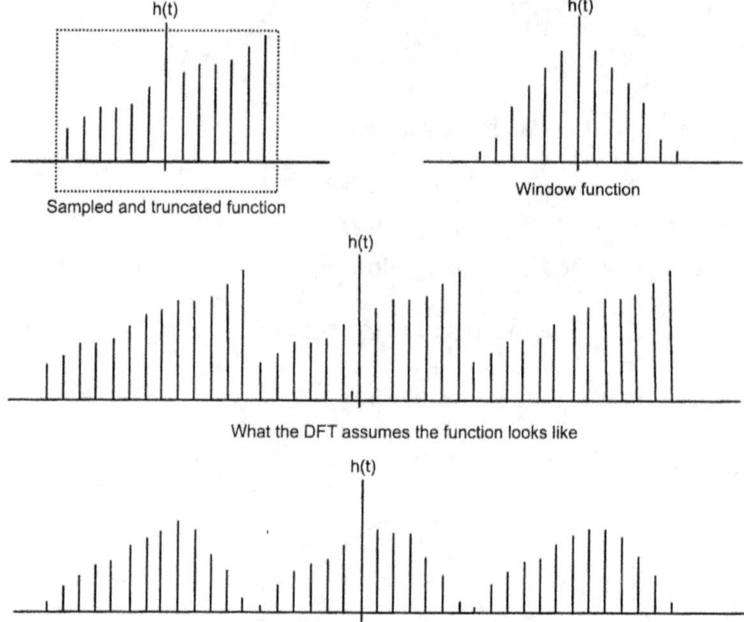

Fig. 2.17 Truncated function, what DFT thinks, results of window operation.

2.7.2 Fast Fourier Transform

The discrete Fourier transform is computationally intensive requiring N^2 complex multiplications for a set of N elements. This problem is exacerbated when working with 2-dimensional data like images [1]. An image of size M x M will require $(M^2)^2$ or M^4 complex multiplications.

Fortunately, in 1942, it was discovered that the Discrete Fourier transform of length N could be rewritten as the sum of two Fourier transforms of length N/2. This concept can be recursively applied to the data set until it is reduced to transforms of only two points [7]. Due partially to the lack of computing power, it wasn't until the mid 1960s that this discovery was put into practical application. In 1965, JW. Cooley and J.W. Tukey applied this finding at Bell Labs to filter noisy signals.

This divide and conquer technique is known as the Fast Fourier transform (FFT). It reduces the number of complex multiplications from N^2 to the order of $N\log_2 N$. Table 2.1 shows the computations and time required to perform the DFT directly and via the FFT. It is assumed that each complex multiply takes 1 microsecond.

Table 2.1 Savings when using the FFT on 1-dimensional data

Size of data set	DFT multiplication	DFT time	FFT multiplication	FFT Time
1024	1E6	1 sec	10,240	0.01 sec
8192	67E6	67 sec	106,496	0.1 sec
65536	4E9	71 min	1,048,576	1.0 sec
1048576	1E12	305 hr	20.971.520	20.9 sec

This savings is substantial especially when processing images. The FFT is separable, which makes Fourier transforms even easier to do [19]. Because of the separability, we can reduce the FFT operation from a 2-dimensional operation to two 1-dimensional operations. First we compute the FFT of the rows of an image and then follow up with the FFT of the columns. For an image of size M x N, this requires N + M FFTs to be computed. The order of $NM\log_2 NM$ computations are required to transform our image. Table 2.2 shows the computations and time required to perform the DFT directly and via the FFT on two-dimensional data.

Table 2.2 Savings when using the FFT on 2-dimensional data

Image size	DFT multiplication	DFT time	FFT multiplication	FFT Time
256*256	4.3E 9	71 min	1,048,576	1.0 sec
512*512	6.8E10	19 hr	4,718,592	4.8 sec
1024*1024	1.1E12	12 days	20,971,520	21.0 sec
2048*2048	1.8 E 13	203 days	92,274,688	92.2 sec

There are some considerations to keep in mind when transforming data to the frequency domain via the FFT. First, since the FFT algorithm recursively divides the data down, the dimensions of the image must be powers of 2 ($N = 2^j$ and $M = 2^k$ where j and k can be any number). Chances are pretty good that your image dimensions are not a power of 2. Your image data set can be expanded to the next legal size by surrounding the image with zeros. This is called zero-padding. You could also scale the image up to the next legal size or cut the image down at the next valid size. For algorithms that remove this power of 2 restriction, see the last section of this chapter.

The 1-dimensional FFT function can be broken down into two main functions. The first is the scrambling routine. Proper reordering of the data can take advantage of the periodicity and symmetry of recursive DFT computation [19]. The scrambling routine is very simple. A bit reversed index is computed for each element in the data array. The data is then swapped with the data pointed to by the bit-reversed index. For example, suppose you are computing the FFT for an 8 element array. The data element at address 1 (001) will be swapped with the data at address 4 (100). Not all data is swapped since some indices are bit-reversals of themselves (000, 010, 101, and 111) (Fig. 2.18).

000	data 0	data 0
001	data 1	data 4
010	data 2	data 2
011	data 3	data 6
100	data 4	data 1
101	data 5	data 5
110	data 6	data 3
111	data 7	data 0

Fig. 2.18 Bit-reversal operation

The second part of the FFT function is the butterflies function. The butterflies function divides the set of data points down and performs a series of two point discrete Fourier transforms. The function is named after the flow graph that represents the basic operation of each stage: one multiplication and two additions (Fig. 2.19).

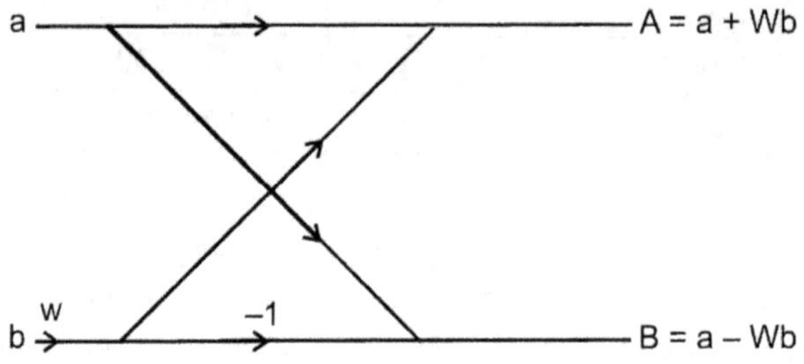

Fig. 2.19 Basic butterfly flow graph.

Remember that the FFT is not a different transform than the DFT, but a family of more efficient algorithms to accomplish the data transform. Usually when one speeds up an algorithm, this speed up comes at a cost [53]. With the FFT, the cost is complexity. There is complexity in the bookkeeping and algorithm execution. The computational savings, however, do not come at the expense of accuracy.

Now that you can generate image frequency data, it's time to display it. There are some difficulties to overcome when displaying the frequency spectrum of an image. The first arises because of the wide dynamic range of the data resulting from the discrete Fourier transform. Each data point is represented as a floating point number and is no longer limited to values from 0 to 255. This data must be scaled back down to put in a displayable format. A simple linear quantization does not always yield the best results, as many times the low amplitude data points get lost. The zero frequency term is usually the largest single component. It is also the least interesting point when inspecting the image spectrum. A common solution to this problem is to display the logarithm of the spectrum rather than the spectrum itself. The display function is

$$D(u,v) = x \log\left[1 + |H(u,v)|\right]$$

where x is a scaling constant and $|H(u, v)|$ is the magnitude of the frequency data to display. The addition of 1 ensures that the pixel value 0 does not get passed to the logarithm function.

Sometimes the logarithm function alone is not enough to display the range of interest. If there is high contrast in the output spectrum using only the logarithm function, you can clamp the extreme values. The rest of the data can be scaled appropriately using the logarithm function above.

Since scientists and engineers were brought up using the Cartesian coordinate system, they like image spectra displayed that way. An unaltered image spectrum will have the zero component displayed in the upper left hand corner of the image corresponding to pixel zero [32]. The conventional way of displaying image spectra is by shifting the image both horizontally and vertically by half the image width and height. Figure 2.20 shows the image spectrum before and after this shifting. All spectra shown thus far have been displayed in this conventional way. This format is referred to as ordered (as opposed to unordered).

Now that we can view the image frequency data, how do we interpret it? Each pixel in the spectrum represents a change in the spatial frequency of one cycle per image width. The origin (at the center of the ordered image) is the constant term, sometimes referred to as the DC term (from electrical engineering's direct current). If every pixel in the image were gray, there would only be one value in the frequency spectrum. It would be at the origin. The next pixel to the right of the origin represents 1 cycle per image width. The next pixel to the right represents 2 cycles per image width and so forth. The further from the origin a pixel value is, the higher the spatial frequency it represents. You will notice that typically the higher values cluster around the origin [56]. The high values that are not clustered about the origin are usually close to the u or v axis.

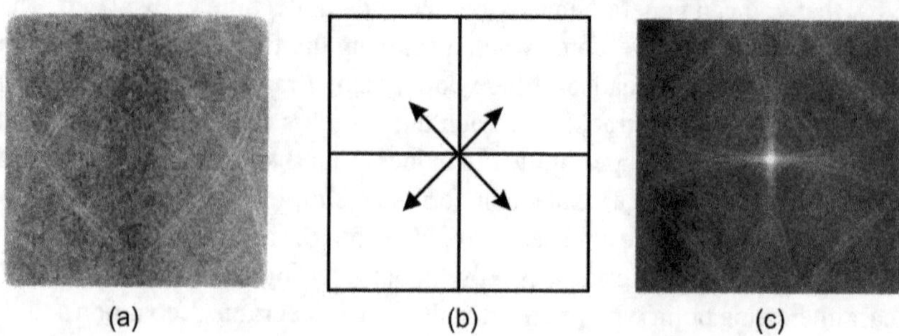

Fig. 2.20 (a) Image spectrum (unordered);

(b) remapping of spectrum quadrants;

(c) conventional view of spectrum (ordered).

2.7.3 Discrete Cosine Transform

The Discrete Cosine Transform (DCT) is the basis for many image compression algorithms. One clear advantage of the DCT over the DFT is that there is no need to manipulate complex numbers. The equation for a forward DCT is

$$H(u,v) = \frac{2}{\sqrt{MN}} C(u)C(v) \sum_{x=0}^{M-1} \sum_{y=0}^{N-1} h(x,y) \cos\left[\frac{(2x+1)u\pi}{2M}\right] \cos\left[\frac{(2y+1)v\pi}{2N}\right]$$

and for the reverse DCT

$$h(x,y) = \frac{2}{\sqrt{MN}} C(u)C(v) \sum_{x=0}^{M-1} \sum_{y=0}^{N-1} H(u,v) \cos\left[\frac{(2x+1)u\pi}{2M}\right] \cos\left[\frac{(2y+1)v\pi}{2N}\right]$$

where

$$C(\gamma) = \begin{cases} \dfrac{1}{\sqrt{2}} & for \quad \gamma = 0 \\ 1 & for \quad \gamma > 0 \end{cases}$$

Just like with the Fourier series, images can be decomposed into a set of basis functions with the DCT (Fig. 2.21 and 2.22). This means that an image can be created by the proper summation of basis functions. In the next chapter, the DCT will be discussed as it applies to image compression.

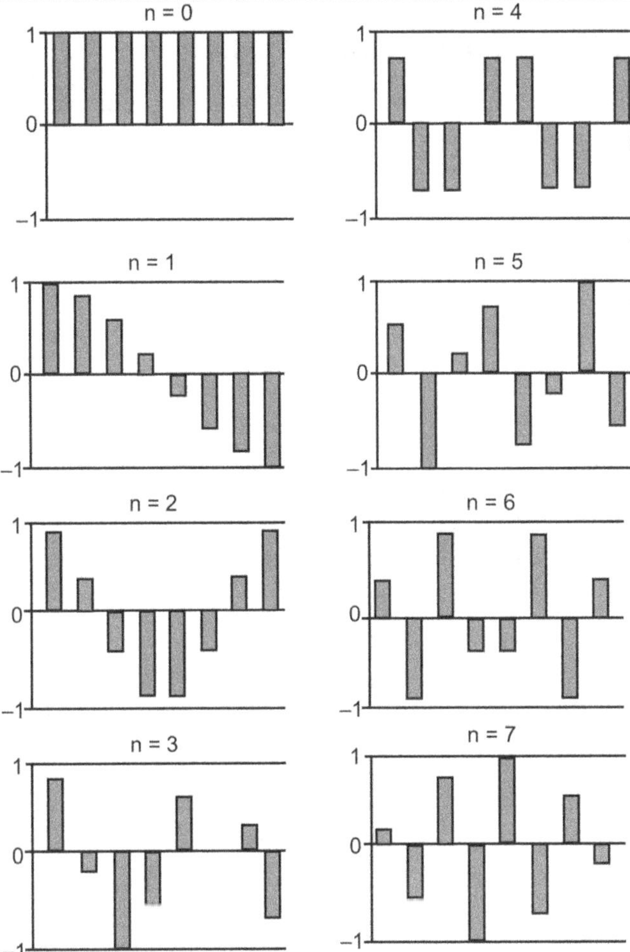

Fig. 2.21 1- D cosine basis functions.

Fig. 2.22 2-DCT basis functions.

2.7.4 Hadamard Transform (Walsh Transform)

The *Hadamard transform* is based on the *Hadamard matrix*, which is a square array of plus and minus 1s whose rows and columns are orthogonal.

A normalized $N \times N$ Hadamard matrix satisfies the relation

$$HH^T = I \tag{a}$$

The smallest orthonormal Hadamard matrix is the 2×2 Hadamard matrix given by

$$
H_4 = \frac{1}{2}
\begin{bmatrix}
1 & 1 & 1 & 1 \\
1 & -1 & 1 & -1 \\
1 & 1 & -1 & -1 \\
1 & -1 & -1 & 1
\end{bmatrix}
\begin{matrix}
\text{Sign} \\ \text{Changes} \\ 0 \\ 3 \\ 1 \\ 2
\end{matrix}
$$

$$
H_8 = \frac{1}{2\sqrt{2}}
\begin{bmatrix}
1 & 1 & 1 & 1 & 1 & 1 & 1 & 1 \\
1 & -1 & 1 & -1 & 1 & -1 & 1 & -1 \\
1 & 1 & -1 & -1 & 1 & 1 & -1 & -1 \\
1 & -1 & -1 & 1 & 1 & -1 & -1 & 1 \\
1 & 1 & 1 & 1 & -1 & -1 & -1 & -1 \\
1 & -1 & 1 & -1 & -1 & 1 & -1 & 1 \\
1 & 1 & -1 & -1 & -1 & -1 & 1 & 1 \\
1 & -1 & -1 & 1 & -1 & 1 & 1 & -1
\end{bmatrix}
\begin{matrix}
\text{Sign} \\ \text{Changes} \\ 0 \\ 7 \\ 3 \\ 4 \\ 1 \\ 6 \\ 2 \\ 5
\end{matrix}
$$

Fig. 2.23 Nonordered Hadamard matrices of size 4 and 8.

$$
H2 = \frac{1}{\sqrt{2}}
\begin{bmatrix}
1 & 1 \\
1 & -1
\end{bmatrix}
\tag{b}
$$

It is known that if a Hadamard matrix of size N exists ($N > 2$), then $N = 0$ modulo 4 (22). The existence of a Hadamard matrix for every value of N satisfying this requirement has not been shown, but constructions are available for nearly all permissible values of N up to 200. The simplest construction is for a Hadamard matrix of size $N = 2n$, where n is an integer. In this case, if is a Hadamard matrix of size N, the matrix

$$H_{2N} = \frac{1}{\sqrt{2}} \begin{bmatrix} H_N & H_N \\ H_N & -H_N \end{bmatrix} \tag{c}$$

is a Hadamard matrix of size 2N. Figure 2.23 shows Hadamard matrices of size 4 and 8 obtained by the construction of Eq. (c).

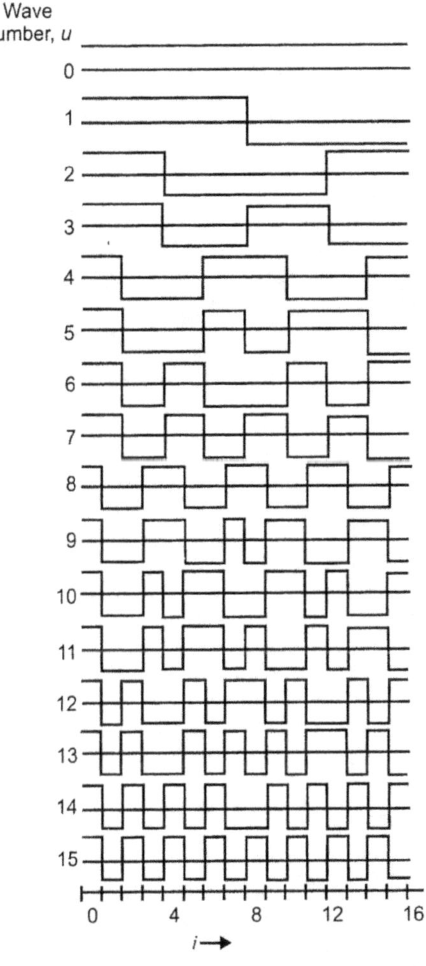

Fig. 2.24 Hadamard transform basis functions, $N = 16$.

Harmuth (25) has suggested a frequency interpretation for the Hadamard matrix generated from the core matrix of Eq. 2.23 the number of sign changes along each row of the Hadamard matrix divided by 2 is called the *sequency* of the row. It is possible to construct a Hadamard matrix of order $N = 2^n$ whose number of sign changes per row increases from 0 to $N - 1$. This attribute is called the *sequency property* of the unitary matrix.

The rows of the Hadamard matrix of Eq. (c) can be considered to be samples of rectangular waves with a subperiod of $1/N$ units. These continuous functions are called *Walsh functions*. In this context, the Hadamard matrix merely performs the decomposition of a function by a set of rectangular waveforms rather than the sine–cosine waveforms with the Fourier transform. A series formulation exists for the Hadamard transform.

Hadamard transform basis functions for the ordered transform with $N = 16$ are shown in Figure 2.24. The ordered Hadamard transform of the test image in shown in Figure 2.25 (a).

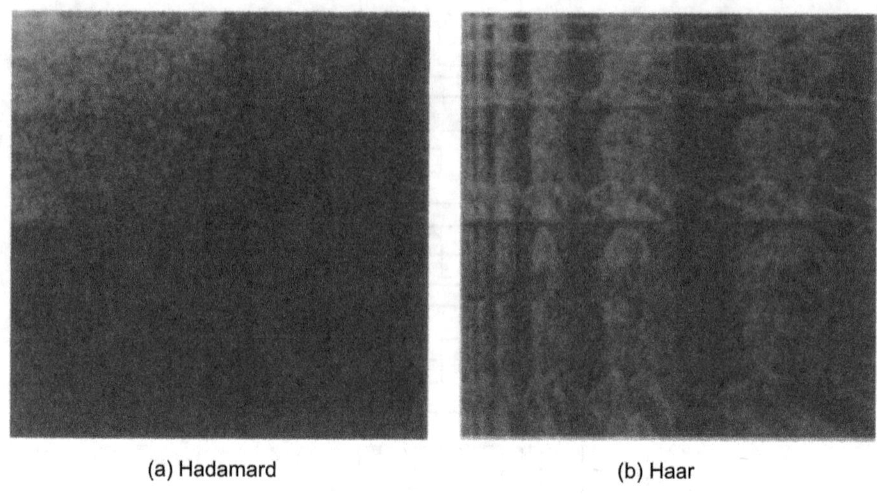

(a) Hadamard   (b) Haar

Fig. 2.25 Hadamard and Haar transforms of a image, log magnitude displays.

2.7.5 Haar Transforms

Originally described by A. Haar (1909). Each step creates two channels: one simply averages adjacent elements (i.e., low-pass channel); and one takes difference between adjacent elements (i.e., a high-pass channel) as shown in the figure below. Both are down-sampled by 2.

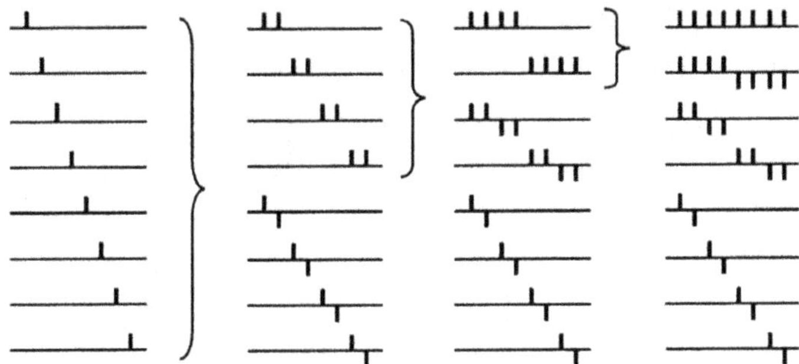

Fig. 2.26 Creation of channels at each step in Haar Transform.

Properties:

1. critically-sampled and self-inverting (orthogonal)

2. local in space (compact) but not continuously differentiable

3. broad ringing frequency spectrum due to top-hat spatial window, and therefore massive aliasing in each band (like blocked DCT).

4. very efficient to compute with pyramid scheme and addition

Analysis / Synthesis Diagram :

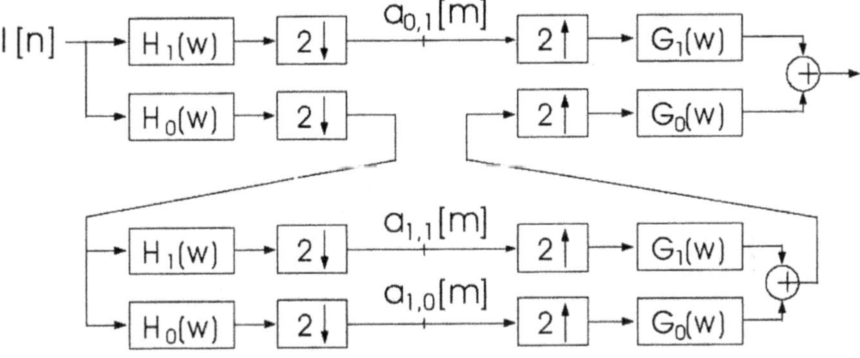

Analysis/Synthesis system diagram for a 2-level cascaded pyramid filter bank

This is an analysis-synthesis diagram for a general 2-level cascaded pyramid (where the low-pass portion is further filtered). It shows the recursive construction of the transform. For the Haar transform, H_0 and H_1 are low-pass and high-pass filters that compute sums and differences (respectively) of adjacent pixels. Moreover, $G_j(\omega) = H_j(-\omega)$, and so the transform can be shown to be selfinverting. Finally, although there is aliasing in the individual channels of the Haar transform, one can show that, upon reconstruction, the aliasing in the transform channels, so the reconstruction is exact.

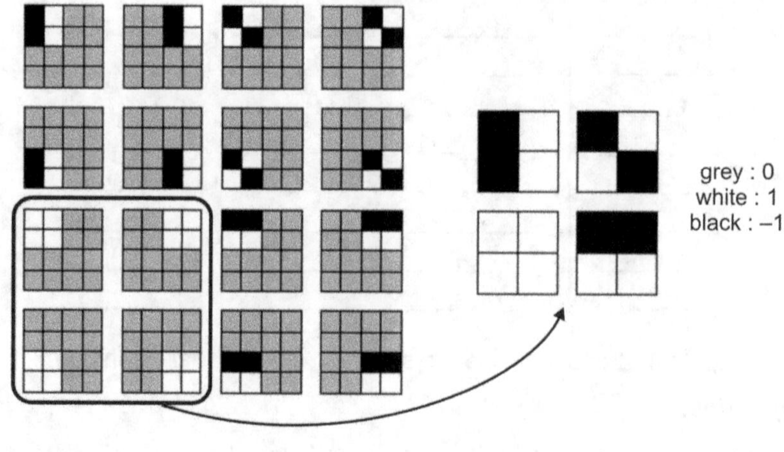

$$\begin{pmatrix}1\\1\end{pmatrix}^{(1\ \ 1)} \qquad \begin{pmatrix}1\\1\end{pmatrix}^{(1\ \ -1)} \qquad \begin{pmatrix}1\\-1\end{pmatrix}^{(1\ \ 1)} \qquad \begin{pmatrix}1\\-1\end{pmatrix}^{(1\ \ -1)}$$

(b) Separable 2D filters:

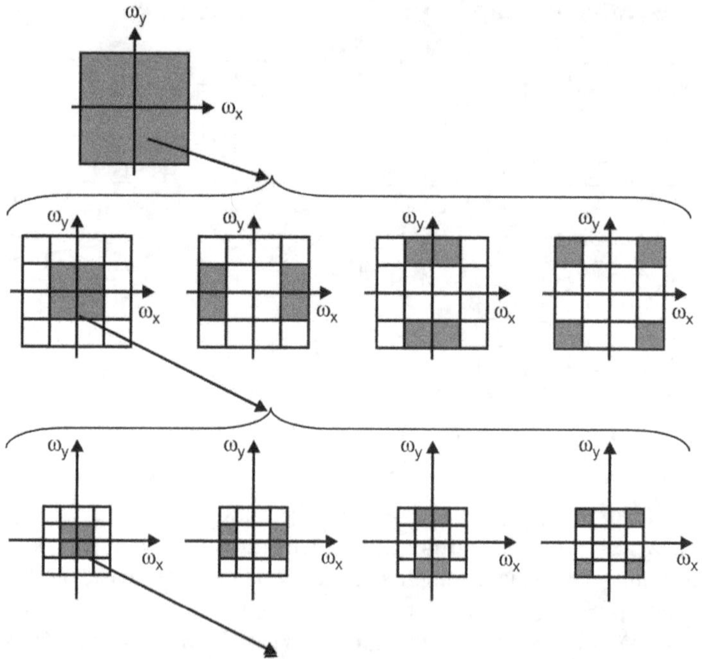

(c) Idealized band-splitting in the frequency domain:

Fig. 2.27 Haar transforms.

2.7.6 Hotelling Transform

KL transform was originally introduced as a series expansion for continuous random processes by Karhunen and Loeve. For discrete random processes, Hotelling was the first person studied what was called a method of principal components, a discrete version of KL series expansion. Consequently, KL Transform is called Hotelling Transform or Method of Principal Components.

The Karhunen-Loeve Transform (KLT) or Hotelling transform is a rotation transformation that aligns the data with the eigen vectors, by the other hand this alignment is precisely the mechanism that decorrelates the data. The transformed image may make evident features not discernable in the original data or alternatively it might be possible to preserve the essential information content of the image for a given application with a reduced number of the transformed dimensions. The KLT can be considered by the eigenvalues and eigen vectors for developing a new co-ordinate system in the multispectral vector space, in which the data can be represented without correlation as defined by:

$$Y = GX \tag{1}$$

where y   is a new co-ordinate system,

G is a linear transformation of the original co-ordinates that is the transposed matrix of eigenvector of the pixel data's covariance in x space

x is an original co-ordinate system

By (1), we can get the principal components and choose the first principal component from this transformation that seems to be the best monochrome representation of the input image.

Processing details

The Karhunen-Loeve transformation is based on statistical property of vector representations. The Karhunen-Loeve transformation has several useful properties that make it an important tool for image processing.

Consider a population of random vectors of the form

$$x = [x1\ x2\ x3\ x4\ x5... \ xn]^T$$

The mean vector of the population is defined as

$$m_x = E\{x\}$$

where $E\{arg\}$ is the expected value of the argument, and the subscript denotes that m is associated with the population of x vectors. Recall that the expected value of a vector or matrix is obtained by taking the expected value of each element.

The covariance matrix of the vector population is defined as

$$C_x = E\{(x - m_x)(x - m_x)^T\}$$

Where T indicates vector transposition. Because x is n dimensional, C_x and $(x - m_x)(x - m_x)^T$ are matrices of order n ´ n . Element c_{ij} of C_x is the variance of x_i , the ith component of the x vectors in population, and element c_{ij} of C_x is the covariance between element x_i and x_j of these vectors. The matrix C_x is real and symmetric. If elements x_i and x_j are uncorrelated , their covariance is zero and, therefore, $c_{ij} = c_{ji} = 0$.

For M vector samples from a random population, the mean vector and covariance matrix can be approximated from the samples by

$$m_x = (1/M) \sum_{k=1}^{M} x_k$$

and
$$C_x = (1/M) \sum_{k=1}^{M} x_k x_k^T - m_x m_x^T$$

Because C_x is real and symmetric, finding a set of n orthonormal eigen-vector always is possible. Let e_i and λ_i, where i = 1, 2, ..., n, be the eigen vectors and corresponding eigen values of C_x , arranged in descending order so that $\lambda_j \geq \lambda_{j+1}$ for j = 1, 2, ... n-1. Let A be a matrix whose rows are formed from the eigen vectors of C_x , ordered so that the first row of A is the the eigen vector corresponding to the largest eigen value, and the last row is the eigen vector corresponding to the smallest eigen value.

Suppose that A is a transformation matrix that maps the x's into vectors denoted by y's, as follows

$$y = A(x - m_x)$$

The mean of y vectors resulting from this transformation is zero; That is

$$m_y = 0$$

and the covariance matrix of y's can be obtained in terms of A and C_x by

$C_y = A C_x A^T$ Furthermore, C_y is a diagonal matrix whose elements along the main diagonal are the eigen values of C_x; that is

$$C_y = diag\{\lambda 1, \lambda 2, ..., \lambda n\}$$

The off-diagonal elements of the covariance matrix are 0, so the elements of the y vectors are uncorrelated. Keep in mind that the λj's are the eigenvalues of C_x and that the elements along the main diagonal of a diagonal matrix are its eigen values.

Thus C_x and C_y have the same eigen values. In fact, the same is true for the eigen vectors.

Example : The following section illustrates the concepts just discussed. The binary object shown is treated as a 2-D population in other words, each pixel in the object is treated as a 2-D vector $x = (a, b)^T$, where a and b are the coordinate values of that pixel with respect to the x1 and x2 axes. These vectors are used to compute the mean vector and covariance matrix of the population (object).

The net effect of using this transformation is to establish a new coordinate system whose origin is at the centroid of the population and whose axes are in the direction of the eigen vectors of C_x, as shown in the figure. This coordinate system clearly shows that the transformation is a rotation transformation that aligns the data with the eigen vectors. In fact, this alignment is precisely the mechanism that decorrelate the data. Furthermore, as the eigen values appear along the main diagonal of C_y, λ_I is the variance of component y_i along eigen vector e_i.

Another important property of this transformation deals with the reconstruction of x from y. Because the rows of A are orthonormal vectors. $A^{-1} = A^T$, and any vector x can be recovered from its corresponding y by using the relation

$$X = A^T Y + M_X$$

Suppose, however, that instead of using all the eigen values of C_x we form matrix A_k from the K eigen vectors corresponding to the K largest eigen values, yielding a transformation matrix order $K \times n$. the y vectors would then be K dimensional, and the reconstruction given above would no longer be exact. The vector reconstructed by using A_k is

$$X' = A_k{}^T Y + M_X$$

It can be shown that the mean square error between x and x' is given by the expression

$$e_{ms} = \sum_{j=1}^{n} \lambda_j - \sum_{j=1}^{k} \lambda_j = \sum_{j=k+1}^{n} \lambda_j$$

The first part of above expression indicates that the error is zero if $k = n$ (that is, if all the eigenvalues are used in the transformation).Because the λ_j 's decrease monotonically. It also shows that the error can be minimized by selecting the K eigen values associated with the largest eigen values. Thus the Karhunen-Loeve transformation is optimal in the sense that it minimizes the mean square error between the vector x and their approximation x'.

Theorem proof

Theorem (Karhunen-Loeve transformation for continuous pictures).

Let $-A/2 \leq x \leq A/2$, $-B/2 \leq y \leq B/2$ define a region ∂ of the xy-plane. Let φ mn (x, y) be a complete family of orthonormal functions defined over the region ∂. A random field f(x, y) may then be expanded in region ∂ as follows

$$f(x, y) = \sum_{m=0}^{\infty} \sum_{n=0}^{\infty} a_{mn} \varphi_{mn}(x, y)$$

where   the summation on the right-hand side converges to f(x,y) in some sense and where

$$a_{mn} = \int_{-B/2}^{B/2} \int_{-A/2}^{A/2} f(x, y) \varphi^{*}_{mn}(x, y)\, dx\, dy$$

for zero-mean random fields the functions $\varphi_{mn}(x, y)$ that result in uncorrelated samples amn must satisfy the following integral equation :

$$\int_{-B/2}^{B/2} \int_{-A/2}^{A/2} R(x, y, x', y') \varphi_{mn}(x', y')\, dx'\, dy' = g_{mn} \varphi mn(x, y)$$

for $-A/2 \leq x \leq A/2$, $-B/2 \leq y \leq B/2$, where $g_{mn} = E\{|a_{mn}|^2\}$

Theorem (Karhunen-Loeve transformation for discrete pictures).

Let R(m, n, p, q) be the autocorrelation function of [f], that is

$$R(m, n, p, q) = E\{f(m, n)\, f(p, q)\}$$

For zero-mean random fields, the orthonormal matrices $[\varphi^{(u,v)}]$ that result in uncorrelated F(u,v) in (20) satisfy the equation

$$\sum_{p=0}^{N-1} \sum_{q=0}^{N-1} R(m, n, p, q) \varphi^{(u,v)}(p, q) = \gamma_{uv} \varphi^{(u,v)}(m, n)$$

where $\varphi^{(u,v)}(p, q)$ and $\varphi^{(u,v)}(m,n)$ are the $(p, q)^{th}$ and the $(m, n)^{th}$ elements, respectively, of the matrix $[\varphi^{(u, v)}]$, and where

$$\gamma_{uv} = E\{|F(u, v)|^2\}$$

the matrices $[\varphi^{(u,v)}]$ are called the eigen matrices or the basis matrices of R (m, n, p, q).

2.8 Image Enhancement Techniques

Image enhancement techniques are application oriented. There are two basic types of methods - *spatial domain methods* and *frequency domain methods*.

Spatial domain methods : methods that directly modify pixel values, possibly using intensity information from a neighborhood of the pixel. Examples include image negatives, contrast stretching, dynamic range compression, histogram specification, image subtraction, image averaging, and various spatial filters.

It is best suited for smoothing, sharpening, noise removal and edge detection.

Frequency domain methods : methods that modify the Fourier transform of the image. First, compute the Fourier transform of the image. Then alter the Fourier transform of the image by multiplying a filter transfer function. Finally, use inverse transform to get the modified image (steps are described later in the text). The key is the filter transfer function - examples include lowpass filter, highpass filter, and Butterworth filter.

2.8.1 Filtering in the Frequency Domain

Convolution Theorem :

The Fourier Transform is used to convert images from the spatial domain into the frequency domain and vice-versa. Convolution is one of the most important concepts in Fourier theory. Mathematically, a convolution is defined as the integral over all space of one function at x times another function at u-x.

$$f * g = \int_{-\infty}^{\infty} f(\tau)g(t-\tau)d\tau = \int_{-\infty}^{\infty} g(\tau)f(t-\tau)d\tau$$

We are interested in what happens if we convolve two functions in frequency domain. This is stated by the convolution theorem. The convolution theorem is useful because it gives us a way to simplify many calculations. Convolutions can be very difficult to calculate directly, but are often much easier to calculate using Fourier transforms and multiplication.

There are two ways of expressing the convolution theorem :

1. The Fourier transform of a convolution is the product of the Fourier transforms.

2. The Fourier transform of a product is the convolution of the Fourier transforms.

Let F be the operator performing the Fourier transform such that e.g. F is the Fourier transform of f (can be 1-D or 2- D). Then

$$\Im(f * g) = \Im(f). \, \Im(g) = F.G \tag{2.1.1}$$

Where denotes the element-by-element multiplication. Also, the Fourier transform of a product is the convolution of the Fourier transforms:

$$\Im(f. g) = \Im(f) * \Im(g) = F * G. \tag{2.1.2}$$

By using the inverse Fourier transform F^{-1}, we can write

$$\Im^{-1}(F. G) = f * g \tag{2.1.3}$$

$$\Im^{-1}(F * G) = f. g. \tag{2.1.4}$$

Proof of convolution theorem (1-D)

$$F(f(x)) * g(x)) = F\left(\int_{-\infty}^{\infty} f(x-t)g(t)dt \right)$$

$$= \int_{-\infty}^{\infty} \int_{-\infty}^{\infty} f(x-t)g(t)dt\, e^{-i2\pi\mu x}\, dx$$

$$= \int_{-\infty}^{\infty} \int_{-\infty}^{\infty} f(x-t)g(t)e^{-i2\pi\mu x}\, dtdx$$

Substituting $s = x - t$ and $ds = dx$,

$$F(f(x)) * g(x)) = \int_{-\infty}^{\infty} \int_{-\infty}^{\infty} f(x-t)g(t)e^{-i2\pi\mu x}\, dtdx$$

$$= \int_{-\infty}^{\infty} \int_{-\infty}^{\infty} f(\delta)g(t)e^{-i2\pi\mu(\delta+t)}\, dtd\delta$$

$$= \int_{-\infty}^{\infty} \int_{-\infty}^{\infty} f(\delta)e^{-i2\pi\mu\delta} g(t)e^{-i2\pi\mu t}\, dtd\delta$$

$$= \int_{-\infty}^{\infty} f(\delta)e^{-i2\pi\mu\delta}\, d\delta \int_{-\infty}^{\infty} f(t)e^{-i2\pi\mu t}\, dt$$

and since we may freely change the variable of integration,

$$F(f(x)) * g(x)) = \int_{-\infty}^{\infty} f(x)e^{-i2\pi\mu x}\, dx \int_{-\infty}^{\infty} g(x)e^{-i2\pi\mu x}\, dx$$

$$= F(f(x)) \, F(g(x))$$

Thus,

$$F(f(x) * g(x)) = F(f(x)) F(g(x))$$

Likewise,

$$F(f(x) g(x)) = F(f(x)) * F(g(x))$$

2.8.2 Basics of filtering in the frequency domain

Before we discuss filtering, it's important to understand what is high and low frequency mean in a image:

If an image has large values at high frequency components then the data (grey level) is changing rapidly on a short distance scale. e.g. a page of text, edges and noise.

If the image has large low frequency components then the large scale features of the picture are more important. e.g. a single fairly simple object which occupies most of the image. For color images, the measure the frequency content is with regard to color: this shows if values are changing rapidly or slowly.

Filtering in the frequency domain is a common image and signal processing technique. It can smooth, sharpen, de-blur, and restore some images. Essentially, filtering is equal to convolving a function with a specific filter function. So one possibility to convolve two functions could be to transform them to the frequency domain, multiply them there and transform them back to spatial domain. The filtering procedure is summarized in Figure 2.28.

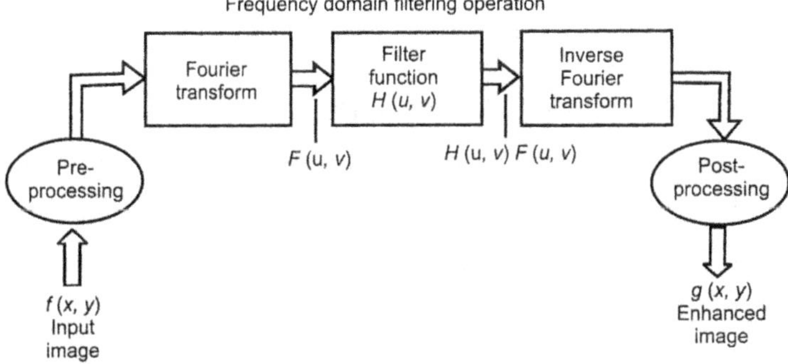

Fig. 2.28 Frequency domain filtering procedure.

Basic steps of filtering in the frequency domain:

1. Multiply the input image $f(x, y)$ by $(-1)^{(x+y)}$ to center the transform, as indicated as following eqaution : $\Im [f(x, y) (-1)^{(x+y)}] = F(u - M/2, v - N/2)$.

2. Compute $F(u, v)$, the DFT of the input image from (1).

3. Multiply $F(u, v)$ by a *filter* function $H(u, v)$.

4. Compute the inverse DFT of the result in (3).

5. Obtain the real part (better take the magnitude) of the result in (4).

6. Multiply the result in (5) by $(-1)^{(x+y)}$.

In step 2, the Two-Dimensional DFT :

$$F(u, v) = \frac{1}{MN} \sum_{x=0}^{M-1} \sum_{x=0}^{N-1} f(x, y)e^{-j2\pi(ux/M + vy/N)} \ ,$$

and its inverse :

$$f(x, y) = \frac{1}{MN} \sum_{u=0}^{M-1} \sum_{v=0}^{N-1} f(u, v)e^{j2\pi(ux/M + vy/N)} \ .$$

In equation form, the Fourier transform of the filtered image in step 3 is given by:

$$G(u, v) = F(u, v) H(u, v) \tag{2.2.1}$$

Where $F(u, v)$ and $H(u, v)$ denote the Fourier transform of the input image $f(x, y)$, and the filter function $h(x, y)$, respectively. And $G(u, v)$ is the Fourier Transform of the filtered image, which is the multiplication of two two-dimensional functions H and F on an element-by-element basics.

The important point to keep in mind is that the filtering process is based on modifying the transform of an image (frequency) in some way via a filter function, and then taking the inverse of the result to obtain the filtered image:

Filtered Image $= \mathfrak{J}^{-1}[G(u, v)]$.

Filtering in the Spatial and Frequency Domains

The most fundamental relationship between spatial and frequency domain is established by a well-known result called convolution theorem (as describe in sec 2.8.1). Formally, the discrete convolution of two functions f(x, y) and h(x, y) of size M x N is defined by the expression:

$$f(x, y) * h(x, y) = \frac{1}{MN} \sum_{m=0}^{M-1} \sum_{n=0}^{N-1} f(m, n)h(x - m, y - n). \tag{2.3.1}$$

From the convolution theorem, we know that the same result of Equation (2.3.1) can also be obtained via the frequency domain by taking the inverse transform of the product of the transforms of the two Equations as shown in Equation (2.1.3). A question that often arises in the development of frequency domain technique is the issue of computational complexity. Why do in the frequency domain for what could be done in the spatial domain using small spatial masks? First, since the frequency carries with a significant degree of intuitiveness regarding how to specify filters. Second part of the answer is depends on the size of the spatial masks and is usually answered with respect to comparable implementations. For example, use both approaches for running software on the same machine, it turns out that the frequency domain implementation runs faster for surprisingly small value of M and N. Also, some experiments shown that some enhancement tasks that would be exceptionally difficult or impossible to formulate directly in the spatial domain become almost trivial in the frequency domain.

An image can be filtered either in the frequency or in the spatial domain. In theory, all frequency filters can be implementing as a spatial filter, but in practice, the frequency filters can only be approximated by the filtering mask in spatial domain. If there exist a simple mask for the desired filter effect, it is computationally less expensive to perform the filtering in the spatial domain. And if there is no straight forward mask can be found in the spatial domain, frequency filtering is more appropriate.

2.8.3 Smoothing frequency domain filters

As discussed in section 2.8.2 about the different between the high and low frequency, we know that edges and noises and other sharp transitions in the grey level contribute significantly to the high frequency. Hence smoothing/blurring is achieved by attenuating a specified range of high frequency components in the transform of a given image, which can be done using a lowpass filter.

Lowpass filter is a filter that attenuates high frequencies and retains low frequencies unchanged. This results a smoothing filter in the spatial domain since high frequencies are blocked. Three types of lowpass filters will be discussed in this report are Ideal, Gaussian and Butterworth.

2.8.3.1 Ideal lowpass filter

The most simple lowpass filter is the ideal lowpass. It suppresses all frequencies higher than the cut-off frequency r_0 and leaves smaller frequencies unchanged:

$$\begin{cases} 1, \text{ if } D\,(u,\,v) \le r_0 \\ H\,(u,\,n) = 0, \text{ if } D\,(u,\,v) > r_0 \end{cases}$$

r_0 is called the cutoff frequency (nonnegative quantity), and $D\,(u,\,n)$ is the distance from point $(u,\,n)$ to the frequency rectangle. If the image is of size $M \times N$, then

$$D\,(u,\,v) = \sqrt{(u - \frac{M}{2})^2 + (v - \frac{N}{2})^2}\,.$$

The lowpass filters considered here are radially symmetric about the origin. Use Fig. 2.29 as the cross section that extending as a function of distance from the origin along a radial line, we get Fig. 2.30, which is the perspective plot of an Ideal LPF transfer function. And Fig. 2.31 is the filter displayed as an image.

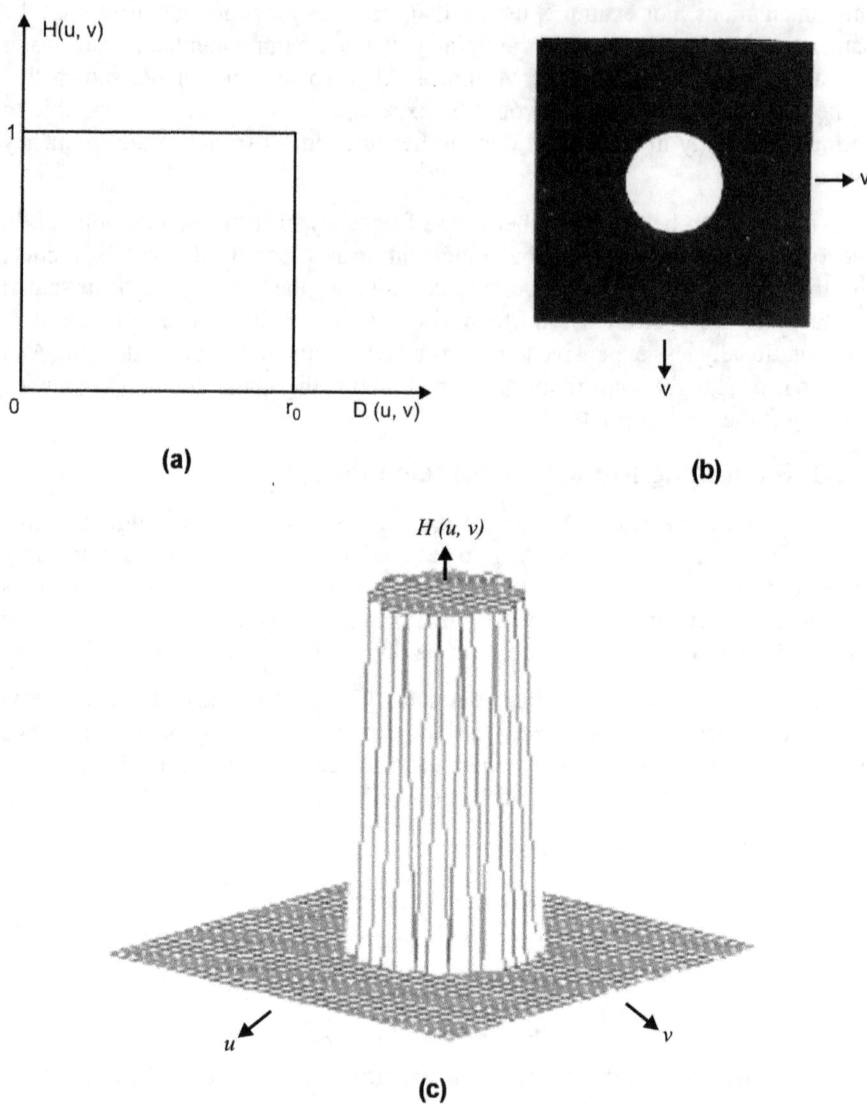

Fig. 2.29 Shows the Ideal low pass filter as (a) cross section (b) image (c) perspective plot

The drawback of the ideal lowpass filter function is a ringing effect that occurs along the edges of the filtered image. In fact, ringing behavior is a characteristic of ILPF (Ideal Low Pass Filter). As mentioned earlier, multiplication in the Fourier domain corresponds to a convolution in the spatial domain. Due to the multiple peaks of the ideal filter in the spatial domain, the filtered image produces ringing along intensity edges in the spatial domain.

The cutoff frequency r_0 of the ILPF determines the amount of frequency components passed by the filter. Smaller the value of r_0, more the number of image components eliminated by the filter (see example below).

In general, the value of r_0 is chosen such that most components of interest are passed through, while most components not of interest are eliminated.

Example 1 : **Ideal low pass filtering :**

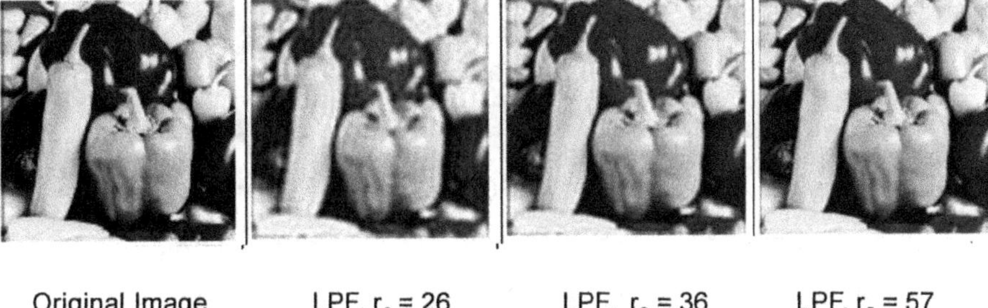

Fig. 2.30 Shows the change in image quality with r_0 value.

As we can see, the filtered image is blured and ringing is more severe as r_0 become smaller. It is clear from this example that ILPF is not very practical.

2.8.3.2 Butterworth lowpass filter

A commonly used discrete approximation to the Gaussian (next section) is the Butterworth filter. Applying this filter in the frequency domain shows a similar result to the Gaussian smoothing in the spatial domain. The transfer function of a Butterworth lowpass filter (BLPF) of order n, and with cutoff frequency at a distance r_0 from the origin, is defined as

$$H(u, v) = \frac{1}{1 + \left[\dfrac{D(u,v)}{r_0}\right]^{2n}} \qquad (3.2.1)$$

Where $D(u, v)$ is defined in 3.1.1.

As we can see from Figure 2.31, frequency response of the BLPF does not have a sharp transition as in the ideal LPF. And as the filter order increases, the transition from the pass band to the stop band gets steeper. Which means as the order of BLPF increase, it will exhibits the characteristics of the ILPF. See example below to see the differences between two images with different orders but the same cutoff frequency. In fact, order of 20 already shows the ILPF characteristic.

***Example 2 :* BLPF with different orders but the same cut-off frequency :**

Fig. 2.31 Effect of passing BLPF on a test image.

Using Figure 2.32 as the cross section that as a function of distance from the origin along a radial line, we get Figure 2.34. And Figure 2.33 is the filter displayed as an image.

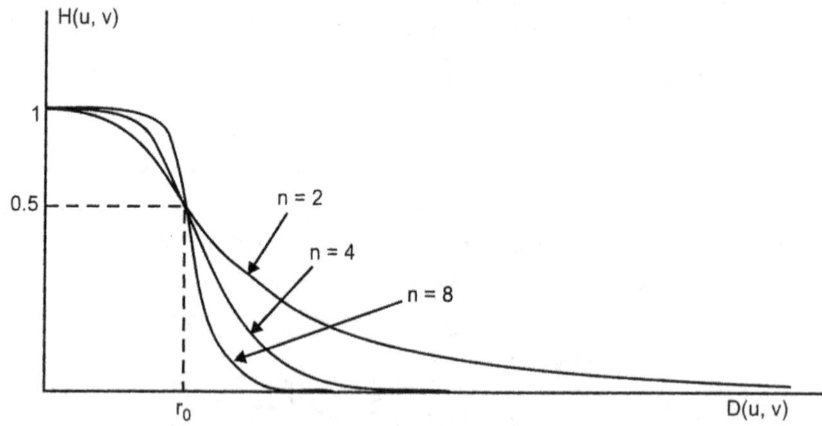

Fig. 2.32 Filter with radial cross sections of order n = 2, 4 and 8.

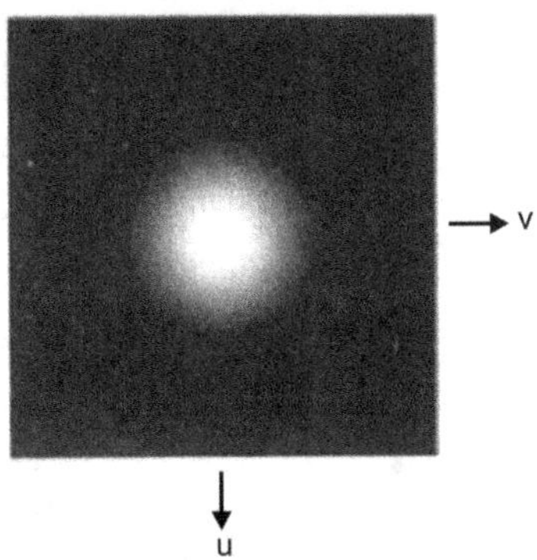

Fig. 2.33 Filter displayed as an image.

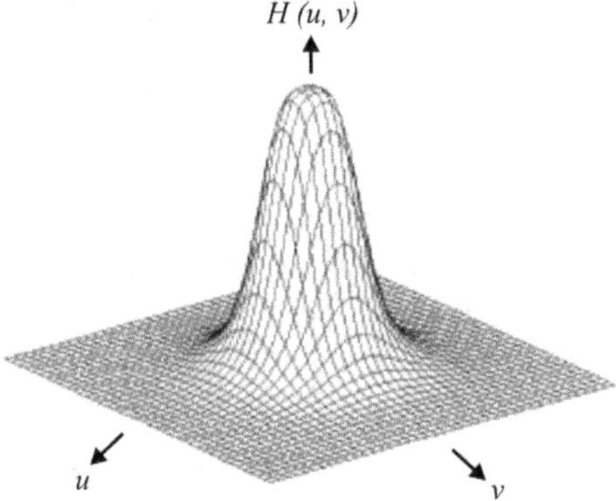

Fig. 2.34 Perspective plot of a Butteerworth LPF transfer function.

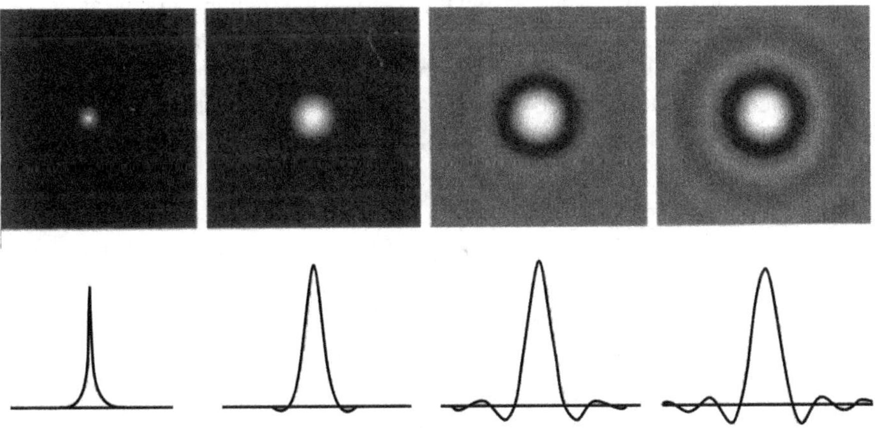

Fig. 2.35 BLPF of order 1, 2, 5, and 20 respectively with their corresponding gray-level images.

Figure 2.35 shows the comparison between the spatial representations of various orders with cutoff frequency of 5 pixels, also the corresponding gray level profiles through the center of the filter. As we can see, BLPF of order 1 has no ringing. Order of 2 has mild ringing. So, this method is more appropriate for image smoothing than the ideal lowpass filter. Ringing in the BLPF becomes significant for higher order.

Example 3 : **Butterworth lowpass filtering :**

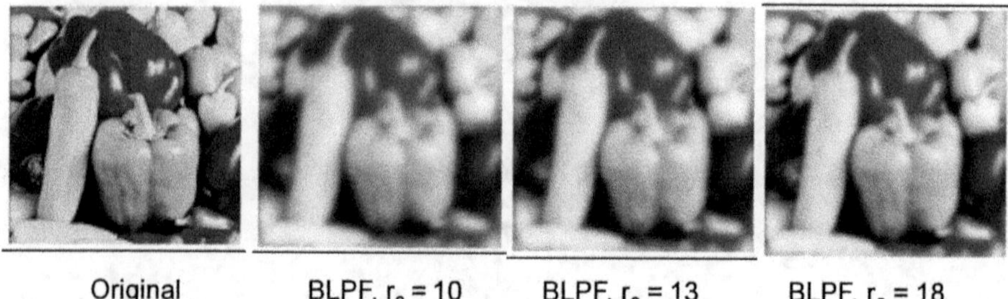

Original   BLPF, $r_0 = 10$ BLPF, $r_0 = 13$ BLPF, $r_0 = 18$

2.8.3.3 Gaussian lowpass filter

Gaussian filters are important in many signal processing, image processing and communication applications. These filters are characterized by narrow bandwidths, sharp cutoffs, and low overshoots. A key feature of Gaussian filters is that the Fourier transform of a Gaussian is also a Gaussian, so the filter has the same response shape in both the spatial and frequency domains.

The form of a Gaussian lowpass filter in two-dimensions is given by

$$H(u, n) = e^{-D2(u, v)/2\sigma 2} \tag{3.3.1}$$

Where $D(u, n)$ is the distance from the origin in the frequency plane as defined in Equation 3.1.1. The parameter σ measures the spread or dispersion of the Gaussian curve see Figure 2.36. Larger the value of σ, larger the cutoff frequency and milder the filtering is. See example at the end of this section.

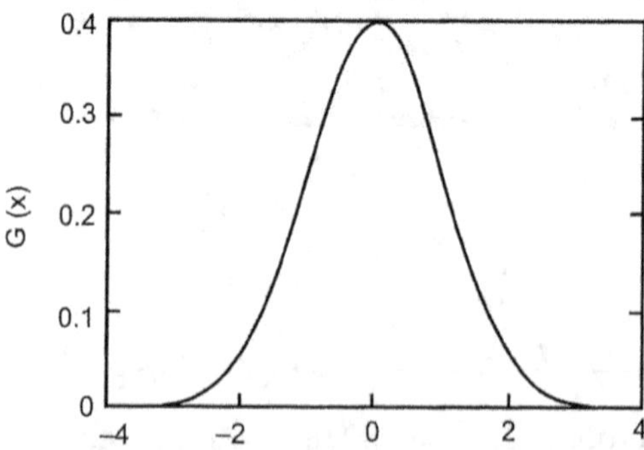

Fig. 2.36 1-D Gaussian distribution with mean 0 and $\sigma = 1$

When letting $\sigma = r_0$, which leads a more familiar form as previous discussion. So Equation 3.3.1 becomes:

$$H(u, v) = e^{-D^2(u, v)/2r_0^2} \tag{3.3.2}$$

When $D(u, v) = r_0$, the filter is down to 0.607 of its maximum value of 1.

A perspective plot, image display, and radial cross section of a GLPF function are shown in Figure 2.37, 2.38 and 2.39.

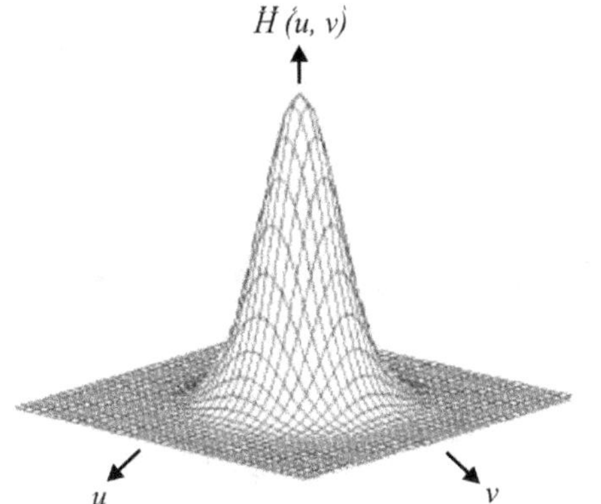

Fig. 2.37 Perspective plot of a GLPF transfer function.

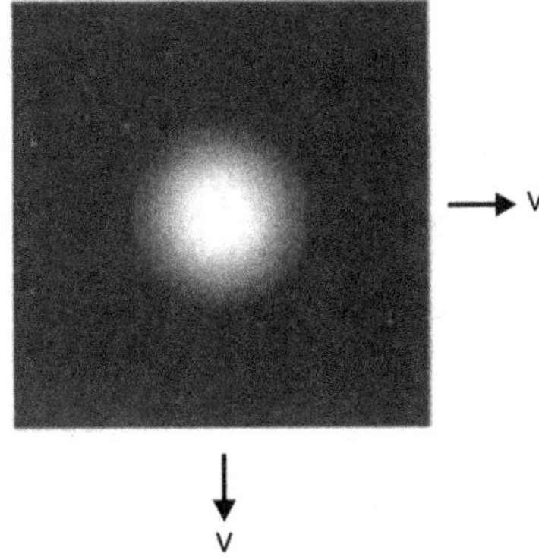

Fig. 2.38 Filter displayed as a image.

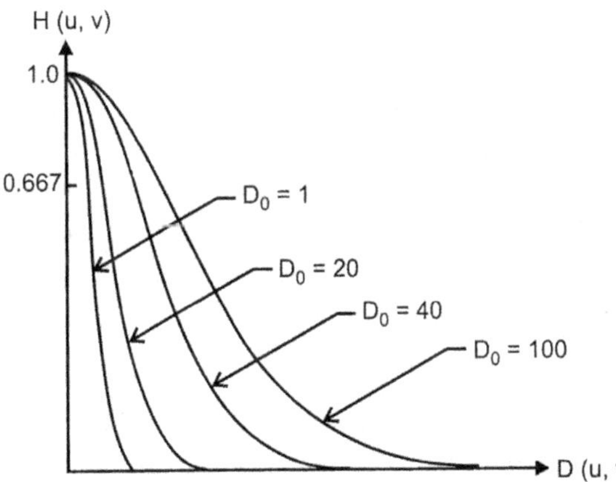

Fig. 2.39 Filter radial cross sections for various values of $D_0 = r_0$.

Example 4 : **Gaussian lowpass filtering :**

 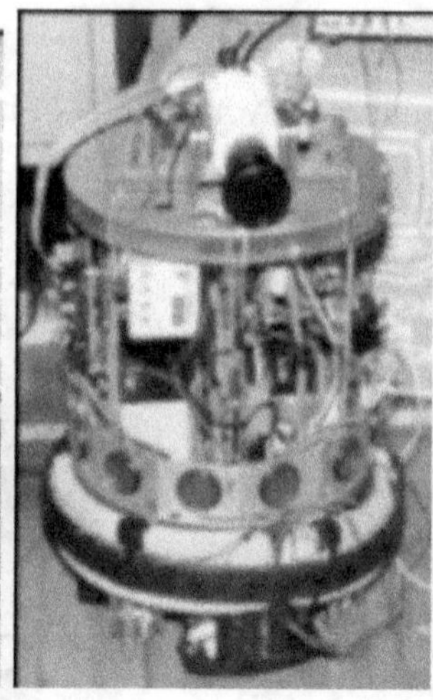 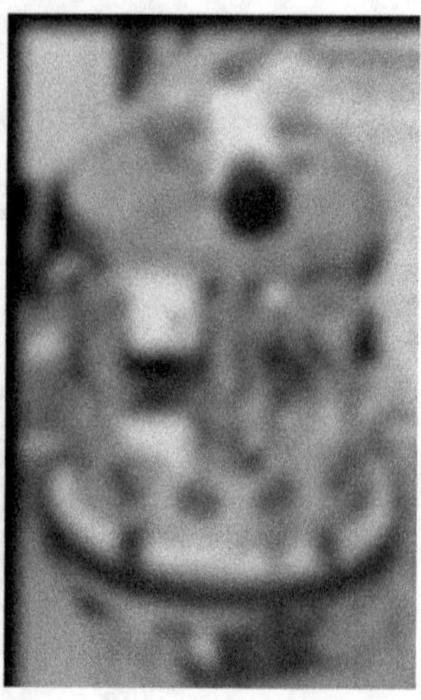

Original   σ = 1.0 (kernel size 5×5)   σ = 4.0 (kernel size 15×15)

As mentioned earlier, the Gaussian has the same shape in the spatial and Fourier domains and therefore does not incur the ringing effect in the spatial domain of the filtered image. This is a advantage over ILPF and BLPF, especially in some situations where any type of artifact is not acceptable, such as medical image. In the case where tight control over transition between low and high frequency needed, Butterworth lowpass filter provides better choice over Gaussian lowpass filter; however, tradeoff is ringing effect.

The Butterworth filter is a commonly used discrete approximation to the Gaussian. Applying this filter in the frequency domain shows a similar result to the Gaussian smoothing in the spatial domain. But the difference is that the computational cost of the spatial filter increases with the standard deviation (e.g the size of the filter kernel), whereas the costs for a frequency filter are independent of the filter function. Hence, the Butterworth filter is a better implementation for wide lowpass filters, while the spatial Gaussian filter is more appropriate for narrow lowpass filters.

2.8.4 Sharpening frequency domain filters

Sharpening filters emphasize the edges, or the differences between adjacent light and dark sample points in an image. A highpass filter yields edge enhancement or edge detection in the spatial domain, because edges contain many high frequencies. Areas of rather constant gray level consist of mainly low frequencies and are therefore suppressed. We obtain a highpass filter function by inverting the corresponding lowpass filter, e.g. an ideal highpass filter blocks all frequencies smaller than r_0 and leaves the others unchanged. The transfer function of lowpass filter and highpass filter can be related as follows:

$$H_{hp}(u, v) = 1 - H_{lp}(u, v) \qquad (4.1.1)$$

Where $H_{hp}(u, n)$ and $H_{lp}(u, n)$ are the transfer function of highpass and lowpass filter respectively.

2.8.4.1 Ideal highpass filter

The transfer function of an ideal highpass filter with the cutoff frequency r_0 which follow Equation 4.1.1

$$H(u, n) = \begin{cases} 0, & \text{if } D(u, n) \leq r_0 \\ 1, & \text{IF } D(U, N) > R_0 \end{cases}$$

Again, r_0 is the cutoff frequency and $D(u, n)$ is define in Equation 3.1.1.

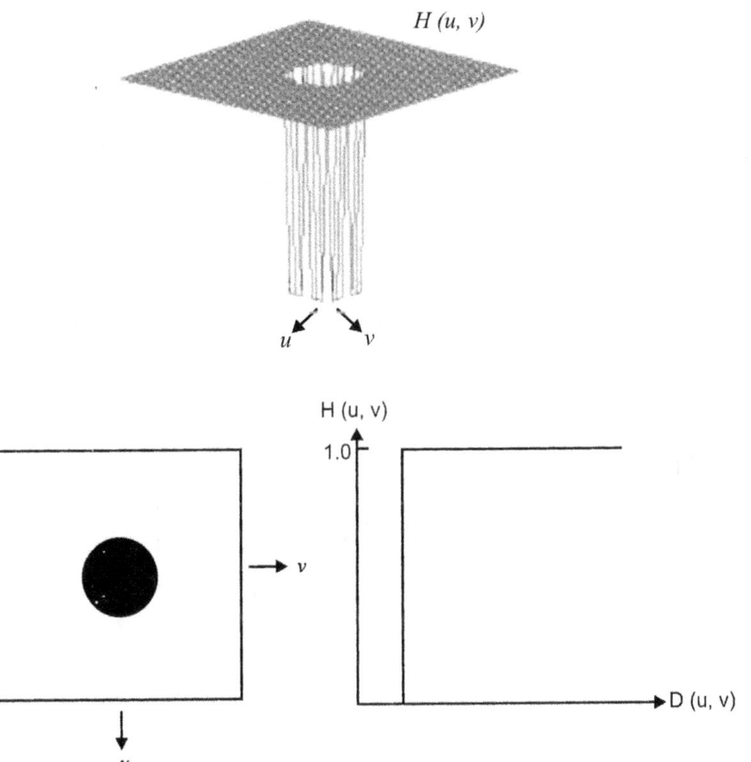

Fig. 2.40 Perspective plot, image representation, and cross section of an IHPF.

Because the transfer functions of lowpass filter and highpass filter are related as shown in Equation 4.1.1, we can expect IHPF to have the same ringing properties as ILPF. This is demonstrated clearly in the example below.

Example 5 : **Ideal highpass filtering :**

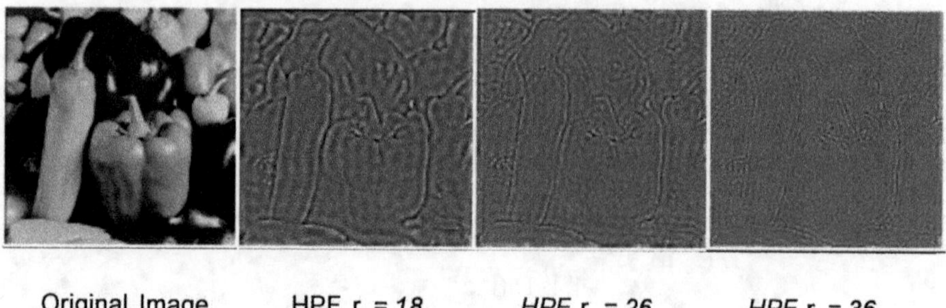

Original Image   HPF, $r_0 = 18$ *HPF, $r_0 = 26$*   *HPF, $r_0 = 36$*

2.8.4.2 Butterworth highpass filter

The transfer function of Butterworth highpass filter (BHPF) of order n and with cutoff frequency r_0 is given by:

$$H(u, v) = \frac{1}{1 + \left[\dfrac{r_0}{D(u,v)}\right]^{2n}} \tag{4.2.1}$$

Where $D(u, n)$ is define in Equation 3.1.1. Again, Equation 4.2.1 also follows Equation 4.1.1 and 4.2.1. Figure 2.41 shows perspective plot, image representation, and cross section of a BHPF.

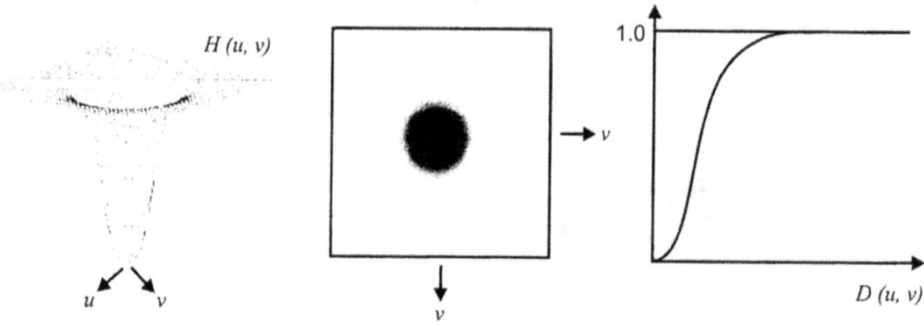

Fig. 2.41 Perspective plot, image representation, and cross section of a BHPF.

Example 6 : **Butterworth highpass filtering with order of 2 :**

Original Image   BHPF, $r_0 = 18$ BHPF, $r_0 = 26$ BHPF, $r_0 = 36$

The frequency response does not have a sharp transition as in the IHPF. As we compare example 5 and 6 with $r_0 = 18$, we can see that BHPF behave smoother and less distortion than IHPF. Therefore, BHPF is more appropriate for image sharpening than the IHPF. Also less ringing is introduced with small value of the order n of BHPF.

Example 7 : **BHPF with different orders but same cutoff frequency :**

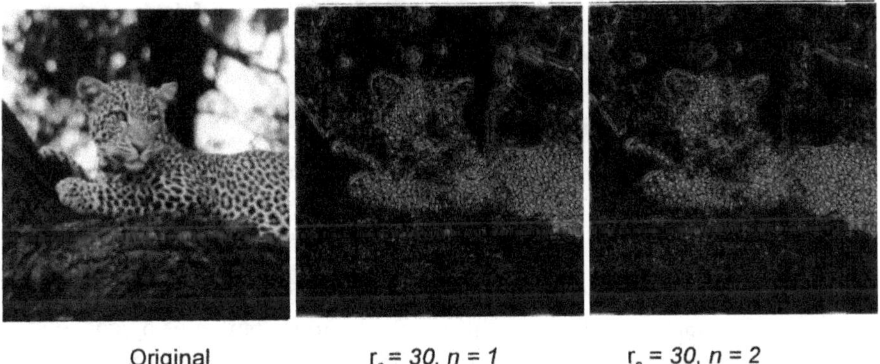

Original $r_0 = 30, n = 1$ $r_0 = 30, n = 2$

2.8.4.3 Gaussian highpass filter

The transfer function of a Gaussian highpass filter (GHPF) with the cutoff frequency r_0 is given by:

$$H(u, v) = 1 - e^{-D2(u, v)/2r02} \tag{4.3.1}$$

Where $D(u, v)$ is define in Equation 3.1.1, and r_0 is the distance from the origin in the frequency plane. Again, Equation 4.3.1 follows Equation 4.1.1.

The parameter σ, measures the spread or dispersion of the Gaussian curve. Larger the value of σ, larger the cutoff frequency and milder the filtering is.

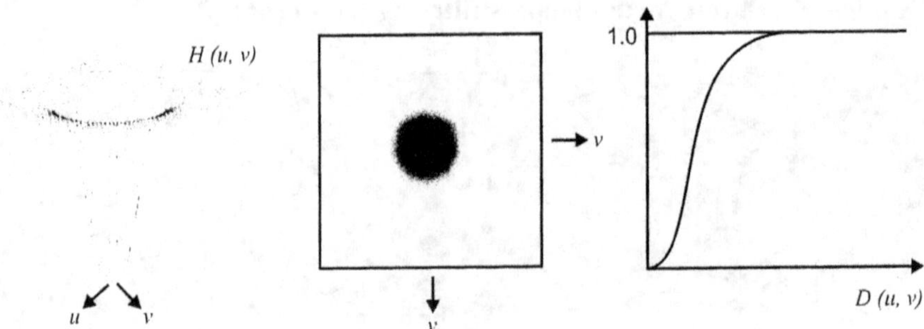

Fig. 2.42 Perspective plot, image representation, and cross section of a GHPF.

***Example 8 :* Results of highpass filtering the image using GHPF of order 2:**

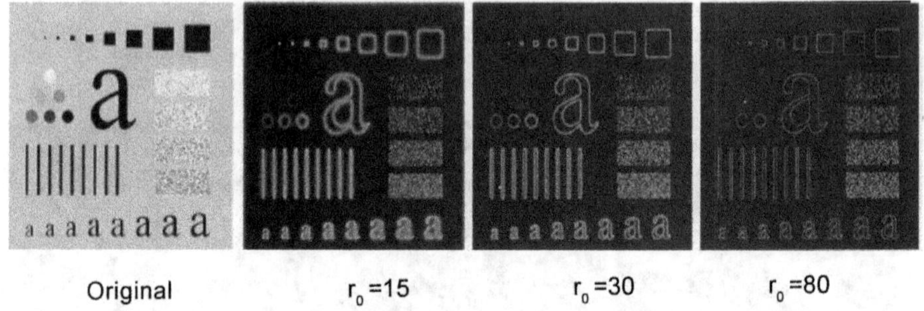

2.8.5 The Laplacian in the frequency Domain

Since edges consist of mainly high frequencies, we can, in theory, detect edges by applying a highpass frequency filter in the Fourier domain or by convolving the image with an appropriate kernel in the spatial domain. In practice, edge detection is performed in the spatial domain, because it is computationally less expensive and often yields better results. As we can see later, we also can detect edges very efficiently using Laplacian filter in the frequency domain.

The Laplacian is a very useful and common tool in image process. This is a second derivative operator designed to measure changes in intensity without being overly sensitive to noise. The function produces a peak at the start of the change in intensity and then at the end of the change. As we know, the mathematical definition of derivative is the rate of change in a continuous function. But in digital image processing, image is a discrete function $f(x, y)$ of integer spatial coordinates. As a result the algorithms will only be seen as approximations to the true spatial derivatives of the original spatial-continuous image. The Laplacian of an image will highlight regions of rapid intensity change and is therefore often used for edge detection (usually called the Laplacian edge detector). Figure 2.43 shows a 3-D plot of Laplacian in the frequency domain.

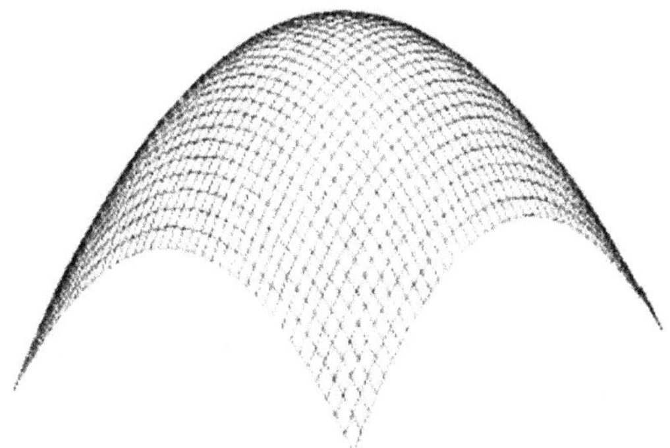

Fig. 2.43 3-D plot of Laplacian in the frequency domain.

The Laplacian is often applied to an image that has first been smoothed with something approximating a Gaussian smoothing filter in order to reduce its sensitivity to noise, and hence the two variants will be described together here. The operator normally takes a single gray level image as input and produces another gray level image as output.

The Laplacian of an image with pixel intensity values f(x, y) *(original image) is given by:*

$$\nabla^2 f(x, y) = \frac{\partial^2 f(x, y)}{\partial x^2} + \frac{\partial^2 f(x, y)}{\partial y^2} \qquad (4.4.1)$$

Since

$$\Im\left[\frac{d^n f(x)}{dx^n}\right] = (ju)^n\, F(u) \qquad (4.4.2)$$

Combine Equation 4.4.1 and 4.4.2

$$\Im\left[\nabla^2 f(x, y)\right] = (ju)^2\, F(u,v) + (jv)^2\, F(u,v)$$

$$= -(u^2 + v^2)\, F(u, v) \qquad (4.4.3)$$

So, from Equation 4.4.3, we know that Laplacian can be implemented in the frequency domain by using the filter:

$$H(u, v) = -(u^2 + v^2).$$

For size of M x N image, the filter function at the center point of the frequency rectangle will be:

$$H(u, v) = -\left[\left(u - \frac{M}{2}\right)^2 + \left(v - \frac{N}{2}\right)^2\right]$$

(4.4.4)

Use Equation 4.4.4 for the filter function, the Laplacian-filtered image in the spatial domain can be obtained by:

$$\nabla^2 f(x, y) = \Im^{-1}[H(u, v)\, F(u, v)]$$

(4.4.5)

So, how we use the Laplacian for image enhancement in the spatial domain? Here are the basic ways where the $g(x, y)$ *is the enhanced image*:

$$g(x, y) = \begin{cases} f(x, y) - \nabla^2 f(x, y) & \text{If the center coefficient of the mask is } \textit{negative} \\ f(x, y) + \nabla^2 f(x, y) & \text{If the center coefficient of the mask is } \textit{positive} \end{cases}$$

In frequency domain, g(x, y) the enhance image is also possible to be obtained by taking the inverse Fourier transform of a single mask (filter)

$$H(u, v) = [1 + [(u - M/2)^2 + (v - N/2)^2]]$$

(4.4.6)

and the original image $f(x, y)$

$$g(x, y) = \Im^{-1}\{[1 + [(u - M/2)^2 + (v - N/2)^2]]\, F(u, v)\}$$

(4.4.7)

Let's see some of the examples of the Laplacian filtered image shown in example 9.

Example 9 : **Example of the Laplacian filtering shows up more detail of in the ring of the Saturn.**

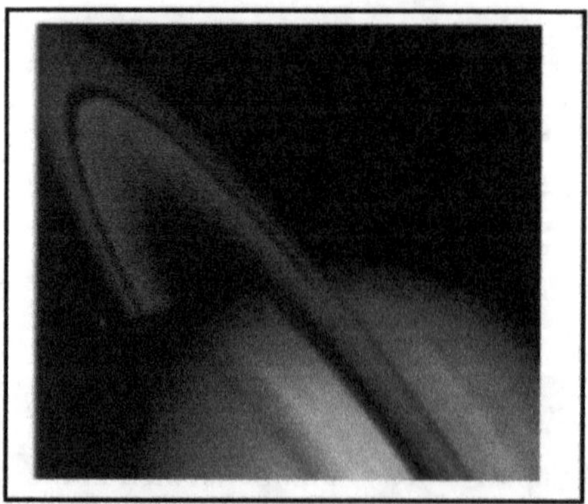 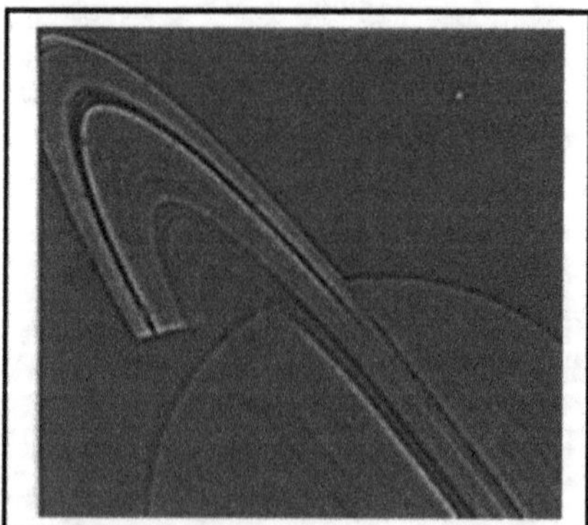

In practice, the result image are identical when compute using only spatial domain techniques or using only frequency domain technique.

2.9 Image Restoration

One of the fundamental problems of signal processing is the restoration of the signal. The deterioration may originate due to passing through a distorting or noisy system. The ultimate goal of restoration techniques is to reconstruct the acquired signal to recover the original signal. It's an objective process which tries to recover the original signal from its measured deteriorated version on the basis of some knowledge of the properties of deterioration. This is oriented towards modeling the degradation and applying the inverse process in order to recover the original image.

No image capture system is perfect. Image is called degraded when presence of redundant information corrupts the useful information content. Causes of degradation can be

- Defects of optical lenses
- Non-linearity of the Electro-optical sensor
- Relative motion between object and camera
- Wrong focus
- Turbulence in atmosphere (remote sensing and astronomy)
- Misalignment
- Vibration during capture, etc.

Hence the objective of image restoration is to reconstruct the original image from its degraded version. To achieve this some knowledge about the degradation function is required. This function can be generated by priori knowledge of the degradation phenomena or it can be extracted from the degraded image itself. Most image restoration methods are based on convolution applied globally to the whole image.

Image restoration techniques can be divided into two groups: Deterministic methods and stochastic methods. Deterministic methods can be applicable to images with little noise and a known degradation function in which case the original image is obtained from the degraded one by a transformation inverse to the degradation. In case of stochastic methods the best restoration is sought according to some stochastic criterion, e.g., a least squares method.

Image restoration techniques can be implemented in spatial and frequency domains. Spatial domain techniques are applicable when major degradation is due to additive noise. While in case of degradation due to image blur are implemented in frequency domain.

Starting with a brief review of the model of deterioration, we would be discussing the inverse filtering and Weiner filtering techniques to restore the signal.

2.9.1 Model of Image Degradation/Restoration

A realistic model in many practically important cases is the combination of distortion by a linear time-invariant system and interference, by additive noise, as shown in the Fig. 2.44.

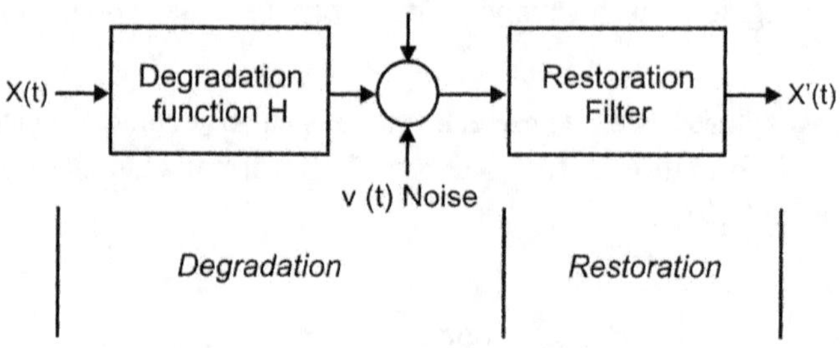

Fig. 2.44 Degradation model.

The model has the form

$$y(t) = \int_{-\infty}^{\infty} h(t-\tau)x(\tau)\, d\tau + v(\tau),$$

where h(t) is the impulse response of the distorting system, x(t) the original signal and v(t) a realization of the noise process. This for discrete process would be:

$$y_n = \sum_{i=0}^{\infty} h_i\, x_{n-i} + v_n$$

The corresponding model in frequency domain would be:

$$Y(s) = H(s)\, X(s) + N(s) \text{ or } Y(\omega) = G(\omega)\, X(\omega) + N(\omega),$$

where $\qquad Y(\omega) = Y(s)\,|\,s = j\omega,\ G(\omega) = H\,(j\omega).$

Given Y(s), some knowledge about the degradation function H and some knowledge about N(s), the objective of the restoration process is to obtain an estimate X(s) of the original image such that the estimate is as close to the original as possible.

The relationship between the degree of signal distortion owing to passing the linear system and to noise interference is very different in practical tasks. If linear distortion prevails, the restoration problem is called deconvolution, whereas if the noise prevails then the restoration aims at increasing the signal-to-noise ratio (SNR). The requirements of removing both are usually conflicting because of the character of common distorting systems.

Lets look at Inverse Filtering followed by Weiner filtering:

2.9.2 Inverse Filtering

This technique is used if the degradation model H(s) is known and the noise level is low. The transfer function of such a filter is given by the inverse of the transfer function of the distorting system.

$$M(\omega) = 1/G(\omega),$$

So the Original image would be

$$X'(\omega) = 1/G(\omega) \{G(\omega) X(\omega) + N(\omega)\} = X(\omega) + N(\omega) / G(\omega)$$

If the distorting system is purely recursive, of the order m, its transfer function is:

$$H(z) = 1/\{\sum_{i=0}^{m} a_i \ z^{-i}\} ; a_0 = 1$$

and its poles must lie inside the unit circle if the distorting system is stable. In such a case, the restoration filter is of an FIR type with all zeros inside the unit circle, with transfer function

$$M(z) = \sum_{i=0}^{m} a_i \ z^{-i}$$

In the absence of noise the term $N(\omega) / G(\omega)$ reduces to zero which gives $X'(\omega) = X(\omega)$. But in presence of noise the output of the exact inverse filter suffers from error due to the second term in the equation. The magnitude of the error is dependent on the noise level at the given frequency and on the relevant value of the frequency response of the distorting system. The second term increases without limits for small values of $G(\omega)$. The restoration of signals distorted by the channels or systems with zero or very small values in the frequency response is therefore very difficult, because even an imperceptible noise is strongly amplified in frequency bands where $G(\omega)$ is zero. One approach to solve this problem is to limit the filter frequencies to values near the origin.

Let's explore two methods of inverse filtering:

1. Thresholding:

2. Iterative Procedure.

Thresholding :

Since in the absence of noise, the blurred image can be modeled as $Y(s) = X(s) L(s)$, where $L(s)$ is some kind of low pass filter, the original image can be reconstructed by using some kind of high pass filter $H(s)$ as:

$$X(s) = Y(s) H(s).$$

We can get $H(s)$ by either taking the DFT of L or by inverting all the elements of L. If L has values very close to zero, then inverting it would give us very high values. Thus to avoid this we will need to set some sort of a threshold on the inverted element. Thus the filter can be modeled as:

$$H(s) = 1/L(s) \qquad \text{if } 1/L(s) < \lambda$$

$$= \lambda \qquad\qquad \text{else}$$

The higher we set λ, the closer it is to a full inverse filter.

Implementation and Results :

Since Matlab does not deal well with infinity, threshold L before taking the inverse. So the following is done:

$$L(s) = L(s) \quad \text{if } L(s) > n$$

$$= n \qquad \text{else}$$

where $n = 1/\lambda$ and is set arbitrarily close to zero for noiseless cases.

Because an inverse filter is a high pass filter, it does not perform well in the presence of noise. There is a definite tradeoff between de-blurring and de-noising.

Iterative Procedure :

The idea behind the iterative procedure is to make some initial guess of X based on Y and to update that guess after every iteration. The procedure is:

$$X'_0(s) = \lambda Y(s)$$

$$X'_{k+1}(s) = X'_k(s) + \lambda \{Y(s) - X'_k(s) * L(s)\}$$

where X'_0 is an initial guess based on Y. If our X'_k is a good guess, eventually X'_k convolved with L will be close to Y. When that happens the second term in the X'_{k+1} equation will disappear and X'_k and X'_{k+1} will converge. λ is our convergence factor and it lets us determine how fast X'_k and X'_{k+1} converge.

Solving recursively for X'_k, we get

$$X'_k(s) = Y(s) / L(s) \{1 - [1 - \lambda L(s)]^{k+1}\}$$

So if $(1 - \lambda L(s))^{k+1}$ goes to zero as k goes to infinity, we would get the result as obtained by the inverse filter. In general, this method will not give the exact same results as inverse filtering, but can be less sensitive to noise in some cases.

Implementation and Results :

The first thing we have to do is pick a λ. λ must satisfy the following:

$$| 1 - \lambda L(s) | < 1$$

and thus will be a positive integer in the range of 0 to 1. The bigger λ is, the faster X'_k and X'_{k+1} will converge. However, picking too large a λ may also make X'_k and X'_{k+1} diverge instead of converge. Imagine that we're walking along a path and the end of the path is a cliff. λ is the size of of the steps we take. We want to go to the edge of the path as fast as possible without falling off. Taking large steps will ensure that we will get there fast but we'd probably first. Taking small will ensure that we get there without falling off but it could take an infinite amount of time. So the compromise would be to take big steps at the start and decrease our step size as we get close to our destination.

2.9.3 Weiner Filtering

Weiner filtering unlike Inverse filtering takes into account the noise and degradation function while restoring the image. The method is formulated considering original signal, observed signal and the noise as stochastic processes. The main objective of the process is to find an estimate X' of the uncorrupted image X such that the mean square error between them is minimal. The error is given by: $e^2 = E\{(X - X')^2\}$, where $E\{.\}$ is the expected value of the argument. The task is to find a universal approach which minimizes the mean quadratic error in every time instant and on average for all possible realizations.

The assumptions made for the process are:

1. Noise and image are uncorrelated
2. Noise or image has zero mean.
3. Gray levels in the estimate are a linear function of the levels in the degraded image.

The estimation will be done in a suboptimal way, by linear superposition operator

$$X'_w(t) = \int_{-\infty}^{\infty} m(t, \tau)\, y_w(\tau)\, d\tau,$$

Where the indices indicate which of the functions are realizations of stochastic processes controlled by an associated stochastic experiment w. The function $m(t, \tau)$ is a time-variable weighting function which is to be determined based on the optimization criterion of reducing the mean square error. Our aim is to derive a time-invariant system; therefore, we shall introduce the first limiting condition that the concerned stochastic processes are stationary. If the characteristics of the processes used for filter design do not change in time, then the filter need not be time variant. So the integral will simplify into a convolution:

$$X'_w(t) = \int_{-\infty}^{\infty} m(t-\tau) \, y_w(t) \, d\tau,$$

The restoration system is thus a linear time-invariant filter with the impulse response m(t), which is to be determined.

According to the above equation, the values of $X'_w(t)$ are estimated linearly based on values of y(s), and considering the orthogonality principle, we see that it must be valid for all t and s.

$$E_w \{(x_w(t) - x'_w(t)) \, y_w(s)\} = 0$$

Simplifying the above two equations, we get,

$$-\int_{-\infty}^{\infty} m(t-\tau) \, E_w \{Y_w(\tau) \, y_w(s)\} \, d\tau + E_w \{x_w(t) \, y(s)\} = 0$$

The first mean value can be recognized as the autocorrelation function $R_{yy}(\tau, s)$ and the second one the crosscorrelation function $R_{xy}(t, s)$. Therefore we have,

$$\int_{-\infty}^{\infty} m(t-\tau) \, R_{yy}(\tau - s)d = R_{xy}(t - s)$$

and introducing t' = τ − s and t" = t − s, we obtain

$$\int_{-\infty}^{\infty} m(t"-t') \, R_{yy}(t') \, dt' = R_{xy}(t")$$

The Left Hand side of (17) can be transformed into frequency domain as:

$$M(\omega) \, S_{yy}(\omega) = S_{xy}(\omega) \text{ or } M(\omega) = S_{xy}(\omega) / S_{yy}(\omega) \qquad (4.4.8)$$

Where $M(\omega)$ is the frequency response of the restoration filter, $S_{yy}(\omega) = F\{R_{yy}(t)\}$ is the power spectrum of the deteriorated signals and $S_{xy}(\omega) = F\{R_{xy}(t)\}$ is the cross-spectrum betwteen original and observed signals. Eqn. (4.4.8) enables designing Weiner filter in its most general form.

The autocorrelation function $R_{yy}(t)$ or the power spectrum $S_{yy}(\omega)$ is easy to measure whereas the crosscorrelation function $R_{xy}(t)$ or the cross-spectrum

$S_{xy}(\omega)$ is very difficult to measure. Hence we shall try to find a more practically suitable filter which would allow us to determine the filter characteristics on the basis of more easily available measurements.

The Cross Correlation function $R_{xy}(t - s)$ can be represented as:

$$R_{xy}(t - s) = \int_{-\infty}^{\infty} h(s - \tau)\, E\{x_w(t)\, x_w(\tau)\}\, d\tau, \qquad (4.4.9)$$

Which can be further written as :

$$Rxy(t') = \int_{-\infty}^{\infty} h(\tau' - t')\, R_{xx}(\tau')\, d\tau' \qquad (4.4.10)$$

By transforming (20) we get,

$$S_{xy}(\omega) = H^*(\omega)\, S_{xx}(\omega) \qquad (4.4.11)$$

The power spectrum of the input signal y(t) is given by the sum of the original-signal power spectrum and power spectrum of noise. Thus,

$$S_{yy}(\omega) = |H(\omega)|^2\, S_{xx}(\omega) + S_{vv}(\omega) \qquad (4.4.12)$$

By substituting (4.4.11) and (4.4.12) in (4.4.9) we get,

$$M(\omega) = \{H^*(\omega)\, S_{xx}(\omega)\} \,/\, \{|H(\omega)|^2 + (S_{xx}(\omega)\,/\,S_{vv}(\omega))\}$$

$$= \{1\,/\,H(\omega)\} * \{|H(\omega)|^2 + \{|H(\omega)|^2 + (S_{vv}(\omega)\,/\,S_{xx}(\omega))\}\}$$

where $|H(\omega)|^2 \,/\, \{|H(\omega)|^2 + (S_{vv}(\omega)\,/\,S_{xx}(\omega))\}$ is called the correction factor.

The product can be interpreted as characterizing a cascade connection of two subsystems: the first one is obviously a plain inverse filter and the other subsystem is so-called Weiner correction factor, the effect of which we shall analyse in detail.

In the absence of noise the second term is 1 and hence the filter corresponds to a inverse filter. If the noise is not negligible, transfer of the filter will be reduced in some bands, which can have two causes. On one hand, the value of the correction factor will obviously decrease markedly at frequencies where the transfer of the distorting system is approaching zero and in the same range of frequencies the power level of the noise spectrum is non zero. On the other hand, the correction factor will also drop when the power noise-to-signal ratio as expressed by the second term of the denominator is high.

The correction factor of the Wiener filter is related to the low frequency aspect of the Wiener filter. The Wiener filter behaves as a bandpass filter, where the highpass filter is due to the inverse filter and the lowpass filter to the parameter correction factor.

Although this filter looks theoretically feasible, practically its very difficult to get the power spectrum of the original signal. Thus the filter can be modified using the above equations to give,

$$M(\omega) = \{1 / H(\omega)\} * \{(S_{yy}(\omega) - S_{vv}(\omega)) / S_{yy}(\omega)\}$$

2.9.4 Noise Models

For most practical cases noise is considered white (zero mean) and uncorrelated (independent of the spatial coordinates).The noise is generally described as its probability density function (PDF) which indicates the statistical distribution of the noise in the grey level range. Following are a few examples of noise PDF's found in image processing:

Gaussian Noise provides a good model of noise in many imaging systems. Its probability density function (pdf) for Gaussian random variable 'n' with zero mean is given by:

$$P_n(n) = \frac{1}{\sqrt{\pi\sigma^2}} e^{-\frac{z^2}{\sigma^2}}$$

where z = intensity levels and σ is the standard deviation.

The frequency domain counterpart of a spatial domain Gaussian model is also Gaussian distribution.Hence it is mathematically easy to use and thus is frequently used for noise modelling. To estimate the mean of a stationary Gaussian random variable, one can't do any better than the linear average. This makes Gaussian noise a worst-case scenario for nonlinear image restoration filters.

Uniform Noise has a pdf given by

$$p(z) = 1/(b-a) \text{ if } a \leq z \leq b = 0 \text{ other wise}$$

The mean of the density function is given by

$$\mu = (a+b)/2$$

and variance is given by

$$\sigma^2 = (b-a)^2/12$$

Uniform noise is not often encountered in real-world imaging systems, but provides a useful comparison with Gaussian noise. The linear average is a comparatively poor estimator for the mean of a uniform distribution. This implies that nonlinear filters should be better at removing uniform noise than Gaussian noise.

2.10 Questions

1. Given an image of size 3×3 as shown below:

$$\begin{bmatrix} 1 & 0 & 3 \\ 4 & 2 & 1 \\ 0 & 2 & 5 \end{bmatrix}$$

   (a) Find the output image using power-law transformation function when $C = 2$ and g (gamma) $= 1$.

   (b) Draw the histogram of the original and transformed (output) images.

2. (a) What is the general form of gray-level transformation function. Explain the terms involved in it?

   (b) Explain how the

      (i) Contrast stretching and

      (ii) Thresholding functions are implemented.

3. (a) What are the steps involved in the design of median filter.

   (b) List the circumstances in which the median filters are most suitable.

   (c) Distinguish the averaging and median filters.

4. (a) How the direction and magnitude at an identified location are computed in an image.

   (b) Derive the Prewitt operators and show the corresponding 3×3 spatial masks.

5. (a) Prove or disprove that the histogram equalization is an invertible function.

   (b) What would be the effect on the histogram if we set to zero the higher order bits.

6. (a) Suppose the convolution of two finite digital functions is to be performed, determine how many elementary actions (additions and multiplications) are required for the given sized domains.How many operations are required if convolution theorem is exploited.

   (b) Explain the aliasing effect in terms of Fourier frequency overlaps.

7. Two images $f(x,y)$ and $g(x,y)$ have histograms hf and hg. Give the condition under which you can determine the histogram of

      (a) $f(x,y) + g(x,y)$ (b) $f(x,y) - g(x,y)$

      (c) $f(x,y) * g(x,y)$ (d) $f(x,y) \div g(x,y)$

   interms of hf ad hg. Explain how to obtain histogram in each case.

8. (a) State and explain convolution theorem on images.

    (b) Discuss various factors that influence the brightness of a pixel in an image.

9. (a) What is the objective of splitting in image processing.

    (b) Device an approach for the automatic selection of grey level for splitting.

10. (a) State and prove the Laplacian and convolution properties of 2-D DFT.

    (b) Find the kernel coefficients for N = 8 of Hardmard tranform.

11. (a) Prove that histogram equalization gives uniform histogram for continuous image.

    (b) Explain how image averaging is used to reduce noise due to sensors?

12. (a) Discuss the use of Laplacian mask in image enhancement.

    (b) Give the differences between gray level and color image processing.

13. Explain the following filters how they are used for Image restoration?

    (a) Inverse filter

    (b) Geometric Mean filter

    (c) Adaptive filter

    (d) Band pass filter.

14. (a) Give expression, properties and applications of discrete cosine transform.

    (b) What are the properties and applications of Hotelling transform.

15. (a) Explain the various sharpening spatial filters.

    (b) What is image padding? Explain why it is needed in image processing?

16. What is the principle of constrained least square filter? Explain how it is used for image on and compare it with wiener filter.

17. (a) Find the kernel coefficients for N=8 of walsh transform.

    (b) Prove that FFT can perform with less number of computations compared to DFT.

18. (a) Explain why the discrete histogram equalization technique does not in general give a flat histogram.

    (b) Explain how local statistics are used to enhance the image.

19. (a) What is Restoration in image processing? Draw and explain the model of Restoration process.

    (b) Explain how a wiener filter is used for image restoration?

20. (a) Explain the basic principle of KL Transform and gives its applications?

    (b) Show that the DFT of convolution of two functions is the product of their DFTS.

21. (a) Explain the method which is used to generate a processed image has a specified histogram.

    (b) Explain how logical operations are used to enhance the image.

22. (a) Explain how a high-boost filter is used in image enhancement.

    (b) Explain the smoothing filters in frequency domain.

23. (a) Explain the methods to estimate the degraded function in image restoration.

    (b) Compare wiener and constrained least squares filter in image restoration.

24. Give a note about the techniques followed in grey-level transformations.

25. Discuss the limiting effect of repeatedly applying a 3×3 low pass filter to a digital image. Ignore the border effects.

26. (a) What is the expression for performing convolution of images. Explain the terms involved in it.

    (b) If the template T is defined as

$$\begin{bmatrix} 1 & 0 \\ 0 & 1 \end{bmatrix}$$

    and the image I is defined as

$$\begin{bmatrix} 1 & 1 & 3 & 3 \\ 1 & 1 & 4 & 4 \\ 2 & 1 & 3 & 3 \\ 1 & 1 & 1 & 4 \end{bmatrix}$$

    find the resulting convolved image T * I.

27. Write short notes on the following :

    (a) Global thresholding   (b) Adaptive thresholding.

28. (a) What are the transformation functions and properties of the following gray level transformations:

    (i) Contrast stretching   (ii) thresholding

    (iii) log transformations   (iv) power law transformations.

29. (a) Obtain the Hadamand transform kernel for N=8.

    (b) Explain the applications of Hotelling transform.

30. (a) What are circulant and block circulant matrices? What is the effect of diagonalization on the degradation model? Explain.

   (b) Derive an expression for restored image using wiener filtering.

31. What are the fundamental steps in image processing? Explain with a block diagram.

32. (a) Show that 1-D discrete Fourier transform and its inverse transform are periodic functions.

   (b) Develop an FFT algorithm using successive doubling method.

33. (a) What are isopreference curves? What is their significance? Explain with an example.

   (b) Explain the effect of reducing spatial resolution and gray level quantization.

34. (a) State and prove any two properties of 2-D fourier transform.

   (b) Obtain 1-D DCT Kernel coefficients for N=8.

35. (a) State and prove the following properties 2-D Fourier Transform

   (i) Seperability   (ii) Translation

   (b) Derive the kernal coefficients for 1-D walsh Transform.

36. (a) Prove or disprove that the histogram equalization is an invertible function.

   (b) What would be the effect on the histogram if we set to zero the higher order bits.

37. (a) Suppose the convolution of two finite digital functions is to be performed, determine how many elementary operations (additions and multiplications) are required for the given sized domains. How many operations are required if convolution theorem is exploted.

   (b) Explain the aliasing effect in terms of Fourier frequency overlaps.

38. (a) What is the objective of splitting in image processing.

   (b) Device an approach for the automatic selection of grey level for splitting.

39. (a) How the second derivative is computed using gray-values of an image.

   (b) What are the Sobel's operations for a 3×3 region of an image.

40. (a) Find the kernel coefficient for $N = 8$ of walsh transform.

   (b) Explain the successing doubling method of finding FFT for $N = 8$.

41. (a) How do you find power density spectrum and energy density spectrum of an image ? Explain.

   (b) Prove the given properties of DFT.

   (i) Laplacian   (ii) Translation

42. Explain about various smoothing and sharpening methods in spatial domain.

43. (a) Explain the effect of diagonalization on the degradation model.

   (b) Explain the principle of inverse filtering.

44. Explain various steps involved in digital image processing.

45. (a) How do you find power density spectrum and energy density spectrum of an image ? Explain.

   (b) Derive the Kernel coefficients for N = 8 of DCT.

46. The array (A) represents a small grayscale image. Compute the image that result when the image in convolved with a given mask (M)

$$A = \begin{bmatrix} 20 & 20 & 20 & 10 & 10 & 10 & 10 & 10 & 10 \\ 20 & 20 & 20 & 20 & 20 & 20 & 20 & 20 & 10 \\ 20 & 20 & 20 & 10 & 10 & 10 & 10 & 20 & 10 \\ 20 & 20 & 10 & 10 & 10 & 10 & 10 & 20 & 10 \\ 20 & 10 & 10 & 10 & 10 & 10 & 10 & 20 & 10 \\ 10 & 10 & 10 & 10 & 20 & 10 & 10 & 20 & 10 \\ 10 & 10 & 10 & 10 & 10 & 10 & 10 & 10 & 10 \\ 20 & 10 & 20 & 20 & 10 & 10 & 10 & 20 & 20 \\ 20 & 10 & 10 & 20 & 10 & 10 & 20 & 10 & 20 \end{bmatrix} \quad M = \begin{bmatrix} -1 & 2 & -1 \\ -1 & 2 & -1 \\ -1 & 2 & -1 \end{bmatrix}$$

47. (a) Enumerate the differences between image enhancement and image restoration.

   (b) Explain the principle of inverse filtering.

48. (a) Show that the DFT and its inverse. DFT are periodic functions. (Assume 1-D function).

   (b) Obtain the slant transforms matix for N = 8.

49. (a) Explain the basic principle of KL Transforms. What are its applications.

   (b) Prove that walsh transforms of f(x) and inverse walsh transforms constitute a transforms pair.

50. Explain about various smoothing and sharpening methods in spatial domain.

51. (a) Explain the properties of discrete Foruier transforms of 2-D signal.

   (b) Obtain the Haar transform matrix for N = 8.

52. (a) Find the Kernel coefficient for N = 8 of hadamard transform.

   (b) Show that the F.T of convolution of two functions is the product of their Fourier transforms.

53. Explain about smoothing and sharpening methods in frequency domain.

54. (a) Compare histogram equalization and specification methods.

    (b) Show that histogram equalization method gives uniform histogram for continuous images.

55. (a) Enumerate the differences between image enhancement and image restorations methods.

    (b) Explain the principle of Wiener filtering method.

56. (a) Show that a high-pass filtered image can be obtained in the spatial domain as:

    High pass = original - low pass

    Assume 3×3 filters.

    (b) Discuss the properties of Butterworth filter.

CHAPTER 3

Segmentation and Edge Detection

3.1 Introduction

The central aim of segmentation is to distinguish objects from their background. Segmentation subdivides an image into its respective regions or objects. Segmentation of complex images is one of the most difficult tasks in image processing. Segmentation accuracy determines the eventual success or failure of computerized image analysis procedures. For intensity images (i.e., gray scale images) four popular approaches are; region-oriented techniques, edge-based methods, connectivity-preserving relaxation methods and threshold techniques.

A region-oriented method usually proceeds as follows: the image is partitioned into connected regions by grouping neighboring pixels of similar intensity levels. Adjacent regions are then merged under some criterion involving homogeneity or sharpness of region boundaries. Overstringent criteria create fragmentation, lenient ones overlook blurred boundaries and over merge.

Edge-based methods center around contour detection: their weakness in connecting together broken contour lines make them prone to failure in the presence of blurring. Hybrid techniques using a mix of the methods above are also popular.

Threshold techniques, which make decisions based on local pixel information, are effective when the intensity levels of the objects fall squarely outside the range of levels in the background. Because spatial information is ignored, however, blurred region boundaries can create problems.

3.2   Region Operations

Discovering regions can be a very simple exercise, as illustrated in 3.2.1. However, more often than not, regions are required that cover a substantial area of the scene rather than a small group of pixels [52].

3.2.1 Crude Edge Detection

USE. To reconsider an image as a set of regions.

OPERATION. There is no operation involved here. The regions are simply identified as containing pixels of the same gray level, the boundaries of the regions (contours) are at the cracks between the pixels rather than at pixel positions [40].

Such a region detection may give far many regions to be useful (unless the number of gray levels is relatively small). So a simple approach is to group pixels into ranges of near values (quantizing or bunching). These ranges can be considered on the image histogram in order to identify good bunching for region purposes results in a merging of regions based on overall gray-level statistics rather than on gray levels of pixels that are spatially near one another.

3.2.2 Region Merging

It is often useful to do the rough gray-level split and then to perform some techniques on the cracks between the regions – not to enhance edges but to identify when whole regions are worth combining – thus reducing the number of regions from the crude region detection above.

USE. Reduce number of regions, combining fragmented regions, determining which regions are really part of the same area.

OPERATION. Let 'S' be crack difference, i.e. the absolute difference in gray levels between two adjacent (above, below, left, right) pixels. Then give the threshold value 'T', we can identify, for each crack

$$w = \begin{cases} 1, & if \ \ s < T \\ 0, & otherwise \end{cases}$$

i.e. 'w' is 1 if the crack is below the threshold (suggesting that the regions are likely to be the same), or 0 if it is above the threshold.

Now measure the full length of the boundary of each of the region that meet at the crack. These will be b_1 and b_2 respectively. Sum the w values that are along the length of the crack between the regions and calculate:

$$\frac{\sum w}{min(b_1, b_2)}$$

If this is greater than a further threshold, deduce that the two regions should be joined [36]. Effectively this is taking the number of cracks that suggest that the regions should be merged and divided by the smallest region boundary. Of course a particularly irregular shape may have a very long region boundary with a small area. In that case it may be preferable to measure areas (count how many pixels there are in them).

Measuring both boundaries is better than dividing by the boundary length between two regions as it takes into account the size of the regions involved [50]. If one region is very small, then it will be added to a larger region, whereas if both regions are large, then the evidence for combining them has to be much stronger.

3.2.3 Region Splitting

Just as it is possible to start from many regions and merge them into fewer, large regions. It is also possible to consider the image as one region and split it into more and more regions [46]. One way of doing this is to examine the gray level histograms. If the image is in color, better results can be obtained by the examination of the three color value histograms.

USE. Subdivide sensibly an image or part of an image into regions of similar type.

OPERATION. Identify significant peaks in the gray-level histogram and look in the valleys between the peaks for possible threshold values. Some peaks will be more substantial than others: find splits between the "best" peaks first.

Regions are identified as containing gray-levels between the thresholds. With color images, there are three histograms to choose from. The algorithm halts when no peak is significant.

LIMITATION. This technique relies on the overall histogram giving good guidance as to sensible regions. If the image is a chessboard, then the region splitting works nicely. If the image is of 16 chessboard well spaced apart on a white background sheet, then instead of identifying 17 regions, one for each chessboard and one for the background, it identifies 16 x 32 black squares, which is probably not what we wanted.

3.3 Basic Edge Detection

The edges of an image hold much information in that image. The edges tell where objects are, their shape and size, and something about their texture [51]. An edge is where the intensity of an image moves from a low value to a high value or vice versa.

There are numerous applications for edge detection, which is often used for various special effects. Digital artists use it to create dazzling image outlines. The output of an edge detector can be added back to an original image to enhance the edges.

Edge detection is often the first step in image segmentation. Image segmentation, a field of image analysis, is used to group pixels into regions to determine an image's composition.

A common example of image segmentation is the "magic wand" tool in photo editing software. This tool allows the user to select a pixel in an image. The software then draws a border around the pixels of similar value. The user may select a pixel in a sky region and the magic wand would draw a border around the complete sky region in the image. The user may then edit the color of the sky without worrying about altering the color of the mountains or whatever else may be in the image.

Edge detection is also used in image registration. Image registration aligns two images that may have been acquired at separate times or from different sensors.

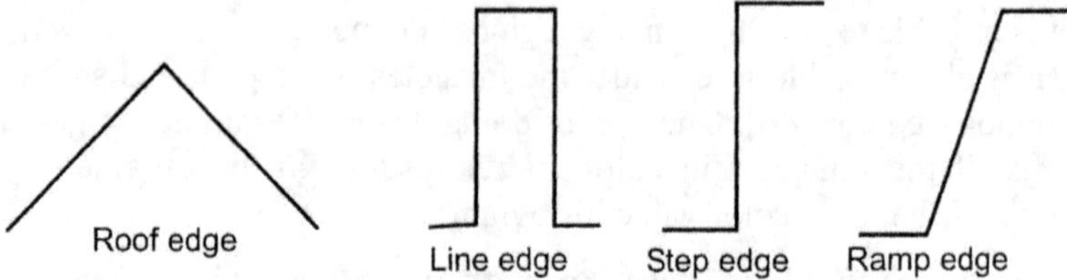

Fig. 3.1 Different edge profiles [21].

There is an infinite number of edge orientations, widths and shapes (Fig. 3.1). Some edges are straight while others are curved with varying radii. There are many edge detection techniques to go with all these edges, each having its own strengths [20]. Some edge detectors may work well in one application and perform poorly in others. Sometimes it takes experimentation to determine what is the best edge detection technique for an application.

The simplest and quickest edge detectors determine the maximum value from a series of pixel subtractions. The homogeneity operator subtracts each 8 surrounding pixels from the center pixel of a 3×3 window as in Fig. 3.2. The output of the operator is the maximum of the absolute value of each difference.

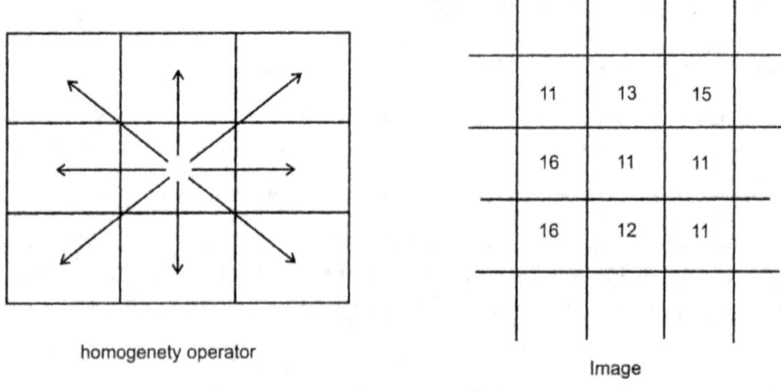

new pixel = maximum{ |11-11|, |11-13|, |11-15|, |11-16|, |11-11|, |11-16|, |11-12|, |11-11| } = 5

Fig. 3.2 How the homogeneity operator works.

Similar to the homogeneity operator is the difference edge detector [5]. It operates more quickly because it requires four subtractions per pixel as opposed to the eight needed by the homogeneity operator. The subtractions are upper left - lower right, middle left - middle right, lower left - upper right, and top middle - bottom middle (Fig. 3.3).

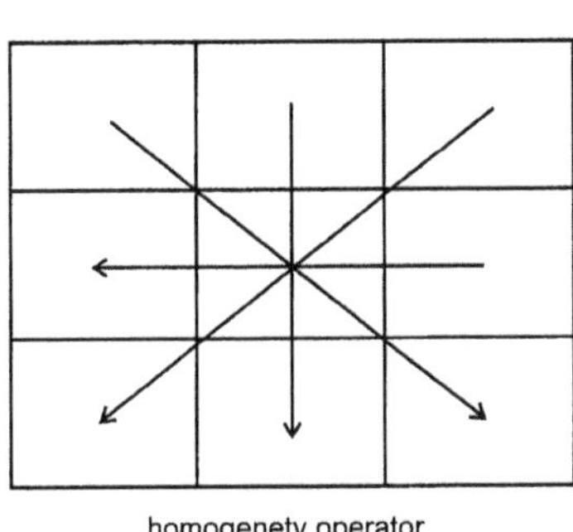

homogenety operator

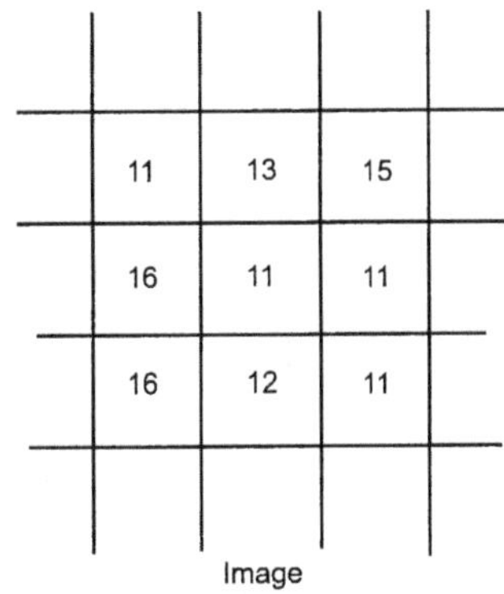

Image

new pixel = maximum { |11-11|, |13-12|, |15-16|, |11-16| } = 5

Fig. 3.3 How the difference operator works.

3.3.1 First Order Derivative for Edge Detection

If we are looking for any horizontal edges it would seem sensible to calculate the difference between one pixel value and the next pixel value, either up or down from the first (called the crack difference), i.e. assuming top left origin

$$H_c = \text{y\_difference } (x, y) = \text{value } (x, y) - \text{value } (x, y + 1)$$

In effect this is equivalent to convolving the image with a 2 x 1 template

$$\begin{matrix} 1 \\ -1 \end{matrix}$$

Likewise

$$H_r = X\_difference(x, y) = value(x, y) - value(x - 1, y)$$

uses the template

$$\begin{matrix} -1 & 1 \end{matrix}$$

H_c and H_r are column and row detectors. Occasionally it is useful to plot both X_difference and Y_difference, combining them to create the gradient magnitude (i.e. the strength of the edge). Combining them by simply adding them could mean two edges canceling each other out (one positive, one negative), so it is better to sum absolute values (ignoring the sign) or sum the squares of them and then, possibly, take the square root of the result [19].

It is also possible to divide the Y_difference by the X_difference and identify a gradient direction (the angle of the edge between the regions)

$$gradient\_direction = \tan^{-1}\left\{\frac{Y\_difference(x, y)}{X\_difference(x, y)}\right\}$$

The amplitude can be determined by computing the sum vector of H_c and H_r

$$H(x, y) = \sqrt{H_r^2(x, y) + H_c^2(x, y)}$$

Sometimes for computational simplicity, the magnitude is computed as

$$H(x, y) = |H_r(x, y)| + |H_c(x, y)|$$

The edge orientation can be found by

$$\theta = \tan^{-1}\frac{H_c(x, y)}{H_r(x, y)}$$

In real image, the lines are rarely so well defined, more often the change between regions is gradual and noisy.

The following image represents a typical read edge. A large template is needed to average at the gradient over a number of pixels, rather than looking at two only.

0	0	0	0	0	0	2	0	3	3
0	0	0	1	0	0	0	2	4	2
0	0	2	0	3	4	3	3	2	3
0	0	1	3	3	4	3	3	3	3
0	1	0	4	3	3	2	4	3	2
0	0	1	2	3	3	4	4	4	3

3.3.2 Sobel Edge Detection

The Sobel operator is more sensitive to diagonal edges than vertical and horizontal edges [15]. The Sobel 3×3 templates are normally given as

X-direction

−1	−2	1
0	0	0
1	2	1

Y-direction

−1	0	1
−2	0	2
−1	0	1

Original image	0	0	0	0	0	0	2	0	3	3
	0	0	0	1	0	0	0	2	4	2
	0	0	2	0	2	4	3	3	2	3
	0	0	1	3	3	4	3	3	3	3
	0	1	0	4	3	3	2	4	3	2
	0	0	1	2	3	3	4	4	4	3

absA + absB	4	6	4	10	14	12	14	4
	6	8	10	20	16	12	6	0
	4	10	14	10	2	4	2	4
	2	12	12	2	2	4	8	8

Threshold at 12	0	0	0	0	1	1	1	1
	2	0	0	1	1	1	0	0
	0	0	1	0	0	0	0	0
	0	1	1	0	0		0	0

3.3.3 Other First Order Operation

The Roberts operator has a smaller effective area than the other mask [6], making it more susceptible to noise.

$$H_r = \begin{bmatrix} 0 & 0 & -1 \\ 0 & 1 & 0 \\ 0 & 0 & 0 \end{bmatrix} \qquad H_c = \begin{bmatrix} -1 & 0 & 0 \\ 0 & 1 & 0 \\ 0 & 0 & 0 \end{bmatrix}$$

The Prewit operator is more sensitive to vertical and horizontal edges than diagonal edges.

$$H_r = \begin{bmatrix} -1 & -1 & -1 \\ 0 & 0 & 0 \\ 1 & 1 & 1 \end{bmatrix} \qquad H_c = \begin{bmatrix} 1 & 0 & -1 \\ 1 & 0 & -1 \\ 1 & 0 & -1 \end{bmatrix}$$

The Frei-Chen mask

$$H_r = \begin{bmatrix} 0 & 0 & -1 \\ \sqrt{2} & 0 & \sqrt{2} \\ 0 & 0 & -1 \end{bmatrix} \qquad H_c = \begin{bmatrix} -1 & -\sqrt{2} & -1 \\ 0 & 0 & 0 \\ 1 & \sqrt{2} & 1 \end{bmatrix}$$

3.4   Second Order Detection

In many applications, edge width is not a concern. In others, such as machine vision, it is a great concern [17]. The gradient operators discussed above produce a large response across an area where an edge is present. This is especially true for slowly ramping edges. Ideally, an edge detector should indicate any edges at the center of an edge. This is referred to as localization. If an edge detector creates an image map with edges several pixels wide, it is difficult to locate the centers of the edges. It becomes necessary to employ a process called thinning to reduce the edge width to one pixel. Second order derivative edge detectors provide better edge localization.

Example. *In an image such as*

$$
\begin{array}{ccccccccc}
1 & 2 & 3 & 4 & 5 & 6 & 7 & 8 & 9 \\
1 & 2 & 3 & 4 & 5 & 6 & 7 & 8 & 9 \\
1 & 2 & 3 & 4 & 5 & 6 & 7 & 8 & 9 \\
1 & 2 & 3 & 4 & 5 & 6 & 7 & 8 & 9 \\
1 & 2 & 3 & 4 & 5 & 6 & 7 & 8 & 9
\end{array}
$$

The basic Sobel vertical edge operator (as described above) will yield a value right across the image. For example if

$$
\begin{array}{ccc}
-1 & 0 & 1 \\
-2 & 0 & 2 \\
-1 & 0 & 1
\end{array}
$$

is used then the results is

$$
\begin{array}{ccccccc}
8 & 8 & 8 & 8 & 8 & 8 & 8 \\
8 & 8 & 8 & 8 & 8 & 8 & 8 \\
8 & 8 & 8 & 8 & 8 & 8 & 8
\end{array}
$$

Implementing the same template on this "all eight image" would yield

$$0\ 0\ 0\ 0\ 0\ 0\ 0\ 0$$

This is not unlike the differentiation operator to a straight line, e.g., if $y = 3x-2$

$$\frac{dy}{dx} = 3 \quad and \quad \frac{d^2 y}{dx^2} = 0$$

Once we have gradient, if the gradient is then differentiated and the result is zero, it shows that the original line was straight.

Images often come with a gray level "trend" on them, i.e. one side of a regions is lighter than the other, but there is no "edge" to be discovered in the region, the shading is even, indicating a light source that is stronger at one end, or a gradual color change over the surface.

Another advantage of second order derivative operators is that the edge contours detected are closed curves [7]. This is very important in image segmentation. Also, there is no response to areas of smooth linear variations in intensity.

The Laplacian is a good example of a second order derivative operator. It is distinguished from the other operators because it is omnidirectional. It will highlight edges in all directions. The Laplacian operator will produce sharper edges than most other techniques. These highlights include both positive and negative intensity slopes.

The edge Laplacian of an image can be found by convolving with masks such as

$$
\begin{array}{ccc}
0 & -1 & 0 \\
-1 & 4 & -1 \\
0 & -1 & 0
\end{array}
\quad \text{or} \quad
\begin{array}{ccc}
-1 & -1 & -1 \\
-1 & 8 & -1 \\
-1 & -1 & -1
\end{array}
$$

The Laplacian set of operators is widely used. Since it effectively removes the general gradient of lighting or coloring from an image it only discovers and enhances much more discrete changes than, for example, the Sobel operator [32]. It does not produce any information on direction which is seen as a function of gradual change. It enhances noise, though larger Laplacian operators and similar families of operators tend to ignore noise.

Determining Zero Crossings

The method of determining zero crossings with some desired threshold is to pass a 3 x 3 window across the image determining the maximum and minimum values within that window [56]. If the difference between the maximum and minimum value exceed the predetermined threshold, an edge is present. Notice the larger number of edges with the smaller threshold. Also notice that the width of all the edges are one pixel wide.

A second order derivative edge detector that is less susceptible to noise is the Laplacian of Gaussian (LoG). The LoG edge detector performs Gaussian smoothing before application of the Laplacian. Both operations can be performed by convolving with a mask of the form

$$
LoG(x, y) = \frac{1}{\pi \pi \sigma^4}\left[1 - \frac{x^2 + y^2}{2\sigma^2}\right] e^{\frac{-(x^2 + y^2)}{2\sigma^2}}
$$

where x, y present row and column of an image, s is a value of dispersion that controls the effective spread.

Due to its shape, the function is also called the Mexican hat filter. Fig. 3.4 shows the cross section of the LoG edge operator with different values of s [40]. The wider the function, the wider the edge that will be detected. A narrow function will detect sharp edges and more detail.

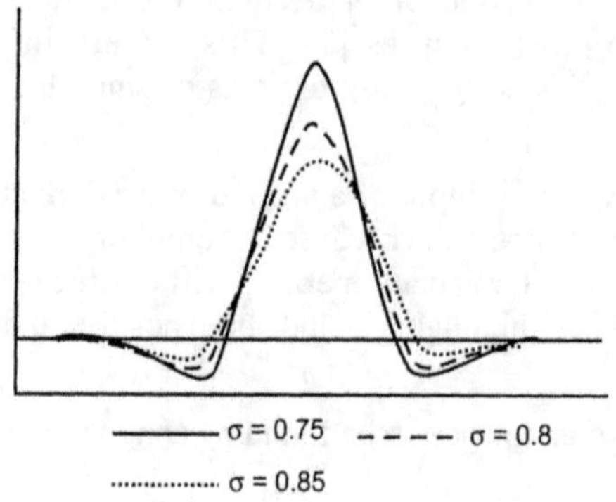

Fig. 3.4 Cross selection of LoG with various s.

The greater the value of σ, the wider the convolution mask necessary. The first zero crossing of the LoG function is at $\sqrt{2}\sigma$ The width of the positive center lobe is twice that. To have a convolution mask that contains the nonzero values of the LoG function requires a width three times the width of the positive center lobe (8.49σ).

Edge detection based on the Gaussian smoothing function reduces the noise in an image [53]. That will reduce the number of false edges detected and also detects wider edges.

Most edge detector masks are seldom greater than 7×7. Due to the shape of the LoG operator, it requires much larger mask sizes. The initial work in developing the LoG operator was done with a mask size of 35×35.

Because of the large computation requirements of the LoG operator, the Difference of Gaussians (DoG) operator can be used as an approximation to the LoG. The DoG can be shown as

$$DoG(x, y) = \frac{e^{-\left(\frac{x^2+y^2}{2\pi\sigma_1^2}\right)}}{2\pi\sigma_1^2} - \frac{e^{-\left(\frac{x^2+y^2}{2\pi\sigma_2^2}\right)}}{2\pi\sigma_2^2}$$

The DoG operator is performed by convolving an image with a mask that is the result of subtracting two Gaussian masks with different a values. The ratio $s_1 / s_2 = 1.6$ results in a good approximation of the LoG. Fig. 3.5 compares a LoG function (s = 12.35) with a DoG function ($s_1 = 10$, $s_2 = 16$).

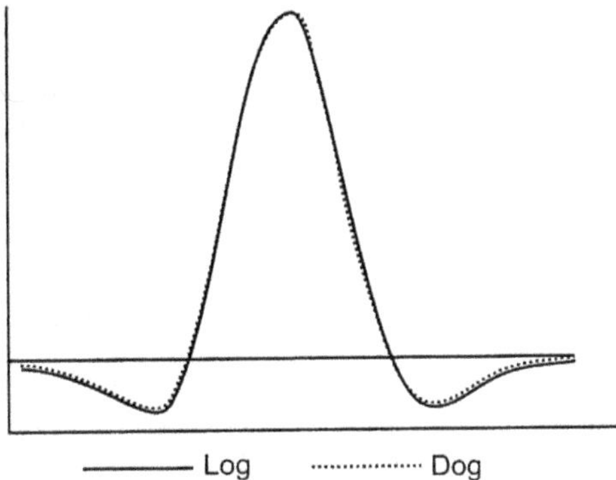

Fig. 3.5 LoG vs. DoG functions.

One advantage of the DoG is the ability to specify the width of edges to detect by varying the values of s_1 and s_2. Here are a couple of sample masks. The 9×9 mask will detect wider edges than the 7×7 mask.

For 7×7 mask, try

$$
\begin{array}{rrrrrrr}
0 & 0 & -1 & -1 & -1 & 0 & 0 \\
0 & -2 & -3 & -3 & -3 & -2 & 0 \\
-1 & -3 & 5 & 5 & 5 & -3 & -1 \\
-1 & -3 & 5 & 16 & 5 & -3 & -1 \\
-1 & -3 & 5 & 5 & 5 & -3 & -1 \\
0 & -2 & -3 & -3 & -3 & -2 & 0 \\
0 & 0 & -1 & -1 & -1 & 0 & 0
\end{array}
$$

For 9×9 mask, try

$$
\begin{array}{rrrrrrrrr}
0 & 0 & 0 & -1 & -1 & -1 & 0 & 0 & 0 \\
0 & -2 & -3 & -3 & -3 & -3 & -2 & -2 & 0 \\
0 & -3 & -2 & -1 & -1 & -1 & -3 & -3 & 0 \\
-1 & -3 & -1 & 9 & 9 & 9 & -1 & -3 & -1 \\
-1 & -3 & -1 & 9 & 19 & 9 & -1 & -3 & -1 \\
-1 & -3 & -1 & 9 & 9 & 9 & -1 & -3 & -1 \\
0 & -3 & -2 & -1 & -1 & -1 & -3 & -3 & 0 \\
0 & -2 & -3 & -3 & -3 & -3 & -2 & -2 & 0 \\
0 & 0 & 0 & -1 & -1 & -1 & 0 & 0 & 0
\end{array}
$$

Color Edge Detection

The method of detecting edges in color images depends on your definition of an edge [36]. One definition of an edge is the discontinuity in an image's luminance. Edge detection would then be done on the intensity channel of a color image in HSI space.

Another definition claims an edge exists if it is present in the red, green, and blue channel. Edge detection can be done by performing it on each of the color components [51]. After combining the color components, the resulting image is still in color, see Fig. 3.6.

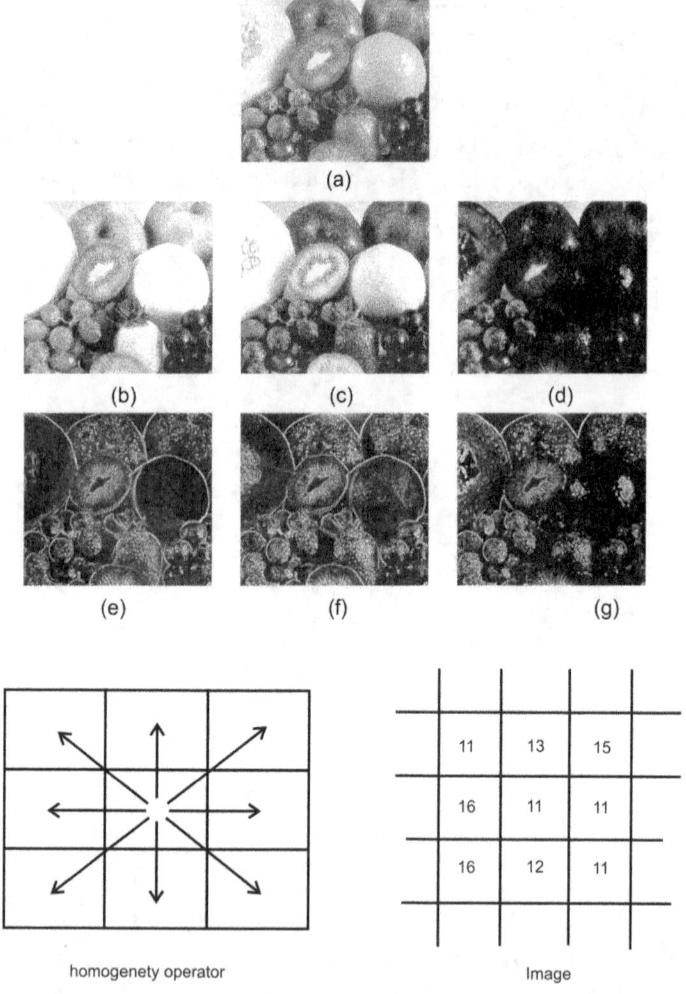

Fig. 3.6 (a) original image; (b) red channel; (c) green channel; (d) blue channel; (e) red channel edge; (f) green channel edge; (g) blue channel edge.

Edge detection can also be done on each color component and then the components can be summed to create a gray scale edge map. Also, the color components can be vector summed to create the gray scale edge map.

$$G(x, y) = \sqrt{G_{red}^2 + G_{green}^2 + G_{blue}^2}$$

It has been shown that the large majority of edges found in the color elements of an image are also found in the intensity component. This would imply that edge detection done on the intensity component alone would be sufficient [22]. There is the case of low contrast images where edges are not detected in the luminance component but found in the chromatic components. The best color edge detector again depends on the application.

3.5 Pyramid Edge Detection

Often it happens that the significant edges in an image are well spaced apart from each other and relatively easy to identify. However, there may be a number of other strong edges in the image that are not significant (from the user's point of view) because they are short or unconnected [7]. The problem is how to enhance the substantial ones but ignore the other shorter ones.

USE. To enhance substantial (strong and long) edges but to ignore the weak or short edges.

THEORY. The image is cut down to the quarter of the area by halving the length of the sides (both horizontally and vertically). Each pixel in the new quarter-size image is an average of the four corresponding pixels in the full size image. This is repeated until an image is created where the substantial edges are still visible but the other edges have been lost.

Now the pyramid is traversed in the other direction. An edge detector is applied to the small image and where edge pixel have been found, an edge detector is applied to the corresponding four pixels in the next large image – and so on to the full-size image.

OPERATION. Let the original image be of size m x n.

Create a second image of size m/2 × n/2 by evaluating for each $0 < i < m$ and $0 < j < n$.

$$newI\left(\frac{i}{2}, \frac{j}{2}\right) = \frac{1}{4}\left[I(i, j) + I(i + 1, j) + I(i, j + 1) + I(i + 1, j + 1)\right]$$

i.e. the corresponding square of four elements in the original image are averaged to give a value in the new image.

This is repeated (possibly recursively) x times, and each generated image is kept [1]. (The generated images will not be larger, in total, than the original image, so only one extra plane is required to hold the image).

Now with the smallest image, perform some edge detection operation – such as Sobel. In pixels where edges are discovered (some threshold is required to identity an "edge" pixel) perform an edge detection operation on the group of four corresponding pixels in the next largest image. Continue to do this following the best edges down through the pyramid of images until the main edges in the original image have been discovered.

3.6 Crack Edge Detection

Crack edge detection is also a popular and effective method of edge enhancement. This involves allocating a likelihood value to all of the cracks between pixels as to whether they lie either side of an edge [19].

6	8	7
7	7	4
3	2	3

if the gray-level range is 0,9, then the crack probabilities in ninths are :

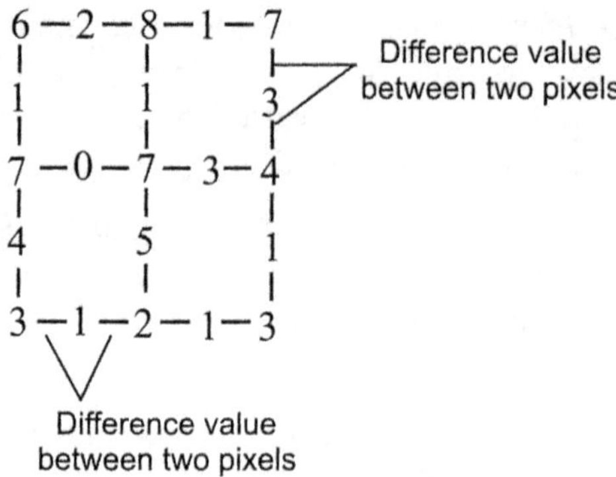

thresholding at 2 gives the edge, where the crack values are bigger than 2.

USE. Find substantial edges from an original image, and depending on the number of iterations that can be selected by the user, will find edges not only by simple statistics on a small local group, but will make sensible decisions about edges being connected to one another [19].

OPERATION. Determine the values of the cracks between the pixels. This is $|I(x, y) - I(x + 1, y)|$ for the vertical cracks and $|I(x, y) - I(x, y + 1)|$ for the horizontal cracks.

Then, classify every pixel cracks depending on how many of the cracks connected to it at both ends are likely to be "significant" cracks, i.e. likely to represent real edges on the picture. Since there are three continuation cracks at each end of every crack, each crack can be classified as having 0, 1, 2 or 3 significant cracks hanging off it at each end. Fig. 3.7 shows a selection of crack edge types.

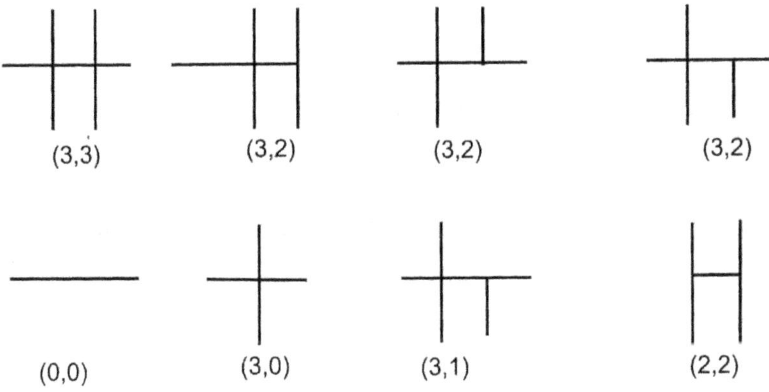

Fig. 3.7 A selection of crack edge types.

If a, b, c are the values of the hanging-off cracks at one end of the crack being classified, and they are ordered such that a ³ b ³ c, and m = max(a, b, c, N/10), where N is the number of gray levels supported by the system, then calculate the maximum of

(m-a)(m-b)(m-c)	Likelihood value for 0 "significant" cracks
a(m-b)(m-c)	Likelihood value for 1 "significant" cracks
ab(m-c)	Likelihood value for 2 "significant" cracks
abc	Likelihood value for 3 "significant" cracks

Choose the most likely number of cracks – i.e. the one with the highest likelihood value. Do this for both ends, allocating a class such as (3, 2) to the crack being considered. Increment the crack value if the crack is of type (1,1), (1,2), (2,1), (1,3), (3,1). Intuitively these will probably be the parts of an edge. Decrement the crack value if the crack is of type (0,0), (0,2), (0,1), (2,0), (3,0). Do nothing for the others. Repeat this enhancement process until adequate edge detection has been performed.

Create an edge detected image by allocating to each pixel a value dependent on the value of the crack above it and the crack to the right of it. This could be a simple sum or the maximum of the two or a binary value from some combined threshold.

This is edge enhancement, using as initial estimate of the edges the cracks between the pixels. It then removes the unlikely ones, enhancing the more likely ones.

3.7   Edge Following

If it is known that an object in an image has a discrete edge all around it, then once a possible position on the edge has been found, it is to follow the code around the object and back to the beginning [5]. Edge following is a very useful operation, particularly as a stepping stone to making decision by discovering region positions in images. This is effectively the dual of segmentation by region detection.

There are a number of edge following techniques. There are many levels of sophistication associated with edge following and the reader may well see how sophistication can be added to the simple technique described [20].

Simple Edge Following

USE. Knowing that a pixel is on an edge, the edge will be followed so that an object is outlined [6]. This is useful prior to calculating the area of a particular shape. It is also useful if the enclosed region is made up of many regions that the user whishes to combine.

OPERATION. It is assumed that a position on the edge of a region has been identified, call it (x, y).

Now flag this position as "used" (so that it is not used again) and evaluate all the 3×3 (or larger) Sobel gradient values centered on each of the eight pixels surrounding (x, y).

Choose the three pixels with the greatest absolute gradient magnitude. Put three pixels positions in a three columns array, one column for each pixel position, order them in the row according to gradient magnitude. Choose the one with greatest gradient magnitude.

Now this pixel will be in one of the directions 0-7 with respect to the pixel (x, y) given by the following map, where * is the position of pixel (x, y).

$$
\begin{array}{ccc}
0 & 1 & 2 \\
7 & * & 3 \\
6 & 5 & 4
\end{array}
$$

For example, if the maximum gradient magnitude was found from the Sobel operator centered round the pixel $(x + 1, y)$ then the direction would be 3. Call the direction of travel d.

Assuming that the shape is not very irregular, repeat the above algorithm but instead of looking at all the pixels around the new pixel, look only in direction a, $(d+1)$ mod 8, and $(d-1)$ mod 8. If no suitably high value of gradient magnitude is found, remove the pixel from the list and choose the next one of the three sorted. If all three have been removed from the list, then move up a row and choose the next best from the previous row. Stop when the travel reaches the original pixel, or excursion has gone on too long or the number of rows in the list is very large.

As suggested in the description of the technique, the problem may be the amount of time to reach a conclusion. Various heuristic techniques, including adding weights and creating more substantial trees can be included [32].

3.8 Thresholding

This technique is based upon a simple concept. A parameter called the brightness threshold is chosen and applied to the image a[m,n] as follows:

$$
\begin{aligned}
&\textit{If } a[m, n] \geq \theta \qquad a[m, n] = object = 1 \\
&\textit{Else} \qquad\qquad\quad a[m, n] = background = 0
\end{aligned}
$$

This version of the algorithm assumes that we are interested in light objects on a dark background. For dark objects on a light background we would use:

$$
\begin{aligned}
&\textit{If } a[m, n] < \theta \qquad a[m, n] = object = 1 \\
&\textit{Else} \qquad\qquad\quad a[m, n] = background = 0
\end{aligned}
$$

The output is the label "object" or "background" which, due to its dichotomous nature, can be represented as a Boolean variable "1" or "0". In principle, the test condition could be based upon some other property than simple brightness (for example, *If*

$(Redness \ \{a[m, n]\} \geq \theta_{red})$, but the concept is clear.

The central question in thresholding then becomes: How do we choose the threshold? While there is no universal procedure for threshold selection that is guaranteed to work on all images, there are a variety of alternatives.

Fixed threshold : One alternative is to use a threshold that is chosen independently of the image data. If it is known that one is dealing with very high-contrast images where the objects are very dark and the background is homogeneous and very light, then a constant threshold of 128 on a scale of 0 to 255 might be sufficiently accurate. By accuracy we mean that the number of falsely-classified pixels should be kept to a minimum.

Histogram-derived thresholds : In most cases the threshold is chosen from the brightness histogram of the region or image that we wish to segment. An image and its associated brightness histogram are shown in Figure 1. A variety of techniques have been devised to automatically choose a threshold starting from the gray-value histogram, $\{h[b] \mid b = 0, 1, \dots, 2^B-1\}$. Some of the most common ones are presented below. Many of these algorithms can benefit from a smoothing of the raw histogram data to remove small fluctuations but the smoothing algorithm must not shift the peak positions. This translates into a zero-phase smoothing algorithm given below where typical values for W are 3 or 5:

$$h_{smooth}[b] = \frac{1}{W} \sum_{w=-(w-1)/2}^{(w-1)/2} h_{raw}[b-w] \quad \text{where } W \text{ is odd} \qquad (3.1)$$

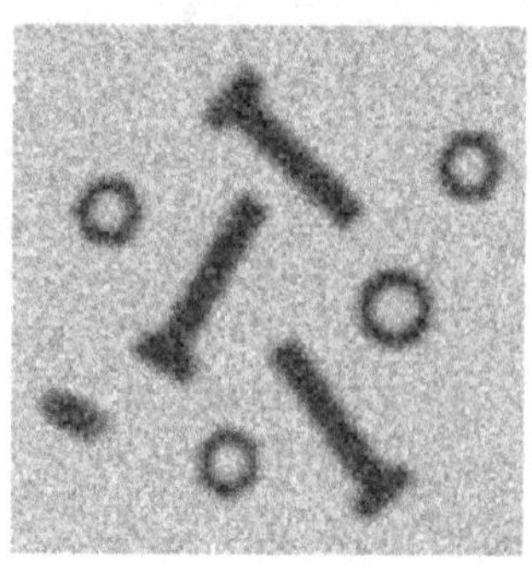

(a) Image to be thresholded

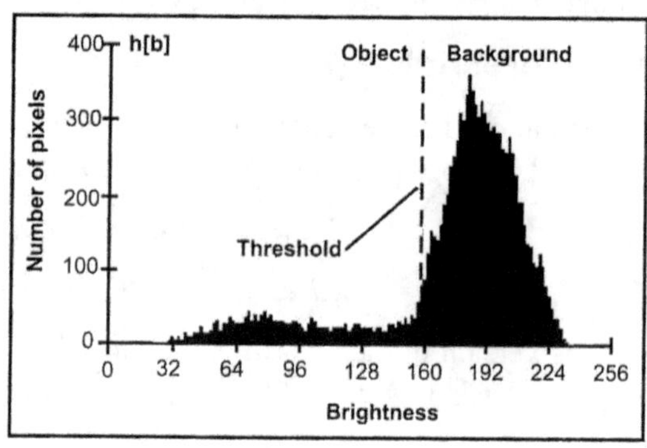

(b) Brightness histrogram of the image

Fig. 3.8 Pixels below the threshold ($a[m, n] < q$) will be labeled as object pixels; those above the threshold will be labeled as background pixels.

Isodata algorithm – This is an iterative technique for choosing a threshold. The histogram is initially segmented into two parts using a strating threshold value such as $q_o = 2^{B-1}$, half the maximum dynamic range. The sample mean (mf,0) of the gray values associated with the foreground pixels and the sample mean (mb,0) of the gray values associated with the background pixels are computed. A new threshold value q1 is now computed as the average of these two sample means. The process is repeated, based upon the new threshold, until the threshold value does not change any more. In formula (2) :

$$\theta_k = (m_{f,k-1} + m_{b,k-1})/2 \text{ until } \theta_k = \theta_{k-1} \qquad (3.2)$$

Background-symmetry algorithm – This technique assumes a distinct and dominant peak for the background that is symmetric about its maximum. The technique can benefit from smoothing as in equation 1. The maximum peak (*maxp*) is found by searching for the maximum value in the histogram. The algorithm then searches on the *non-object pixel side* of that maximum to find a $p\%$ point. In Fig. 3.8 (b), where the object pixels are located to the *left* of the background peak at brightness 183, this means searching to the right of that peak to locate, as an example, the 95% value. At this brightness value, 5% of the pixels lie to the *right* (are above) that value. This occurs at brightness 216 in Figure 1b. Because of the assumed symmetry, we use as a threshold a displacement to the *left* of the maximum that is equal to the displacement to the right where the $p\%$ is found. For Figure 1b this means a threshold value given by 183 - (216 - 183) = 150. In formula (3):

$$\theta = \max P - (p\% - \max p) \qquad (3.3)$$

This technique can be adapted easily to the case where we have light objects on a dark, dominant background. Further, it can be used if the object peak dominates and we have reason to assume that the brightness distribution around the object peak is symmetric. An additional variation on this symmetry theme is to use an estimate of the sample standard deviation (stdev.) based on one side of the dominant peak and then use a thershold based on $\theta = maxp$ +/- 1.96 **stdev*. (at the 5% level) or $\theta = maxp$ +/- 2.57 * *stdev*. (at the 1% level). The choice of "+" or "–" depends on which direction from *maxp* is being defined as the object/ background threshold. Should the distributions be approximately Gaussian around maxp, then the values 1.96 and 2.57 will, in fact, correspond to the 5% and 1% level.

Triangle algorithm – This technique is illustrated in Figure 3.9. A line is constructed between the maximum of the histogram at brightness b_{max} and the lowest value $b_{min} = (p = 0)\%$ in the image. The distance **d** between the line and the histogram $h[b]$ is computed for all values of b from $b = b_{min}$ to $b = b_{max}$. The brightness vlaue b_o where the distance between $h[b_0]$ and the line is maximal is the threshold value, that is, $\theta = b_o$. This technique is particularly effective when the object picels produce a weak peak in the histogram.

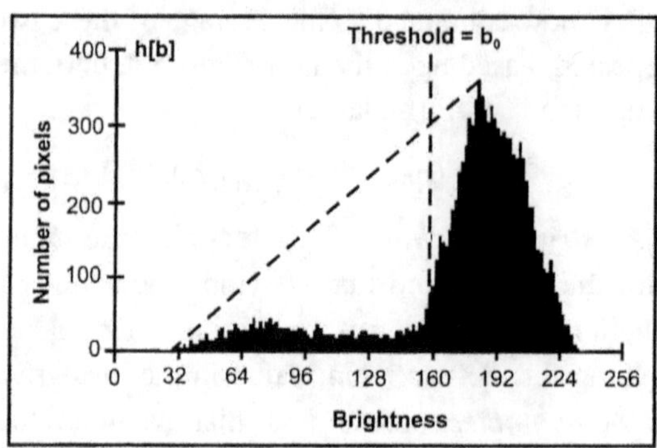

Fig. 3.9 The triangle algorithm is based on finding the value of b that gives the maximum distance d.

The three procedures described above give the values $\theta = 139$ for the Isodata algorithm, $\theta = 150$ for the background symmetry algorithm at the 5% level, and $\theta = 152$ for the triangle algorithm for the image in Fig. 3.10.

Optimal Threshold :

Suppose an image contains two principal gray-level regions. Let z denote the grey-level values. Viewing their values as random quantities and their histogram may be considered an estimate of their probability density function, $p(z)$. This overall density function is the sum or mixture of two densities, one for the light and one for the dark regions in the image. If the form of the densities is known or assumed, it is possible to establish an optimal threshold for segmenting the image into two distinct regions.

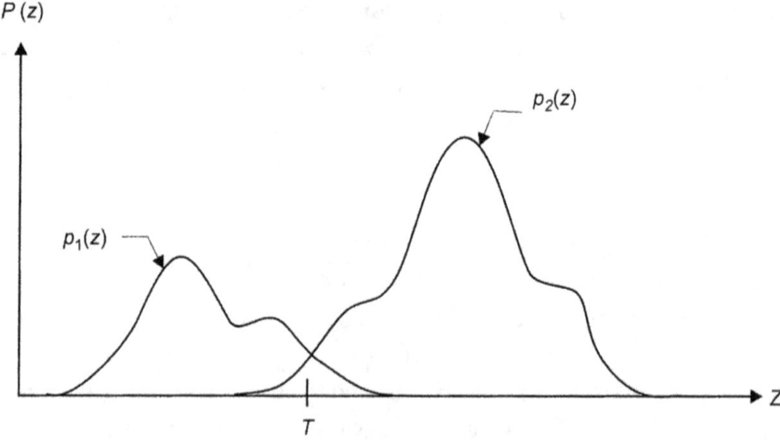

Fig. 3.10 Gray level pdf of two regions in an image.

The mixture probability density function describing the overall gray level variation of the image is given by:

$$p(z) = P_1\, p_1(z) + P_2\, p_2(z) \tag{3.4}$$

P_1 and P_2 are the probabilities of occurrence of the two classes of pixels. P_1 is the probability that a random pixel is an object pixel, whereas, P_2 is the probability that the pixel is a background pixel. This allows the assumption that:

$$P_1 + P_2 = 1 \tag{3.5}$$

If the probability density function is assumed to be a Gaussian density, then,

$$p(z) = \frac{P_1}{\sqrt{2\pi}\sigma_1} e^{\frac{(z-\mu_1)^2}{2\sigma_1^2}} + \frac{P_2}{\sqrt{2\pi}\sigma_2} e^{\frac{(z-\mu_2)^2}{2\sigma_2^2}} \tag{3.6}$$

If this is the case, then the optimal threshold is given by

$$T = \frac{\mu_1 + \mu_2}{2} + \frac{\sigma^2}{\mu_1 - \mu_2} \ln\left(\frac{P_2}{P_1}\right) \tag{3.7}$$

Thresholding does not have to be applied to entire images but can be used on a region by region basis. Such methods are called Adaptive Thresholding methods. Chow and Kaneko developed a variation in which the M x N image is divided into non-overlapping regions. In each region a threshold is calculated and the resulting threshold values are put together (interpolated) to form a thresholding surface for the entire image. The regions should be of "reasonable" size so that there are a sufficient number of pixels in each region to make an estimate of the histogram and the threshold.

3.9 Questions

1. Write short notes on the following:

    (a) Global thresholding   (b) Adaptive thresholding.

2. Find the edge corresponding to the minimum-cost path in the subimage shown.The numbers in brackets are gray levels and the outer numbers are spatial coordinates.Assume that the edge starts in the first column and ends in the last column.

	1	2	3
1	•	•	•
	[2]	[1]	[0]
2	•	•	•
	[1]	[1]	[7]
3	•	•	•
	[6]	[8]	[2]

3. (a)   Discuss the differences between thinning and skeletonization. Explain the skeletonization with an example.

    (b)   What is pruning? Explain with a neat diagram.

4. (a)   Explain the basic types of gray-level discontinuties in a digital image.

    (b)   Explain the role of thresholding in segmentation.

5. (a)   Explain the region split and merge algorithm for segmentation.

    (b)   What are the basic data redundancies in image processing? Explain how they are overcome?

6. (a)   Explain the various basic gray level transformation methods.

    (b)   Explain how averaging and subtraction are used for image enhancement.

7. (a)   Explain how derivative operators are used for edge detection.

    (b)   Find the edge corresponding to the minimum cost path in the subimage shown. The numbers in brackets are gray levels and the outer numbers are spatial coordinates. Assume that edge starts in the first column and ends in the last column.

$$
\begin{array}{ccc}
\bullet & \bullet & \bullet \\
2 & 1 & 0 \\
\bullet & \bullet & \bullet \\
1 & 1 & 6 \\
\bullet & \bullet & \bullet \\
5 & 8 & 1
\end{array}
$$

8.   Explain the various smoothing spatial filters.

9. (a) Give prewitt and sobel masks and explain how these are used in image segmentation.

    (b) Explain the segmentation based on Region Growing.

10. Explain how logical operations are used to enhance the images.

11. (a) What is image segmentation? Why is it needed in image processing?

     (b) What is the basic principle of Hough tranform and explain how it is employed for edge detection?

12. Explain various discontinuity detection methods in detail with suitable examples.

13. Discuss about the following edge detection techniques
    (a) Laplacean
    (b) Laplacean of Gaussian (LOG) and
    (c) Zero crossing.

14. A sample image of 5×5 is shown below.

$$\begin{bmatrix} 3 & 2 & 3 & 4 & 1 \\ 0 & 2 & 4 & 3 & 7 \\ 3 & 4 & 2 & 1 & 0 \\ 4 & 1 & 3 & 3 & 7 \\ 5 & 4 & 5 & 4 & 6 \end{bmatrix}$$

   Apply the Sobel's diagonal operators in both the directions and show the turncated output image of size 3×3.

15. (a) Explain the characteristics of the following smoothing filters.
        (i) Thresholding   (ii) averaging filters (iii) median filters.
    (b) Discuss their relative advantages and disadvantages.

16. Write short notes on the following:
    (a) Optimal thresholding   (b) Role of Illumination in thresholding.

17. (a) Explain how the directional smoothing is performed.
    (b) Explain the steps involved in median filtering.

18. (a) Enumerate the basic formulation of the region-based segmentation.
    (b) Explain the concept of region growing procedure with suitable example.

19. Distinguish first-order derivative and second-order derivative of a 2-D function. Give the example operators for each of the derivatives.

20. (a) What is meant by image segmentation? Explain the features that are considered for segmentation.
    (b) Explain with an example how derivative operators are useful for edge detection.

21. (a) Explain the basic principle of Hough transform and how it is employed for edge detection.
    (b) Explain the concept of region split and merge algorithm for segmentation.

22. Explain about various spatial filters for image smoothing and sharpening operations.

23. What are circulant and block circulant matrices? What is the effect of diagonalization on the degradation model? Explain.

24. Describe the procedure for image segmentation based on
    (a) region growing and
    (b) region splitting & merging
    with relevant examples.

25. (a) Distinguish between spatial and frequency domain methods of image enhacement.
    (b) Briefly explain about image enhancement using point processing techniques.

26. (a) What are circulant and block circulant matrices? What is the effect of diagonalization on the degradation model? Explain?
    (b) Explain the method of inverse filtering for image restoration.

27. (a) Explain with an example how derivative operators are use that are considered for segmentation.
    (b) What is the role of thresholding in segmentation? Explain. .

28. (a) Explain with an example how derivative operators are useful for edge detection.
    (b) What is the role of thresholding in segmentation? Explain

29. (a) What is the general form of gray-level transformation function. Explain the terms involved in it?
    (b) Explain how the
         i. Contrast stretching and
         ii. Thresholding functions are implemented.

30. (a) How the direction and magnitude at an identified location are computed in an image.
    (b) Derive the Prewitt operators and show the corresponding 3×3 spatial masks.

31. (a) Explain the algorithm for edge following.
    (b) What are the applications of edge following.

32. (a) How the second derivative is computed using gray-values of an image.
    (b) What are the Sobel's operations for a 3×3 region of an image.

33. The mean and standard deviation of the background pixels in the image shown are 110 and 15 respectively. The object pixels have mean and standard deviation values of 200 and 40 respectively. Give a thresholding solution for segmenting the objects of the image.

34. (a) What are the derivative operators useful in image segementation ? Explain their role in segmentation.

    (b) Explain about region growing methods in segmentation.

35. (a) What are the derivative operators useful in image segmentation ? Explain their role in segmentation.

    (b) Explain the segmentation method based on similarities in gray level.

36. (a) Explain various methods of detecting discontinuities in an image.

    (b) Find the edge corresponding to the minimum lost path in the subimage given below, Where the numbers in paranthesis indicate intensity. Assume that the edge starts in the first column and ends in the last column.

$$
\begin{array}{ccc}
* & * & * \\
(2) & (1) & (0) \\
* & * & * \\
(1) & (1) & (7) \\
* & * & * \\
(6) & (8) & (2)
\end{array}
$$

CHAPTER 4

Morphological and Other Area Operations

The word morphology means "the form and structure of an object", or the arrangements and interrelationships between the parts of an object. Morphology is related to shape, and digital morphology is a way to describe or analyze the shape of a digital (most often raster) object [56].

4.1 Basic Morphological Operations

Binary morphological operations are defined on bilevel images; that is, images that consist of either black or white pixel only. For the purpose of beginning, consider the image seen in Fig. 4.1a. The set of black pixels from a square object. The object in 4.1b is also square, but is one pixel larger in all directions. It was obtained from the previous square by simply setting all white neighbors of any black pixel to black. This amounts to a simple binary dilation, so named

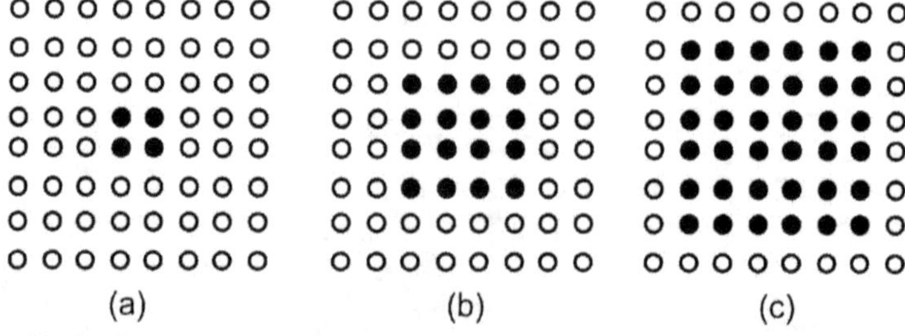

Fig. 4.1 The effects of a simple binary dilation on a small object. (a) Original image. (b) Dilation of the original by 1 pixel, (c) Dilation of the original by 2 pixels (dilation of (b) by 1).

because it causes the original object to grow larger. Fig. 4.1c shows the result of dilating Fig. 4.1b by one pixel, which is the same as dilating Fig. 4.1a by two pixels, this process could be continued until the entire image consisted entirely of black pixels, at which point the image would stop showing any change.

4.1.1 Binary dilation

Now some definition of simple set operations are given, with the goal being to define dilation in a more general fashion in terms of sets [40]. The translation of the set A by the point x is defined, in set notation, as :

$$(A)_x = \{c|c = -a, a \in A\}$$

For example, if x were at (1, 2) then the first (upper left) pixel in $(A)_x$ would be (3,3) + (1,2) = (4,5); all of the pixels in A shift down by one row and right by two columns in this case. This is a translation in the same sense that is seen in computer graphics - a change in position by specified amount.

The reflection of a set A is defined as:

$$\hat{A} = \{c = -a, a \in A\}$$

This is really a rotation of the object A by 180 degree about the origin. The complement of the set A is a set of pixels not belonging to A. This would correspond to the white pixels in the figure, or in the language of set theory:

$$A^c = \{c|c \notin A\}$$

The *intersection* of two sets A and B is the set of elements (pixels) belonging to both A and B:

$$A \cap B = \{c|(c \in A) \wedge (c \in B)\}$$

The *union* of two sets A and B is the set of pixels that belong to either A or B or to both:

$$A \cup B = \{c|(c \in A) \vee (c \in B)\}$$

Finally, completing this collection of basic definitions, the *difference* between the set A and the set B is:

$$A - B = \{c|(c \in A) \wedge (c \notin B)\}$$

which is the set of pixels belonging to A but not to B. This can also be expressed as the intersection of A with the complement of B or, $A \cap B^c$.

It is now possible to define more formally what is meant by a dilation. *A dilation of the set A by the set B is:*

$$A \oplus B = \{c|c = a + b, a \in A, b \in B\}$$

where A represents the image being operated on, and B is a second set of pixels, a shape that operates on the pixels of A to produce the result; the set B is called a structuring element, and its composition defines the nature of the specific dilation [52].

To explore this idea, let A be the set of Figure 4.1a, and let B be the set of {(0,0)(0,1)}. The pixels in the set C = A + B are computed using the last equation which can be rewritten in this case as:

$$A \oplus B = (A + (0,0)) \cup (A + (0,1))$$

There are four pixels in the set A, and since any pixel translated by (0,0) does not change, those four will also be in the resulting set C after computing C = A + {(0,1)}:

$$(3,3) + (0,0) = (3,3) \quad (3,4) + (0,0) = (3,4)$$
$$(4,3) + (0,0) = (4,3) \quad (4,4) + (0,0) = (4,3)$$

The result A + {(0,1)} is

$$(3,3) + (0,1) = (3,4) \quad (3,4) + (0,1) = (3,5)$$
$$(4,3) + (0,1) = (4,4) \quad (4,4) + (0,1) = (4,5)$$

The set C is the result of the dilation of A using structuring element B, and consists of all of the pixels above (some of which are duplicates). Figure 4.2 illustrates this operation, showing graphically the effect of the dilation. The pixels marked with an "X," either white or black, represent the origin of each image [36]. The location of the origin is important. In the example above, if the origin of B were the rightmost of the two pixels, the effect of the dilation would be to add pixels to the left of A, rather than to the right. The set B in this case would be {(0,-1)(0,0)}.

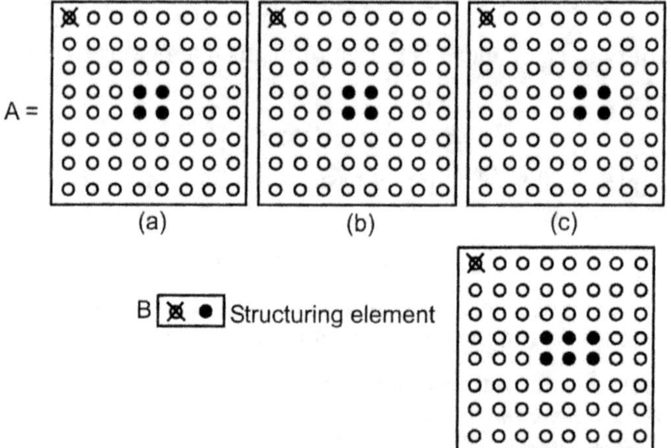

Fig. 4.2. Dilation of the set A of (Fig. 4.1(a)) by the set B; (a) The two sets; (b) The set obtained by adding (0,0) to all element of A; (c) The set obtained by adding (0,1) to all elements of A; (d) The union of the two sets is the result of the dilation.

Moving back to the simple binary dilation that was performed in Fig. 4.1, one question that remains is "What was the structuring element that was used?" Note that the object increases in size in all directions, and by a single pixel. From the example just completed it was observed that if the structuring element has a pixel to the right of the origin, then a dilation that uses that structuring element 4 grows a layer of pixels on the right of the object. To grow a layer of pixels in all directions, we can use a structuring element having one pixel on every side of the origin; that is, a 3 x 3 square with the origin at the center. This structuring element will be named simple in the ensuing discussion, and is correct in this instance (although it is not always easy to determine the shape of the structuring element needed to accomplish a specific task).

As a further example, consider the object and structuring element shown in Figure 4.3. In this case, the origin of the structuring element B, contains a white pixel, implying that the origin is not included in the set B. There is no rule against this, but it is more difficult to see what will happen, so the example will be done in detail. The image to be dilated, A_1, has the following set representation:

$$A_1 = \{(1,1)(2,2)(2,3)(3,2)(3,3)(4,4)\}$$

The structuring element B_1 is :

$$B_1 = \{(0, -1)(0,1)\}$$

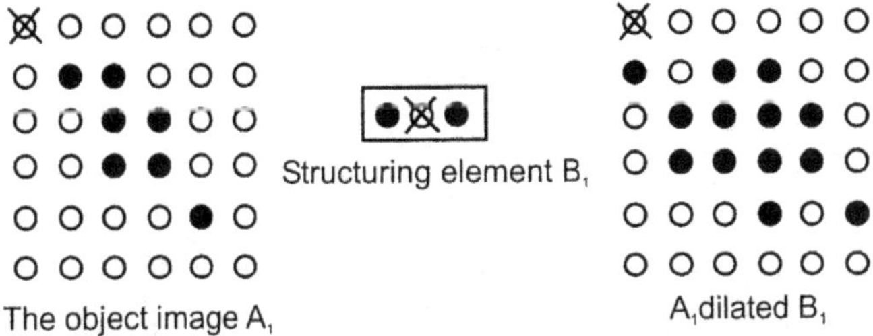

Fig. 4.3. Dilation by a structuring element that does not include the origin. Some pixels that are set in the original image are not set in the dilated image.

The translation of A_1 by (0,-1) yields

$$(A_1)_{(0, -1)} = \{(1,0)(2,1)(2,2)(3,1)(3,2)(4,3)\}$$

and the translation of A, by (0,1) yields:

$$(A_1)_{(0, -1)} = \{(1,2)(2,3)(2,4)(3,3)(3,4)(4,5)\}.$$

The dilation of A_1 by B_1 is the union of $(A_1)_{(0,-1)}$ with $(A_1)_{(0,1)}$, and is shown in Figure 4.3. Notice that the original object pixels, those belonging to A_1 are not necessarily set in the result; (1,1) and (4,4), for example, are set in A_1 but not in $A_1 + B_1$. This is the effect of the origin not being a part of B_1.

The manner in which the dilation is calculated above presumes that a dilation can be considered to be the union of all of the translations specified by the structuring element [43]; that is, as

$$A \oplus B = \bigcup_{b \in B} (A)_b$$

Not only is this true, but because dilation is commutative, a dilation can also be considered to be the union of all translations of the structuring element by all pixels in the image:

$$A \oplus B = \bigcup_{a \in A} (B)_a$$

This gives a clue concerning a possible implementation for the dilation operator as shown in Fig. 4.4. Think of the structuring element as a template, and move it over the image. When the origin of the structuring element aligns with a black pixel in the image, all of the image pixels that correspond to black pixels in the structuring element are marked, and will later be changed to black. After the entire image has been swept by the structuring element, the dilation calculation is complete. Normally the dilation is not computed in place. A third image, initially all white, is used to store the dilation while it is being computed.

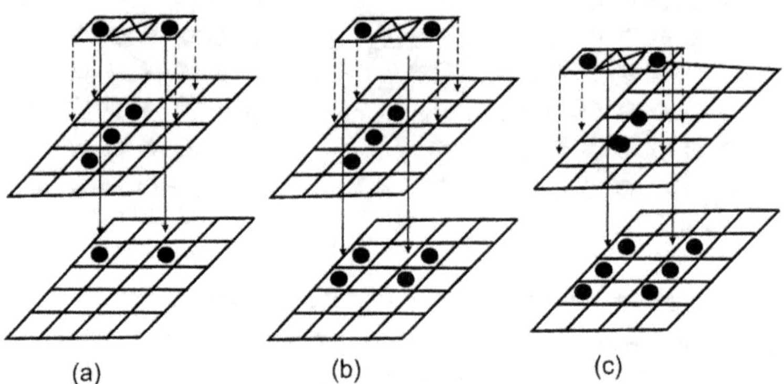

(a)   (b)   (c)

Fig. 4.4 Dilating an image using a structuring element. (a) The origin of the structuring element is placed over the first black pixel in the image, and the pixels in the structuring element are copied into their corresponding positions in the result image. (b) Then the structuring element is placed over the next black pixel in the image and the process is repeated. (c) This is done for every black pixel in the image.

4.1.2 Binary Erosion

If dilation can be said to add pixels to an object, or to make it bigger, then erosion will make an image smaller [50]. In the simplest case, a binary erosion will remove the outer layer of pixels from an object. For example, Fig. 4.1b is the result of such a simple erosion process applied to Fig. 4.1c. This can be implemented by marking all black pixels having at least one white neighbor, and then setting to white all of the marked pixels. The structuring element implicit in this implementation is the same 3×3 array of black pixels that defined the simple binary dilation.

In general, the erosion of image A by structuring element B can be defined as:

$$A \ominus B = \left\{ c \middle| (B)_c \subseteq A \right\}$$

In other words, it is the set of all pixels c such that the structuring element B translated by c corresponds to a set of black pixels in A. That the result of an erosion is a subset of the original image seems clear enough, any pixels that do not match the pattern defined by the black pixels in the structuring element will not belong to the result. However, the manner in which the erosion removes pixels is not clear (at least at first), so a few examples are in order, and the statement above that the eroded image is a subset of the original is not necessarily true if the structuring element does not contain the origin.

Simple example

Consider the structuring element B = {(0,0)(1,0)} and

the object image $\qquad$ A = {(3,3)(3,4)(4,3)(4,4)}

The set A − B is the set of translations of B that align B over a set of black pixels in A. This means that not all translations need to be considered, but only those that initially place the origin of B at one of the members of A. There are four such translations:

$$B_{(3,3)} = \{(3,3)(4,3)\}$$

$$B_{(3,4)} = \{(3,4)(4,4)\}$$

$$B_{(4,3)} = \{(4,3)(5,3)\}$$

$$B_{(4,4)} = \{(4,4)(5,4)\}$$

In two cases, $B_{(3,3)}$ and $B_{(3,4)}$, the resulting (translated) set consists of pixels that are all members of A, and so those pixels will appear in the erosion of A by B. This example is illustrated in Fig. 4.5.

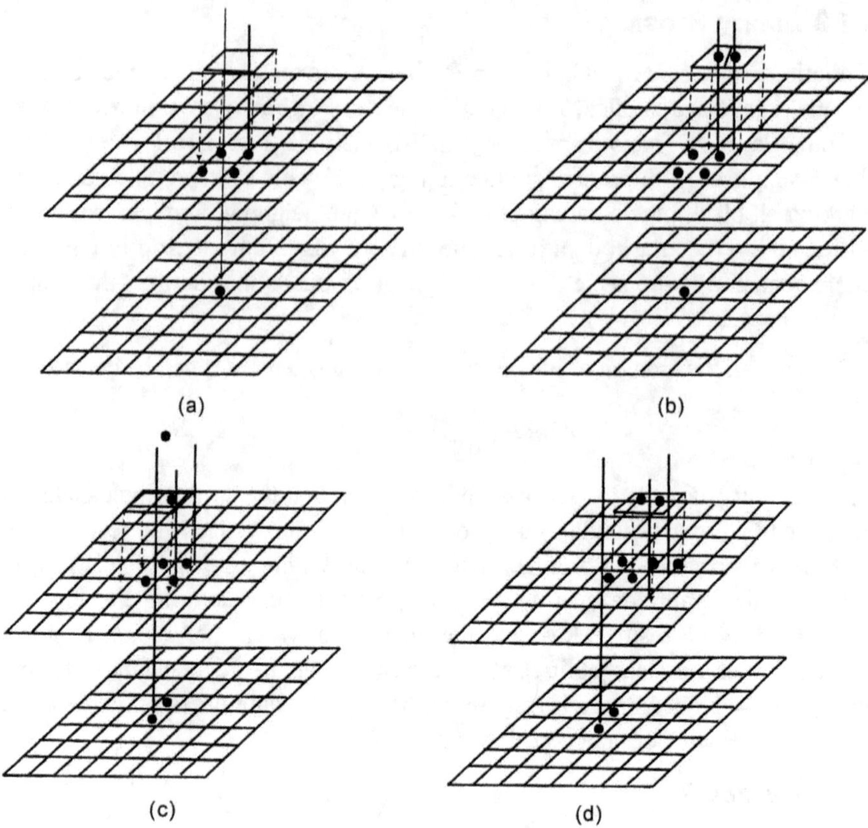

Fig. 4.5 Binary erosion using a simple structuring element.

(a) The structuring element is translated to the position of a black pixel in the image. In this case all members of the structuring element correspond to black image pixels so the result is a black pixel.

(b) Now the structuring element is translated to the next black pixel in the image, and there is one pixel that does not match. The result is a white pixel.

(c) At the next translation there is another match so, again the pixel in the output image that corresponds to the translated origin of the structuring element is set to black.

(d) The final translation is not a match, and the result is a white pixel. The remaining image pixels are white and could not match the origin of the structuring element; they need not be considered.

Now consider the structuring element $B_2 = \{(1,0)\}$; in this case the origin is not a member of B_2. The erosion $A - B$ can be computed as before, except that now the origin of the structuring element need not correspond to a black pixel in the image. There are quite a few legal positions, but the only ones that result in a match are :

$$B_{(2,3)} = \{(3,3)\}$$
$$B_{(2,4)} = \{(3,4)\}$$
$$B_{(3,3)} = \{(4,3)\}$$
$$B_{(3,4)} = \{(4,4)\}$$

This means that the result of the erosion is $\{(2,3)(2,4)(3,3)(3,4)\}$, which is not a subset of the original.

Note

It is important to realize that erosion and dilation are not inverse operations. Although there are some situations where an erosion will undo the effect of a dilation exactly, this is not true in general [51]. Indeed, as will be observed later, this fact can be used to perform useful operations on images. However, erosion and dilation are dual of each other in the following sense:

$$(A\ominus B)^c = A^c \oplus B^{\hat{c}}$$

This says that the complement of an erosion is the same as a dilation of the complement image by the reflected structuring element. If the structuring element is symmetrical then reflecting it does not change it, and the implication of the last equation is that the complement of an erosion of an image is the dilation of the background, in the case where simple is the structuring element.

The proof of the erosion-dilation duality is fairly simple, and may yield some insights into how morphological expressions are manipulated and validated. The definition of erosion is :

$$A\ominus B = \left\{ z \mid (B)_z \subseteq A \right\}$$

so the complement of the erosion is :

$$(A\ominus B)^c = \left\{ z \mid (B)_z \subseteq A \right\}^c$$

If $(B)_z$ is a subset of A, then the intersection of $(B)_z$ with A is not empty :

$$(A\ominus B)^c = \left\{ z \mid \left((B)_z \cap A \right) \neq 0 \right\}^c$$

but the intersection with A^c will be empty:

$$= \left\{ z \mid \left((B)_z \cap A \right) \neq 0 \right\}^c$$

and the set of pixels not having this property is the complement of the set that does:

$$= \left\{ z \mid \left((B)_z \cap A^c \right) \neq 0 \right\}$$

By the definition of translation, if $(B)_z$, intersects A^c then

$$= \left\{ z \mid (b+z) \in A^c, b \in B \right\}$$

which is the same thing as

$$= \left\{ z \mid b+z = a, a \in A^c, b \in B \right\}$$

Now if $a = b + z$ then $z = a - b$:

$$= \left\{ z \mid b+z = a, a \in A^c, b \in B \right\}$$

Finally, using the definition of reflection, if b is a member of B then A member of the reflection of B:

$$= \left\{ z \mid z = a-b, a \in A^c, b \in B \right\}$$

which is the definition of $A^c \oplus B^{\hat{c}}$

The erosion operation also brings up an issue that was not a concern at dilation; the idea of a "don't care" state in the structuring element. When using a strictly binary structuring element to perform an erosion, the member black pixels must correspond to black pixels in the image in order to set the pixel in the result, but the same is not true for a white (0) pixel in the structuring element. We don't care what the corresponding pixel in the image might be when the structuring element pixel is white.

4.2   Opening and Closing Operators

Opening

The application of an erosion immediately followed by a dilation using the same structuring element is referred to as an *opening* operation [5]. The name opening is a descriptive one, describing the observation that the operation tends to "open" small gaps or spaces between touching objects in an image. This effect is most easily observed when using the simple structuring element. Figure 4.6 shows image having a collection of small objects, some of them touching each other. After an opening using simple the objects are better isolated, and might now be counted or classified.

Figure 4.6 also illustrates another, and quite common, usage of opening: the removal of noise. When a noisy gray-level image is thresholded some of the noise pixels are above the threshold, and result in isolated pixels in random locations. The erosion step in an opening will remove isolated pixels as well as boundaries of objects, and the dilation step will restore most of the boundary pixels without restoring the noise. This process seems to be successful at removing spurious black pixels, but does not remove the white ones.

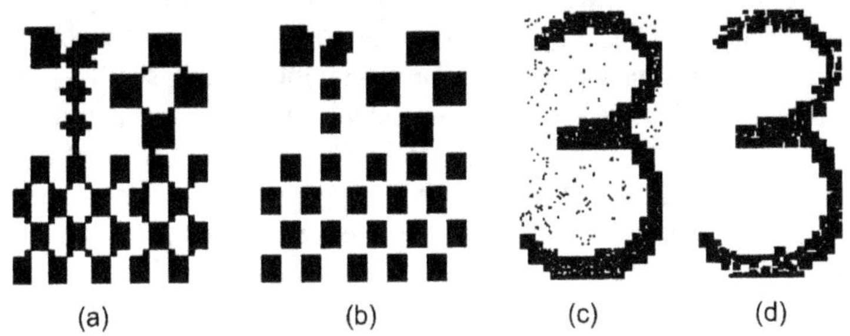

(a)   (b)   (c)   (d)

Fig. 4.6 The use of opening: (a) An image having many connected objects, (b) Objects can be isolated by opening using the simple structuring element, (c) An image that has been subjected to noise, (d) The noisy image after opening showing that the black noise pixels have been removed.

Closing

A closing is similar to an opening except that the dilation is performed first, followed by an erosion using the same structuring element [20]. If an opening creates small gaps in the image, a closing will fill them, or "close" the gaps. Figure 4.7 shows a closing applied to the image of Figure 4.6d, which you may remember was opened in an attempt to remove noise. The closing removes much of the white pixel noise, giving a fairly clean image.

Fig. 4.7 The result of closing Figure 4.6d using the simple structuring element

Closing can also be used for smoothing the outline of objects in an image [1]. Sometimes digitization followed by thresholding can give a jagged appearance to boundaries; in other cases the objects are naturally rough, and it may be necessary to determine how rough the outline is. In either case, closing can be used. However, more than one structuring element may be needed, since the simple structuring element is only useful for removing or smoothing single pixel irregularities. Another possibility is repeated application of dilation followed by the same number of erosions; N dilation/erosion applications should result in the smoothing of irregularities of N pixels in size.

First consider the smoothing application, and for this purpose Figure 4.7 will be used as an example. This image has been both opened and closed already, and another closing will not have any effect. However, the outline is still jagged, and there are still white holes in the body of the object. An opening of depth 2 (that is two dilations followed by two erosions) gives Figure 4.8a. Note that the holes have been closed, and that most of the outline irregularities are gone. On opening of depth 3 very little change is seen (one outline pixel is deleted), and no figure improvement can be hoped for.

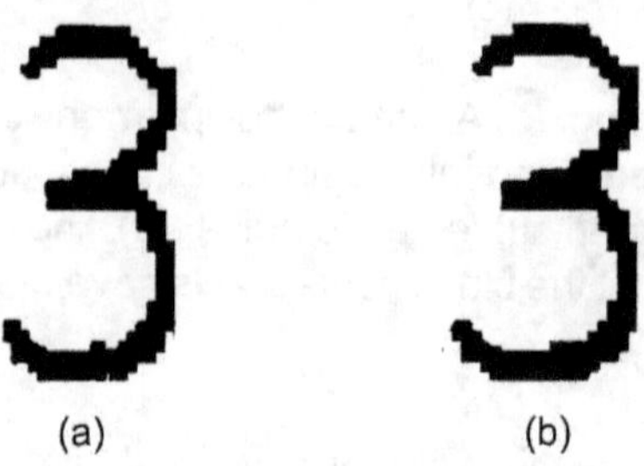

(a)   (b)

Fig. 4.8 Multiple closings for outline smoothing. (a) glyph from Fig. 4.7 after a depth 2 closing, (b) after a depth 3 closing.

Most opening and closings use simple structuring element in practice. The traditional approach to computing an opening of depth N is to perform N consecutive binary erosions followed by N binary dilations. This means that computing all of the openings of an image up to depth ten requires that 110 erosions or dilations be performed [7]. If erosion and dilation are implemented in a naive fashion, this will require 220 passes through the image. The alliterative is to save each of the ten erosions of the original image, each of these is then dilated by the proper number of iterations to give the ten opened images. The amount of storage required for the latter option can be prohibitive, and if file storage is used the I/O time can be large also.

A fast erosion method is based on the distance map of each object, where the numerical value of each pixel is replaced by a new value representing the distance of that pixel from the nearest background pixel [14]. Pixels on a boundary would have a value of 1, being that they are one pixel width from a background pixel; pixels that are two widths from the background would be given a value of 2, and so on. The result has the appearance of a contour map, where the contours represent the distance from the boundary. For example, the object shown in Fig. 4.9 (a) has the distance map shown in Fig. 4.9 (b). The distance map contains enough information to perform an erosion by any number of pixels in just one pass through the image; in other words, all erosions have been encoded into one image. This globally eroded image can be produced in just two passes through the original image, and a simple thresholding operation will give any desired erosion.

There is also a way, similar to that of global erosion, to encode all possible openings as one gray-level image, and all possible closings can be computed at the same time. First, as in global erosion, the distance map of the image is found. Then all pixels that do NOT have at least one neighbor nearer to the background and one neighbor more distant are located and marked: These will be called nodal pixels. Fig. 4.9 (c) shows the nodal pixels associated with the object of Fig. 4.9 (a). If the distance map is thought of as a three-dimensional surface where the distance from the background is represented as height, then every pixel can be thought of as being the peak of a pyramid having a standardized slope. Those peaks that are not included in any other pyramid are the nodal pixels. One way to locate nodal pixels is to scan the distance map, looking at all object pixels; find the minimum (or MIN) and maximum (or MAX) value of all neighbors of the target pixel, and compute MAX-MIN. If this value is less than the maximum possible, which is 2 when using 8-distance, then the pixel is nodal.

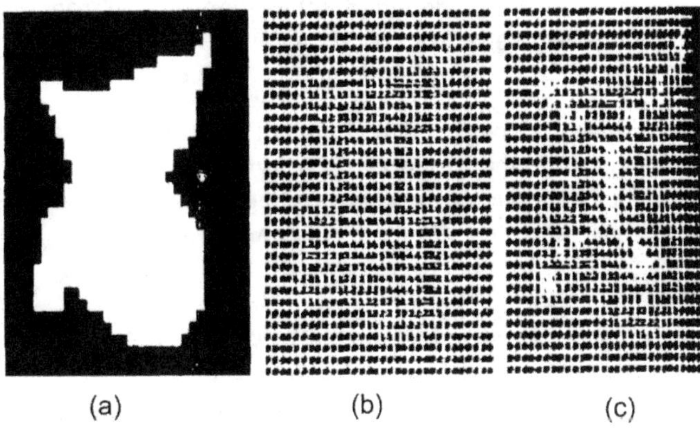

(a)   (b)   (c)

Fig. 4.9. Erosion using a distance map. (a) A blob as an example of an image to be eroded, (b) The distance map of the blob image, (c) Nodal pixels in this image are shown as periods (".").

To encode all openings of the object, a digital disk is drawn centered at each nodal point. The pixel values and the extent of the disk are equal to the value the nodal pixel [15]. If a pixel has already been drawn, then it will take on the larger of its current value or the new one being painted. The resulting object has the same outline as the original binary image, so the object can be recreated from the nodal pixels alone. In addition, the gray levels of this globally opened image represent an encoding of all possible openings. As an example, consider the disk shaped object in Fig. 4.10 (a) and the corresponding distance map of Fig. 4.10 (b). There are nine nodal points: Four have the value 3, and the remainders have the value 5. Thresholding the encoded image yields an opening having depth equal to the threshold.

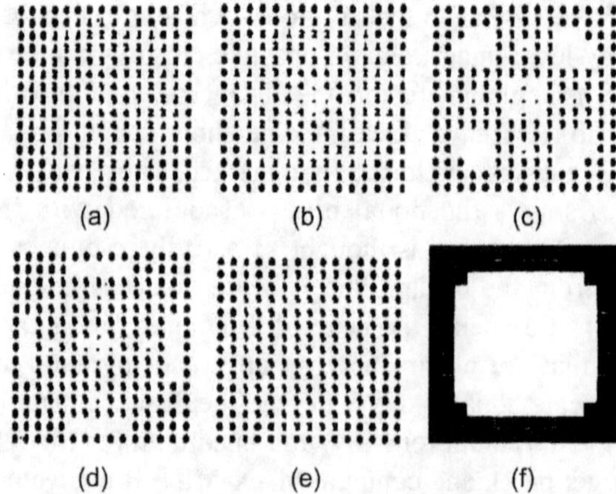

(a)   (b)   (c)

(d)   (e)   (f)

Fig. 4.10 Global opening of a disk-shaped object. (a) Distance map of the original object. (b) Nodal pixels identified. (c) Regions grown from the pixels with value 3. (d) Regions grown from pixels with value 5. (e) Globally opened image. (f) Globally opened image drawn as pixels.

All possible closings can be encoded along with the openings if the distance map is changed to include the distance of background pixels from an object. Closings are coded as values less than some arbitrary central value (say, 128) and openings are coded as values greater than this central value [6].

4.3 Questions

1. (a) What is granulometry? Explain the different morphological operations used in granulometry?

    (b) A gray scale image, $f(x,y)$, is corrupted by overlapping noise spikes that can be modeled as small, cylindrical artifacts of radii $R_{min} \leq r \leq R_{max}$ and amplitude $A_{min} \leq a \leq A_{max}$. Develop a morphological filtering approach for cleaning up the image.

2. (a) With necessary diagrams explain the operation of opening.

    (b) Let A and B are two sets in Z^2. Show that $A \odot B = \underset{b \in B}{\cap} (A)_{-b}$

3. (a) Explain with necessary diagrams, the operation of closing

    (b) With examples, explain how morphology operations are used in region filling.

4. Expalin how the following morphological operations can be extended to gray scale images

    (a) erosion   (b) opening.

5. (a) Explain with an example the boundary extraction using morphology operations.

    (b) Write short notes on opening and closing.

CHAPTER 5

Image Compression (Image Coding)

5.1 Introduction

The purpose of compression is to code the image data into a compact form, minimizing both the number of bits in the representation, and the distortion caused by the compression [40]. The importance of image compression is emphasized by the huge amount of data in raster images: a typical gray-scale image of 512×512 pixels, each represented by 8 bits, contains 256 kilobytes of data. With the color information, the number of bytes is tripled. If we talk about video images of 25 frames per second, even a one second of color film requires approximately 19 megabytes of memory. Thus, the necessity for compression is obvious.

There exists a number of universal data compression algorithms that can compress almost any kind of data, of which the best known are the family of Ziv-Lempel algorithms. These methods are lossless in the sense that they retain all the information of the compressed data. However, they do not take advantage of the 2-dimensional nature of the image data. Moreover, only a small portion of the data space can be saved by a lossless compression method, and thus lossy methods are more widely used in image compression. In the use of lossy compression, there is always a trade-off between the bit rate and the image quality.

A common characteristic of most images is that the neighboring pixels are correlated and therefore contain redundant information. The foremost task then is to find less correlated representation of the image. Two fundamental components of compression are redundancy and irrelevancy reduction. *Redundancy reduction* aims at removing duplication from the signal source (image/video) [32]. *Irrelevancy reduction* omits parts of the signal that will not be noticed by the signal receiver, namely the Human Visual System (HVS).

In general, three types of redundancy can be identified:

- **Spatial Redundancy** or correlation between neighboring pixel values.

- **Spectral Redundancy** or correlation between different color planes or spectral bands.

- **Temporal Redundancy** or correlation between adjacent frames in a sequence of images (in video applications).

Image compression research aims at reducing the number of bits needed to represent an image by removing the spatial and spectral redundancies as much as possible. Since we will focus only on still image compression, we will not worry about temporal redundancy.

Compression Ratio

Compression ratios are commonly present in discussions of data compression. A compression ratio is simply the size of the original data divided by the size of the compressed data. A technique that compresses a 1 megabyte image to 100 kilobytes has achieved a compression ratio of 10 [40].

compression ratio = original data/compressed data = 1 M bytes/ 100 k bytes = 10.0

For a given image, the greater the compression ratio, the smaller the final image will be.

5.2 Principle of Compression

A typical lossy image compression system is shown in Fig. 5.1. There are three components for the encoder namely Source Encoder, Quantizer and Entropy Encoder.

Source Encoder (Linear Transforms)

Over the years, a variety of linear transforms have been developed which include Discrete Fourier Transform (DFT), Discrete Cosine Transform (DCT), Discrete Wavelet Transform (DWT) and many more, each with its own advantages and disadvantages.

Quantizer

A quantizer simply reduces the number of bits needed to store the transformed coefficients by reducing the precision of those values. Since this is a many-to-one mapping, it is a lossy process and is the main source of compression in an encoder. Quantization can be performed on each individual coefficient, which is known as Scalar Quantization (SQ). Quantization can also be performed on a group of coefficients together, and this is known as Vector Quantization (VQ) [54].

Entropy Encoder

An entropy encoder further compresses the quantized values losslessly to give better overall compression. It uses a model to accurately determine the probabilities for each quantized value and produces an appropriate code based on these probabilities so that the resultant output code stream will be smaller than the input stream. The most commonly used entropy encoders are the Huffman encoder and the arithmetic encoder.

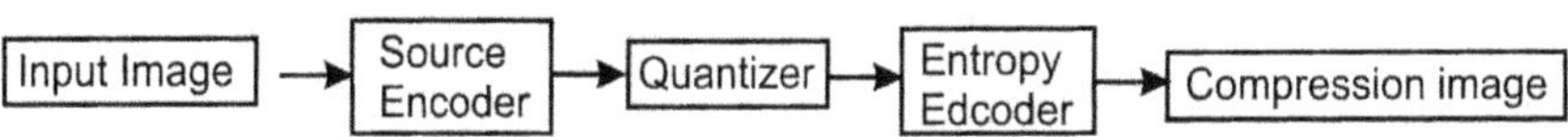

Fig. 5.1 Lossy Image Compression System.

5.3 Types of Compression

Two ways of classifying compression techniques are :

(a) *Lossless vs. Lossy compression :* In lossless compression schemes, the reconstructed image, after compression, is numerically identical to the original image. However lossless compression can only achieve a modest amount of compression. An image reconstructed following lossy compression contains degradation relative to the original [46]. Often this is because the compression scheme completely discards redundant information. However, lossy schemes are capable of achieving much higher compression. Under normal viewing conditions, no visible loss is perceived (visually lossless).

(b) *Predictive vs. Transform coding :* In predictive coding, information already sent or available is used to predict future values, and the difference is coded. Since this is done in the image or spatial domain, it is relatively simple to implement and is readily adapted to local image characteristics. Differential Pulse Code Modulation (DPCM) is one particular example of predictive coding. Transform coding, on the other hand, first transforms the image from its spatial domain representation to a different type of representation using some well-known transform and then codes the transformed values (coefficients). This method provides greater data compression compared to predictive methods, although at the expense of greater computation [60].

Lossy compression schemes allow redundant and nonessential information to be lost. Typically with lossy schemes there is a tradeoff between compression and image quality. You may be able to compress an image down to an incredibly small size but it looks so poor that it isn't worth the trouble. Though not always the case, lossy compression techniques are typically more complex and require more computations.

Lossy image compression schemes remove data from an image that the human eye wouldn't notice. This works well for images that are meant to be viewed by humans. If the image is to be analyzed by a machine, lossy compression schemes may not be appropriate. Computers can easily detect the information loss that the human eye may not. The goal of lossy compression is that the final decompressed image be visually lossless. Hopefully, the information removed from the image goes unnoticed by the human eye.

Many people associate huge degradations with lossy image compression. What they don't realize is that the most of the degradations are small if even noticeable. The entire imaging operation is lossy, scanning or digitizing the image is a lossy process, and displaying an image on a screen or printing the hardcopy is lossy. The goal is to keep the losses indistinguishable.

Which compression technique to use depends on the image data. Some images, especially those used for medical diagnosis, cannot afford to lose any data. A lossless compression scheme will need to be used. Computer generated graphics with large areas of the same color compress well with simple lossless schemes like run length encoding or LZW [10]. Continuous tone images with complex shapes and shading will require a lossy compression technique to achieve a high compression ratio. Images with a high degree of detail that can't be lost, such as detailed CAD drawings, cannot be compressed with lossy algorithms.

When choosing a compression technique, you must look at more than the achievable compression ratio. The compression ratio alone tells you nothing about the quality of the resulting image. Other things to consider are the compression/ decompression time, algorithm complexity, cost and availability of computational resources, and how standardized the technique is. If you use a compression method that achieves fantastic compression ratios but you are the only one using it, you will be limited in your applications. If your images need to be viewed by any hospital in the world, it is better to use a standardized compression technique and file format.

If the compression/decompression will be limited to one system or set of systems you may wish to develop your own algorithm. Perhaps there are different aspects you wish to draw from different algorithms and optimize them for your specific application (Fig. 5.2).

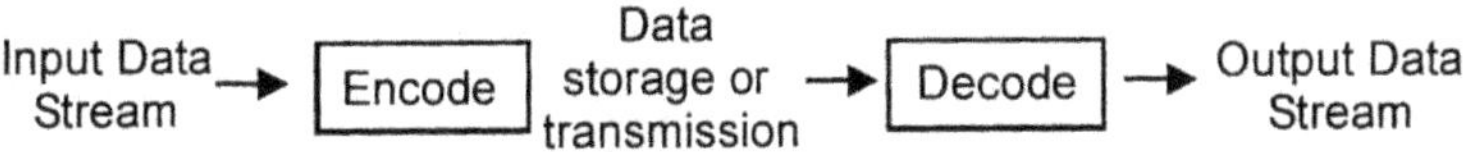

Fig. 5.2 A typical data compression system.

Before presenting the compression algorithms, it is needed to define a few terms used in the data compression world.

A *character* is a fundamental data element in the input stream. It may be a single letter of text or a pixel in an image file.

Strings are sequences of characters.

The *input stream* is the source of the uncompressed data to be compressed. It may be a data file or some communication medium.

Codewords are the data elements used to represent the input characters or character strings. Also the term *encoding* to mean compressing is used. As expected, decoding and decompressing are the opposite terms.

In many of the following discussions, ASCII strings is used as data set. The data objects used in compression could be text, binary data, or in our case, pixels. It is easy to follow a text string through compression and decompression examples.

5.4 Run Length Encoding

Run-length encoding (RLE) is a very simple form of data compression in which runs of data (that is, sequences in which the same data value occurs in many consecutive data elements) are stored as a single data value and count, rather than as the original run. This is most useful on data that contains many such runs; for example, simple graphic images such as icons and line drawings.

For example, consider a screen containing plain black text on a solid white background. There will be many long runs of white pixels in the blank space, and many short runs of black pixels within the text. Let us take a hypothetical single scan line, with B representing a black pixel and W representing white:

W W W W W W W W W W W W B W W W W W W W W W W W W BB
B W W W W W W W W W WW W W WW W W W W W W W W W W W B W W
W W W W W W W W W W W W

If we apply a simple run-length code to the above hypothetical scan line, we get the following :

12WB12W3B24WB14W

Interpret this as twelve W's, one B, twelve W's, three B's, etc. The run-length code represents the original 67 characters in only 16. Of course, the actual format used for the storage of images is generally binary rather than ASCII characters like this, but the principle remains the same. Even binary data files can be compressed with this method; file format specifications often dictate repeated bytes in files as padding space. However, newer compression systems often use *deflation* or other LZ77-based algorithms, which can take advantage of runs of strings of characters (such as B W W B W W B W W B W W) [56].

Common formats for run-length encoded data include PackBits, PCX and ILBM.

Run-length encoding performs lossless data compression and is well suited to palette-based iconic images. It does not work well at all on continuous-tone images such as photographs, although JPEG uses it quite effectively on the coefficients that remain after transforming and quantizing image blocks.

Data that has long sequential runs of bytes (such as lower-quality sound samples) can be RLE compressed after *Delta encoding* is applied to it.

Run length encoding is one of the simplest data compression techniques, taking advantage of repetitive data. Some images have large areas of constant color. These repeating characters are called runs. The encoding technique is a simple one. Runs are represented with a count and the original data byte. For example, a source string of

A A A A B B B B B C C C C C C C C D E E E

could be represented with

4 A 5 B 8 C 1 D 4 E

Four As are represented as 4A. Five Bs are represented as 5 B and so forth. This example represents 22 bytes of data with 10 bytes, achieving a compression ratio of:

22 bytes / 10 bytes = 2.2.

That works fine and dandy for my hand-picked string of ASCII characters. You will probably never see that set of characters printed in that sequence outside of this book. What if we pick an actual string of English like:

MyDogHasFleas

It would be encoded

l M l y l D l o l g l H l a l s l F l l l e l a l s

Here we have represented 13 bytes with 26 bytes achieving a compression ratio of 0.5. We have actually expanded our original data by a factor of two. We need a better method and luckily, one exists. We can represent unique strings of data as the original strings and run length encode only repetitive data. This is done with a special prefix character to flag runs. Runs are then represented as the special character followed by the count followed by the data. If we use a + as our special prefix character, we can encode the following string

A B C D D D D D D D D D E E E E E E E E E

as

ABC + 8D + 9E

achieving a compression ratio of 2.11 (19 bytes/9 bytes). Since it takes three bytes to encode a run of data, it makes sense to encode only runs of 3 or longer. Otherwise, you are expanding your data. What happens when your special prefix character is found in the source data? If this happens, you must encode your character as a run of length 1. Since this will expand your data by a factor of 3, you will want to pick a character that occures infrequently for your prefix character [59].

The MacPaint image file format uses run length encoding, combining the prefix character with the count byte (Fig. 5.3). It has two types of data strings with corresponding prefix bytes. One encodes runs of repetitive data. The other encodes strings of unique data. The two data strings look like those shown in Fig. 5.3.

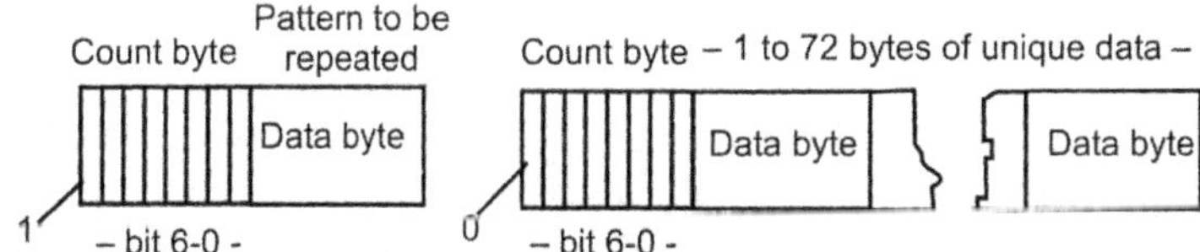

Fig. 5.3 MacPaint encoding format.

The most significant bit of the prefix byte determines if the string that follows is repeating data or unique data. If the bit is set, that byte stores the count (in twos complement) of how many times to repeat the next data byte. If the bit is not set, that byte plus one is the number of how many of the following bytes are unique and can be copied verbatim to the output. Only seven bits are used for the count. The width of an original MacPaint image is 576 pixels, so runs are therefore limited to 72 bytes.

The PCX file format run length encodes the separate planes of an image. It sets the two most significant bits if there is a run. This leaves six bits, limiting the count to 63. Other image file formats that use run length encoding are RLE and GEM. The TIFF and TGA file format specifications allow for optional run length encoding of the image data.

Run length encoding works very well for images with solid backgrounds like cartoons. For natural images, it doesn't work as well. Also because run length encoding capitalizes on characters repeating more than three times, it doesn't work well with English text. A method that would achieve better results is one that uses fewer bits to represent the most frequently occurring data. Data that occurs less frequently would require more bits. This variable length coding is the idea behind Huffman coding.

5.5 Huffman Coding

In 1952, a paper by David Huffman was published presenting Huffman coding. This technique was the state of the art until about 1977. The beauty of Huffman codes is that variable length codes can achieve a higher data density than fixed length codes if the characters differ in frequency of occurrence. The length of the encoded character is inversely proportional to that character's frequency. Huffman wasn't the first to discover this, but his paper presented the optimal algorithm for assigning these codes.

Huffman codes are similar to the Morse code. Morse code uses few dots and dashes for the most frequently occurring letter. An E is represented with one dot. A T is represented with one dash. Q, a letter occurring less frequently is represented with dash-dash-dot-dash [36].

Huffman codes are created by analyzing the data set and assigning short bit streams to the datum occurring most frequently. The algorithm attempts to create codes that minimize the average number of bits per character. Table 5.1 shows an example of the frequency of letters in some text and their corresponding Huffman code. To keep the table manageable, only letters were used. It is well known that in English text, the space character is the most frequently occurring character.

As expected, E and T had the highest frequency and the shortest Huffman codes. Encoding with these codes is simple. Encoding the word *toupee* would be just a matter of stringing together the appropriate bit strings, as follows:

$$\begin{array}{cccccc} T & 0 & U & P & E & E \\ 111 & 0100 & 10111 & 10110 & 100 & 100 \end{array}$$

One ASCII character requires 8 bits. The original 48 bits of data have been coded with 23 bits achieving a compression ratio of 2.08.

Table 5.1 Huffman codes for the alphabet letters.

Letter	Frequency	Code
A	8.23	0000
B	1.26	110000
C	4.04	1101
D	3.40	01011
E	12.32	100
F	2.28	11001
G	2.77	10101
H	3.94	00100
I	8.08	0001
J	0.14	110001001
K	0.43	1100011
L	3.79	00101
M	3.06	10100
N	6.81	0110
O	7.59	0100
P	2.58	10110
Q	0.14	1100010000
R	6.67	0111
S	7.64	0011
T	8.37	111
U	2.43	10111
V	0.97	0101001
W	1.07	0101000
X	0.29	11000101
Y	1.46	010101
Z	0.09	1100010001

During the codes creation process, a binary tree representing these codes is created. Figure 5.4 shows the binary tree representing Table 5.1. It is easy to get codes from the tree. Start at the root and trace the branches down to the letter of interest. Every branch that goes to the right represents a 1. Every branch to the left is a 0. If we want the code for the letter R, we start at the root and go left-right-right-right yielding a code of 0111 [15].

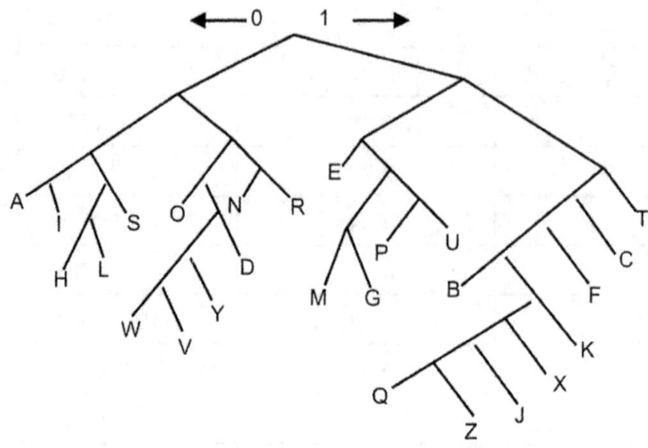

Fig. 5.4 Binary tree of alphabet [18].

Using a binary tree to represent Huffman codes insures that our codes have the prefix property. This means that one code cannot be the prefix of another code. (Maybe it should be called the non-prefix property.) If we represent the letter e as 01, we could not encode another letter as 010. Say we also tried to represent b as 010. As the decoder scanned the input bit stream 0 10 .... as soon as it saw 01, it would output an e and start the next code with 0. As you can expect, everything beyond that output would be garbage. Anyone who has debugged software dealing with variable length codes can verify that one incorrect bit will invalidate all subsequent data. All variable length encoding schemes must have the prefix property.

The first step in creating Huffman codes is to create an array of character frequencies. This is as simple as parsing your data and incrementing each corresponding array element for each character encountered. The binary tree can easily be constructed by recursively grouping the lowest frequency characters and nodes. The algorithm is as follows :

1. All characters are initially considered free nodes.
2. The two free nodes with the lowest frequency are assigned to a parent node with a weight equal to the sum of the two free child nodes.

3. The two child nodes are removed from the free nodes list. The newly created parent node is added to the list.

4. Steps 2 through 3 are repeated until there is only one free node left. This free node is the root of the tree.

When creating your binary tree, you may run into two unique characters with the same frequency. It really doesn't matter what you use for your tie-breaking scheme but you must be consistent between the encoder and decoder.

Let's create a binary tree for the image below. The 8 × 8 pixel image is small to keep the example simple. In the section on JPEG encoding, you will see that images are broken into 8 × 8 blocks for encoding. The letters represent the colors Red, Green, Blue, Cyan, Magenta, Yellow, and Black (Fig. 5.5).

R	K	K	K	K	K	K	K
K	K	K	R	R	K	K	K
K	K	R	R	R	R	G	G
K	K	B	C	C	C	R	R
G	G	G	M	C	B	R	R
B	B	B	M	Y	B	B	R
G	G	G	G	G	G	G	R
G	R	R	R	R	G	R	R

Fig. 5.5 Sample 8 × 8 screen of red, green, blue, cyan, magenta, yellow, and black pixels.

Before building the binary tree, the frequency table (Table 5.2) must be generated.

Table 5.2 Frequency table for Fig. 5.5

Color	Frequency
red	19
black	17
green	14
blue	7
cyan	4
magenta	2
yellow	1

Fig. 5.6 shows the free nodes table as the tree is built. In step 1, all values are marked as free nodes. The two lowest frequencies, magenta and yellow, are combined in step 2. Cyan is then added to the current sub-tree; blue and green are added in steps 4 and 5. In step 6, rather than adding a new color to the sub-tree, a new parent node is created.

This is because the addition of the black and red weights (36) produced a smaller number than adding black to the sub-tree (45). In step 7, the final tree is created. To keep consistent between the encoder and decoder, I order the nodes by decreasing weights. You will notice in step 1 that yellow (weight of 1) is to the right of magenta (weight of 2). This protocol is maintained throughout the tree building process (Fig. 5.6). The resulting Huffman codes are shown in Table 5.3.

Table 5.3 Huffman codes for Fig. 5.5.

Color	Frequency
red	00
black	01
green	10
blue	111
cyan	1100
magenta	11010
yellow	11011

When using variable length codes, there are a couple of important things to keep in mind. First, they are more difficult to manipulate with software. You are no longer working with ints and longs. You are working at a bit level and need your own bit manipulation routines. Also, variable length codes are more difficult to manipulate inside a computer. Computer instructions are designed to work with byte and multiple byte objects. Objects of variable bit lengths introduce a little more complexity when writing and debugging software. Second, as previously described, you are no longer working on byte boundaries. One corrupted bit will wipe out the rest of your data. There is no way to know where the next codeword begins. With fixed-length codes, you know exactly where the next codeword begins.

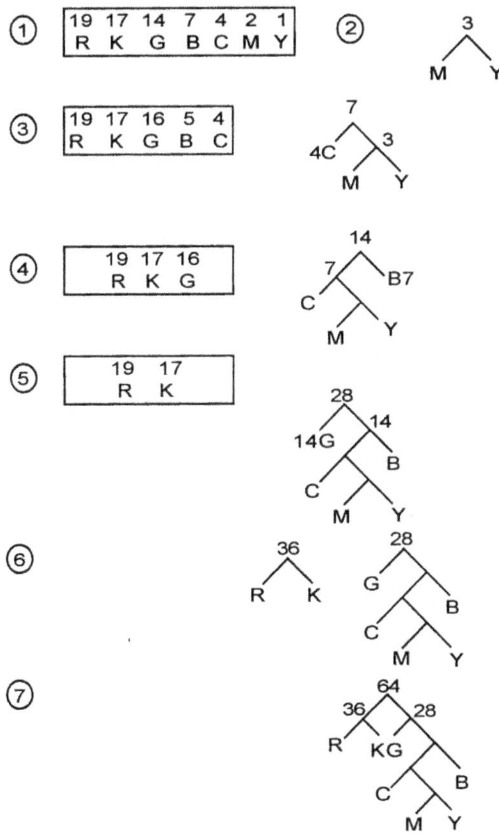

Fig. 5.6 Binary tree creation.

One drawback to Huffman coding is that encoding requires two passes over the data. The first pass accumulates the character frequency data, which is then compressed on the second pass. One way to remove a pass is to always use one fixed table. Of course, the table will not be optimized for every data set that will be compressed. The modified Huffman coding technique in the next section uses fixed tables.

The decoder must use the same binary tree as the encoder. Providing the tree to the decoder requires using a standard tree that may not be optimum for the code being compressed. Another option is to store the binary tree with the data. Rather than storing the tree, the character frequency could be stored and the decoder could regenerate the tree. This would increase decoding time. Adding the character frequency to the compressed code decreases the compression ratio [50].

The next coding method has overcome the problem of losing data when one bit gets corrupted. It is used in fax machines which communicate over noisy phone lines. It has a synchronization mechanism to minimize data loss to one scanline.

5.6   Modified Huffman Coding

Modified Huffman coding is used in fax machines to encode black on white images (bitmaps). It is also an option to compress images in the TIFF file format. It combines the variable length codes of Huffman coding with the coding of repetitive data in run length encoding [52].

Since facsimile transmissions are typically black text or writing on white background, only one bit is required to represent each pixel or sample. These samples are referred to as white bits and black bits. The runs of white bits and black bits are counted, and the counts are sent as variable length bit streams.

The encoding scheme is fairly simple. Each line is coded as a series of alternating runs of white and black bits. Runs of 63 or less are coded with a *terminating code*. Runs of 64 or greater require that a *makeup code* prefix the terminating code. The makeup codes are used to describe runs in multiples of 64 from 64 to 2560. This deviates from the normal Huffman scheme which would normally require encoding all 2560 possibilities [59]. This reduces the size of the Huffman code tree and accounts for the term *modified* in the name.

Studies have shown that most facsimiles are 85 percent white, so the Huffman codes have been optimized for long runs of white and short runs of black. The protocol also assumes that the line begins with a run of white bits. If it doesn't, a run of white bits of 0 length must begin the encoded line. The encoding then alternates between black bits and white bits to the end of the line. Each scan line ends with a special EOL (end of line) character consisting of eleven zeros and a 1 (000000000001). The EOL character doubles as an error recovery code. Since there is no other combination of codes that has more than seven zeroes in succession, a decoder seeing eight will recognize the end of line and continue scanning for a 1. Upon receiving the 1, it will then start a new line. If bits in a scan line get corrupted, the most that will be lost is the rest of the line. If the EOL code gets corrupted, the most that will get lost is the next line.

Tables 5.4 and 5.5 show the terminating and makeup codes. Fig. 5.7 shows how to encode a 1275 pixel scanline with 53 bits.

Table 5.4 Terminating codes

Run Length	White bits	Black bits	Run Length	White bits	Black bit
0	00110101	0000110111	32	00011011	000001101010
1	000111	010	33	00010010	000001101011
2	0111	11	34	00010011	000011010010
3	1000	10	35	00010100	000011010011
4	1011	011	36	00010101	000011010100
5	1100	0011	37	00001110	000011010101
6	1110	0010	38	00010111	000011010110
7	1111	00011	39	00101000	000011010111
8	10011	000101	40	00101001	000001101100
9	10100	000100	41	00101010	000001101101
10	00111	0000100	42	00101011	000011011010
11	01000	0000101	43	00101100	000011011011
12	001000	0000111	44	00101101	000001010100
13	000011	00000100	45	00000100	000001010101
14	110100	00000111	46	00000101	000001010110
15	110101	000011000	47	00001010	000001010111
16	101010	0000010111	48	00001011	000001100100
17	101011	0000011000	49	01010010	000001100101
18	0100111	0000001000	50	01010011	000001010010
19	0001100	00001100111	51	01010100	000001010011
20	0001000	00001101000	52	01010101	000000100100
21	0010111	00001101100	53	00100100	000000110111
22	0000011	00000110111	54	00100101	000000111000
23	0000100	00000101000	55	01011000	000000100111
24	0101000	00000010111	56	01011001	000000101000
25	0101011	00000011000	57	01011010	000001011000
26	0010011	000011001010	58	01011011	000001011001
27	0100100	000011001011	59	01001010	000000101011
28	0011000	000011001100	60	01001011	000000101100
29	00000010	000011001101	61	00110010	000001011010
30	00000011	000001101000	62	001110011	000001100110
31	00011010	000001101001	62	00110100	000001100111

Table 5.5 Makeup code words

Run Length	White bits	Black bits
64	11011	000000111
128	10010	00011001000
192	010111	000011001001
256	0110111	000001011011
320	00110110	000000110011
384	00110111	000000110100
448	01100100	000000110101
512	01100101	0000001101100
576	01101000	0000001101101
640	01100111	0000001001010
704	011001100	0000001001011
768	011001101	0000001001100
832	011010010	0000001001101
896	101010011	0000001110010
960	011010100	0000001110011
1024	011010101	0000001110100
1088	011010110	0000001110101
1152	011010111	0000001110110
1216	011011000	0000001110111
1280	011011001	0000001010010
1344	011011010	0000001010011
1408	011011011	0000001010100
1472	010011000	0000001010101
1536	010011001	0000001011010
1600	010011010	0000001011011
1664	011000	0000001100100
1728	010011011	0000001100101
1792	00000001000	00000001000
1856	00000001100	00000001100
1920	00000001101	00000001101
1984	000000010010	000000010010
2048	000000010011	000000010011
2112	000000010100	000000010100
2170	000000010101	000000010101
2240	000000010110	000000010110
2304	000000010111	000000010111
2368	000000011100	000000011100
2432	000000011101	000000011101
2496	00000011110	00000011110
2560	00000011111	000000011111
EOL	000000000001	000000000001

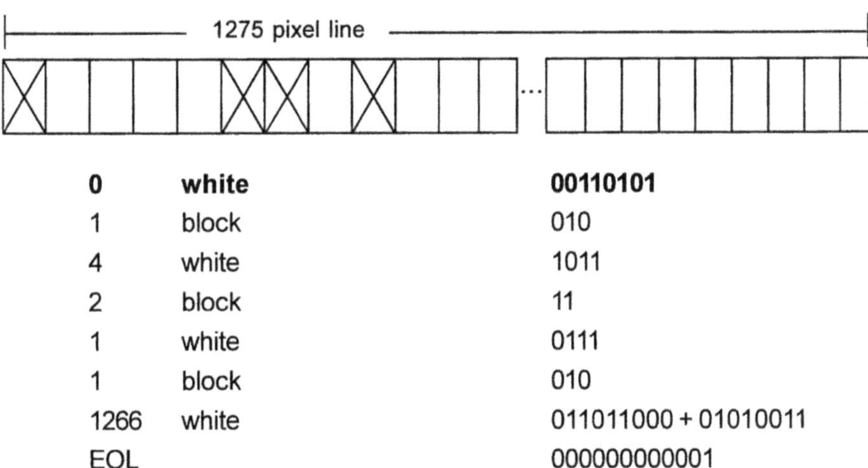

0	**white**	**00110101**
1	block	010
4	white	1011
2	block	11
1	white	0111
1	block	010
1266	white	011011000 + 01010011
EOL		000000000001

Fig. 5.7 Example encoding of a scanline.

5.7 Modified READ

Modified READ is a 2-dimensional coding technique also used for bilevel bitmaps. It is also used by tax machines. The Modified READ (Relative Element Address Designate) is a superset of the modified Huffman coding (Fig. 5.8).

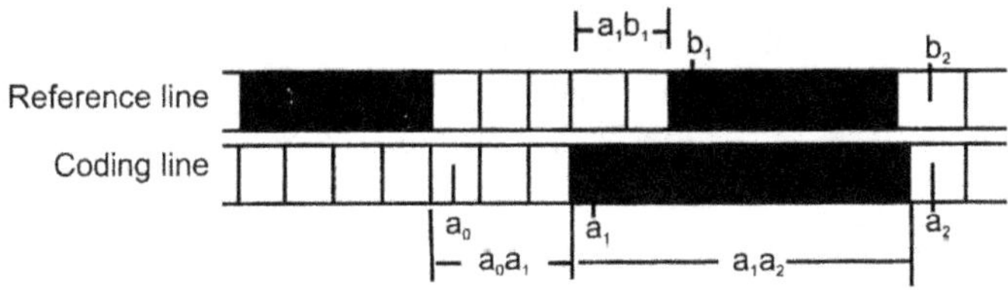

Fig. 5.8 Reference point and lengths used during modified READ encoding

Research shows that 75 percent of all transitions in bilevel fax transmissions occur one pixel to the right or left or directly below a transition on the line above. The Modified READ algorithm exploits this property.

The first line in a set of K scanlines is encoded with modified Huffman and the remaining lines are encoded with reference to the line above it. The encoding uses bit transitions as reference points. These transitions have names :

1. a_o This is the starting changing element on the scan line being encoded. At the beginning of a new line, this position is just to the left of the first element.

2. a_1 This is the next transition to the right of a_o on the same line. This has the opposite color of a_0 and is the next element to be coded.

3. a_2 This is the next transition to the right of a_1 on the same line.

4. b_1 This is the next changing element to the right of a_0 but on the reference line. This bit has the same color as a_1.

5. b_2 This is the next transition to the right of b_1 on the same line.

With these transitions there are three different coding modes:

1. *Pass mode coding* : This mode occurs when b_2 lies to the left of a_1. This mode ignores pairs of transitions that occur on the reference line but not on the coding line.

2. *Vertical mode coding* : This mode is used when the horizontal position of a_1 *is* within three pixels to the left or right of b_1

3. *Horizontal mode coding* : This mode is used when vertical mode coding cannot be used. In this case, the flag word 001 is followed by the modified Huffman encoding of $a_0a_1 + a_1a_2$

The codes for these modes can be summarized as shown in Table 5.6.

Table 5.6

S.No.	Modes	Codes
1.	Pass	0001
2.	Vertical	
	a_1 under b_1	1
	a_1 one pixel to the right of b_1	011
	a_1 two pixels to the right of b_1	000011
	a_1 three pixels to the right of b_1	0000011
3.	Horizontal	$001 + M(a_0a_1) + M(a_1a_2)$

where $M(x)$ is the modified Huffman code of x. The encoding is a fairly simple process :

1. Code the first line using the modified Huffman method.

2. Use this line as the reference line.

3. The next line is now considered the coding line

4. If a pair of transitions is in the reference line but not the coding line, use pass mode.

5. If the transition is within three pixels of b_1, use vertical mode.

6. If neither step 4 nor step 5 apply, use horizontal mode.

7. When the coding line is completed, use this as the new reference line.

8. Repeat steps 4, 5, and 6 until K lines are coded.

9. After coding K lines, code a new reference line with modified Huffman encoding.

One problem with the 2-dimensional coding is that if the reference line has an error, every line in the block of K lines will be corrupt. For this reason, facsimile machines keep K small.

Currently, there is a committee to define a compression standard to replace the modified READ standard. This group is the Joint Bi-Level Image Experts Group (JBIG). Its mission is to define a compression standard for lossless compression of black-and-white images. Due to the proliferation of the modified READ in all fax machines today, modified READ should be around for a few more years. The flow chart of the modified READ algorithm is given in Fig. 5.9.

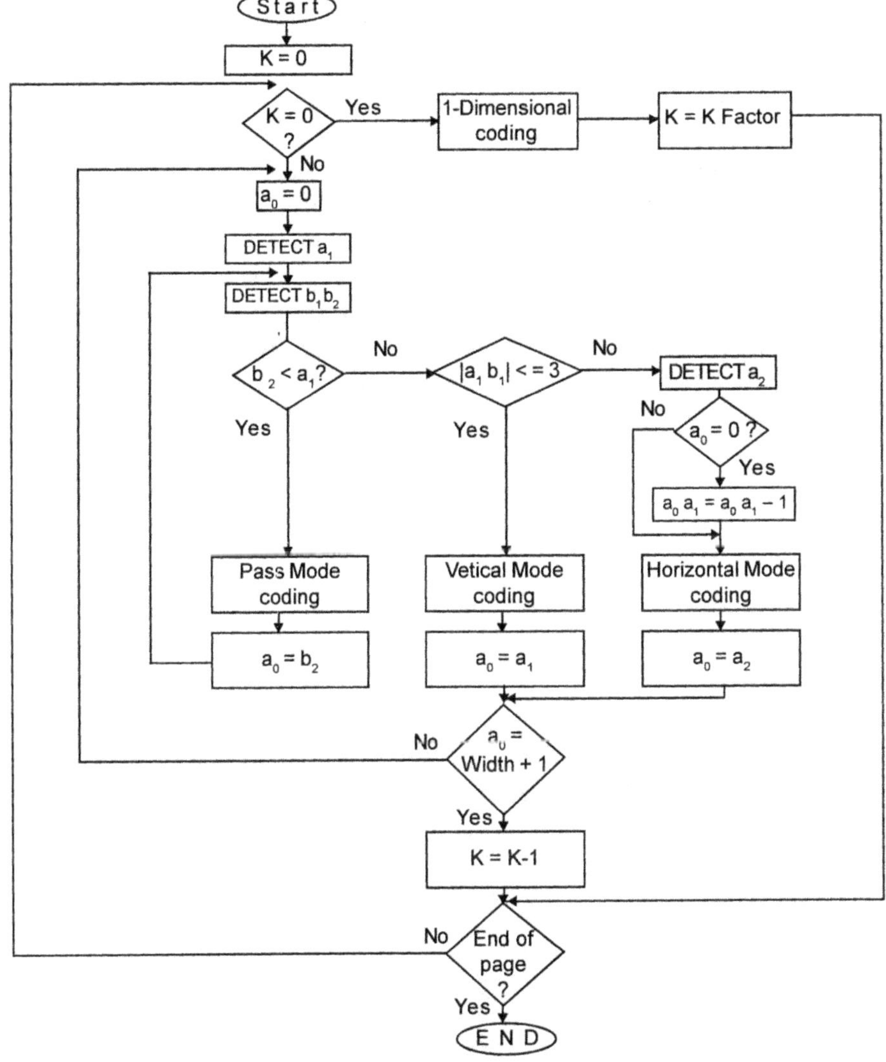

Fig. 5.9 Modified READ flowchart [39].

5.8 LZW

In 1977, a paper was published by Abraham Lempel and Jacob Ziv laying the foundation for the next big step in data compression. While Huffman coding achieved good results, it was typically limited to coding one character at a time. Lempel and Ziv proposed a scheme for encoding strings of data. This technique took advantage of sequences of characters that occur frequently like the word *the* or a period followed by a space in text files.

IEEE Computer published a paper by Terry Welch in 1984 that presented the LZW (Lempel Ziv Welch) algorithm. This paper improved upon the original by proposing a code table that could be created the same way in the compressor and the decompressor. There was no need to include this information with the compressed data. This algorithm was implemented in myriad applications. It is the compression method used in the UNIX compress command. LZW became the technique for data compression in the personal computer world. It is the compression algorithm used in ARC and the basis for compression of images in the GIF file format.

Although the implementation of LZW can get tricky, the algorithm is surprisingly simple. It seeks to replace strings of characters with single codewords that are stored in a string table. Most implementations of LZW used 12-bit codewords to represent 8-bit input characters [50]. The string table is 4096 locations, since that is how many unique locations you can address with a 12-bit index. The first 256 locations are initialized to the single characters (location 0 stores 0, location 1 stores 1, and so on). As new combinations of characters are parsed in the input stream, these strings are added to the string table, and will be stored in locations 256 to 4095 in the table.

The data parser will continue to parse new input characters as long as the string exists in the string table. As soon as an additional character creates a new string that is not in the table, it is entered into it and the code for last known string is output.

The compression algorithm is as follows :

Initialize table with single character strings

STRING = first input character

WHILE not end of input stream

    CHARACTER = next input character

    IF STRING + CHARACTER is in the string table

        STRING = STRING + CHARACTER

ELSE

> **output the code for STRING**
>
> **add STRING + CHARACTER to the string table**
>
> **STRING = CHARACTER**

END WHILE

output code for string

If you hand code a few examples, you quickly get a feel for it. Let's compress the string BABAABAAA.

Following the above algorithm, we set STRING equal to B and CHARACTER equal to A. We then output the code for string (66 for B) and add BA to our string table. Since 0 to 255 have been initialized to single characters in the string table, our first available entry is 256. Our new STRING is set to A and we start at the top of the WHILE loop. This process is repeated until the input stream is exhausted. As we encode the data we output codes and create a string table as shown in Table 5.7.

Table 5.7

Encoder	Output	String	Table
output code	Representing	codeword	string
66	B	256	BA
65	A	257	AB
256	BA	258	BAA
257	AB	259	ABA
65	A	260	AA
260	B		

Our output stream is <66><65><256><257><65><260>.

The LZW decompressor creates the same string table during decompression. It starts with the first 256 table entries initialized to single characters. The string table is updated for each character in the input stream, except the first one. After the character has been expanded to its corresponding string via the string table, the final character of the string is appended to the previous string. This new string is added to the table in the same location as in the compressor's string table.

The decompression algorithm is also simple :

Initialize table with single character strings

OLD_CODE = first input character

output translation of OLD_CODE

WHILE not end of input stream

   NEW_CODE = next input character

   IF NEW_CODE is not in the string table

      STRING = translation of OLD_CODE

      STRING = STRING + CHARACTER

   ELSE

      STRING = translation of NEW_CODE

   output STRING

   CHARACTER = first character of STRING

   add OLD_CODE + CHARACTER to the string table

   OLD_CODE = NEW_CODE

END WHILE

Let's decompress our compressed data <66><65><256><257><65><260>. First we input the first character, 66, into OLD - CODE and output the translation (B). We read (65) into NEW-CODE. Since NEW-CODE is in the string table we set STRING = A. A is then output. CHARACTER is set to A and BA is our first entry in the string table [28]. OLD-CODE gets set to 65 and jump to the beginning of the WHILE loop. The process continues until we have processed all the compressed data. The decompression process yields output and creates a string table like that shown below (Table 5.8).

Table 5.8

Decoder	String	Table
string	codeword	string
B		
A	256	BA
BA	257	AB
AB	258	BAA
A	259	ABA
AA	260	AA

This algorithm compresses repetitive sequences of data well. Since the codewords are 12 bits, any single encoded character will expand the data size rather than reduce it. This is always seen in the early stages of compressing a data set with LZW. In this example, 72 bits are represented with 72 bits of data (compression ratio of 1). After a reasonable string table is built, compression improves dramatically.

During compression, what happens when we have used all 4096 locations in our string table? There are several options. The first would be to simply forget about adding any more entries and use the table as is. Another would be to clear entries 256-4095 and start building the tree again. Some clever schemes clear those entries and rebuild a string table from the last N input characters. N could be something like 1024. The UNIX compress utility constantly monitors the compression ratio and when it dips below the set threshold, it resets the string table.

One advantage of LZW over Huffman coding is that it can compress the input stream in one single pass. It requires no prior information about the input data stream [47]. The string table is built on the fly during compression and decompression. Another advantage is its simplicity, allowing fast execution.

As mentioned earlier, the GIF image file format uses a variant of LZW. It achieves better compression than the technique just explained because it uses variable length codewords. Since the table is initialized to the first 256 single characters, only one more bit is needed to create new string table indices. Codewords are nine bits wide until entry number 511 is created in the string table. At this point, the length of the codewords increases to ten bits. The length can increase up to 12 bits. As you can imagine, this increases compression but adds complexity to GIF encoders and decoders.

GIF also has two specially defined characters. A clear code is used to reinitialize the string table to the first 256 single characters and codeword length to nine bits. An end-of information code is appended to the end of the data stream. This signals the end of the image [50].

5.9 Arithmetic Coding

Arithmetic coding is unlike all the other methods discussed in that it takes in the complete data stream and outputs one specific codeword. This codeword is a floating point number between 0 and 1. The bigger the input data set, the more digits in the number output. This unique number is encoded such that when decoded, it will output the exact input data stream. Arithmetic coding, like Huffman, is a two-pass algorithm. The first pass computes the characters' frequency and generates a probability table. The second pass does the actual compression [51].

The probability table assigns a range between 0 and 1 to each input character. The size of each range is directly proportional to a characters' frequency. The order of assigning these ranges is not as important as the fact that it must be used by both the encoder and decoder. The range consists of a low value and a high value. These parameters are very important to the encode/decode process. The more frequently occurring characters are assigned wider ranges in the interval requiring fewer bits to represent them. The less likely characters are assigned more narrow ranges, requiring more bits.

With arithmetic coding, you start out with the range 0.0-1.0 (Fig. 5.10). The first character input will constrain the output number with its corresponding range. The range of the next character input will further constrain the output number. The more input characters there are, the more precise the output number will be.

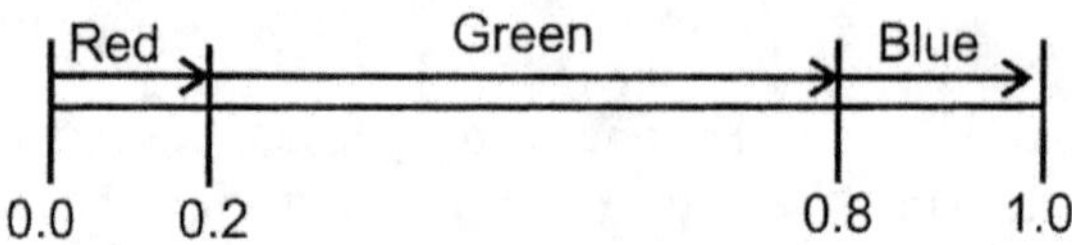

Fig. 5.10 Assignment of ranges between 0 and 1.

Suppose we are working with an image that is composed of only red, green, and blue pixels. After computing the frequency of these pixels, we have a probability table that looks like Table 5.9.

Table 5.9

Pixel	Probability	Assigned Range
Red	0.2	[0.0,0.2)
Green	0.6	[0.2,0.8)
Blue	0.2	[0.8,-1.0)

The algorithm to encode is very simple.

LOW   0. 0

HIGH   1.0

WHILE not end of input stream

    get next CHARACTER

    RANGE = HIGH - LOW

    HIGH = LOW + RANGE   * high range of CHARACTER

    LOW = LOW + RANGE   * low range of CHARACTER

END WHILE

output LOW

Fig. 5.11 shows how the range for our output is reduced as we process two possible input streams.

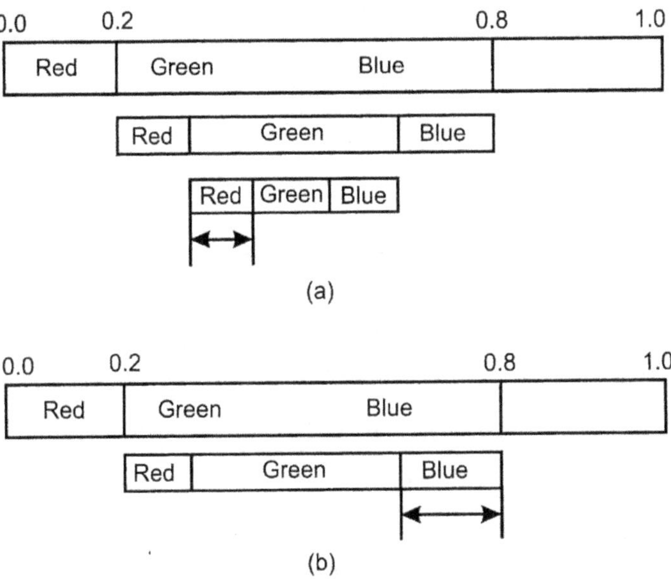

Fig. 5.11 Reduced output range: (a) Green-Green-Red; (b) Green-Blue-Green.

Let's encode the string ARITHMETIC. Our frequency analysis will produce the following probability Table 5.10.

Table 5.10

Symbol	Probability	Range
A	0.100000	0.000000 - 0.100000
C	0.100000	0.100000 - 0.200000
E	0.100000	0.200000 - 0.300000
H	0.100000	0.300000 - 0.400000
I	0.200000	0.400000 - 0.600000
M	0.100000	0.600000 - 0.700000
R	0.100000	0.700000 - 0.800000
T	0.200000	0.800000 - 1.000000

Before we start, LOW is 0 and HIGH is 1. Our first input is A. RANGE = 1 - 0 = 1. HIGH will be (0 + 1) x 0.1 = 0.1. LOW will be (0 + 1) x 0 = 0. These three calculations will be repeated until the input stream is exhausted. As we process each character in the string, RANGE, LOW, and HIGH will look like as Table 5.11.

Table 5.11

Range	Low	High
A range = 1.000000000	low = 0.0000000000	high = 0. 1000000000
R range =0.100000000	low=0.0700000000	high = 0.0800000000
I range =0.010000000	low=0.0740000000	high = 0.0760000000
T range = 0.002000000	low = 0.0756000000	high = 0.0760000000
H range = 0.000400000	low = 0.0757200000	high = 0.0757600000
M range = 0.000000000	low = 0.0757440000	high = 0.0757480000
E range = 0.000004000	low = 0.0757448000	high = 0.0757452000
T range = 0.000000400	low = 0.0757451200	high = 0.0757452000
I range = 0.000000080	low = 0.0757451520	high = 0.0757451680
C range = 0.0000000 16	low = 0.0757451536	high = 0.0757451552

Our output is then 0.0757451536.

The decoding algorithm is just the reverse process.

get NUMBER

DO

    find CHARACTER that has HIGH > NUMBER and LOW <NUMBER

    set HIGH and LOW corresponding to CHARACTER

    output CHARACTER

    RANGE = HIGH - LOW

    NUMBER = NUMBER - LOW

    NUMBER = NUMBER - RANGE

UNTIL no more CHARACTERs

As we decode 0.0757451536, we see

Table 5.12

Number	Character	Range	Low	High
num = 0.075745153600	A	Range = 0. 1	low = 0.0	high = 0. 1
num = 0.757451536000	R	Range = 0. 1	low = 0.7	high = 0.8
num = 0.574515360000	1	Range = 0.2	low = 0.4	high = 0.6
num = 0.872576800000	T	Range = 0.2	low = 0.8	high = 1.0
num = 0.362884000000	H	Range = 0. 1	low = 0.3	high = 0.4
num = 0.628840000000	M	Range = 0. 1	low = 0.6	high = 0.7
num = 0.288400000002	E	Range = 0. 1	low = 0.2	high = 0.3
num = 0.884000000024	T	Range = 0.2	low = 0.8	high = 1.0
num = 0.420000000120	1	Range = 0.2	low = 0.4	high = 0.6
num = 0.100000000598	C	Range = 0. 1	low = 0. 1	high = 0.2

Arithmetic coding is one possible algorithm for use in the entropy coder during JPEG compression. For JPEG compression, see the next part. JPEG achieves slightly higher compression ratios than the Huffman option but is computationally more intensive.

5.10 JPEG

JPEG is a family of compression techniques standardized by the Joint Photographic Experts Group. The 'Joint' in the title refers to the cooperative efforts of ISO and CCITT. ISO is the International Organization for Standardization. CCITT is the International Telegraph and Telephone Consultative Committee. The result of their efforts was the first international digital image compression standard [40].

Through the development of the standard, they had the following goals:

1. The standard would achieve state-of-the-art compression with user-adjustable compression ratios.

2. The standard would be applicable to any continuous tone digital image.

3. It would have manageable computational complexity for widespread implementation.

4. It would have four modes of operation:

    (a) *Sequential encoding :* encode each image in one single scan

    (b) *Progressive encoding :* encode image in multiple scans, decode image in multiple scans with each successive image being a better image

    (c) *Lossless encoding :* the decoded image is exact duplicate of original image

    (d) *Hierarchical encoding :* encode at multiple resolutions for display on different devices

JPEG has three modes of lossy compression and one lossless mode. Much larger compression ratios are achieved using lossy JPEG than the lossless flavor. For this reason, few actual implementations of lossless JPEG exists. The majority of this section will focus on the baseline sequential coding method.

JPEG compression takes advantage of a limitation of the human visual system. The human eye can perceive small changes in brightness better than small changes in color. This allows JPEG to remove some color information.

Impressive compression ratios can be achieved by JPEG, ratios of up to twenty to one can be achieved without noticeable difference from the original image. Although big compression ratios can be achieved with JPEG, it does not do well with all images. Its forte is continuous tone images. Cartoons and most computer generated images lose image quality when compressed with JPEG. JPEG filters out high frequency data and therefore does not do well with images composed of sharp edges.

When compressing images with JPEG, you can specify a quality level (Q or Q factor) for the resulting image. The higher Q is set, the greater the image quality and the larger the file size. Smaller Qs result in smaller files with a reduction in image quality. This is the classic quality versus compression ratio tradeoff present in lossy compression methods. Great compression ratios can be achieved before image quality suffers.

As the quality starts to degrade, you will notice a blocky structure in the image. As the quality gets worse, the image degenerates to a set of squares. These squares will consist of the average value of the pixels that compose that square. It will soon become apparent why this happens. Other artifacts that appear are contouring and ringing. Contouring shows up in regions of gradual shading. Ringing occurs around sharp edges.

JPEG is considered a symmetrical algorithm since it compresses and decompresses an image in the same number of operations (Fig. 5.12).

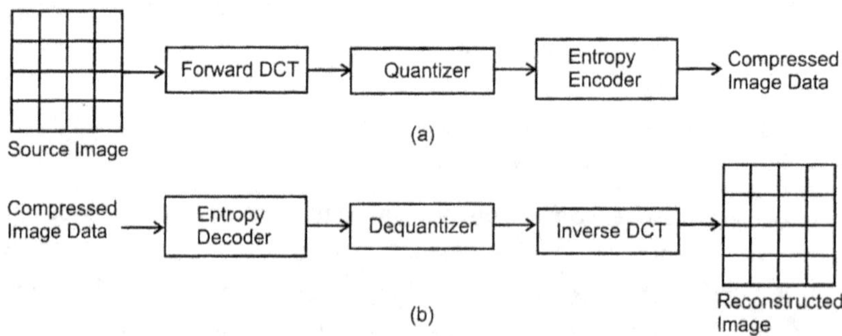

Fig. 5.12 Baseline JPEG (a) encoder, (b) decoder.

It therefore takes the same amount of time for decompression as compression. Baseline JPEG compression consists of five basic steps:

1. Transform image to luminance/chrominance color space ($YC_b C_r$).
2. Reduce the color components (optional).
3. Partition image into 8 x 8 pixel blocks and perform the DCT on each block.
4. Quantize resulting DCT coefficients.
5. Entropy code the reduced coefficients.

Let's take a look at each step. The first step requires us to transform the image from RGB to $YC_b C_r$. If the image is gray scale, no transform is necessary. The reason for the separation of luminance and chrominance is because more information is removed from the chrominance components than the luminance component.

The second step is optional but it is standard practice. While the luminance component is left at full resolution, the color components are subsampled by 2 horizontally and vertically. This is not the only subsampling scheme, but is one of the more popular ones. This subsampling can be done by throwing out every other pixel or averaging blocks of 4 pixels. This step is the first lossy step and the amount of data is reduced to one-half that of the original.

The third step consists of separating image components are broken into arrays or "tiles" of 8 x 8 pixels. The elements within the tiles are converted to signed integers (for pixels in the range of 0 to 255, subtract 128). These tiles are then transformed into the spatial frequency domain via the forward DCT. Element $(0,0)$ of the 8×8 block is referred to as DC. The 63 other elements are referred to as AC_{YX}, where x and y are the position of the element in the array. Here AC is the average value of the 8×8 original pixel values.

The fourth step requires us to quantize these blocks with quantization coefficients. This is the fundamental information losing step. Simply stated, the DCT coefficients are divided by their corresponding quantization coefficient and rounded to the nearest integer.

These coefficients are simply numbers stored in an array. The value of Q determines the quantization coefficients. This step reduces many of the elements to 0, making them ripe for lossless coding.

There are no fixed quantization tables set for JPEG use. Tables 5.13 and 5.14 are provided as examples. They produce good results with images of 8 bits per luminance and chrominance samples. If the values in these tables are divided by 2, the results are even better. The reconstructed image is nearly indistinguishable from the original image.

Table 5.13 Luminance quantization table.

16	11	10	16	24	40	51	61
12	12	14	19	26	58	60	55
14	13	16	24	40	57	69	56
14	17	22	29	51	87	80	62
18	22	37	56	68	109	103	77
24	35	55	64	81	104	113	92
49	64	78	87	103	121	120	101
72	92	95	98	112	100	103	99

Table 5.14 Chrominance quantization table.

17	18	24	47	99	99	99	99
18	21	26	66	99	99	99	99
24	26	56	99	99	99	99	99
47	66	99	99	99	99	99	99
99	99	99	99	99	99	99	99
99	99	99	99	99	99	99	99
99	99	99	99	99	99	99	99
99	99	99	99	99	99	99	99

The eye can't discern fine color detail, so we can remove a considerable amount of high-frequency data. As Q is decreased, more high-frequency data is removed. As Q gets lower and lower, the only frequency data that will remain is element (0,0) of the DCT transform (the average value). Q controls the values in the quantization tables.

The fifth and last step is lossless. String the resulting numbers together and encode them using Huffman codes, which actually represent different runs of different values. You will soon see that it is a form of run length encoding very similar to modified Huffman coding. Though this sounds easy, the method has been optimized for maximum compression which makes implementation more complex.

DC values are encoded as the difference from the DC value of the previous block. This differential coding is possible because there is a strong correlation between adjacent DC values (Fig. 5.13).

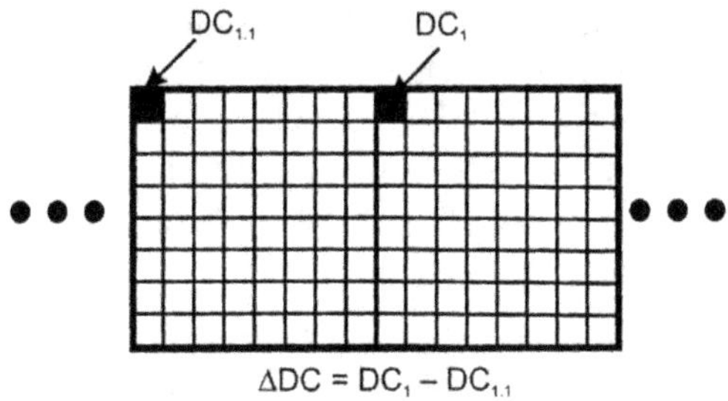

Fig. 5.13 Differential DC computation.

The AC values are then strung together in a zigzag sequence. This irregular ordering keeps low frequency coefficients together. Low frequency coefficients are more likely to be nonzero. Typically, the high-frequency coefficients create long strings of zeros which can be easily run length encoded (Figure 5.14).

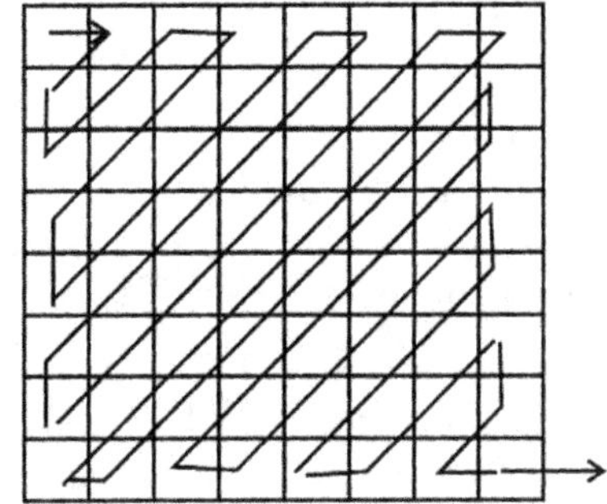

Fig. 5.14 Zigzag sequence of entropy coding DC$_i$, AC$_{01}$, AC$_{10}$...

After the DC component is differentially encoded, the AC coefficients are broken into runs of zeros ending in a nonzero number. This set of numbers is encoded as symbol, symbol-2. Symbol-1 consists of the number of zeros (RUN-LENGTH) and also the number of bits necessary to encode the amplitude of the non-zero number (AMPLITUDE). Symbol-1 is referred to as the variable-length code (VLC). Symbol-2 is the variable-length integer (VLI). Every DC and AC coefficient is encoded as a VI-C followed by a V1-1. VLCs are encoded as Huffman codes and therefore must adhere to the prefix property. The length of the VLI is not known until the VI-C is decoded. Decoding the VI-C will yield the number of zeros to prefix the number and also the number of bits following to encode the amplitude of the non-zero number. At this point, we know how many bits to read in from the bit stream for our amplitude so the VLI does not need to follow the prefix property.

There are a couple of important notes on the implementation of the lossless coding block. First, the run length is restricted to runs of 15 or less. If a longer run is encountered it is encoded with several symbols specifying a RUNLENGTH of 15 and a SIZE of 0. This is interpreted as a runlength of 16. The specification allows up to three sequences of symbol-1 = (15,0). The trailing elements in the symbol string are typically zeros. There is no need to encode this non-information. For this reason, an end-of-block (EOB) symbol is used to specify that the rest of the coefficients are zero. EOB is defined as a RUNLENGTH of 0 and a SIZE of 0. Use of EOB further improves compression.

When encoding DC values, symbol-1s store less information than AC values. DC values are differentially encoded and are not encoded with proceeding runs of zeros. A DC symbol-1 consists only of SIZE-there is no corresponding RUNLENGTH. Table 5.15 shows how SIZE is derived from the amplitude of the differential DC value. There are no default tables for coding the luminance and chrominance values. Tables 5.16 and 5.17 are example tables that are often used.

All of this can be very confusing the first time you are exposed to this process. Let's take an example image through the encoding and decoding process. For simplicity's sake, our example image is an 8 X 8 resolution gray scale image (8 bits/pixel).

Figure 5.15(a) shows our original image. Since the original is gray scale, we will skip the subsampling step. After subtracting 128 from each pixel, the block is run through a DCT. The results are shown in Figure 5.15(b). Fig. 5.15(c) shows the results of quantization using the coefficients from Table 5.19.

The next step is the lossless encoding. DC is the first coefficient to encode. Assuming that the DC value of the previous 8 by 8 block was -34, the difference to encode is +3. From Table 5.15, we see that to encode a 3 requires an amplitude of 2. The VLC is 011. The VLI is 11. The first string to encode of the AC coefficients contains one 0 and nonzero -2. The run of zeros is therefore 1. The amplitude required to encode -2 is 2. Table 5.15 shows how to encode the block losslessly from the DC value to the EOB.

Table 5.15 Baseline entropy coding symbol-2 structure.

Size	Amplitude
1	-1.1
2	-3..-2,2..3
3	-7..-4,4..7
4	-15..-8,8..15
5	-31..-16,16..31
6	-63..-32,32..63
7	-127..-64,64..127
8	-255..-128,128..255
9	-511..-256,256..511
10	-1023..512,512..1023

Table 5.16 Luminance DC values

Length	Code
2	00
3	010
3	011
3	100
3	101
3	110
4	1110
5	11110
6	111110
7	1111110
8	11111110
9	111111110

Our final string is 0111111011010000000001110000001010. We have just represented our image of 512 bits with 34 bits achieving a compression ratio of 15.

Let's reverse the process. Decoding the VLCs and VLIs yields the image shown in Figure 5.16(b). Multiplying the quantized coefficients by the quantization table produces Figure 5.16(a). The inverse DCT yields Figure 5.16(b). How much information is lost in the process? Figure 5.16(c) shows the difference between our original image and our JPEG encoded image. You can see that the losses are small.

```
48 53 58 62 64 64 64 64       -492.4  -1.0 -12.0 -5.2  2.1 -1.7 -2.7  1.3      -31  0 -1 0 0 0 0 0
53 60 62 65 68 65 65 65       -22.6 -17.5  -6.2 -3.2 -2.9 -0.1  0.4 -1.2       -2 -1  0 0 0 0 0 0
59 64 69 72 67 65 65 65       -11.0  -9.3  -1.6  1.5  0.2 -0.9 -0.6 -0.1       -1 -1  0 0 0 0 0 0
68 70 71 69 69 68 68 68        -7.0  -1.9   0.2  1.5  0.9 -0.0 -0.0  0.3       -1  0  0 0 0 0 0 0
68 69 70 71 71 64 64 64        -0.6  -0.8   1.5  1.6 -0.1 -0.7  0.6  1.3        0  0  0 0 0 0 0 0
70 70 70 70 69 66 66 66         1.8  -0.2   1.6 -0.3 -0.8  1.5  1.0 -1.0        0  0  0 0 0 0 0 0
71 71 70 72 71 66 66 66        -1.3  -0.4  -0.3 -1.5 -0.5  1.7  1.1 -0.8        0  0  0 0 0 0 0 0
71 71 70 70 72 67 67 67        -2.6   1.6  -3.8 -1.8  1.9  1.2 -0.6 -0.5        0  0  0 0 0 0 0 0
         (a)                              (b)                                        (c)
```

Fig. 5.15 JPEG encoding example: (a) original image; (b) forward DCT; (c) quantized with Table 5.16.

```
-496   0 -10 0 0 0 0 0     50 52 55 58 60 61 62 62      -2  1  3  4  4  3  2  2
-24 -12    0 0 0 0 0 0     57 58 61 63 64 65 64 64      -4  2  1  2  4  0  1  1
-14 -13    0 0 0 0 0 0     65 66 67 69 69 68 67 66      -6 -2  2  3 -2 -3 -2 -1
-14   0    0 0 0 0 0 0     70 70 71 71 70 68 66 65      -2  0  0 -2 -1  0  2  3
  0   0    0 0 0 0 0 0     70 70 70 70 69 66 64 63      -2 -1  0  1  2 -2  0  1
  0   0    0 0 0 0 0 0     68 69 69 69 68 66 64 62       2  1  1  1  1  0  2  4
  0   0    0 0 0 0 0 0     68 68 69 70 69 68 66 65       3  3  1  2  2 -2  0  1
  0   0    0 0 0 0 0 0     68 69 71 72 72 71 69 68       3  2 -1 -2  0 -4 -2 -1
        (a)                        (b)                              (c)
```

Fig. 5.16 JPEG decoding example: (a) dequantized image; (b) result of inverse DCT; (c) difference image (original minus 5.16b).

Table 5.17 Chrominance DC values.

Length	Code
2	00
2	01
2	10
3	110
4	1110
5	11110
6	111110
7	1111110
8	11111110
9	111111110
10	1111111110
11	11111111110

JPEG also designates arithmetic coding as a method for entropy coding. It is not required for baseline encoding. Arithmetic coding has achieved 5 to 10 percent better compression than Huffman but is not typically used for a couple of reasons. The first is that it is more complex to implement than Huffman. Also, there are several patents associated with arithmetic coding. They are held by such heavy-hitters as AT&T and IBM. Unless you obtain licenses from these companies, you cannot legally use the algorithm for comercial purposes.

The lossless compression method does not use the DCT. It encodes the difference between one pixel and its predicted value. Fig. 5.17 shows a block diagram of the sequence.

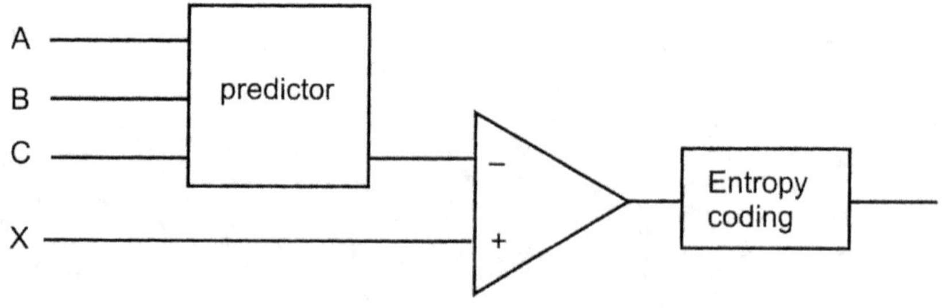

Fig. 5.17 Lossless encoding block.

The predicted value is computed from the pixel to the left, the pixel directly above it and the pixel one row up and one column to the left. Figure 5.18 shows these pixels and the eight possible prediction schemes. Lossless JPEG compression does not achieve good compression ratios (1.6 to 2.5) and therefore sees little use.

Unfortunately, JPEG does not specify a file format. It is only a bitstream format. This has caused the creation of a number of file formats to store JPEG compressed images. None are considered a standard. The closest thing to a standard is the JFIF (JPEG File Interchange Format) and the JPEG extension to TIFF 6.0.

Table 5.18

Scheme	Prediction
0	No prediction (differential encoding)
1	A
2	B
3	C
4	A+B-C
5	A+((A-C)/2)
6	B+((A-C)/2)
7	(A+B)/2

MPEG, named for the Motion Picture Experts Group, is a compression scheme that uses many of the same concepts but applies to multiple images in succession. The scheme takes basic JPEG and adds motion compensation and frame prediction. In general, the process consists of representing all the image data for every 15 or so frames. Using frame difference information and prediction algorithms, the intermediate frames are generated.

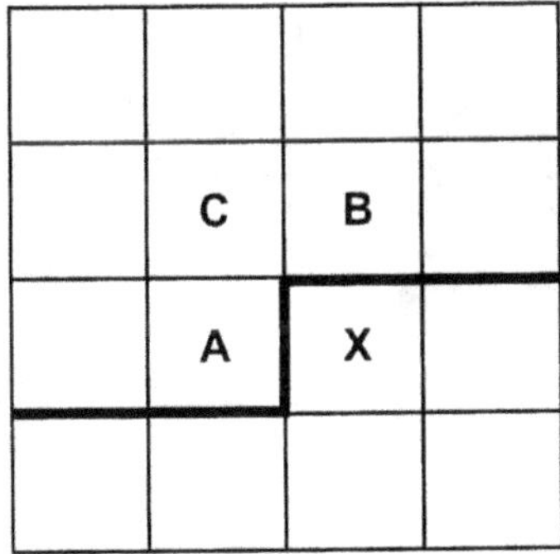

Fig. 5.18 Neighbourhood and algorithms used for predicting the value of the next pixel.

Table 5.19 Lossless encoding of example

Zeros	Amplitude	Coefficient	VLC	VLI
0	2	3	011	11
1	2	-2	11011	01
0	1	-1	00	0
0	1	-1	00	0
0	1	-1	00	0
2	1	-1	11100	0
0	1	-1	00	0
0	0		1010	

5.11 Other State-of-the-Art Image Compression

5.11.1 Vector Quantization

Vector quantization, like JPEG, breaks an image into blocks (or vectors) of $n \times n$ pixels. These blocks are then compared with a set of representative blocks [40]. This collection of representative vectors is called a codebook. A summation of differences between the pixels in the source vector and the codebook vector is computed for each codebook entry. The codebook entry with the smallest difference summation is chosen as the representative vector. The index of that vector is then stored to a file or transmitted (Fig. 5.19).

Fig. 5.19 VQ encoding.

Let's compute the compression ratio achieved using VQ. Say our original image is broken into vectors of 4 x 4 pixels. The original image is 24 bits/pixel. If we use a codebook that has 1024 vectors, we will need 10 bits to uniquely address the representative code vector. Our compression ratio for one vector (and also for the whole image) is

Compress ratio = [24 byte / pixel * 16 pixel] / 10 byte = 38.4

The toughest part of vector quantization is generating codebooks. Many people instinctively think that you can just count the frequency of all vectors in a large set of representative images. The codebook could then be composed of the most frequently occurring vectors. Although this seems like a great idea, it creates a lousy codebook. Vectors that contain much information (like edges) may not occur frequently in an image and may be left out of a codebook. This produces images of poor quality. There are many elaborate schemes for generating good codebooks. Most of them have great computational requirements.

Vector quantization comes in many flavors. One method, recursive VQ, repetitively encodes the image and the difference between the image and its approximation (the value from the codebook). Another method removes the mean of a vector before encoding.

VQ is a lossy algorithm. Artifacts introduced by VQ encoding are blockeness and color posterization. Staircased edges (jaggies) along diagonal lines can also be seen in images that have been encoded with VQ. All VQ algorithms are computationally intensive during the encoding stage, but decode relatively quickly (Figure 5.20). The decode process is merely pulling vectors out of the codebook and building the image. It is a very fast process.

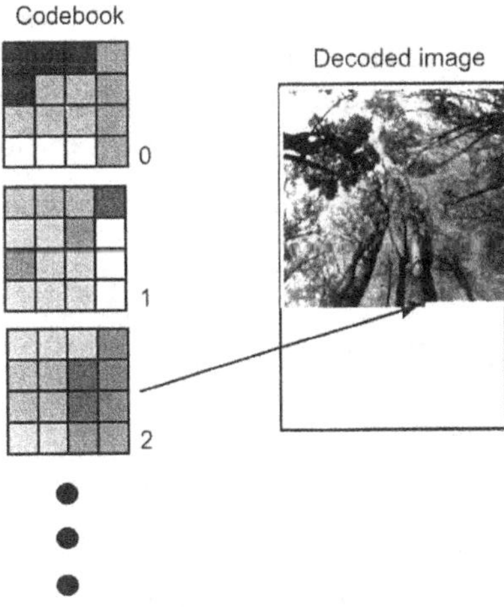

Fig. 5.20 VQ decoding.

5.11.2 Fractal Compression

Fractal compression is a radical departure from the conventional image compression techniques. The difference between it and the other techniques is much like the difference between bitmapped graphics and vector graphics. Rather than storing data for individual pixels, fractal compression stores instructions or formulas for creating the image. Because of that, images compressed with fractal compression are resolution independent. They can be scaled up to a resolution higher than the original image without distracting artifacts associated with scaling (jaggies, smoothing from interpolation, and so on). These scalable images are well suited for graphics systems that are typically composed of devices of differing resolutions (graphics cards, printers, etc.).

Fractals are images that are composed of smaller images. Fractals were first widely introduced (or reintroduced) in the book *The Fractal Geometry of Nature* by Benoit Mandelbrot. Fractal compression does very well with natural scenes and claims to achieve compression ratios greater than 100.

Like vector quantization, fractal compression is asymmetrical. Although it takes a long time to compress an image, decompression is very fast. These asymmetrical methods are well suited to such applications as video on a CD-ROM where the user doesn't care about compression but does expect to see images quickly. Decompression simply reads the mathematical formulas and recreates the image.

The tough part is generating the formulas to correctly represent the image. Fractal compression assumes that every image is composed of smaller images just like them. Blue sky in an image is composed of smaller patches of blue. Tree branches can be broken into smaller branches and then twigs that all have similar structure. The compression technique tries to find as many of these relationships in an image and then describe them with mathematical formulas. This is done within regions of an image called domain regions. These domain regions are determined by using techniques such as frequency analysis, edge detection, and texture-variation analysis.

Like other lossy compression schemes, fractal compression involves a tradeoff, which is a little different from the other methods that have presented. The tradeoff is between image quality and compression time. The longer the encoder has to create the descriptive formulas, the higher the quality of the output image.

Like all other lossy compression schemes, fractal compression also introduces artifacts. These include softness and substitution of details with other details. This substitution is typically undetected in natural images.

Several patents associated with fractal compression have been granted. The techniques are proprietary and not in the public domain. If you wish to use this compression method, you must purchase a development kit from Iterated Systems Incorporated. This may be what is slowing the advancement of fractal compression into the image compression community.

5.11.3 Discrete Wavelet Transforms

Wavelet theory is a new wave in applied mathematics. This far-reaching technology has found applications in numerous sciences including acoustics, crystallography, quantum mechanics and, of course, image compression.

Discrete wavelet transforms are like DCTs in that they will decompose and image into coefficients assigned to basis functions. The DCT is limited to cosine functions that require a lot of arithmetic computations. Wavelets use a wider range of simpler functions. The result is less computational complexity with no sacrifice in image quality [52].

The basic compression idea is a simple one. First, the discrete wavelet transform of the image is computed. The resulting coefficients are compared with a threshold. Coefficients below the threshold are set to zero. As with the DCT-based image compression, compression comes from the information being packed into a small number of coefficients. The non-zero coefficients are then encoded using a lossless encoding scheme.

Compression ratios of up to 40 have been achieved with no noticeable difference between the original and compressed image. Beyond that, artifacts are introduced in the process. Wavelet artifacts are marked by softness, subtle random noise, and halos along edges.

5.12 Image Compression Standard File Formats

Introduction

Images that may be used by PC computers are saved in various formats. Different image file formats are capable of holding different quantities of colors. Each file format will have a reference to the number of "bits per pixel" that the format is capable of supporting.

Images are stored in different formats depending on the application and requirements of the user. Image formats can be very broadly classified into

(i) Platform dependent formats

(ii) Platform independent formats

5.12.1 Platform Dependent Formats

Many graphical/imaging applications create their own file format particular to the systems they are executed upon. The following are a few popular system dependent formats:

Microsoft Windows : BMP

BMP is a lossless image format. BMP will handle 24 bit data but it cannot be compressed. BMP uses RLE (Run Length Encoding) to compress 8 bit data, which is effective in graphics, but much less effective in continuous tones like photos. A system standard graphics file format for Microsoft Windows

Used in PC Paintbrush and other programs, it is capable of storing 24-bit bitmap images

Macintosh: PAINT and PICT

PAINT was originally used in MacPaint program, initially only for 1-bit monochrome images.

PICT format is used in MacDraw (a vector based drawing program) for storing structured graphics .

X-windows: XBM

Primary graphics format for the X Window system

Supports 24-bit color bitmap

Many public domain graphic editors, e.g., xv

Used in X Windows for storing icons, pixmaps, backdrops, etc.

5.12.2   Platform Independent formats

There are several graphics file formats which run with equal ease on almost all platforms. Some of the most popular ones are described below

TIFF - Tag Image File Format (.TIF files)

TIFF has been the format of choice for use for master copies of our scanned data for several years. TIFF was developed by Aldus, before Adobe bought them, and is the most widely supported format across other platforms. TIFF writes a large file, and it uses lossless compression, just meaning there are no losses, meaning that you can always read back in what you wrote out, without data corruption. If you might ever be modifying and writing the file a second time, then use a non-lossy format like TIFF. TIFF is primarily designed for raster data interchange. TIFF is based on file-offsets, so that it is not easily "streamable" in the way JPEG JFIF streams are.

TIFF is the most universal format, about any program on any platform will handle TIFF. However, there are many TIFF variations, for example TIFF F format is used for sending all fax documents. And certainly not all programs can read all variations. LZW compression (Lempel-Ziv-Welch, same compression as used by PKZIP) for TIFF is an option available in many programs (LZW is found under the Option Button in the TIF SAVE-AS dialog).

Still, LZW TIF files are generally far too large to email. JPEG files are very much more suitable size for email purposes.

Limitations :

1. No provisions for storing vector graphics, text annotation, etc (although such items could be easily constructed using TIFF extensions).
2. The TIFF format permits both MSB ("Motorola") and LSB ("Intel") byte order data to be stored, with a header item indicating which order is used. There are old, poorly written TIFF programs on the PC which rebelled against this and assume that all TIFF files are Intel byte order.
3. TIFF uses 4-byte integer file offsets to store image data, with the consequence that a TIFF file cannot have more than 4 Gigabytes of raster data

Strengths :

1. Highly flexible and platform independent format.
2. Ability to decompose an image by tiles rather than scanlines which permits much more efficient access to very large imagery which has been compressed.
3. Theoretically, TIFF can support imagery with multiple bands (up to 64K bands), arbitrary # bits per pixel, data cubes, and multiple images per file, including thumbnail subsampled images.

JPEG - Joint Photographic Experts Group

This is the best format for scanned photographs used on websites or for sending your photographic images in email, because the file is wonderfully small, often compressed to only 1/10 or 1/20 size. However, this fantastic compression efficiency comes with a price. JPG uses a lossy compression, that is, some quality is lost when the file is written (saved), and it cannot be recovered. Even worse, a little more quality is lost EVERY TIME the JPG file is compressed and saved again.

Because of quality problems, JPG is NOT suitable for storing a master copy of your data. A JPG file can be read and viewed a jillion times without affecting the data, like on a web page say, but EVERY TIME THE FILE IS SAVED, the JPG compression causes additional image quality to be lost.

JPG is mathematically complex, very similar in process to digitizing sound, and requires considerable CPU processing power to decompress an image. A 486/33 will slow noticeably loading a large JPG.

Good JPG compression values for routine use are 75-80% Quality, or 20-25% Compression. Too little Quality or too much Compression will affect image quality visibly. But JPG is a very poor Master Copy for your images.

Limitations

1. Small images often end up larger than small GIFs.
2. Does not allow less than 16.7 million colors
3. Very high level of compression creates very ugly images
4. Lossy process

Strengths

1. Huge compression ratios are possible , for faster download speeds
2. Gives excellent results in most photographs and medical images
3. Supports full color images(24-bit true color) images

3 GIF - Graphic Interchange Format.

This is an older format developed by CompuServe, with relatively small compressed file sizes (but nothing like JPG). However, GIF is limited to only 256 colors, a great match for the older 8 bit video boards, but which makes it poorly suited today for photographic purposes. The file is also large for photographic images.

GIF is still the smallest file for 16 or 256 color data like graphic art or screen captures or 2 color Line art, and is the format of choice for that kind of graphic images. Simple images like a company logo should be reduced to 16 colors if possible and saved as a GIF for smallest size on the web The fewer colors, the smaller the GIF file. Size is important to web pages.

GIF uses lossless compression, like TIF. JPG is much better for photographic images, the file is very much smaller (although lossy). But GIF files will be smaller for graphic artwork.

Also, you will not even be offered the GIF format as a choice until you have reduced the image to 256 colors or less.

The 256 colors in a GIF image can be any 256 colors from the set of 16.7 million colors. Each color is a 24 bit RGB value, and each GIF file contains its own color palette. The actual image data contains the 8 bit index to this color in the palette, and each pixel in the images specifies one of the palette colors, maybe "color number 82". If a 8-bit 256 color video mode is used, then Windows reloads its Palette Manager to the palette in the image so that it can map the color correctly.

This of course disrupts the palette of all other 8 bit images simultaneously on your screen, and you may see some flashes and bizarre colors.

For that reason (8 bit video mode), all the GIF files in one HTML document should use the same color palette. There are several ways to choose a GIF indexed palette, and Netscape and other browsers use only one special palette to solve this problem. The Netscape palette is called "6-6-6" colors, denoting that 6 standard equally spaced shades of each Red, Green, and Blue are present, generally a wide choice for any image (but perfect for no one image). 6x6x6 is 216 colors, and if the image uses one of the 216 Netscape index colors, it is used.

GIF is the most widely supported graphics format on the Web.

Limitations

1. Limited to only 256 colors
2. Lossy file format which removes bits of color to compress

Strengths

1. All graphic Web viewers support Gif format for inlined images.
2. GIFs of diagrammatic images look better than JPEGs.
3. GIF supports transparency and interlacing

FlashPix

FPX is a multi-resolution image format in which the image is stored as a series of independent arrays, each representing the image at a different spatial resolution. In other words, there would be many different images at different distances/ resolutions. Usually when a user zooms in on an image the image will loose quality. With FPX, the array of images all at different resolutions will allow the computer to create a clear representation of the zoomed picture on different output devices at different resolutions with minimal resizing of the image. With an intelligent software layer on top of the format, this multi-resolution ability is achieved transparently to the user.

Limitations

1. Requires more file space

Strengths

1. Much less RAM for viewing
2. Less time for modifying
3. requires much less RAM for viewing; approximately 20% of the RAM required for a TIFF file
4. It takes much less time to modify an image and store the revision

In summary, a FPX file requires a less powerful computer. Less data is stored in RAM and less data is processed. FPX files offer a significant speed advantage to the computer user. Images burst upon the screen and are quickly modified regardless of their maximum resolution.

Capabilities

As Flashpix is not very common as yet , it is explained in detail here. The FPX image file provides a common foundation upon which to build products that can be universally connected ... computers, applications software, capture products, sharing networks, printing, and services. In addition, it is more than a format. It requires products to use images differently.

In addition to specifying the organization of image data, FPX also defines a resolution-independent coordinate system for describing the locations of points in the image.

A structured storage format was chosen as the "wrapper" for FPX files. FPX structured storage format provides compatibility with Microsoft? structured storage format and other structured storage paradigms. Structured storage can be likened to a "file system in a file"; a structured storage file contains both storages (directories) and streams (files). Any application that understands the structured storage format can add additional storages and streams to any structured storage file at will, which will be "invisible" to the original application. A FPX file consists of a number of storages and streams, which can provide independent access to different parts of the file, such as a file system can provide access to multiple files at once.

The FPX file format provides an extensible color format that includes two unambiguous color space definitions, and optional support for the International Color Consortium (ICC) color management scheme.

The FPX file format provides a strong format for the encoding and storage of colors within an image. The format is intended to be extensible and to address many of the concerns of today and some of the concerns of tomorrow.

As with almost all existing image formats, the ability to compress image data is important, It is especially important in FPX, as the hierarchy of resolutions combined with the small disks often found on low-end machines can produce an unusable system if the image data in not sufficiently compressed. The basic compression block in FPX is the tile. It is important that a reader be able to access individual tiles, so any compression must not preclude accessing only a single tile. FPX allows three compression methods:

1. Uncompressed
2. Single Color Compression
3. JPEG Compression

Each tile is compressed individually from all other tiles, both in its present resolution and in all other resolutions. Each tile may be compressed using a different compression method, which allows an output device to determine the best method (for either size or reconstruction speed) depending on the data in that file.

PNG - Portable Network Graphics (.PNG files, pronounced Ping)

PNG was intended to be the replacement for GIF due to LZW patent problems, and due to GIF being limited to only 256 colors. However, being designed later with the advantage of knowing all that went before, PNG also supports 24 and 48 bit color, and an awesome set of technical specifications and features, sort of the modern universal "be all, end all" of file formats, including superior lossless compression of specific interest here. The PNG basic compression is called the ZIP method, and is like the "deflate" method in PKZIP, but PNG also incorporates special preprocessing filters that improve the compression efficiency, especially for gradient data often found in photographs.

PNG is of great interest today, because it has lossless compression well suited for master copy data, and PNG is noticeably smaller than LZW TIF. It looks like about 30% smaller than TIF LZW for 24 bit files, and is said to be 10% to 30% smaller than 8 bit GIF files.

Most graphics applications like PhotoImpact, Photoshop, Paint Shop Pro already support PNG, so compatibility transferring files is probably not an issue.

For the Web, PNG really has three main advantages over GIF: alpha channels (variable transparency), gamma correction (cross-platform control of image brightness), and two-dimensional interlacing (a method of progressive display). PNG also compresses better than GIF in almost every case, but the difference is generally only around 5% to 25%, not a large enough factor to encourage folks to switch on that basis alone.

For image editing, PNG provides a useful format for the storage of intermediate stages of editing. Since PNG's compression is fully lossless—and since it supports up to 48-bit truecolor or 16-bit grayscale—saving, restoring and re-saving an image will not degrade its quality, unlike standard JPEG (even at its highest quality settings). Although JPEG's lossy compression can introduce visible artifacts, these can be minimized, and the savings in file size even at high quality levels is much better than is generally possible with a lossless format like PNG

PNG's compression is among the best that can be had without losing image information and without paying patent fees, but not all implementations take full advantage of the available power. Even those that do can be thwarted by unwise choices on the part of the user.

PNG supports three main image types: truecolor, grayscale and palette-based ("8-bit"). JPEG only supports the first two; GIF only the third (although it can fake grayscale by using a gray palette).

Limitations

1. Does not support animation and is not supported by all browsers
2. Substantially bigger than GIF and JPEG

Strengths

1. Lossless compression   2. Faster download times
3. Non patented   4. Supports gamma information

Here are some representative file sizes for a 9.9 megabyte 1943x1702 color image :

File type	File size	
TIFF	9.9 megs	
TIFF LZW	8.4 megs	
PNG	6.5 megs	
JPG	1.0 megs	1.0 / 9.9 is 10% file size
BMP	9.9 megs	
PCX	9.2 megs	

Best file types for these general purposes :

	Photographic images	Graphics, Logos, Line art and Screen Captures
Properties	Continuous tones, 24 bit color or 8 bit Gray, no text, few lines and edges	Solid colors, up to 256 colors, with text or lines and sharp edges
Best Quality for Master Copy	TIF or PNG	PNG or GIF or TIF
Smallest File Size	JPG, 75% to 80% Quality factor is good. Normal useful range is 90% to 60% (JPG is not suitable for master copy)	PNG or GIF, maybe TIF LZW. Graphics/logos usually permit 2 to 16 colors for smallest file
Maximum Compatibility (PC, Mac, Unix)	TIF without LZW	TIF without LZW
Poor Choice	256 color GIF is limited color, and is a larger file than 24 bit JPG	JPG compression adds artifacts, smears text and lines and edges

5.13 Questions

1. (a) What do you mean by bandwidth compression?

   (b) Explain the two different types of image compression techniques and their applications.

   (c) In digital image compression how different types of redundancies are applicable? Explain.

2. (a) What is meant by statistical coding? Classify.

   (b) Explain briefly about the types of statistical coding.

3. (a) What is meant by compression ? What is its need ? Waht are the variuos ways to achieve compression ? Explain briefly.

   (b) Compare lossless and lossy predictive coding methods.

4. (a) What is meant by image compression ? What is its need ? What are the various ways to achieve compression ? Explain briefly.

5. (a) Explain the concept of homomorphic filtering.

   (b) Explain the properties of butter worth filter.

6. (a) Compare lossless and lossy coding methods.

   (b) For the given source symbol generate the corresponding Huffman code. Original Source

Symbol	Probability
a_2	0.35
a_3	0.20
a_6	0.15
a_7	0.10
a_1	0.1
a_5	0.05
a_4	0.05

7. (a) Compare lossless and lossy predictive coding methods.

   (b) Explain the concept of bit plane coding method.

8. (a) What do you mean by compression? Briefly explain its requirement.

   (b) Differentiate lossy compression and lossless compression. Mention their applications.

   (c) What do you mean by improved Gray Scale Quantization?

   (d) Explain the fidelity criteria in image compression.

9.   (a) Explain about

        (i) slope overload

        (ii) granular noise.

  (b) List out the advandages and drawbacks of different types of lossy compression techniques.

10.   (a) Explain about

        (i) two dimensional run length coding

        (ii) contour coding.

  (b) What do you mean by reversible in compression.

11.   (a) Mention different types of coding used in error free compression.

  (b) Discuss about Huffman coding.

12.   (a) With a neat block diagram, describe the image compression system model

  (b) What do you mean by mapper in source encoder ?

  (c) Compare the statistical Compression and spatial Compression.

13.   (a) What is false contouring ?

  (b) Differentiate

        (i) compression and decompression

        (ii) coding and decoding and

        (iii) mapper and demapper

  (c) How the word distance is related with hamming code ?

14. How statistical coding is differentiated from spatial coding ? Give one example for both the coding. Explain.

15. Write a short notes on the following with respect to Digital Image.

  (a) Error-free compression

  (b) Lossy compression.

16.   (a) Draw and explain the general compression system model.

  (b) Explain the methods of measuring the quality of image.

17. Write a short note on the following:

  (a) Arithmatic coding

  (b) Lossy predictive coding.

18.   (a) What is coding redundancy? Explain how variable-length code is used for image compression with example.

  (b) Give the differences between channel, source encoder and decoder.

19. Explain the following coding techniques.

    (a) Huffman coding

    (b) Lossless predictive coding.

20. (a) What is fidelity criteria? Explain the different classes of criteria.

    (b) What is compression? Why is it needed? Mention some methods to acheive compression.

21. Write a short notes on the following:

    (a) Variable-length coding

    (b) Transform coding.

22. (a) Describe about Transform coding.

    (b) Write notes on optimal quantization.

23. (a) Write about the Huffman coding.

    (b) What do you mean by error free compression.

    (c) Explain about near optimal variable length coding.

24. (a) Define

    (i) Compression ratio

    (ii) Relative data redundancy

    (iii) Mappings

    (iv) Quantization in Psychovisual redundancy.

    (b) How the interpixel redundancy is differentiated from the coding redundancy and psychovisual redundancy?

25. (a) Explain how subimage selection and bit allocation effects the compression and quality of an image.

    (b) Compare and contrast lossless and lossy compression methods in all aspects.

26. (a) Obtian the arithmetic code for the message sequence a e e o i u ! given the code model:

Symbol	Probability
a	0.2
e	0.3
i	0.1
o	0.2
u	0.1
!	0.1

    (b) For the above code model develope an Huffman code.

27. (a) Describe the principle of lossless and lossy predictive coding methods.

    (b) Explain with a block diagram about transform coding system.

28. (a) What is meant by image compression? What is the need for compression? Explain, with an example, in terms of storage and transmission requirements.

    (b) What are the various data redundancies? Explain.

29. (a) What is bit-plane slicing? How it is used for achieving compression? Explain.

    (b) The arithmetic decoding process is the reverse of the encoding procedure. Decode the message 0.234 given the coding model:

Symbol	Probability
a	0.2
e	0.3
i	0.1
o	0.2
u	0.1
!	0.1

30. (a) Consider an 8-pixel line of gray-scale data, {12, 12, 13, 13, 10, 13, 57, 54}, which has been uniformly quantized with 6-bit accuracy. Construct its 3-bit IOS code.

    (b) Explain the principle of 2-D ran length coding with an example.

CHAPTER 6

Pattern Recognition (Object Recognition)

6.1 Introduction

A pattern recognition system finds objects in the real world from an image of the world, using object models, which are known a priori(beforehand). This task is surprisingly difficult. In this chapter we will discuss different steps in pattern recognition and introduce some techniques that have been used for pattern recognition in many applications.

The pattern recognition problem can be defined as a labeling problem based on models of known objects. Formally, given an image containing one or more patterns of interest (and background) and a set of labels corresponding to a set of models known to the system, the system should assign correct labels to regions, or a set of regions, in the image [44]. The pattern recognition problem is closely tied to the segmentation problem: without at least a partial recognition of patterns, segmentation cannot be done, and without segmentation, pattern recognition is not possible.

6.2 System Component

An pattern recognition system must have the following components to perform the task [10] :

- Model database (also called modelbase)
- Feature detector
- Hypothesizer
- Hypothesis verifier

A block diagram showing interactions and information flow among different components of the system is given in Figure 6.1.

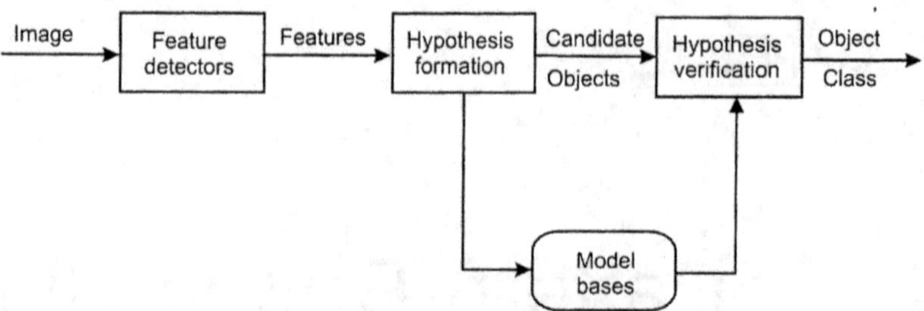

Fig. 6.1 Different components of a pattern recognition system are shown

The model database contains all the models known to the system [6]. The information in the model database depends on the approach used for the recognition. It can vary from a qualitative or functional description to precise geometric surface information. In many cases, the models of objects are abstract feature vectors, as discussed later in this Chapter. A feature is some attribute of the object that is considered important in describing and recognizing the object in relation to other objects. Size, color, and shape are some commonly used features.

The feature detector applies operators to images and identifies locations of features that help in forming object hypotheses. The features used by a system depend on the types of objects to be recognized and the organisation of the model database. Using the detected features in the image, the hypothesizer assigns likelihoods to objects present in the scene. This step is used to reduce the search space for the recognizer using certain features. The modelbase is organized using some type of indexing scheme to facilitate elimination of unlikely object candidates from possible consideration. The verifier then uses object models to verify the hypotheses and refines the likelihood of objects. The system then selects the object with the highest likelihood, based on all the evidence, as the correct object.

A pattern recognition system must select appropriate tools and techniques for the steps discussed above. Many factors must be considered in the selection of appropriate methods for a particular application [49]. The central issues that should be considered in designing a pattern recognition system are :

- *Object or model representation :* How should objects be represented in the model database? What are the important attributes or features of objects that must be captured in these models? For some objects, geometric descriptions may be available and may also be efficient, while for another class one may have to rely on generic or functional features. The representation of an object should capture all relevant information without any redundancies and should organize this information in a form that allows easy access by different components of the pattern recognition system.

- *Feature extraction :* Which features should be detected, and how can they be detected reliably? Most features can be computed in two-dimensional images but they are related to three-dimensional characteristics of objects. Due to the nature of the image formation process, some features are easy to compute reliably while others are very difficult.

- *Feature-model matching :* How can features in images be matched to models in the database? In most object recognition tasks, there are many features and numerous objects. An exhaustive matching approach will solve the recognition problem but may be too slow to be useful. Effectiveness of features and efficiency of a matching technique must be considered in developing a matching approach.

- *Hypotheses formation :* How can a set of likely objects based on the feature matching be selected, and how can probabilities be assigned to each possible object? The hypothesis formation step is basically a heuristic to reduce the size of the search space. This step uses knowledge of the application domain to assign some kind of probability or confidence measure to different objects in the domain. This measure reflects the likelihood of the presence of objects based on the detected features.

- *Object verification :* How can object models be used to select the most likely object from the set of probable objects in a given image? The presence of each likely object can be verified by using their models. One must examine each plausible hypothesis to verify the presence of the object or ignore it. If the models are geometric, it is easy to precisely verify objects using camera location and other scene parameters. In other cases, it may not be possible to verify a hypothesis.

Depending on the complexity of the problem, one or more modules in Figure 6.1 may become trivial. For example, pattern recognition-based pattern recognition systems do not use any feature-model matching or object verification; they directly assign probabilities to objects and select the object with the highest probability.

6.3 Complexity of Pattern Recognition

Since an object must be recognized from images of a scene containing multiple entities, the complexity of object recognition depends on several factors [27]. A qualitative way to consider the complexity of the object recognition task would consider the following factors:

- *Scene constancy :* The scene complexity will depend on whether the images are acquired in similar conditions (illumination, background, camera parameters, and viewpoint) as the models. Under different scene conditions, the performance of different feature detectors will be significantly different. The nature of the background, other objects, and illumination must be considered to determine what kind of features can be efficiently and reliably detected.

- *Image-models spaces* : In some applications, images may be obtained such that three-dimensional objects can be considered two-dimensional. The models in such cases can be represented using two-dimensional characteristics. If models are three-dimensional and perspective effects cannot be ignored, then the situation becomes more complex. In this case, the features are detected in two-dimensional image space, while the models of objects may be in three-dimensional space. Thus, the same three-dimensional feature may appear as a different feature in an image. This may also happen in dynamic images due to the motion of objects.

- *Number of objects in the model database* : If the number of objects is very small, one may not need the hypothesis formation stage. A sequential exhaustive matching may be acceptable. Hypothesis formation becomes important for a large number of objects. The amount of effort spent in selecting appropriate features for object recognition also increases rapidly with an increase in the number of objects.

- *Number of objects in an image and possibility of occlusion* : If there is only one object in an image, it may be completely visible. With an increase in the number of objects in the image, the probability of occlusion increases. Occlusion is a serious problem in many basic image computations. Occlusion results in the absence of expected features and the generation of unexpected features. Occlusion should also be considered in the hypothesis verification stage. Generally, the difficulty in the recognition task increases with the number of objects in an image. Difficulties in image segmentation are due to the presence of multiple occluding objects in images.

The object recognition task is affected by several factors. We classify the object recognition problem into the following classes.

Two-dimensional

In many applications, images are acquired from a distance sufficient to consider the projection to be orthographic. If the objects are always in one stable position in the scene, then they can be considered two-dimensional. In these applications, one can use a two-dimensional modelbase. There are two possible cases:

- Objects will not be occluded, as in remote sensing and many industrial applications.

- Objects may be occluded by other objects of interest or be partially visible, as in the bin of parts problem.

In some cases, though the objects may be far away, they may appear in different positions resulting in multiple stable views. In such cases also, the problem may be considered inherently as two-dimensional pattern recognition.

Three-dimensional

If the images of objects can be obtained from arbitrary viewpoints, then an object may appear very different in its two views. For pattern recognition using three-dimensional models, the perspective effect and viewpoint of the image have to be considered. The fact that the models are three-dimensional and the images contain only two-dimensional information affects pattern recognition approaches. Again, the two factors to be considered are whether objects are separated from other objects or not.

For three-dimensional cases, one should consider the information used in the pattern recognition task. Two different cases are:

- *Intensity :* There is no surface information available explicitly in intensity images. Using intensity values, features corresponding to the three-dimensional structure of objects should be recognized.

- *2.5-dimensional images :* In many applications, surface representations with viewer-centered coordinates are available, or can be computed, from images. This information can be used in pattern recognition. Range images are also 2.5-dimensional. These images give the distance to different points in an image from a particular viewpoint.

Segmented

The images have been segmented to separate objects from the background. Pattern recognition and segmentation problems are closely linked in most cases. In some applications, it is possible to segment out an object easily. In cases when the objects have not been segmented, the recognition problem is closely linked with the segmentation problem.

6.4 Object Representation

Images represent a scene from a camera's perspective. It appears natural to represent objects in a camera-centric, or viewer-centered, coordinate system [33]. Another possibility is to represent objects in an object-centered coordinate system. Of course, one may represent objects in a world coordinate system also. Since it is easy to transform from one coordinate system to another using their relative positions, the central issue in selecting the proper coordinate system to represent objects is the ease of representation to allow the most efficient representation for feature detection and subsequent processes.

A representation allows certain operations to be efficient at the cost of other operations. Representations for pattern recognition are no exception [52]. Designers must consider the parameters in their design problems to select the best representation for the task. The following are commonly used representations in pattern recognition.

6.4.1 Observer-Centered Representations

If objects usually appear in a relatively few stable positions with respect to the camera, then they can be represented efficiently in an observer-centered coordinate system. If a camera is located at a fixed position and objects move such that they present only some aspects to the camera, then one can represent objects based on only those views. If the camera is far away from objects, as in remote sensing, then three-dimensionality of objects can be ignored. In such cases, the objects can be represented only by a limited set of views-in fact, only one view in most cases. Finally, if the objects in a domain of applications are significantly different from each other, then observer-centered representations may be enough.

Observer-centered representations are defined in image space. These representations capture characteristics and details of the images of objects in their relative camera positions [33].

One of the earliest and most rigorous approaches for pattern recognition is based on characterizing objects using a feature vector. This feature vector captures essential characteristics that help in distinguishing objects in a domain of application. The features selected in this approach are usually global features of the images of objects. These features are selected either based on the experience of a designer or by analyzing the efficacy of a feature in grouping together objects of the same class while discriminating it from the members of other classes. Many feature selection techniques have been developed in pattern classification. These techniques study the probabilistic distribution of features of known objects from different classes and use these distributions to determine whether a feature has sufficient discrimination power for classification.

In Figure 6.2 we show a two-dimensional version of a feature space. An object is represented as a point in this space. It is possible that different features have different importance and that their units are different. These problems are usually solved by assigning different weights to the features and by normalizing the features.

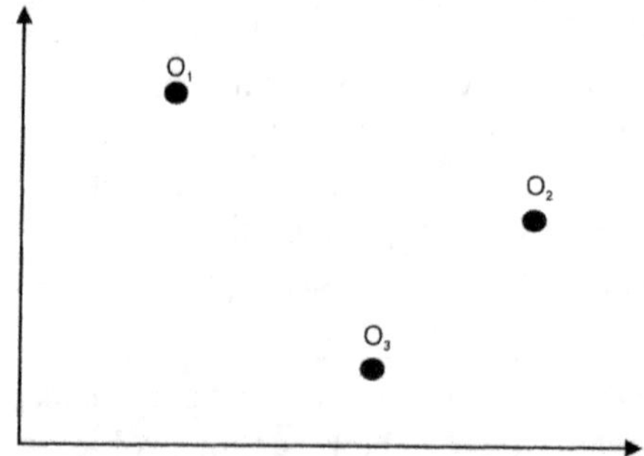

Fig. 6.2 Two-dimensional feature space for pattern recognition. Each object in this space is a point. Features must be normalized to have uniform units so that one may define a distance measure for the feature space.

Most so-called approaches for two-dimensional pattern recognition in the literature are the approaches based on the image features of objects [2]. These approaches try to partition an image into several local features and then represent an object as image features and relations among them. This representation of objects allows partial matching also. In the presence of occlusion in images, this representation is more powerful than feature space. In Figure 6.3 we show local features for an object and how they will be represented.

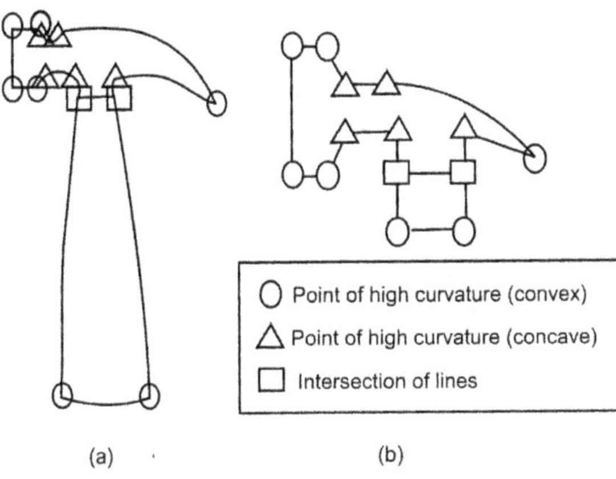

Fig. 6.3 In (a) an object is shown with its prominent local features highlighted. A graph representation of the object is shown in (b). This representation is used for object recognition using a graph matching approach.

6.4.2 Object-Centered Representations

An object-centered representation uses description of objects in a coordinate system attached to objects. This description is usually based on three-dimensional features or description of objects.

Object-centered representations are independent of the camera parameters and location. Thus, to make them useful for object recognition, the representation should have enough information to produce object images or object features in images for a known camera and viewpoint. This requirement suggests that object-centered representations should capture aspects of the geometry of objects explicitly.

Constructive Solid Geometry (CSG)

A CSG representation of an object uses simple volumetric primitives, such as blocks, cones, cylinders, and spheres, and a set of boolean operations: union, intersection, and difference [18]. Since arbitrarily curved objects cannot be represented using just a few chosen primitives, CSG approaches are not very useful in object recognition. These representations are used in object representation in CAD/CAM applications. In Fig. 6.4, a CSG representation for a simple object is shown.

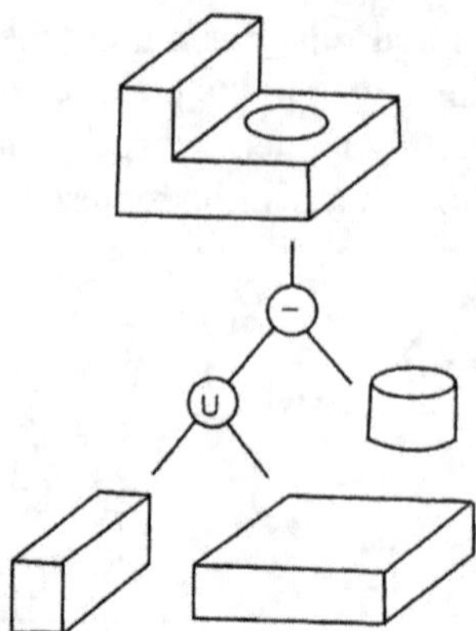

Fig. 6.4 A CSG representation of an object uses some basic primitives and operations among them to represent an object.

Spatial Occupancy

An object in three-dimensional space may be represented by using non-overlapping subregions of the three-dimensional space occupied by an object. There are many variants of this representation such as voxel representation, octree, and tetrahedral cell decomposition. In Figure 6.5, we show a voxel representation of an object.

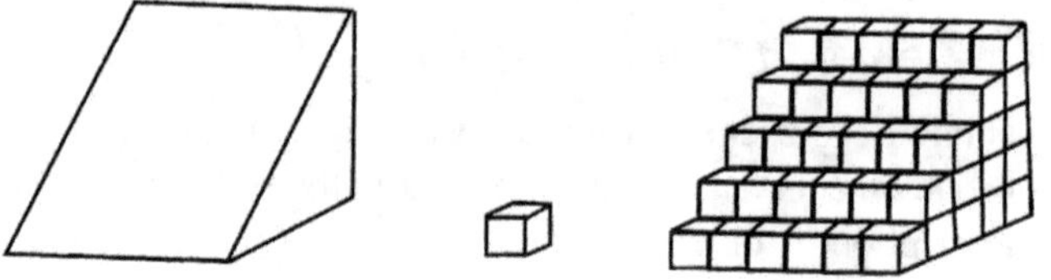

Fig. 6.5 A voxel representation of an object.

A spatial occupancy representation contains a detailed description of an object, but it is a very low-level description. This type of representation must be processed to find specific features of objects to enable the hypothesis formation process.

Multiple-View Representation

Since objects must be recognized from images, one may represent a three-dimensional object using several views obtained either from regularly spaced viewpoints in space or from some strategically selected viewpoints. For a limited set of objects, one may consider arbitrarily many views of the object and then represent each view in an observer-centered representation [4].

A three-dimensional object can be represented using its aspect graph. An aspect graph represents all stable views of an object. Thus, an aspect graph is obtained by partitioning the view-space into areas in which the object has stable views. The aspect graph for an object represents a relationship among all the stable views. In Fig. 6.6 we show a simple object and its aspect graph, each node in the aspect graph represents a stable view. The branches show how one can go from one stable view through accidental views.

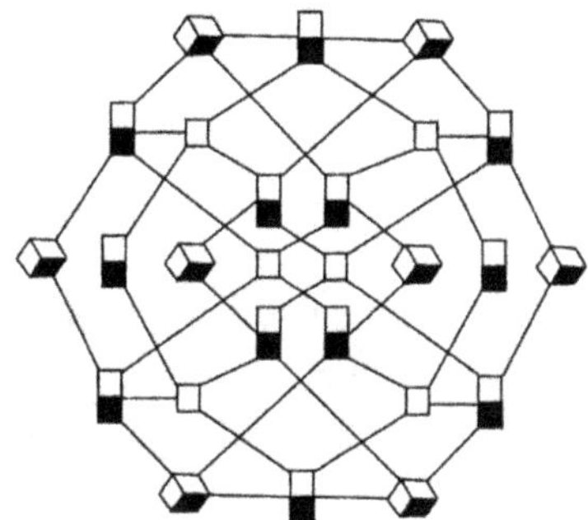

Fig. 6.6 An object and its aspect graph.

Surface-Boundary Representation

A solid object can be represented by defining the surfaces that bound the object. The bounding surfaces can be represented using one of several methods popular in computer graphics. These representations vary from triangular patches to non-uniform rational B-splines (NURBS).

Sweep Representations : Generalized Cylinders

Object shapes can be represented by a three-dimensional space curve that acts as the spine or axis of the cylinder, a two-dimensional cross-sectional figure, and a sweeping rule that defines how the cross section is to be swept along the space curve. The cross section can vary smoothly along the axis. This representation is shown in Fig. 6.7, the axis of the cylinder is shown as a dash line, the coordinate axes are drawn with respect to the cylinder's central axis, and the cross sections at each point are orthogonal to the cylinder's central axis.

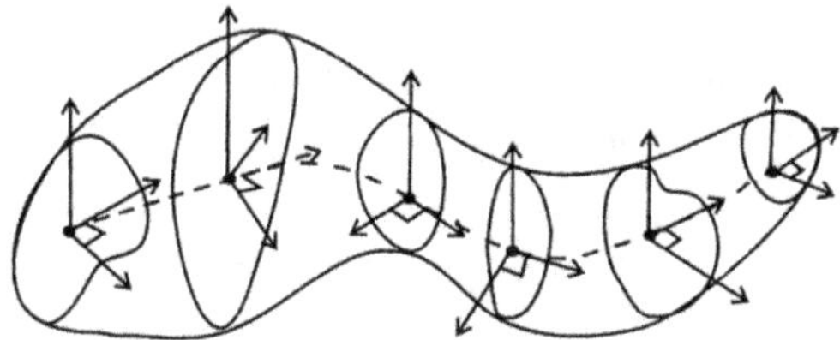

Fig. 6.7 An object and its generalized cylinder representation.

For many industrial and other objects, the cross section of objects varies smoothly along an axis in space, and in such cases this representation is satisfactory. For arbitrarily shaped objects, this condition is usually not satisfied, making this representation unsuitable.

6.5 Feature Detection

Many types of features are used for object recognition. Most features are based on either regions or boundaries in an image. It is assumed that a region or a closed boundary corresponds to an entity that is either an object or a part of an object [10]. Some of the commonly used features are as follows.

Global Features

Global features usually are some characteristics of regions in images such as area (size), perimeter, Fourier descriptors, and moments. Global features can be obtained either for a region by considering all points within a region, or only for those points on the boundary of a region. In each case, the intent is to find descriptors that are obtained by considering all points, their locations, intensity characteristics, and spatial relations.

Local Features

Local features are usually on the boundary of an object or represent a distinguishable small area of a region. Curvature and related properties are commonly used as local features. The curvature may be the curvature on a boundary or may be computed on a surface. The surface may be an intensity surface or a surface in 2.5-dimensional space. High curvature points are commonly called corners and play an important role in object recognition. Local features can contain a specific shape of a small boundary segment or a surface patch. Some commonly used local features are *curvature, boundary segments, and corners.*

Relational Features

Relational features are based on the relative positions of different entities, either regions, closed contours, or local features. These features usually include distance between features and relative orientation measurements. These features are very useful in defining composite objects using many regions or local features in images. In most cases, the relative position of entities is what defines objects. The exact same feature, in slightly different relationships, may represent entirely different objects.

In Fig. 6.8, an object and its description using features are shown. Both local and global features can be used to describe an object. The relations among objects can be used to form composite features.

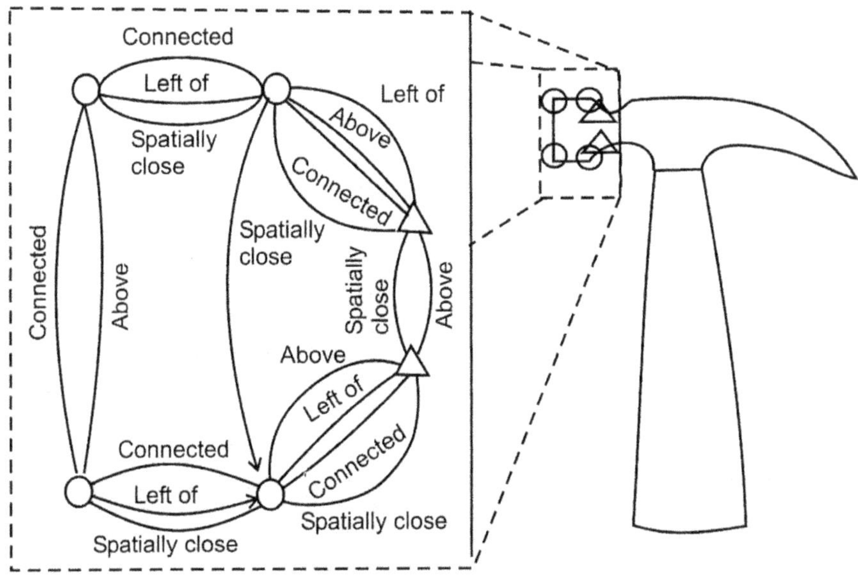

Fig. 6.8 An object and its partial representation using multiple local and global features.

6.6 Recognition Strategies

Pattern recognition is the sequence of steps that must be performed after appropriate features have been detected. As discussed earlier, based on the detected features in an image, one must formulate hypotheses about possible objects in the image [6]. These hypotheses must be verified using models of objects. Not all object recognition techniques require strong hypothesis formation and verification steps. Most recognition strategies have evolved to combine these two steps in varying amounts. As shown in Fig. 6.9, one may use three different possible combinations of these two steps. Even in these, the application contest, characterized by the factors discussed earlier in this section, determines how one or both steps are implemented. In the following, we discuss a few basic recognition strategies used for recognizing objects in different situations.

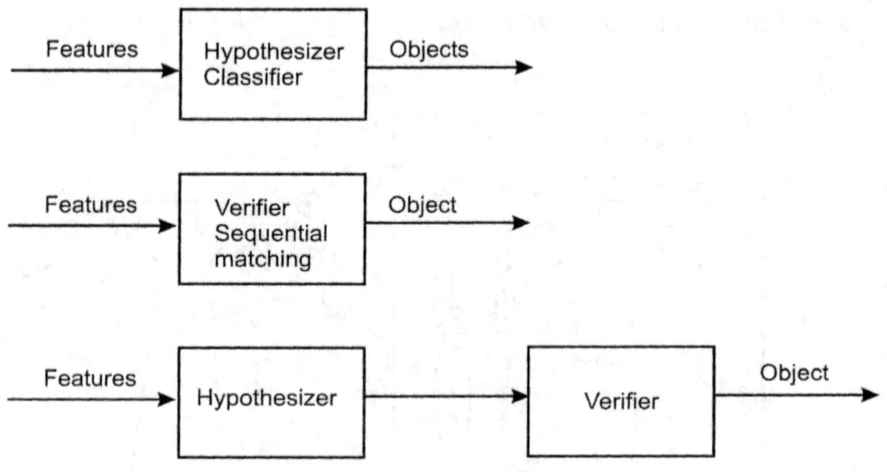

Fig. 6.9 Depending on the complexity of the problem, a recognition strategy may need to use either or both the hypothesis formation and verification steps.

6.6.1 Classification

The basic idea in classification is to recognize objects based on features. Pattern recognition approaches fall in this category, and their potential has been demonstrated in many applications. Neural net-based approaches also fall in this class. Some commonly used classification techniques are discussed briefly here. All techniques in this class assume that N features have been detected in images and that these features have been normalized so that they can be represented in the same metric space [39]. We will briefly discuss techniques to normalize these features after classification. In the following discussion, it will be assumed that the features for an object can be represented as a point in the N-dimensional feature space defined for that particular pattern recognition task.

Nearest Neighbour Classifiers

Suppose that a model object (ideal feature values) for each class is known and is represented for class i as f_{ij}, $j = 1, \ldots , N$. Now suppose that we detect and measure features of the unknown object U and represent them as u_j, $j = 1, \ldots, N$. For a 2-dimensional feature space, this situation is shown in Fig. 6.10.

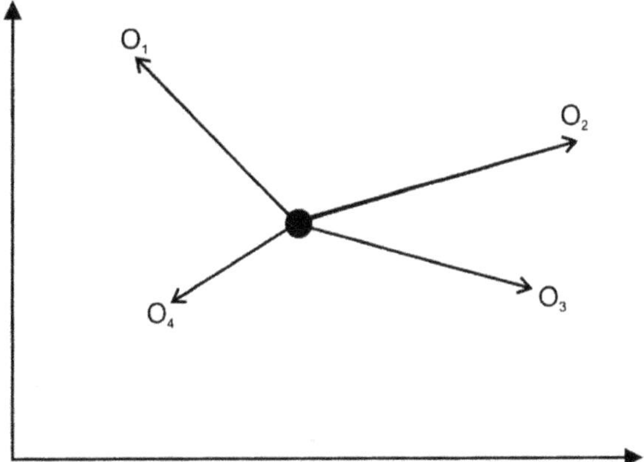

Fig. 6.10 The prototypes of each class are represented as points in the feature space. An unknown object is assigned to the closest class by using a distance measure in this space.

To decide the class of the object, we measure its similarity with each class by computing its distance from the points representing each class in the feature space and assign it to the nearest class [18]. The distance may be either Euclidean or any weighted combination of features. In general, we compute the distance d_j of the unknown object from class j as given by

$$d_j = \left[\sum_{i=1}^{N} \left(u_j - f_{ij} \right)^2 \right]^{1/2}$$

then the object is assigned to the class R such that

$$d_R = \min_{j=1}^{N} \left[d_j \right]$$

In the above, the distance to a class was computed by considering distance to the feature point representing a prototype object. In practice, it may be difficult to find a prototype object. Many objects may be known to belong to a class. In this case, one must consider feature values for all known objects of a class. This situation is shown in Fig. 6.11, each class is represented by a cluster of points in the feature space. Either the centroid of the cluster representing the class or the closest point of each class is considered the prototype for classification. Two common approaches in such a situation are :

1. Consider the centroid of the cluster as the prototype object's feature point, and compute the distance to this.

2. Consider the distance to the closest point of each class.

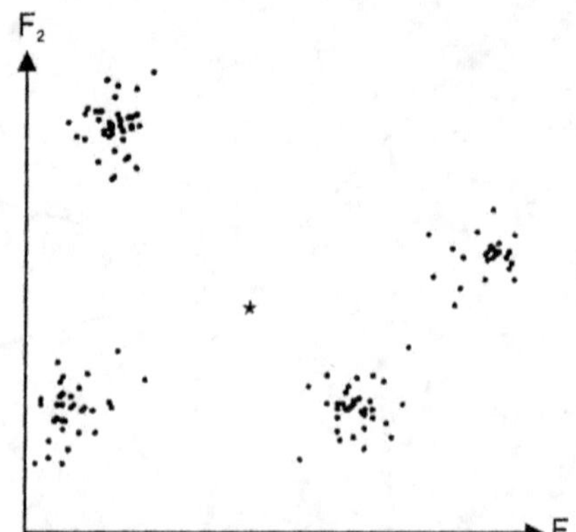

Fig. 6.11 All known objects of each class are represented as points in the feature space.

Bayesian Classifier

A Bayesian approach has been used for recognizing objects when the distribution of objects is not as straightforward as shown in the cases above. In general, there is a significant overlap in feature values of different objects. Thus, as shown for the one-dimensional feature space in Fig. 6.12, several objects can have same feature value. For an observation in the feature space, multiple-object classes are equally good candidates. To make a decision in such a case, one may use a Bayesian approach to decision making.

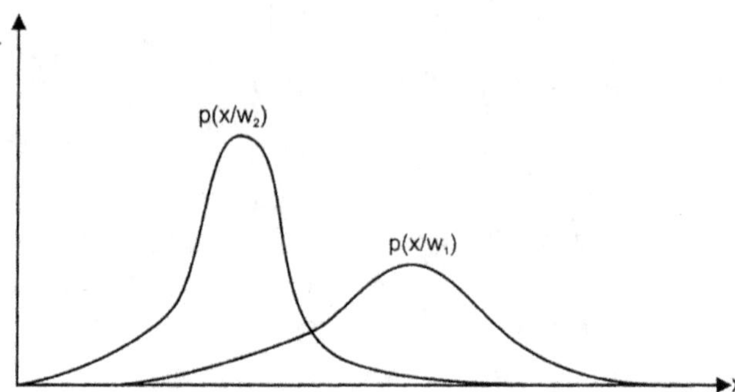

Fig. 6.12 The conditional density function for $p(x \mid w_j)$. This shows the probability of the feature values for each class.

In the Bayesian approach, probabilistic knowledge about the features for objects and the frequency of the objects is used [25]. Suppose that we know that the probability of objects of class j is $P(w_j)$. This means that a priori we know that the probability that an object of class j will appear is $P(w_j)$, and hence in absence of any other knowledge we can minimize the probability of error by assigning the unknown object to the class for which $P(w_j)$ is maximum.

Decisions about the class of an object are usually made based on feature observations. Suppose that the probability $P(x|w_j)$ is given and is as shown in Fig. 6.12. The conditional probability $P(x|w_j)$ tells us that, based on the probabilistic information provided, we know that if the feature value is observed to be x, then the probability that the object belongs to class j is $P(x|w_j)$. Based on this knowledge, we can compute the a posteriori probability $P(x|w_j)$ for the object. The a posteriori probability is the probability that, for the given information and observations, the unknown object belongs to class j.

Using Bayes' rule, this probability is given as :

$$P(w_j|x) = \frac{p(x|w_j)P(w_j)}{p(x)}$$

where
$$p(x) = \sum_{j=1}^{N} p(x|w_j)P(w_j).$$

The unknown object should be assigned to the class with the highest a posteriori probability $P(w_j|x)$. As can be seen from the above equations, and as shown in Fig. 6.13, a posteriori probability depends on prior knowledge about the objects [26]. If a priori probability of the object changes, so will the result.

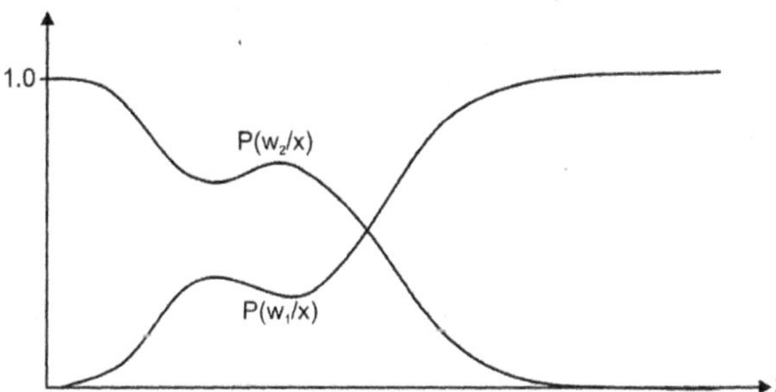

Fig. 6.13 A posteriori probabilities for two different values of a priori probabilities for objects [26].

We discussed the Bayesian approach above for one feature. It can be easily extended to multiple features by considering conditional density functions for multiple features.

Off-Line Computations

The above classification approaches consider the feature space, and then, based on the knowledge of the feature characteristics of objects, a method is used to partition the feature space so that a class decision is assigned to each point in the feature space [18]. To assign a class to each point in the feature space, all computations are done before the recognition of unknown objects begins. This is called off-line computation. These off-line computations reduce the computations at the run time. The recognition process can be effectively converted to a look-up table and hence can be implemented very quickly.

Neural Nets

Neural nets have been proposed for object recognition tasks. Neural nets implement a classification approach. Their attraction lies in their ability to partition the feature space using nonlinear boundaries for classes. These boundaries are obtained by using training of the net. During the training phase, many instances of objects to be recognized are shown. If the training set is carefully selected to represent all objects encountered later during the recognition phase, then the net may learn the classification boundaries in its feature space [33]. During the recognition phase, the net works like any other classifier.

The most attractive feature of neural nets is their ability to use nonlinear classification boundaries and learning abilities. The most serious limitations have been the inability to introduce known facts about the application domain and difficulty in debugging their performance.

6.6.2 Matching

Classification approaches use effective features and knowledge of the application. In many applications, a priori knowledge about the feature probabilities and the class probabilities is not available or not enough data is available to design a classifier. In such cases one may use direct matching of the model to the unknown object and select the best-matching model to classify the object. These approaches consider each model in sequence and fit the model to image data to determine the similarity of the model to the image component. This is usually done after the segmentation has been done. In the following we discuss basic matching approaches.

Feature Matching

Suppose that each object class is represented by its features. As above, let us assume that the jth feature's value for the ith class is denoted by f_{ij}. For an unknown object the features are denoted by u_j. The similarity of the object with the ith class is given by

$$S_i = \sum_{j=1}^{N} w_j s_j$$

where w_j is the weight for the jth feature. The weight is selected based on the relative importance of the feature. The similarity value of the jth feature is s_j. This could be the absolute difference, normalized difference, or any other distance measure. The most common method is to use

$$s_j = \left| u_j - f_{ij} \right|$$

and to account for normalization in the weight used with the feature.

The object is labeled as belonging to class k if S_k is the highest similarity value. Note that in this approach, we use features that may be local or global. We do not use any relations among the features.

Symbolic Matching

An object could be represented not only by its features but also by the relations among features. The relations among features may be spatial or some other type. An object in such cases may be represented as a graph. As shown in Fig. 6.6, each node of the graph represents a feature, and arcs connecting nodes represent relations among the objects. The object recognition problem then is considered as a graph matching problem.

A graph matching problem can be defined as follows. Given two graphs G_1 and G_2 containing nodes N_{ij}, where i and j denote the graph number and the node number, respectively, the relations among nodes j and k is represented by R_{ijk}. Define a similarity measure for the graphs that considers the similarities of all nodes and functions.

In most applications of machine vision, objects to be recognized may be partially visible [6]. A recognition system must recognize objects from their partial views. Recognition techniques that use global features and must have all features present are not suitable in these applications. In a way, the partial view object recognition problem is similar to the graph embedding problem studied in graph theory. The problem in pattern recognition becomes different when we start considering the similarity of nodes and relations among them. We discuss this type of matching in more detail later, in the section on verification.

6.6.3 Feature Indexing

If the number of objects is very large and the problem cannot be solved using feature space partitioning, then indexing techniques become attractive. The symbolic matching approach discussed above is a sequential approach and requires that the unknown object be compared with all objects. This sequential nature of the approach makes it unsuitable with a number of objects. In such a case, one should be able to use a hypothesizer that reduces the search space significantly. The next step is to compare the models of each object in the reduced set with the image to recognize the object.

Feature indexing approaches use features of objects to structure the modelbase. When a feature from the indexing set is detected in an image, this feature is used to reduce the search space. More than one feature from the indexing set may be detected and used to reduce the search space and in turn reduce the total time spent on pattern recognition.

The features in the indexing set must be determined using the knowledge of the modelbase. If such knowledge is not available, a learning scheme should be used. This scheme will analyze the frequency of each feature from the feature set and, based on the frequency of features, form the indexing set, which will be used for structuring the database.

In the indexed database, in addition to the names of the objects and their models, information about the orientation and pose of the object in which the indexing feature appears should always be kept. This information helps in the verification stage.

Once the candidate object set has been formed, the verification phase should be used for selecting the best object candidate.

6.7   Verification

Suppose that we are given an image of an object and we need to find how many times and where this object appears in an image. Such a problem is essentially a verification, rather than an pattern recognition problem. Obviously a verification algorithm can be used to exhaustively verify the presence of each model from a large modelbase, but such an exhaustive approach will not be a very effective method. A verification approach is desirable if one, or at most a few, objects are possible candidates. There are many approaches for verification. Here we discuss some commonly used approaches [27].

6.7.1 Template Matching

Suppose that we have a template $g[i, j]$ and we wish to detect its instances in an image $f[i,j]$. An obvious thing to do is to place the template at a location in an image and to detect its presence at that point by comparing intensity values in the template with the corresponding values in the image. Since it is rare that intensity values will match exactly, we require a measure of dissimilarity between the intensity values of the template and the corresponding values of the image. Several measures may be defined :

$$\max_{[i,j]\in R} \left| f - g \right|$$

$$\sum_{[i,j]\in R} \left| f - g \right|$$

$$\sum_{[i,j]\in R} \left(f - g \right)^2$$

where R is the region of the template.

The sum of the squared errors is the most popular measure. In the case of template matching, this measure can be computed indirectly and computational cost can be reduced. We can simplify :

$$\sum_{[i,j]\in R} \left(f - g \right)^2 = \sum_{[i,j]\in R} f^2 + \sum_{[i,j]\in R} g^2 - 2 \sum_{[i,j]\in R} fg$$

Now if we assume that f and g are fixed, then Σfg gives a measure of mismatch. A reasonable strategy for obtaining all locations and instances of the template is to shift the template and use the match measure at every point in the image. Thus, for an m × n template, we compute

$$M[i,j] = \sum_{k=1}^{m}\sum_{l=1}^{n} g[k,l] f[i+k,j+l]$$

where k and l are the displacements with respect to the template in the image. This operation is called the cross-correlation between f and g.

Our aim will be to find the locations that are local maxima and are above a certain threshold value. However, a minor problem in the above computation was introduced when we assumed that f and g are constant. When applying this computation to images, the template g is constant, but the value of f will be varying. The value of M will then depend on f and hence will not give a correct indication of the match at different locations. This problem can be solved by using normalized cross-correlation. The match measure M then can be computed using

$$C_{fg}[i,j] = \sum_{k=1}^{m}\sum_{l=1}^{n} g[k,l] f[i+k,j+l]$$

$$M[i,j] = \frac{C_{fg}[i,j]}{\left\{\sum_{k=1}^{m}\sum_{l=1}^{n} f^{2}[i+k,j+l]\right\}^{1/2}}$$

It can be shown that M takes maximum value for $[i,j]$ at which $g = cf$.

The above computations can be simplified significantly in binary images. Template matching approaches have been quite popular in optical computing: frequency domain characteristics of convolution are used to simplify the computation.

A major limitation of template matching is that it only works for translation of the template. In case of rotation or size changes, it is ineffective. It also fails in case of only partial views of objects.

6.7.2 Morphological Approach

Morphological approaches can also be used to detect the presence and location of templates. For binary images, using the structuring element as the template and then opening the image will result in all locations where the template fits in. For gray images, one may use gray-image morphology. These results are shown for a template in Fig. 6.14.

(a)

objects in the *real*
bject models. This 1
cognition effortlessl
ask for implement;
:r we will discuss d
echniques that hav.
We will discuss difl

(b)

(c)

Fig. 6.14 (a) A structuring element (b) an image
and (c) the result of the morphological opening.

6.7.3 Symbolic

As discussed above, if both models of objects and the unknown object are represented as graphs, then some approach must be used for matching graphical representations. Here we define the basic concepts behind these approaches.

Graph Isomorphism

Given two graphs (V_1, E_1) and (V_2, E_2), find a 1:1 and onto mapping (an isomorphism) f between V_1 and V_2 such that for $\theta_1, \theta_2 \in V_1, V_2, f(\theta_1) = \theta_2$ and for each edge of E_1 connecting any pair of nodes θ_1 and $\theta_2 \in V_1$, there is an edge of E_2 connecting $f(\theta_1)$ and $f(\theta_1')$.

Graph isomorphism can be used only in cases of completely visible objects. If an object is partially visible, or a 2.5-dimensional description is to be matched with a 3-dimensional description, then graph embedding, or subgraph isomorphisms, can be used.

Subgraph Isomorphisms

Find isomorphisms between a graph (V_1, E_1) and subgraphs of another graph (V_2, E_2).

A problem with these approaches for matching is that the graph isomorphism is an NP problem. For any reasonable object description, the time required for matching will be prohibitive. Fortunately, we can use more information than that used by graph isomorphism algorithms [39]. This information is available in terms of the properties of nodes. Many heuristics have been proposed to solve the graph matching problem. These heuristics should consider:

- Variability in properties and relations
- Absence of properties or relations
- The fact that a model is an abstraction of a class of objects
- The fact that instances may contain extra information.

One way to formulate the similarity is to consider the arcs in the graph as springs connecting two masses at the nodes. The quality of the match is then a function of the goodness of fit of the templates locally and the amount of energy needed to stretch the springs to force the unknown onto the modelence data.

$$C = \sum_{d \in R_1} template\ cost\big(d, F(d)\big)$$

$$+ \sum_{(d,e) \in R_2} spring\ cost\big(F(d), F(e)\big)$$

$$+ \sum_{e \in R_3} missing\ cost\big(c\big)$$

where R_1 = {found in model}, R_2 = {found in model x found in unknown}, and R_3 = {missing in model} $\cup$ {missing in unknown}. This function represents a very general formulation. Template cost, spring cost, and missing cost can take many different forms. Applications will determine the exact form of these functions.

6.7.4 Analogical Methods

A measure of similarity between two curves can be obtained by measuring the difference between them at every point, as shown in Fig. 6.15. The difference will always be measured along some axis. The total difference is either the sum of absolute errors or the sum of squared errors [33]. If exact registration is not given, some variation of correlation-based methods must be used.

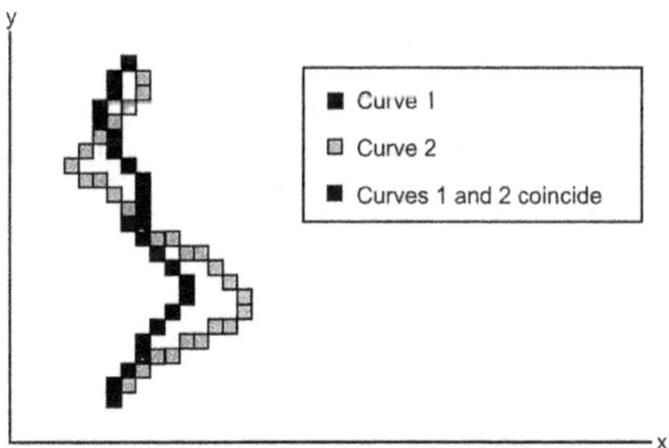

Fig. 6.15 Matching of two entities by directly measuring the errors between them.

For recognizing patterns using three-dimensional models, one may use rendering techniques from computer graphics to find their appearance in an image and then try to compare with the original image to verify the presence of an object. Since the parameters required to render objects are usually unknown, usually one tries to consider some prominent features on three-dimensional models and to detect them and match them to verify the model's instance in an image [26]. This has resulted in development of theories that try to study three-dimensional surface characteristics of objects and their projections to determine *invariants* that can be used in pattern recognition. Invariants are usually features or characteristics in images that are relatively insensitive to an object's orientation and scene illumination. Such features are very useful in detecting three-dimensional patterns from their two-dimensional projections.

6.8　Questions

1. What factors would you consider in selecting an appropriate representation for the modelbase? Discuss the advantages and disadvantages of object-centered and observer-centered representations.

2. What is feature space? How can you recognize objects using feature space?

3. Compare classical pattern recognition approaches based on Bayesian approaches with neural net approaches by considering the feature space, classification approaches, and object models used by both of these approaches.

4. One of the most attractive features of neural nets is their ability to learn. How is their ability to learn used in object recognition? What kind of model is prepared by a neural net? How can you introduce your knowledge about objects in neural nets?

5. Where do you use matching in object recognition? What is a symbolic matching approach?

6. What is feature indexing? How does it improve object recognition?

7. Discuss template matching. In which type of applications would you use template matching? What are the major limitations of template matching? How can you overcome these limitations?

CHAPTER 7

Digital Image Processing
– SOFTWARES

7.1 MATLAB

MATLAB is a high-level technical computing language and interactive environment for algorithm development, data visualization, data analysis, and numeric computation. MATLAB helps solve technical computing problems faster than with traditional programming languages, such as C, C++, and Fortran.

MATLAB can be used in a wide range of applications, including signal and image processing, communications, control design, test and measurement, financial modeling and analysis, and computational biology. Add-on toolboxes extend the MATLAB environment to solve particular classes of problems in these application areas. MATLAB provides a number of features for documenting and sharing of work. MATLAB code can be integrated with other languages and applications, and helps distribute MATLAB algorithms and applications.

MATLAB is a computer program that can be very helpful in solving the sorts of mathematical problems frequently encountered. The built-in features of MATLAB can be effortlessly used to solve a wide variety of numerical problems, from the very basic, such as a system of 2 equations with 2 unknowns to the more complex, such as factoring polynomials, fitting curves to data points, making calculations using matrices, performing signal processing operations such as Fourier transforms, and building and training neural networks. A very powerful and often very useful aspect of MATLAB is that it can be used to plot many different kinds of graphs, enabling you to visualize complex mathematical functions and laboratory data.

7.1.1 Key Features of MATLAB

- High-level language for technical computing
- Development environment for managing code, files, and data
- Interactive tools for iterative exploration, design, and problem solving
- Mathematical functions for linear algebra, statistics, Fourier analysis, filtering, optimization, and numerical integration
- 2-D and 3-D graphics functions for visualizing data
- Tools for building custom graphical user interfaces
- Functions for integrating MATLAB based algorithms with external applications and languages, such as C, C++, Fortran, Java, COM, and Microsoft Excel

7.1.2 Functions of MATLAB

- Data analysis and visualization
- Numeric and symbolic computation
- Engineering and scientific graphics
- Modeling, simulation, and prototyping
- Programming, application development, and GUI design

MATLAB is used in a variety of application areas including signal and image processing, control system design, financial engineering, and medical research. The open architecture makes it easy to use MATLAB and companion products to explore data and create custom tools that provide early insights and competitive advantages.

The Image Processing Toolbox extends the MATLAB computing environment to provide functions and interactive tools for enhancing and analyzing digital images and developing image processing algorithms. In addition, it facilitates the learning and teaching of image processing techniques in both academic and research settings.

Together, MATLAB and the Image Processing Toolbox provide scientists, researchers, and engineers with a diverse, flexible set of tools for solving complex imaging problems in disciplines such as aerospace/defense, astronomy, remote sensing, medical and scientific imaging, and materials science. Most functions are implemented in the open MATLAB language, letting you explore and customize existing toolbox algorithms or develop your own. You can use the toolbox for the restoration of noisy or degraded images, image enhancement for improved intelligibility, blob analysis, and extraction and analysis of image data with 2-D statistics and transforms, as well as to develop complete solutions to challenging image processing problems that involve multidimensional data sets.

The MATLAB development environment allows develop algorithms, interactively analyze data, view data files, and manage projects.

7.1.3 Visualizing Data

All the graphics features that are required to visualize engineering and scientific data are available in MATLAB. These include 2-D and 3-D plotting functions, 3-D volume visualization functions, tools for interactively creating plots, and the ability to export results to all popular graphics formats. It allows to customize plots by adding multiple axes; changing line colors and markers; adding annotation, LaTEX equations, and legends; and drawing shapes.

2-D Plotting

We can visualize vectors of data with 2-D plotting functions that create:

- Line, area, bar, and pie charts
- Direction and velocity plots
- Histograms
- Polygons and surfaces
- *Scatter/bubble plots*
- *Animations*

7.1.4 3-D Plotting and Volume Visualization

MATLAB provides functions for visualizing 2-D matrices, 3-D scalar, and 3-D vector data, which helps visualize and understand large, often complex, multidimensional data. You can specify plot characteristics, such as camera viewing angle, perspective, lighting effect, light source locations, and transparency. 3-D plotting functions include:

- Surface, contour, and mesh
- *Image plots*
- *Cone, slice, stream, and isosurface*

Creating and Editing Plots Interactively

MATLAB provides interactive tools for designing and modifying graphics. From a MATLAB figure window, you can perform the following tasks:

- Drag and drop new data sets onto the figure
- Change the properties of any object on the figure
- Zoom, rotate, pan, and change camera angle and lighting

- Add annotations and data tips
- Draw shapes
- Generate an M-code function that can be reused with different data

7.1.5 Importing and Exporting Graphic Files

MATLAB lets you read and write common graphical and data file formats, such as GIF, JPEG, BMP, EPS, TIFF, PNG, HDF, AVI, and PCX. As a result, you can export MATLAB plots to other applications, such as Microsoft Word and Microsoft PowerPoint, or to desktop publishing software. Before exporting, you can create and apply style templates, covering characteristics such as layout, font, and line thickness, to meet publication specifications.

7.2   EASI/PACE

EASI/PACE is an image processing software used for remote sensing satellite data analysis and interpretation. EASI (Environmental Analysis and Scientific Interface) is a command-based language that is used to setup and run all PACE programs and raster modeling. EASI can also be used as a programming language. The prominent functions available in the software include the pre-processing functions like noise filtering, warping, scene mosaicking, SAR orthorectification, multi-resolution sensor fusion, and co-registration of image, elevation and feature data; photo-textured perspective scenes can be generated using this software; functions are also provided for terrain slope, aspect, sun shading and radar angle of incidence; generation of stereo pairs; numerous feature extraction, imagery exploitation, database and data export capabilities.

EASI/PACE supports 24 USGS map projections and provides satellite image orthorectification with or without an elevation model, ground control point collection from map sheets in any map projection, and transformation of imagery to and from any map projection. It supports 3-D perspective image creation from a DEM, including an option to overlay vector data; wireframe 3-D perspective generation from a DEM; extraction of DEMs from SPOT stereo-pairs; generation of true elevation contours from DEMs; determination of viewable areas from specified points on a DEM; import and export of DEM, DLG, JPEG and SCITEX formats and more.

EASI/PACE has the ability to import 36 raster and 11 vector formats. It includes a Hyperspectral Data Analysis Package with programs based on software developed at the USGS Spectroscopy Lab. Images of up to 1024 bands can be processed. The Satellite Ortho and DEM Package can orthorectify ERS-1 and JERS-1 radar imagery, as well as IRS-1 imagery. EASI/PACE's ImageWorks component includes support for Landsat 7 level 1G data in HDF, GeoTIFF and FAST formats. Source code and a toolkit for writing new applications are also available in EASI/PACE. Links to ARC/INFO, SPANS, Intergraph, PAMAP, AutoCAD and other programs are provided.

7.2.1 EASI / PACE Modules

Image Works : Image Works is a GUI based software which incorporates the most frequently needed image display, enhancement, and data management tools in an easy to learn user interface. The software provides integrated raster and vector display technologies.

GCP Works : This is an interactive, point-and-click tool for performing ground control point collection, image-to-map, image-to-image, and image-to-vector registration, and image mosaicking. Ground control points are collected using multiple image displays. GCP locations are estimated automatically by the software. Mosaics are created from image sources through user specified mosaic cut lines and automatic tone or color balancing. A registration/mosaic preview feature facilitates quality control before registration to disk.

XPACE: XPACE is the Graphical User Interface for EASI/PACE, providing point-and-click access to all applications. This Package is available on Desktop and Workstations, providing a common interface across all platforms.

Ortho Engine : It is an airphoto/satellite imagery orthorectification package. Ortho Engine software generates precise orthoimages from scanned aerial photographs and satellite imagery.

FLY : It is an application allowing a user to create 3-D perspective scene generation and real time fly-through. Flight parameters such as elevation, speed, and direction as well as perspective parameters can be controlled interactively during the flight.

Image Processing : This Package provides fundamental image processing capabilities, such as image arithmetic, several types of filtering, radiometric correction and enhancement, and intensity-hue-saturation and reverse transforms. Mean, median, mode, edge detection, Gaussian, and weighted average filters are supported. Image compression techniques are included in this Package. Data transform using forward and reverse Cosine, Fourier, Hadamard, or Walsh 2D FFT transforms is possible.

Geometric Correction : This Package is used to ensure that images of different resolutions are correctly referenced to the earth. Four types of registration are possible: image to image, image to map, image to vector, and image to terminal coordinates. During ground control point (GCP) collection, extensive error reports are provided to ensure proper results when the final image is produced. Once the GCPs have been collected, up to a 5th order model can be used to rectify the image. Pixel sizes can also be resampled so that input data with varying resolutions can be stored in the same manner for further processing. Images can be mosaicked and blended along arbitrary cut-lines, and histogram matched.

Vector Utilities : Interactively manipulate and modify vectors that are either input from a digitizing table, imported from a vector GIS, or created through raster to vector conversion. Vector input programs allow entering and editing of line and point data, with or without associated attribute values. Gridding programs allow the user to take contours or points with elevations, digitized off a map, and create a raster DEM model. Contouring of raster surfaces such as DEMs is supported.

Multilayer Modeling : This Package is a critical decision support tool that allows the user to combine up to 128 layers (channels) of information, each with up to 256 values (or attributes). Using a powerful modeling language, these layers and associated attributes can be related to produce suitability or site selection maps. As well, images can be queried by simply pointing to a pixel, and up to 16 layers of attribute information is presented interactively. Additional GIS tools include index, matrix, and overlay analysis. Proximity zone maps may be generated. The modeling language is also a very powerful pixel-based image processing language which allows the user to do channel arithmetic, ratios, reports, sub-area totalizations, and to write almost any imaging equation. Looping, "if-then-else" constructs, internal variables, and trigonometric functions are supported.

7.3   ERDAS Imagine Software

Earth Resource Data Analysis System (ERDAS) Imagine is a popular software package widely used in the world for processing digital remote sensing (RS) and Geographic Information System (GIS) data. ERDAS Imagine supports both aerial and satellite RS data right from data ingesting, pre-processing, analysis, post-processing and map printing, The software package accepts data acquired from optical and microwave sensors satellites. The software package is a robust, seasoned, user friendly and easy to use. ERDAS Imagine is powered with accurate mathematical formulae for delivering mapping products to the world standards covering most of the map projections used in the world. In view of high-resolution voluminous remote sensing data processing, the package uses pyramidal data structures for quick display, processing, classification and map-composition with all the latest technologies. The package is equipped with several tools to give wide room for developing customized processing algorithms to meet the operational requirements of the users in the ERDAS Imagine environment. The package supports most of the file structures for importing and exporting RS and GIS data to the other digital image processing software packages. With the raster and vector processing capabilities, the package is provided with virtual GIS, 3D data presentation and 3D measurements. The software package has got the extensibility into photogrammetric suit for generating ortho-maps, DEMs, 3D Modeling and contours from aerial and satellite stereo pairs. The package uses all open GIS system standards.

To cover all the above said capabilities, the package is modularized based on major functionalities. The functionalities of different modules are presented as follows:

Table 7.1 ERDAS IMAGINE® Product Tier Comparison.

Functionality	Essentials	Advantage	Professional
Work with files in geospatially linked viewers	X	X	X
Use over 130 different image formats	X	X	X
Rapidly display and roam through imagery	X	X	X
Digitize Arc Coverage and Shape files on top of images	X	X	X
Create and print maps in over 1000 projected coordinate systems	X	X	X
Display and analyze ESRI Geodatabases	X	X	X
Display and analyze Oracle GeoRaster and geometry	X	X	X
Perform image georeferencing	X	X	X
Schedule batch processing	X	X	X
Mosaic images		X	X
Interpolate surfaces from points		X	X
Orthorectify images		X	X
Advanced spatial, radiometric and spectral enhancement		X	X
Spatial analysis and modeling		X	X
Analyze information in radar images			X
Perform advanced image classification			X
Perform graphical spatial modeling			X
Extract information from hyper spectral imagery			X

7.3.1 IMAGINE Essentials®

Use over 130 different image formats, including JPEG 2000 encoding/recoding

Geospatially linked viewers, including the

IMAGINE Geospatial Light Table™

Rapidly display and roam through imagery

Georeference raw image data

Manage images with the IMAGINE Image Catalog

Unsupervised classification

Digitize Arc coverage and Shape files over images

Display and analyze ESRI Geodatabases

Display and analyze Oracle Spatial GeoRaster and geometries

Create and print maps in over 1000 projected coordinate systems with Map Composer

Easy data access using the CellArray™

Batch processing wizard

Intuitive graphical user interface

Customizable interface with the Preference Editor

Context-sensitive, hypertext-linked on-line help

7.3.2 IMAGINE Advantage®

Orthocorrection

Surface interpolation

Mosaicking

Image processing

Spatial analysis

Pan sharpening

Knowledge Classifier

Spatial Modeling Language (SML)

7.3.3 IMAGINE Professional®

Spectral analysis

Hyperspectral image exploitation

IMAGINE Expert Classifier

Multispectral classification

Area frame sampling

Model Maker

7.3.4 IMAGINE Radar Interpreter™

All the modules are equipped with rich GUI's (Graphical user interface) for easy to use. The functional details of the above modules are discussed below with brief description. Where ever possible examples are also presented along with the functional details.

7.3.5 Image Processing, Vector and Raster GIS Tools

Raster Data Formats : GeoTIFF, ESRI GRID, ESRI GRID Stack, ESRI BIL, BIP and BSQ, JFIF (JPEG), DTED, CIB, CADRG, PIX, Mr.SID, ER Mapper Raster, Silicon Graphics FIT, Bitmap (.bmp), Portable Network Graphics (.png), IRS, Spot, NOAA, MODIS, HYPERION, ASTER, TM, Quick bird, Cartosat, ORBI Image and IKONOS/Cartosat/ORBIView sensor Support. Oracle 10 G support.

Vector Data Formats : ESRI ArcInfo coverages (8.x, 7.x, 6.x & 3.5), ARCGIS Geodatabases, ESRI Shape files, DXF, DWG, DGN/IGN files, ESRI SDE Vectors, TerraModel Project files (.pro). Oracle 10 G support.

Data Visualization tools

- Multiple image display types
- Overlay multiple data types (Unlimited data layers)
- Support for files over 2 GB in size
- Geographic linking
- Dynamic roam
- Fractional zoom, rectangle zoom and continuous zoom
- Continuous rotate
- Zoom to a specific scale
- On-the-fly resampling
- Image histogram modification tools
- Save and reload multiple LUTs

- Recode class values
- Filtering for thematic images (Neighborhood Analysis)
- Visual change detection between any data types
    - Swipe
    - Blend
    - Flicker
- Inquire cursor and inquire box, including MGRS support
- Measurement tool for points, lengths, angles, areas, perimeters, etc
- Profile tools
    - Spectral profile for hyper spectral analysis
    - Spectral reference libraries
    - Spatial profile for cross-section, surface distance, and line-of-sight analysis
- Surface profile for rapid isometric surface views
- GPS live-link
    - Display location in Viewer based on NMEA-0183 communication
    - Drive View based on GPS coordinates in real time
- Batch Processing options (Record and Repeat common Functions)
- Interpolation techniques: linear or non-linear rubber sheeting
- GEO Raster Read/Write into ORACLE 10g (Enterprisae solutions).

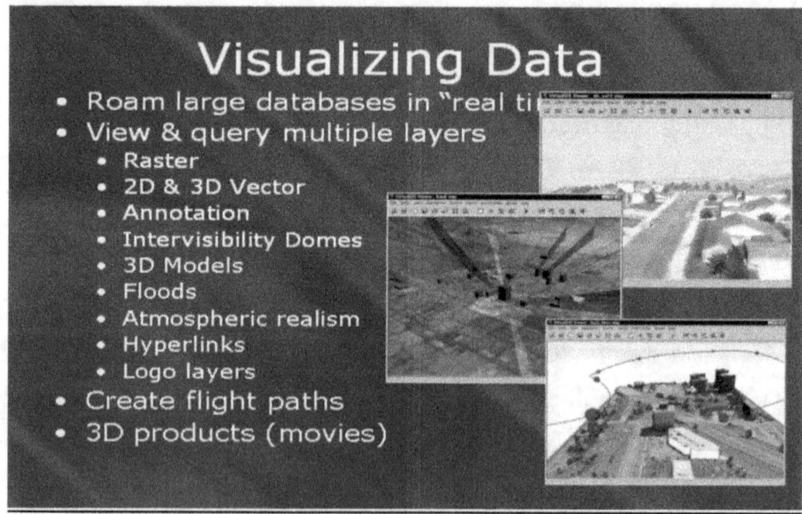

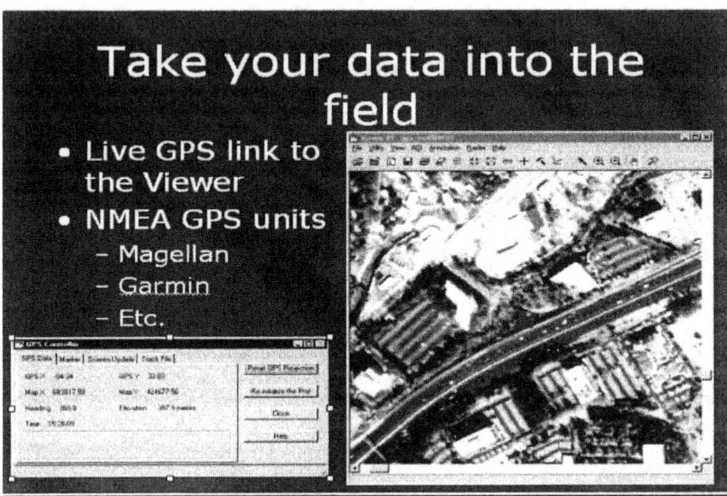

Vector Data handling capabilities

- ESRI Shape file and ArcInfo coverage read/write/create

- ESRI ArcInfo Coverage/Geo database and Shape file coverage formats built directly into the software.

- Integrated vector handling between ArcInfo, Arcview files & SDE vectors

- Create points, arcs, polygons, and tics

- Topology creation for vector coverages.

- Create and enter attribute data

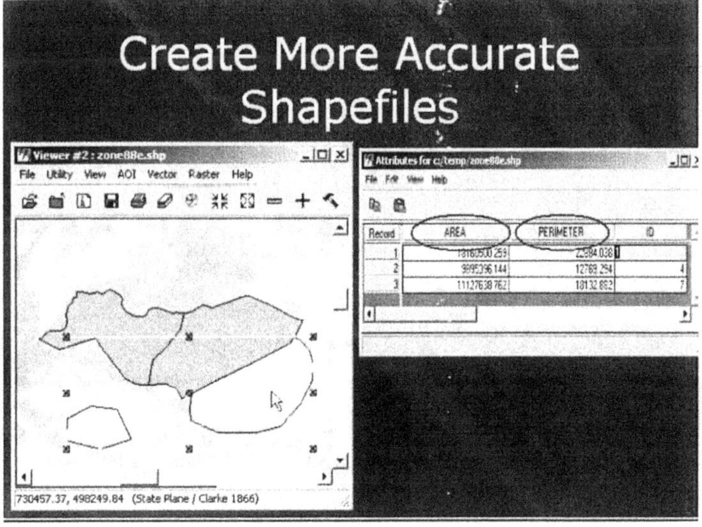

- Cut, copy, paste, and delete
- Splining, densifying, and generalization
- Automatic feature extraction
- Heads-up digitizing in viewer, digitizing tablet input, or keyboard data entry
- Reproject to another projection
- Add Hyperlinks to Windows applications or web pages from vector features
- Read/Write into ORACLE 10g(Enterprise solutions)

Geometric Correction Tools

- Automatic geometric correction from valid ephemeris information
- Manual georeferencing can be applied to any raster data
  - Affine
  - Polynomial (1st to 10th order)
  - Rubber Sheeting
- Reprojection
- Edit Ground Control Points (GCPs)
- GCP selection from map, image, vector, or keyboard
- Automatic coordinate conversion
- Automatic error reporting
- Automatic point prediction
- Image resampling to coordinate system
- Nearest Neighbor, Bilinear, or Cubic Convolution resampling
- User-defined pixel sizes, geographic subsets, etc.
- DLL extendible
- Single Photo/Image Orthocorrection using External DEM.
- Supports more than 55 projections
- Supports more than 45 spheroids and 200 datum's
- Has the capabilities for adding more spheroids and datum's
- Support for both standard and user-defined projection libraries, allowing thousands of projection systems to be defined

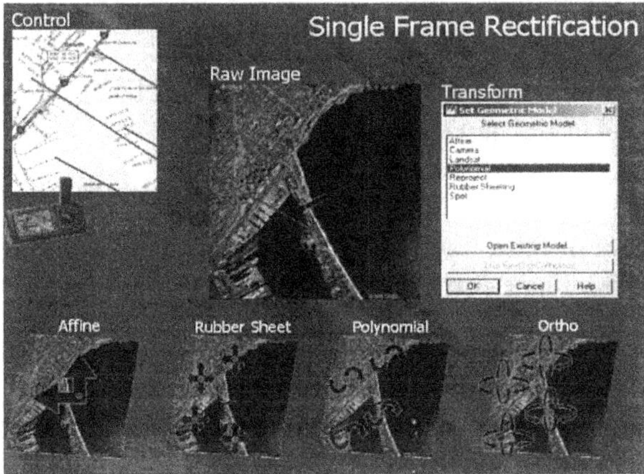

Map Composer Capabilities

Create or access individual custom maps, of user-defined size.

- Add multiple data frames containing one or more data layers each
- Automatically generated grid ticks, lines and graticules
- Titles
- Neat lines, bounding boxes, symbols, etc.
- Annotation
- Logos
- North arrows

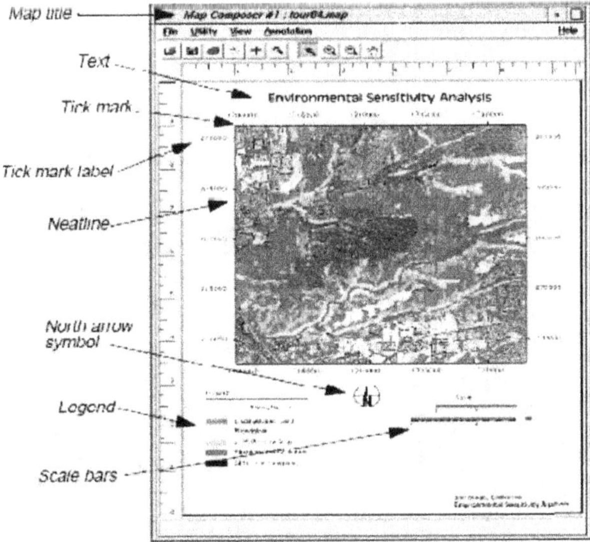

- Scale bars
- Automatically generated legends
- User-definable styles
- Build customized map templates
- Industry-standard printer languages and devices

Advanced Mosaicking Tool

- Advanced color balancing and matching capabilities to produce seamless mosaics.
- Stitch multiple images with:
  - Differing or like resolution (pixel sizes)
  - Differing or like projection systems
  - Geometrically calibrated images
- Color balancing
- Manual or semi-automated
  - Define abnormal areas for exclusion from processing
  - Surface-fitting removes spatially varying illumination effects like Hot spots.
  - Preview color balancing effects
- Histogram matching
- Use existing lookup tables (LUTs) to perform color balancing
- View image outlines, overlap areas, and cutlines
- Full control over the algorithm applied at each image overlap region
- Output into a single file or cut into multiple files based on AOI's.
- Specify output projection cell size and data type

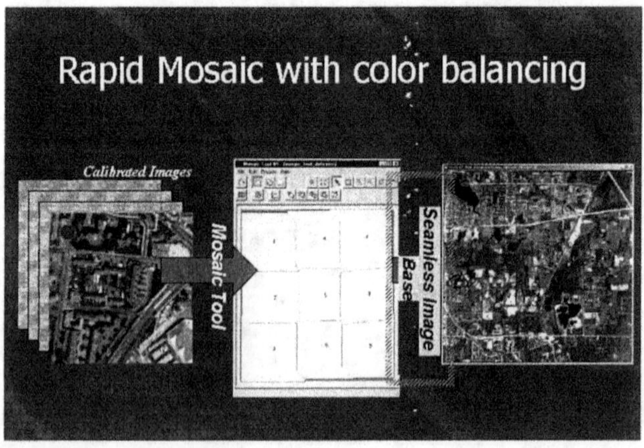

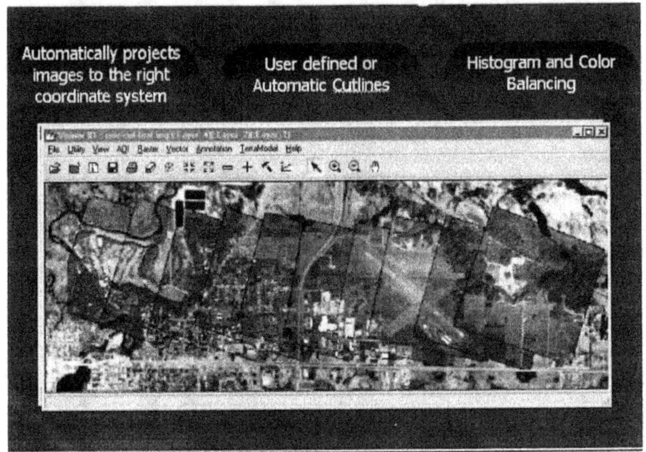

Image Processing and Spatial Analysis Tools

- Convolution filtering
- Resolution merge (PAN + LISS)
- Lookup table stretch
- Histogram equalization
- Histogram match
- Principal components
- Fourier analysis
- Topographic analysis like Slope, Aspect and Shaded relief
- Vector to raster and Vice versa

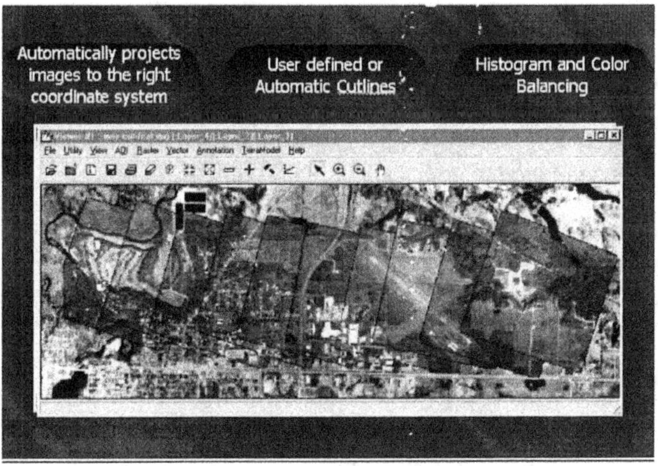

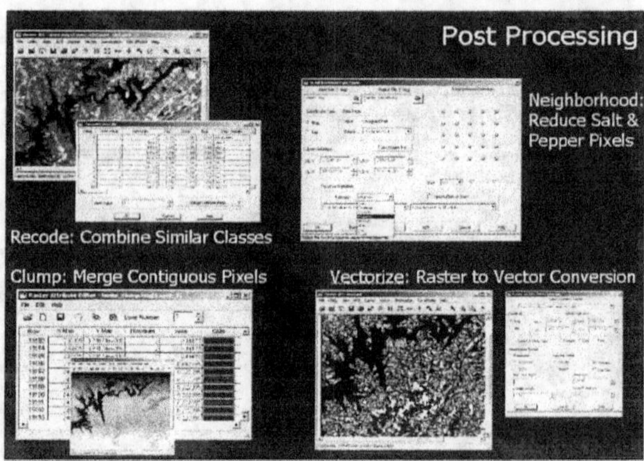

SURFACE Interpolation

A surface tool provides an effective means of interpolating a continuous raster surface from discrete input data.

- Multiple input data sources supported
- Interpolation techniques: linear or non-linear rubber sheeting (Delaunay Triangulation) • User-definable output

Multispectral Classification Tools

- ISODATA Classifier
- Fuzzy classification
- Rule based classification using ancillary information.
- Classifier like maximum likelihood, mahalanobis distance, parallelpiped, or minimum distance rules
- Hybrid parametric/non-parametric classification
- Select, evaluate and edit signatures
- Signature creation
- User-defined AOI point, ellipse, rectangle, polygon, or polyline objects
- Sophisticated feature-space signature editing, extraction and evaluation
- Signature evaluation and manipulation
- Contingency matrices
- Separability measures
- User-specified bands per combiation
- Univariate and covariance statistics
- Feature space (scattergram) plotting
- User-specified band combinations

- Signature ellipse plotting
- Image to feature space linking
- Non-parametric signature extraction
- Signature merge, delete, and replace
- Set layers to use in classification process
- Manual editing of parallelepiped limits
- Set output class values, colors, apriori probabilities, and classification order
- Post-classification class editing
- Classification accuracy assessment
- Random or user-defined ground truth locations
- Automatically generate accuracy reports
- Kappa statistics, error matrices and accuracy totals

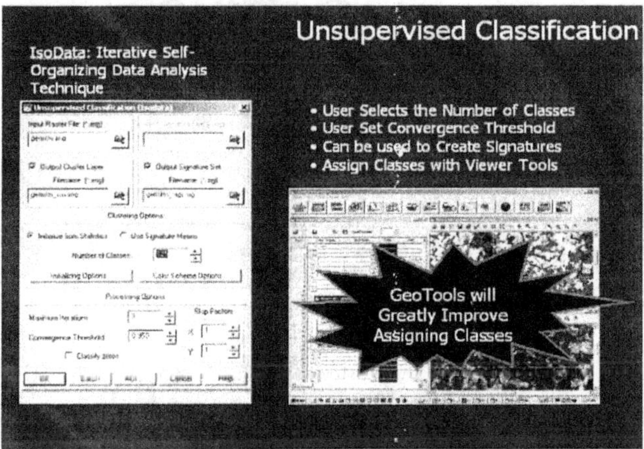

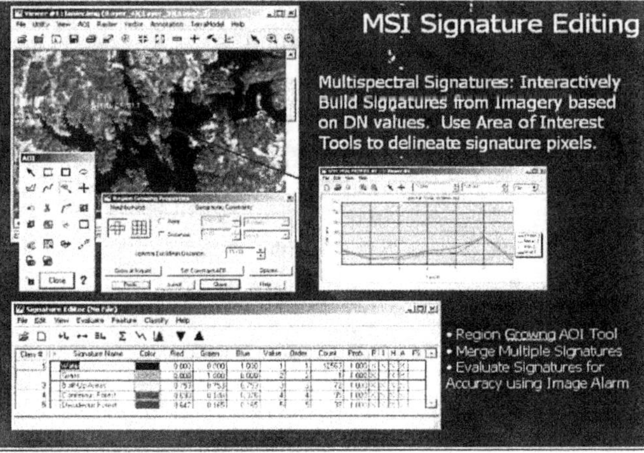

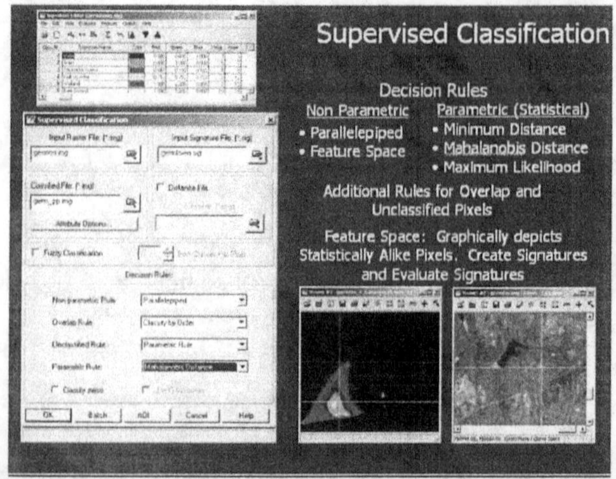

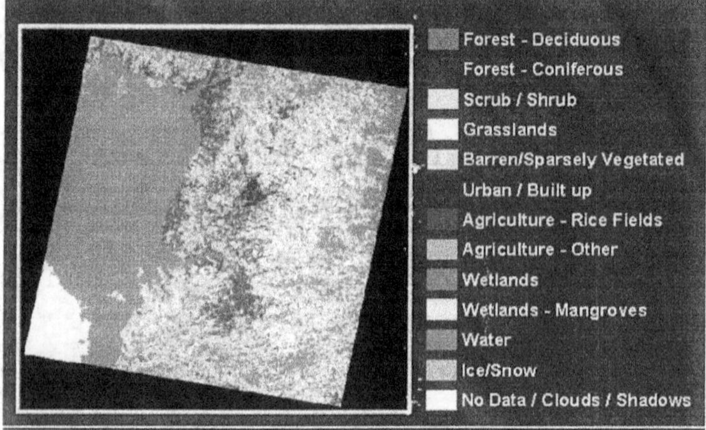

Raster GIS Analysis Tools

Object-based graphical tool for the rapid definition of integrated raster and vector data analyses and spatial modeling.

- Use graphical flow charts to quickly perform sophisticated GIS analysis
- Combine GIS and image processing functions in the same spatial model
- Combine raster, vector and attribute data in a single model
- Apply a model to new data or a different geographical area at the push of a button
- Cut, copy, and paste objects
- Quickly modify and re-run your model
- Run a model directly or generate a script for integration with the main software.

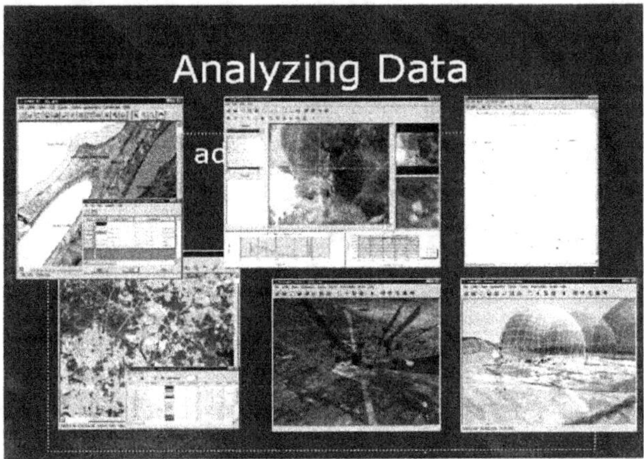

Terrain Visualization and fly-through Module

- 3D raster drape
- Drape Aerial photography, satellite imagery, scanned maps and thematic images
- 3D vector drape using Arc info Coverages.
- Navigate the scene using mouse controls or user-defined
- Create flight paths, create 3D movies, or "fly" automatically to a selected database feature
- Capabilities to add annotation, vector GIS layers, symbols, billboards, and texture mapped 3D objects to create realistic views of the study area.
- Create buildings by extending ArcInfo coverages or annotation in the "Z" direction using a user selected attribute as the height.
- Preprocesses data layers for faster, smoother fly-through and scene manipulation
- Perform intervisibility calculations
- Create 3D movies for presentations
- Overlay and control the opacity of multiple raster, vector, and annotation layers
- Query geographic location and pixel categories/values while moving the cursor across the 3D environment
- Query attributes for vector data rendered as 3D objects
- Modify styling for vector points, lines, or polygons rendered as 3D objects
- Display annotation text and symbols as "billboards"
- Interactive 3D stereo display mode

- Sky background and atmospheric fog options
- Sun position and lens flare simulation
- Simulate night-time and night-vision device environments
- Import realistic 3D models (e.g., 3D DXF, MultiGen OpenFlight, etc.)
- Create flight paths to 3D models.
- Randomly place specified models in polygons
- Simulate fog, mist or smog
- Add water layers(s) to the scene

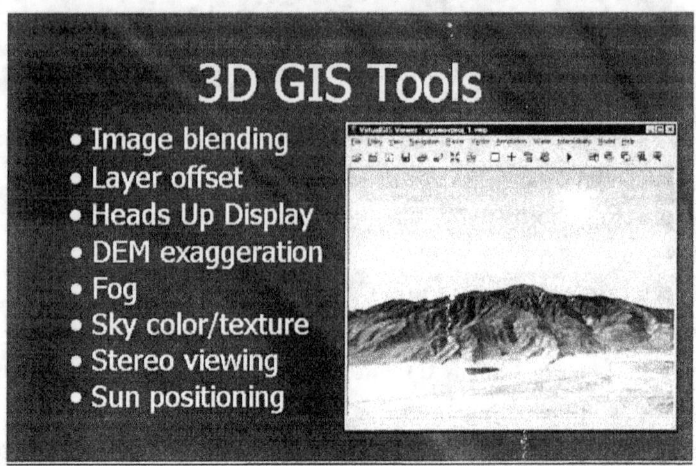

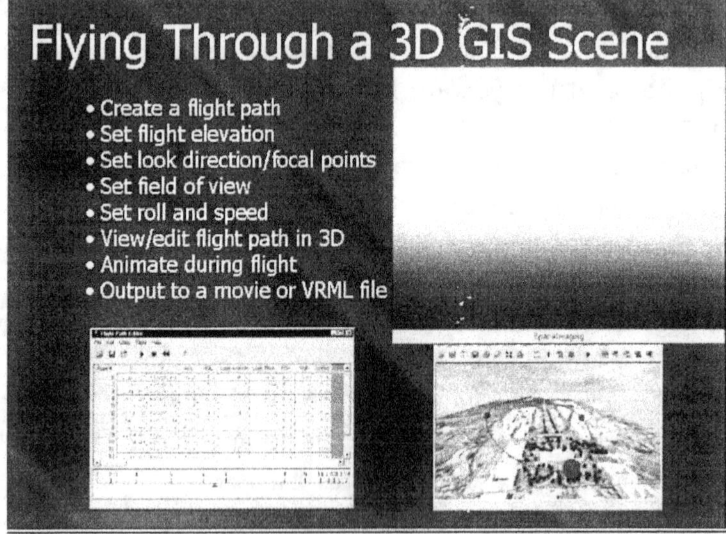

Hyper Spectral Analysis Tools

Any user with access to hyperspectral imagery from which they wish to quickly extract material mapping information with the minimum of user interaction (and without the need for costly training in hyperspectral image processing theory) can benefit from the new Spectral Analysis tools:

- Standard task-based workflows
  - Anomaly Detection
  - Target Detection
  - Material Mapping
  - Material Identification
- Hyperspectral image preprocessing steps
  - Band wavelength/width specification
  - Bad band identification
  - Spectral subset
  - Spatial subset
  - Atmospheric Adjustment
  - Minimum Noise Fraction
- Spectral libraries provided
  - ASTER
  - JPL
  - USGS
  - Import new versions of the above libraries
  - Import SITAC libraries
  - Import SPECMIN libraries
- Spectral Analysis Workstation
  - Multi-pane workspace providing access to all the tools, functionalities and viewers for interactively analyzing hyperspectral imagery, spectral signatures and other data displays
  - Three geospatially-linked views (main view, an overview view of the whole image extent and a zoom view showing magnified detail of a specific location)
  - Embedded Spectral Plot tools - Embedded Spectral Libraries - Drag and drop interaction between image pixels, plots and libraries
  - Access to all preprocessing and task processes

- Spectral Analysis Methodologies
  - Orthogonal Subspace Projection (OSP)
  - Spectral Angle Mapper (SAM)
  - Spectral Correlation Mapper (SCM)
  - Constrained Energy Minimization (CEM)
- Bow and Tie correction (part of Importer)

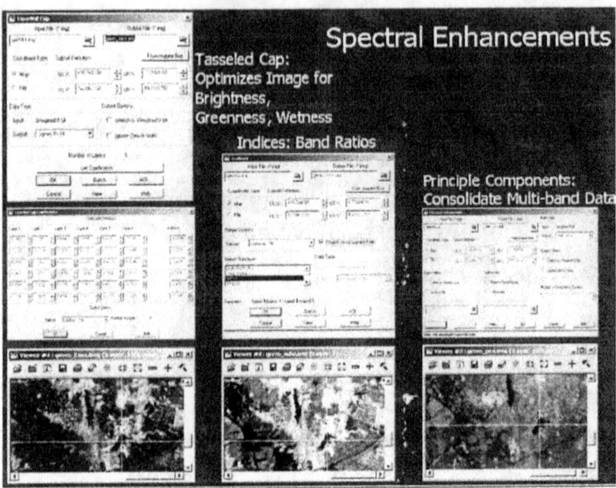

7.3.6 Radar Functionalities

Provides the tools like IFSAR, STEREO SAR & Ortho-correction tools needed to process and enhance SAR images. Because it is data source independent, it allows you to work with any SAR imagery.

- Sensor merge
- Texture analysis
- Speckle removal
- Edge enhancement
- Wallis adaptive filter
- Luminance modification
- Slant-to-ground range adjustment
- Adjust to flat plain or user-defined spheroid
- Sensor model based orthorectification of RADARSAT and ERS-1,-2 imagery
- Optional orbit correction using three-dimensional GCP points

- Optional terrain distortion removal (if DEM is available)

- Optional radiometric correction based on surface slope (sigma-zero)

- A multi-projection capability allows users to translate data to and from different projections

- Automatic, softcopy output options are the best in the industry, and include TIFF or GeoTIFF, Digital Orthoquad (DOQ), GRASS and SDTS raster

- To extract terrain height information from stereo pairs of SAR satellite imagery for the generation of extremely accurate digital elevation models (DEMs).

- Use updated ephemeris data from the major data vendors

- Achieve accurate results without the use of ground controls

- Uses interferometric techniques to quickly create high-resolution digital elevation models (DEMs) from synthetic aperture radar (SAR) image pairs.

- Perform easy, wizard-based interferometric terrain extraction

- Create detailed, accurate terrain information

- Minimize the need for ground control points (GCPs) when creating DEMs

7.3.7 C Developer Tool kit

The IMAGINE Developers' Toolkit™ consists of a set of libraries and documentation that allow you to customize and extend ERDAS IMAGINE®. The Toolkit includes a number of packages, which creates and supports the following types of routines:

- ERDAS IMAGINE object manipulation routines
- Application environment routines
- Low-level file I/O and system access routines
- Abstract object manipulation routines
- EML GUI access routines
- Extensive context-sensitive online help
- Example programs
- 2D visualization routines
- 3D visualization routines

Compression Module

The MrSID Encoder modules enable the MrSID encoding of any raster format supported by ERDAS IMAGINE and is integrated seamlessly into the geographic imaging workflow. The MrSID Workstation Encoder will handle input files over 500 million pixels.

Features

- Unprecedented reduction ratios
- No perceptible loss of visual quality

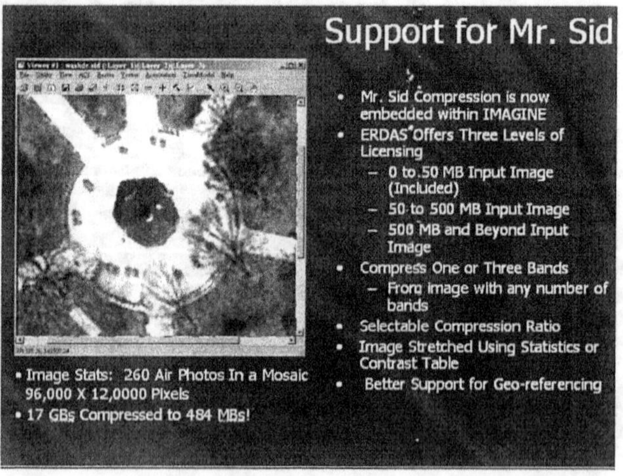

- Simple compression
- Multiple resolutions from single-source files
- Selective decompression
- Seamless roaming/browsing
- Floating license structure
- Access to the Batch Wizard

7.3.8 Automated 2D and 3D Feature extraction tools for High Resolution Imagery

- Provides geospatial professionals with a comprehensive automated feature extraction toolset for collecting 2D and 3D geospatial features from earth imagery and scanned maps.
- Features such as roads, buildings, water bodies, vegetation, pervious-impervious surfaces, multi-class image classification, and land cover are easily extracted using simple one-button workflows.
- Uses multiple spatial attributes (size, shape, texture, pattern, spatial association, and shadow) with spectral information to collect geospatial features from monoscopic and stereo imagery as vector shapefiles.
- Benefits include significantly lower database maintenance costs, increased accuracy in feature collection, and a simpler approach to geospatial data production.
- Provides a complete solution for extracting geospatial features from
  - Panchromatic imagery
  - 3-band color
  - multispectral Imagery
  - radar Imagery
  - hyperspectral imagery.

Features

- Easy-to-use automated feature extraction
- 2D and 3D feature extraction
- Change detection
- Multi-class image classification
- Landcover classification
- Automated clutter removal
- Data fusion with DEMs
- Smart vector editing tools

- Batch processing
- Smooth shapes
- Convert to point, convert to line

FLEXLM licensing advantages

Ability to Float Individual modules.

Ortho Correction, Automatic DEM generation & 3D Feature collection Tools:

Core Photogrammetric Tools

- Project set-up
- Direct Support file read/write
- Import/Export
- Rigorous Sensor Modeling of Various Camera and Satellite Sensors
- Support for aerial frame, digital, video and non-metric cameras, as well as satellite sensors (CARTOSAT, Quick Bird, SPOT, IRS-1C, IKONOS,ASTER and QUICK BIRD)
- Ability to read RPC files for sensors like CARTOSAT, IKONOS, Quick bird.
- Automatic Interior Orientation
- STEREO / MONO GCP Point Measurement
- Satellite Block Triangulation and Ariel Triangulation.
- Orthorectification

- Mosaicking
- 3D Surfacing
- Map Composition
- Data Management tools
- Automatic Tie Point Measurement

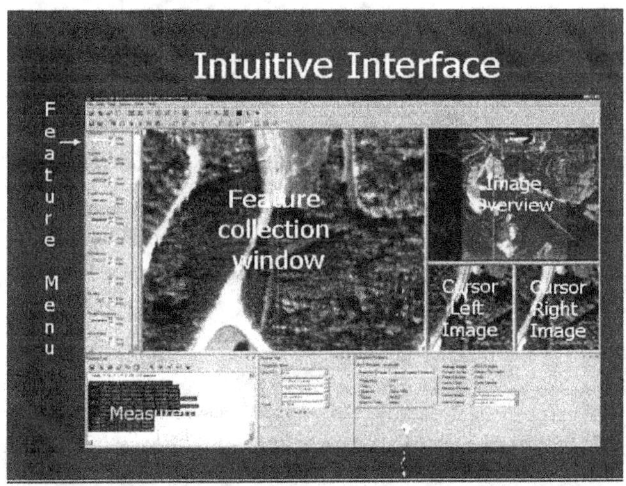

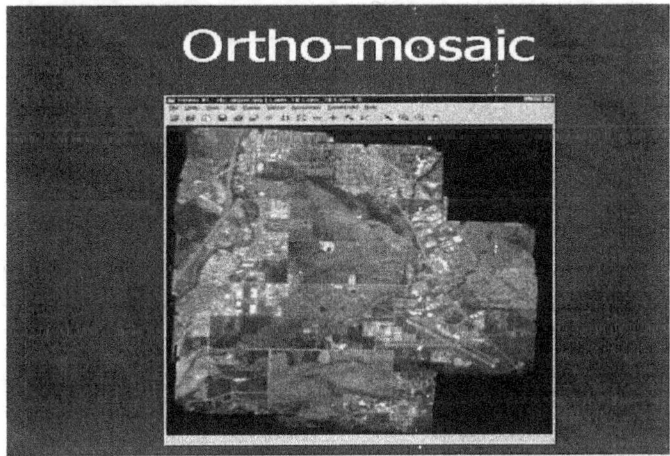

Stereo Visualization

- Unlimited number of stereo windows should be supported
- Stereo, split-panel, tri-view (stereo and split panel) and mono views
- Sub-pixel positioning
- Continuous panning and zooming

- Ergonomic digitizing devices supported (16-button TopoMouse, Mouse-Trak,)
- On-the-fly accuracy reporting
- Fixed Cursor/Moving image support
- Fixed Image/Moving cursor support
- Image contrast/brightness adjustment

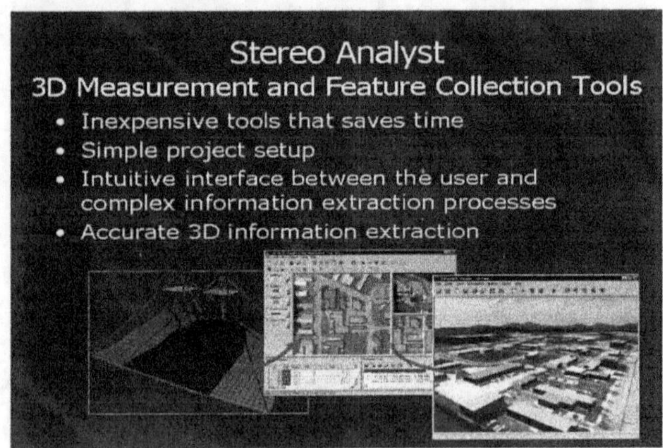

Automatic DEM/DTM Extraction Module

- Ability to extract individual DTMs or an entire DTM for a project consisting of many images
- DTM outputs should be in : Raster DEMs, TINs, 3D Shapefiles, ASCII files
- Output DTMs in different projections

- Automatic accuracy reporting
- Strategy parameter definition
- Ability to define exclusion areas
- Contour line generation

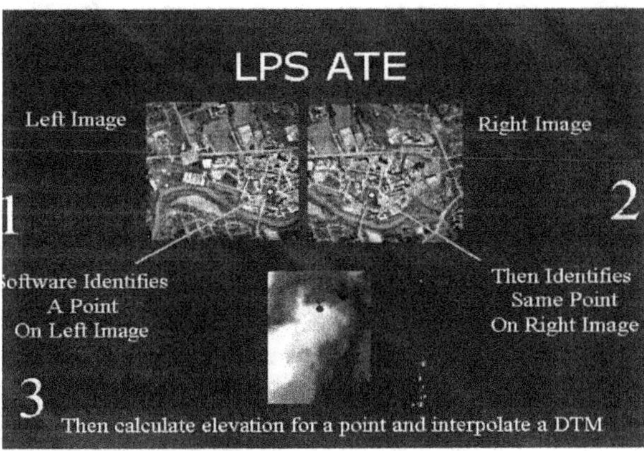

DTM (Terrain) Editing Tools

- Interactively edit DTM's using Stereo Imagery as back drop reference.
- Provides point, area, geomorphic editing tools
- Raster DEMs and TINs can be edited
- Dynamic display of contours, mass points, break-lines and TINs
- Editing by point, lines or area
- Dynamic update of graphics while editing
- Virtually unlimited Undo and Redo

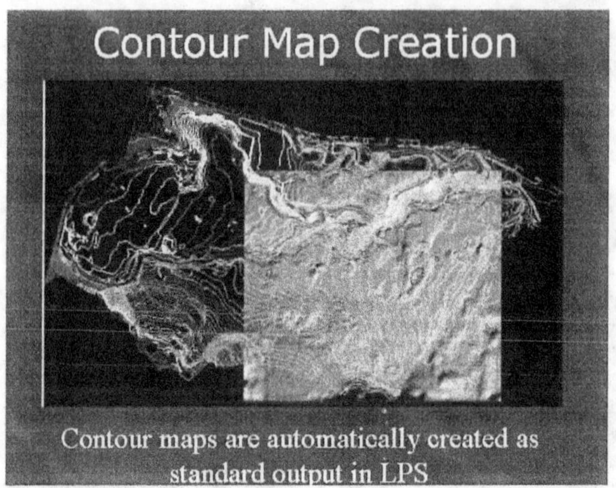

3D Feature capturing Tool

- Collect 3D data from Stereo imagery directly on to Microstation Platform.
- Update the existing GIS data bases by superimposing existing 2D/3D vector layers onto a digital stereo model and then editing and reshaping them to their accurate, real-world positions.
- Automatically attribute spatial geographic information
- Output in Microstation DGN file / ESRI 3D shape files.
- Unparalleled image handling for the display and manipulation of 3D digital stereo models.
- OpenGL and stereo-in-a-window supported
- 16 Button - 3D digitizing devices supported

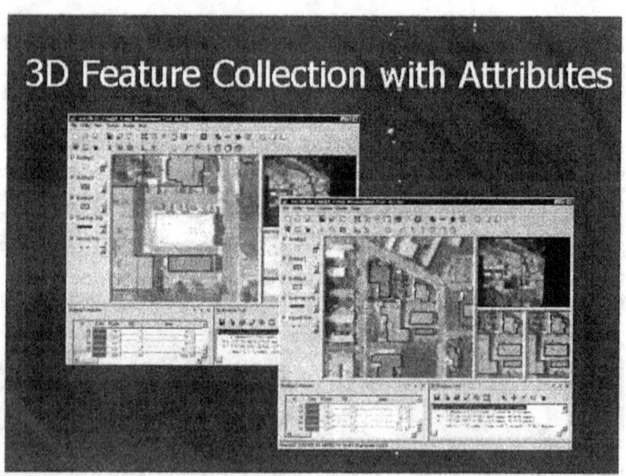

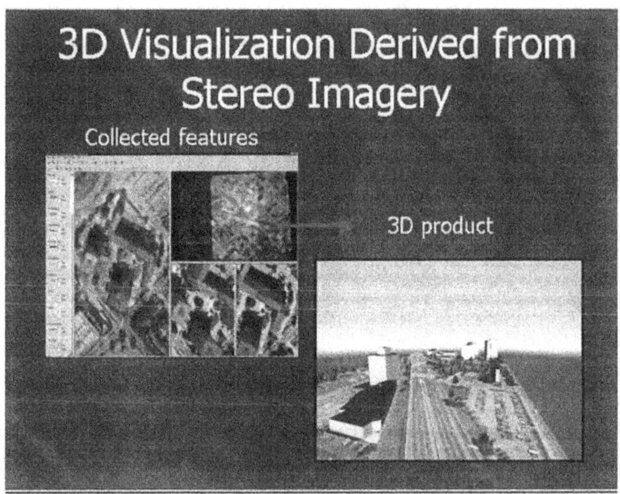

3D devices support

- Infra Red Emitter and Glasses are supported for Stereo Viewing.
- 16 Button - 3D mouse support
- Z-Screen support

High – End Triangulation Software

ORIMA Orientation Management software is a modern, easy-to-use and high productivity solution for orientation and triangulation. It enables you to process large data sets of image coordinates, ground control points and GPS coordinates to detect and climinate blunders, and minimize the need for costly remeasurements.

Features

- State-of-the-art bundle adjustment with self-calibration for frame and ADS40 imagery
- Triangulation in non-3D-cartesian coordinate systems
- Airborne GPS and IMU (Inertial Measurement Unit) data processing
- Powerful statistical techniques for blunder detection and elimination and identification of weak areas
- Easy to understand, easy to use graphics for analysis
- Point numbering, driving to points, interior, relative and absolute orientation
- Fully automatic point measurement and ground control point transfer

7.3.9 File Management System

GeoVault Data Manager (GDM) provides automated, cost-effective and accessible long term storage and management of digital imagery files and geospatial information in a work group, intranet or Internet setting. Implemented as a multi-tiered client-server application, GDM uses an open architecture to exploit off-the-shelf hardware and software. The GDM provides enhanced productivity and resource utilization to the modern geospatial production enterprise.

The GDM open architecture allows service to any networked client. Clients can be customized for specific products including the DSW500 or other scanners, the ground processing systems for the ADS40 and the ALS50 and other digital photogrammetric or image processing products. Further customization is possible by means of standard SQL, ODBC and JDBC database interfaces or the GDM API.

Features

- Multi-user data query, retrieval, and serving
- Manage, catalog, browse, and share images and geospatial data
- Store multiple levels of project data, from flight plans to finished products
- View image thumbnails or geographic boundaries during queries
- Search by metadata such as location, name and date
- Conduct map-based searches
- Compress, build pyramids and do other batch processes automatically during retrieval
- Use wizard-driven tools to reduce data errors during insert, retrieve and update
- User modifiable data model; add tables and other entries as needed
- Open architecture allows service to any networked client
- Customize clients for scanners, ground processing systems and other digital photogrammetric or image processing products

Ease of Use

- Should be completely a GUI software i.e. intuitive graphical user interface throughout
- Common tools used throughout the suite
- Context-sensitive, Hypertext-linked On-Line Help

7.4 Questions

1. Enumerate the key features and functions of MATLAB.
2. Explain 2-D and 3-D plotting features of MATLAB.
3. Enumerate the various modules of EASI/PACE and explain briefly.
4. Enumerate and explain in brief the various modules of ERDAS imagine.
5. Explain the features of automated 2-D and 3-D feature extraction tools for high resolution imagery provided in ERDAS.

Index

References

1   J.F. Abramatic, J. Arvidsson, O.D. Faugeras, G.H. Granlund, R.M. Haralick, T.C. Henderson, H. Knutsson, B. Kruse, S.W. Krusemark, M. Kunt, J.C. Latombe, S. Levialdi, A. Lux, A. Rosenfeld, R. Wilson; Fundamentals in Computer Vision, Cambridge University Press, 1983, ISBN 0-521-250994.

2   P.K. Allen; Robotic Object Recognition Using Vision and Touch, KluwerAcademic Publishers, 1987, ISBN 0-89838-245-9.

3   Y. Aloimonos; Visual Navigation: From Biological Systems to Unmanned Ground Vehicles, Lawrence Erlbaum Associates, Inc, 1996, ISBN 0805820507.

4   H.C. Andrews; Computer Techniques in Image Processing, Academic Press, 1970,

5   G.A. Barnes; Digital Image Processing, Wiley, 1994, ISBN .

6   B.G. Batchelor; Pattern Recognition: Ideas in Practice, PlenumPress, 1978,

7   G.A. Baxes; Digital Image Processing: Principles and Applications, Wiley, 1994, ISBN 0-471-00949-0.

8   E. Bayro Corrochano; Handbook of Geometric Computing with Applications in Pattern Recognition, Computer Vision, Neurocomputing and Robotics, Springer Verlag, 2005, ISBN 3-540-20595-0.

9   J. Beck, B. Hope, A. Rosenfeld; Human and Machine Vision, Academic Press, 1983, ISBN 0-12-084320-x.

10   M. Bennamoun, G.J. Mamic; Object Recognition Fundamentals and Case Studies, Springer-Verlag, 2002, ISBN 1-85233-398-7.

11   A. Bovik; Handbook of Image and Video Processing, Academic Press, 2000, ISBN 0-12-119790-5.

12   R. D. Boyle, R. C. Thomas; Computer vision : a first course, Blackwell Scientific, 1988, ISBN 0632015772.

13   R. N. Bracewell ; Two-dimensional imaging, Prentice-Hall, 1995, ISBN 0-13-062621-X.

14   M. Brady; Computer Vision, North Holland Publishing Company, 1981,

15   C. Brown; Advances in Computer Vision: Volume 2, Lawrence Erlbaum Associates, 1988, ISBN 0-08058-0082-1.

16   Vicki Bruce, Patrick R. Green; Visual Perception: Physiology, Psychology and Ecology, Lawrence Erlbaum Associates, 1990, ISBN 0-86377-146-7.

17   K.R. Castleman; Digital Image Processing, Prentice Hall, 1979,

18   C.H. Chen, P. Wang; Handbook of pattern recognition and computer vision, 3rd edition, World Scientific, 2005, ISBN 981-256-105-6.

19   W. G. Driscoll, W. Vaughn; Handbook of Optics, McGraw-Hill, 1978,

20   E.R. Dougherty; Digital Image Processing Methods, Dekker, 1994 ,

21   M. Fairchild; Color Appearance Models, Prentice-Hall, 1988, ISBN 0-201-63464-3.

22   O. Faugeras ; Fundamentals in Computer Vision, Cambridge University Press, 1983, ISBN 0521250994.

23   M.A. Fischler, O. Firschein; Intelligence: The Eye, the Brain and the Computer, Addison-Wesley, 1987,

24   M.M. Fleck, D. Stevenson; Computer Vision Handbook, Harvey Mudd, 1997,

25   K.S. Fu; Applications of Pattern Recognition, CRC Press, 1982,

26   K.S. Fu; Digital Pattern Recognition,, Springer-Verlag, 1976,

27   K. Fukunaga; Introduction to Statistical Pattern Recognition, Academic Press, 1990, ISBN 0-12-269851-7.

28 L.J. Galbiati; Machine vision and digital image processing fundamentals, Prentice Hall, 1990, ISBN 013542044x.

29 E.B. Goldstein; Sensation and Perception, Wadsworth, 1989, ISBN 0-534-09672-7.

30 R.C. Gonzalez, M.G. Thomason; Syntactic Pattern Recognition: An Introduction, Addison-Wesley, 1978,

31 E. Gose, S. Jost; Pattern Recognition and Image Analysis, Prentice Hall, 1996, ISBN 0-13-236415-8.

32 W.B. Green; Digital Image Processing: A Systems Approach, Van Nostrand-Reinhold, 1982,

33 W.E.L. Grimson; Object Recognition By Computer : The Role of Geometric Constrains, MIT Press, 1990, ISBN 0-262-07130-4.

34 W.R. Hendee, P.N.T. Wells; Perception of Visual Information, Springer-Verlag Berlin and Heidelberg GmbH and Co. KG, 1993, ISBN 3540979042.

35 R.M. Hord; Digital Image Processing of Remotely Sensed Data, Academic Press, 1982,

36 B. Jahne; Digital Image Processing: Concepts, Algorithms, and Scientific Applications, Springer-Verlag, 1995, ISBN 3-540-59298-9.

37 B. Jahne, H. Haussecker, P. Geissler; Handbook of Computer Vision and Applications , Academic Press, 1999, ISBN 0123797705.

38 B. Jahne , H. Haussecker; Computer Vision and Applications: A Guide for Students and Practitioners , Academic Press, 2000, ISBN 0123797772.

39 S. Levialdi, V. Cantoni, V. Roberto; Artificial Vision: Image Description, Recognition and Communication (Signal Processing S.), Academic Press, 1996, ISBN 012444816X.

40 A.A. Low; Introductory Computer Vision and Image Processing, McGraw Hill, 1991, ISBN 0-07-707403-3.

41 F.T. Marchese; Understanding Images: Finding Meaning in Digital Imagery, Springer, 1995, ISBN 0387941487.

42 G. Medioni, M.S. Lee, C.K. Tang; A computational framework for segmentation and grouping, Elsevier,, 2000, ISBN 0444503536.

43 T. Morris; Computer Vision and Image Processing (Cornerstones of Computing), Palgrave Macmillan, 2003, ISBN 0333994515.

44 H.R. Myler; Fundamentals of Machine Vision, SPIE Society of Photo-Optical Instrumentation Engineering, 1999, ISBN 0819430498.

45   V.S. Nalwa; A Guided Tour of Computer Vision, Addison Wesley, 1993, ISBN 0-201-54853-4.

46   W. Niblack; An Introduction to Digital Image Processing, Prentice Hall, 1986,

47   J.R. Parker; Algorithms for image processing and computer vision, Wiley Computer Publishers, New York, 1997, ISBN 0471140562.

48   J. Pauli; Learning-Based Robot Vision , Springer-Verlag, 2001, ISBN 3-540-42108-4.

49   T. Pavlidis; Structural Pattern Recognition, Springer, 1977,

50   M. Petrou, P. Bosdogianni; Image Processing: The Fundamentals, John Wiley and Sons, 1999,

51   W.K. Pratt; Digital image processing, John Wiley and Sons, Inc, 1978, ISBN 0471018880.

52   L.G. Shapiro , A. Rosenfeld ; Computer Vision and Image Processing, Academic Press, 1992,

53   J. Teuber; Digital Image Processing, Prentice Hall, 1993, ISBN 0-13-213364-4.

54   T.Y. Young; Handbook of Pattern Recognition and Image Processing: Computer Vision v. 2 , Academic Press, 1994, ISBN 0127745610.

55   X. S. Zhou, Y. Rui, T. S. Huang; Exploration of visual data, Kluwer Academic Publishers, 2003, ISBN 1402075693.

56   John C. Cruss, The Image Processing Handbook, CRC Press, 1995, ISBN 0-8493-2516-1.

57   Parker J.R., Algorithms for Image Processing and Computer Vision, Wiley Computer Publishing, 1997, ISBN 0-471-14056-2.

58   Ramesh Jain, Rangachar Kasturi, Brian G. Schunck, Machine Vision, McGraw-hill, ISBN 0-07-032018-7, 1995, 549p, ISBN0-13-226616-1.

59   Randy Crane, A simplied approach to Image Processing: clasical and modern technique in C. Prentice Hall, 1997, ISBN 0-13-226616-1.

60   Anji Reddy M,Remote Sensing and Geographical Information Systems, 2005. ISBN-81-7800-018-0